D1927791

# New Perspectives on Firm Growth

Per Davidsson

*Director of the Australian Centre for Entrepreneurship Research; Professor of Entrepreneurship, Queensland University of Technology, Australia, and Jönköping International Business School, Sweden*

Johan Wiklund

*Professor of Entrepreneurship, Syracuse University, Syracuse, NY, USA, and Jönköping International Business School, Sweden*

**Edward Elgar**

Cheltenham, UK • Northampton, MA, USA

Published by
Edward Elgar Publishing Limited
The Lypiatts
15 Lansdown Road
Cheltenham
Glos GL50 2JA
UK

Edward Elgar Publishing, Inc.
William Pratt House
9 Dewey Court
Northampton
Massachusetts 01060
USA

A catalogue record for this book
is available from the British Library

This book is available electronically in the ElgarOnline.com
Business Subject Collection, E-ISBN 978 0 85793 361 4

Library of Congress Control Number: 2012951753

MIX
Paper from
responsible sources
FSC® C018575

ISBN 978 0 85793 360 7 (cased)

Typeset by Servis Filmsetting Ltd, Stockport, Cheshire
Printed and bound by MPG PRINTGROUP, UK

# Contents

*List of figures* vii
*List of contributors* viii
*Acknowledgements* x

Introduction 1
*Per Davidsson and Johan Wiklund*

PART I EXPLAINING WHY AND HOW MUCH FIRMS GROW

1 Building an integrative model of small business growth 15
*Johan Wiklund, Holger Patzelt and Dean A. Shepherd*

2 Aspiring for, and achieving growth: the moderating role of resources and opportunities 56
*Johan Wiklund and Dean A. Shepherd*

3 The effect of small business managers' growth motivation on firm growth: a longitudinal study 82
*Frédéric Delmar and Johan Wiklund*

PART II CHANGING THE FIRM GROWTH RESEARCH AGENDA

4 Are we comparing apples with apples or apples with oranges? Appropriateness of knowledge accumulation across growth studies 115
*Dean A. Shepherd and Johan Wiklund*

5 Advancing firm growth research: a focus on growth mode instead of growth rate 139
*Alexander McKelvie and Johan Wiklund*

6 Towards an integrative framework for future research on small firm growth 176
*Per Davidsson, Leona Achtenhagen and Lucia Naldi*

PART III A CRITICAL LOOK AT THE GROWTH–PROFIT RELATIONSHIP

7 Growing profitable or growing from profits: putting the horse in front of the cart? 187
*Per Davidsson, Paul Steffens and Jason Fitzsimmons*

8 Performance configurations over time: implications for growth- and profit-oriented strategies 221
*Paul Steffens, Per Davidsson and Jason Fitzsimmons*

PART IV THEORY-DRIVEN RESEARCH ON SPECIFIC FORMS OF GROWTH

9 Asset specificity and behavioral uncertainty as moderators of the sales growth–employment growth relationship in emerging ventures 253
*Gaylen N. Chandler, Alexander McKelvie and Per Davidsson*

10 Organic and acquisitive growth: re-examining, testing and extending Penrose's growth theory 291
*Andy Lockett, Johan Wiklund, Per Davidsson and Sourafel Girma*

*Index* 325

# Figures


| | | |
|---|---|---|
| 1.1 | Diagram of the results for the revised model of small business growth | 27 |
| 2.1 | Adapted version of the theory of planned behaviour for studying how growth aspirations influence actual growth | 60 |
| 2.2a | Interaction of aspiration and education on growth | 70 |
| 2.2b | Interaction of aspiration and experience on growth | 70 |
| 2.2c | Interaction of aspiration and dynamism on growth | 71 |
| 2.3 | Four types of firms in terms of resources and opportunities for growth and growth aspirations | 76 |
| 3.1 | Cross-lagged analysis of growth and growth motivation | 88 |
| 6.1 | Alternative foci for studies of small firm growth | 177 |
| 7.1 | Categorization schema of firms by growth and profitability | 194 |
| 8.1 | An integrated model of growth–profitability dynamics | 224 |
| 8.2 | Profitability–growth configurations | 232 |
| 10.1 | Model of firm growth | 302 |
| 10.2 | Linear and quadratic models of the relationship between previous and current organic growth | 311 |

# Contributors

**Leona Achtenhagen** is Professor of Business Administration, Head of the Entrepreneurship, Strategy, Organization and Leadership Department and Assistant Director of the Media Management and Transformation Centre at the Jönköping International Business School, Sweden.

**Gaylen N. Chandler** is the W. Frank Barton Distinguished Chair and Professor at Wichita State University, USA.

**Per Davidsson** is Director of the Australian Centre for Entrepreneurship Research and Professor of Entrepreneurship at Queensland University of Technology, Australia, and Professor of Entrepreneurship at the Jönköping International Business School, Sweden.

**Frédéric Delmar** is Professor of Entrepreneurship at the Sten K. Johnson Centre for Entrepreneurship, School of Economics and Management, Lund University, Sweden.

**Jason Fitzsimmons** is Director of MBA Programmes and Alumni Relations Office, U21 Global, Singapore.

**Sourafel Girma** is Professor of Industrial Economics at the University of Nottingham, UK.

**Andy Lockett** is Professor of Strategy and Entrepreneurship at Warwick Business School, UK.

**Alexander McKelvie** is Assistant Professor of Entrepreneurship at the Whitman School of Management, Syracuse University, USA.

**Lucia Naldi** is Assistant Professor at the Department of Entrepreneurship, Strategy, Organization and Leadership, Jönköping International Business School, Sweden.

**Holger Patzelt** is Professor of Entrepreneurship and holds the Chair of Entrepreneurship at the TUM Entrepreneurship Research Institute, TUM School of Management, Technische Universität München (TUM), Germany.

**Dean A. Shepherd** is Professor of Entrepreneurship and holder of the Randall L. Tobias Chair in Entrepreneurial Leadership at the Kelly

School of Business, Indiana University, USA. He is also Editor-in-Chief of the *Journal of Business Venturing* and Adjunct Professor at the Australian Centre for Entrepreneurship Research.

**Paul Steffens** is Associate Professor and Deputy Director at the Australian Centre for Entrepreneurship Research, Queensland University of Technology, Australia.

**Johan Wiklund** is Professor of Entrepreneurship at Syracuse University, USA, and at Jönköping International Business School, Sweden.

# Acknowledgements

The editors and publishers wish to thank the authors and the following publishers, who have kindly given permission for the use of copyright material.

Blackwell Publishing Ltd for articles: Johan Wiklund and Dean A. Shepherd (2003), 'Aspiring for, and achieving growth: the moderating role of resources and opportunities', *Journal of Management Studies*, **40** (8), December, 1919–41; Frédéric Delmar and Johan Wiklund (2008), 'The effect of small business managers' growth motivation on firm growth: a longitudinal study', *Entrepreneurship Theory and Practice*, **32** (3), May, 437–57; Dean A. Shepherd and Johan Wiklund (2009), 'Are we comparing apples with apples or apples with oranges? Appropriateness of knowledge accumulation across growth studies', *Entrepreneurship Theory and Practice*, **33** (1), January, 105–23; Paul Steffens, Per Davidsson and Jason Fitzsimmons (2009), 'Performance configurations over time: implications for growth- and profit-oriented strategies', *Entrepreneurship Theory and Practice*, **33** (1), January, 125–48; Alexander McKelvie and Johan Wiklund (2010), 'Advancing firm growth research: a focus on growth mode instead of growth rate', *Entrepreneurship Theory and Practice*, **34** (2), March, 261–88; Andy Lockett, Johan Wiklund, Per Davidsson and Sourafel Girma (2009), 'Organic and acquisitive growth: re-examining, testing and extending Penrose's growth theory', *Journal of Management Studies*, **48** (1), January, 48–74.

Elsevier Ltd via the Copyright Clearance Center for articles: Gaylen N. Chandler, Alexander McKelvie and Per Davidsson (2009), 'Asset specificity and behavioral uncertainty as moderators of the sales growth–employment growth relationship in emerging ventures', *Journal of Business Venturing*, **24** (4), July, 373–87; Per Davidsson, Paul Steffens and Jason Fitzsimmons (2009), 'Growing profitable or growing from profits: putting the horse in front of the cart?', *Journal of Business Venturing*, **24** (4), 388–406.

Now Publishers for article: Per Davidsson, Leona Achtenhagen and Lucia Naldi (2010), 'Towards an integrative framework for future research on small firm growth', *Foundations and Trends in Entrepreneurship*, **6** (2), 135–43.

Springer Science and Business Media B.V. for article: Johan Wiklund, Holger Patzelt and Dean A. Shepherd (2009), 'Building an integrative model of small business growth', *Small Business Economics*, **32** (4), 351–74.

Every effort has been made to trace all the copyright holders, but if any have been inadvertently overlooked the publishers will be pleased to make the necessary arrangement at the first opportunity.

# Introduction

## Per Davidsson and Johan Wiklund

The issue of firm growth – how it is achieved and managed, and what consequences it has for different stakeholders – is both theoretically interesting and practically important. It is also an area of scholarly enquiry that has expanded very significantly since we started doing research on it in the 1980s and 1990s. In this volume we present and comment upon the most recent contributions we have made to this field of inquiry – separately, jointly and with various colleagues (who are included in the 'we/us = article authors' used in the remainder of this introduction). While the chapters have been published before in various places, we think it valuable to gather them in one easily accessible place, which also allows space for our reflective commentary across the individual chapters. We hope readers will find the work a useful and worthwhile addition to the extant body of knowledge about firm growth. We also hope they will find that it – as its title suggests – brings new perspectives on firm growth and its study, and that it can inspire future contributions by other researchers. This is important, because despite the growing volume of research on firm growth, many important questions still lack satisfactory answers.

The current volume may be regarded as a follow-up of a previous collection where we – and Frederic Delmar – presented and commented on eight articles on (mostly small) firm growth that we had jointly or separately published up until that time (Davidsson et al., 2006). In that volume we organised the works under three broad themes: *the conceptual and empirical complexity of the firm growth phenomenon; growth aspirations and motivations;* and *patterns and determinants of actual growth.* The current volume builds on and extends these themes. Only one of the chapters in the previous volume directly addressed the issue of drivers of actual growth. We add three more in this book, two of which expand on the 'aspirations and motivations' theme by relating growth aspirations and motivations (or lack thereof) of the owner-manager to the actual growth achieved in the subsequent period. We present these three chapters in *Part I – Explaining why and how much firms grow*.

Not least because of the 'conceptual and empirical complexity', it has been a growing insight of ours that research on firm growth needs to move beyond attempts at trying to explain variance in the (total) amount of growth firms achieve, undertake or undergo. Therefore, *Part II – Changing the firm growth research agenda* presents three chapters providing critical reviews of prior research (including our own) and the growth indicators it has used as well as outlining a research agenda to address the problems and gaps identified through these reviews.

The last two parts and sets of chapters outline beginnings of such a changed research agenda by addressing antecedents and effects of different forms (or modes) of growth; and the outcomes of growth. As our examples far from exhaust these topics, we use somewhat narrower part titles: *Part III – A critical look at the growth–profit relationship* and *Part IV – Theory-driven research on specific forms of growth.* These parts comprise two chapters each.

In the remainder of this Introduction we provide a short summary of each part and the chapters within them, organised in the order they appear in the volume.

## PART I – EXPLAINING WHY AND HOW MUCH FIRMS GROW

In the previous volume (Davidsson et al., 2006) we provided as a background a discussion of our (including Delmar's) respective dissertation works. The first chapter in our current volume, 'Building an integrative model of small business growth', can be seen as the culmination of these works, as it is in effect a refinement of core contents of Wiklund's dissertation study (other parts of the study were published much earlier, e.g., Wiklund, 1999). The work draws on five different streams of literature to arrive at an integrated model that considers individual (growth attitude), environmental (industry; hostility-munificence-dynamism) and firm-level (resources; strategy) drivers of growth. The model puts strategy – specifically, entrepreneurial orientation (Lumpkin and Dess, 1996) – at the centre stage as the most direct driver of growth, but allows for direct effects of individual and environmental factors as well in the empirical analysis.

To us, this chapter represents an example of useful phenomenon-driven research (cf. Wiklund et al., 2011). It is decidedly phenomenon-driven but not atheoretical; instead it takes on the task of integrating several theoretical perspectives. It uses a large sample representing a select set of different industries and size classes, thus allowing for broad generalisation while avoiding some of the heterogeneity and micro-firm dominance of simple random samples. It employs a longitudinal design, thus separating the actual growth in time from its theorised antecedents. It lets both theory and data speak by allowing revision of the theoretical model. It assesses growth with multiple indicators rather than a single measure that may be differentially valid across a broad sample. Finally, it explains a sizeable share of the variance of 'total' growth – not just a statistically significant but possibly practically irrelevant share of a variance that through the researchers' design choices has already been made much smaller than that occurring in the real economy. We agree that the type of carefully designed single-theory research on homogeneous samples of firms that is the current fashion in leading management journals can reach further and deeper as regards both measurement and estimation of the effects of the factors highlighted by that particular theory. However, we hold that it benefits the collective sobriety of academic research on firm growth to once in a while get an idea of where these factors sit in the bigger scheme of things. This first chapter of our current collection is arguably a good example of the latter.

In the previous volume we included two chapters investigating drivers of owner-managers' expectations and/or motivation for future growth (Delmar and Davidsson, 1999; Wiklund et al., 2003). While such studies may yield unexpected and sometimes provocative (to some) results – such as the expected financial outcome of growth being only of secondary importance – they leave unanswered the important question of whether the managers' stated expectations and motivations have any bearing on what actual growth materialises in the following period.

The second chapter, 'Aspiring for, and achieving growth: the moderating role of resources and opportunities' expands on the same theme. Here, we take a more explicit theoretical vantage point than in the *Theory of Planned Behavior* (TBP) (Ajzen, 1991). This also leads to searching for moderator variables representing TBP's notion of 'perceived behavioral control'. In short, we argue that growth aspirations positively affect growth, but more strongly so: (a) for managers with more human capital (HC), that is, more experience and education; (b) where the access to financial capital is better; and (c) under conditions of high environmental dynamism. Assessing growth with a four-indicator index reflecting sales and employment growth relative to firm size and relative to competitors, we find support for (a) and (c) but not for (b). Further, the introduction of the moderator variables led to very considerable increases in the variance explained. Thus, while knowledge about the managers' aspirations or motivations towards growth has some informational value, it appears at least as important to consider the conditions under which these aspirations are supposed to translate into actual growth. The results also shed light on the often surprisingly weak effects on performance that researchers obtain for various aspects of HC (Davidsson and Gordon, 2012; Unger et al., 2009). The implication is that such research is often blind to what the managers are trying to achieve. Having, for example, pursued a long education does not force anyone to pursue growth. However, if a manager wants their firm to expand, then it appears that having extensive education or rich experience is helpful for making such ambitions materialise.

The third chapter, 'The effect of small business managers' growth motivation on firm growth: a longitudinal study', was one of the first to address this problem by following up on the actual growth over the following three to four years. The motivation–actual growth relationship was estimated for two separate samples and in each case using two different measures of growth (in sales and employment, respectively). The analysis applies hierarchical cross-lagged regression with Heckman correction and inclusion of potentially important control variables, thus controlling for issues of reverse causality, survivor bias and alternative explanations. The results thus stand on fairly solid ground. These results show that while the influence is bi-directional (that is, growth in period 1 also influences growth motivation in period 2), growth motivation is a predictor of future growth over and above what past growth (and control variables) can explain. Further, at least with respect to employment growth, the motivation of the founder is the relatively more important predictor. This finding has important implications. First, studies of growth motivation are meaningful even if the 'real interest' should be in actual growth. Second, policies and pedagogical approaches that affect growth motivation are also likely to affect actual firm growth.

## PART II – CHANGING THE FIRM GROWTH RESEARCH AGENDA

While the chapters in the previous part in our (possibly biased) view are examples of well-conceived and well-crafted research on their respective topics, they also represent 'old school' research on firm growth in two important ways. First, they are restricted to trying to explain variance in the 'amount' of growth. Second, although they may use more than one indicator of growth, they conceptually treat growth as a unified or undifferentiated phenomenon. Firm growth is *one* phenomenon, with assumed common antecedents and effects.

The critical reviews that we present in the current part call this into question. There may be more important questions and fruitful research avenues available to researchers than to try to further improve our ability to explain or predict differences in the amount of growth. For example, growth is rarely a sound end in itself, so it would be useful to know under which conditions growth is actually conducive to achieving more terminal goals. Further, the fact that different measures of growth are only weakly correlated is not just a methods problem or peculiarity – it suggests that we are at least in part dealing with different phenomena, which require different theoretical explanations. On a more positive note, this insight also suggests there are great opportunities for researchers to make valuable contributions within a revised agenda of research on firm growth.

Chapter 4 'Are we comparing apples with apples or apples with oranges? Appropriateness of knowledge accumulation across growth studies' first provides a review of past research. This review focuses on which *indicators* of growth researchers have used (sales, employment, assets, equity, profits, other); which growth *formulae* they employ (especially absolute vs. relative or percentage growth) and across what *time span* (for example, one-, three- or five-year periods) growth is measured. The most revealing and troublesome finding in relation to these method choices is that they appear to be made relatively independently of each other and independently of what theoretical perspective is used (Davidsson and Wiklund, 2000). This indicates that the research is often under-conceptualised.

The chapter then moves on to a very comprehensive, longitudinal investigation of how different measures of growth relate to each other. The shorthand summary of the results is that few correlations are above 0.5 and that most are low and many even negative. Interestingly, relative sales growth – often argued the 'best indicator' if one has to pick a single one – is *not* empirically the best compromise candidate for representing the phenomenon of growth 'in its entirety'. Further, the many low and negative correlations suggest that such 'entirety' is a mirage: what the measures represent cannot reasonably be said to reflect one and the same (meaningful) theoretical construct. Hence the suggestion that 'perhaps our theories are too broad, and by narrowing the boundary conditions, we are able to build richer theories that, when empirically tested, better describe *a particular aspect* of growth' (p. 134, emphasis added).

This view is reinforced and elaborated in the next chapter, 'Advancing firm growth research: a focus on growth mode instead of growth rate'. We here start out by observing that theoretical development has been notably slow in research on firm growth, Penrose (1959) still being something of a sole, bright star in otherwise rather dark skies. We then launch the suspicion that a major reason for this is that researchers have been too eager asking 'how much' before answering (or considering) the question 'how' firms grow.

This is then underpinned with a review of three streams of research. The first and largest is *growth as an outcome.* This stream is fraught with problems indicated above: restricting the perspective to the question of 'how much'; applying an undifferentiated view of this phenomenon while operationalising it in any number of ways; and turning a blind eye towards whether growth is always 'good' or not with respect to reaching more terminal growth. *The outcome of growth* theme is associated with the criticised 'stages' or 'life-cycle' stream of research (cf. Levie and Lichtenstein, 2010). We here note that the potential for practical relevance of this perspective is limited not just by lack of empirical evidence, but by limiting the perspective to assuming that the 'problem' at hand is one of an organisational unit that grows organically, leaving little room for acquisition, diversification, and so on. The main problem with the third stream, *growth as a process*, is that it is close to non-existent. Interestingly, the review of extant work includes two works from this volume (Chandler et al., Chapter 9; Lockett et al., Chapter 10) that could alternatively be regarded as research on types or modes of growth. This reflects the dual meaning of 'how' as 'in what form?' and 'through what temporal pattern?'

Most importantly, the chapter suggests a future research agenda for each stream. For growth as outcome the suggestion is a focus on choice between, combination of and sequential pattern of growth modes. For the outcome of growth the managerial and performance implications of different modes of growth are highlighted – questions that arguably are of the highest practical relevance. For growth process research what is suggested can be characterised as it being time to do Penrose all over again, with deep empirical work and theoretical analysis starting from more current business realities.

The third chapter in the part, 'Towards an integrative framework for future research on small firm growth', is a 'conclusions' excerpt from a monograph based on a comprehensive review of the literature on (small) firm growth. Being based largely on the same literature as the previous chapter, and by researchers from a similar background, it is not surprising that some of the conclusions are the same. For example, the chapter's suggested research agenda holds that while how antecedents relate to the 'amount' of growth 'in general' may have been the most common focus in past research, it is only one of at least nine possible foci for growth researchers, and not the most promising path for the future. We make the somewhat pessimistic but possibly realistic remark that 'the most relevant "growth factor" in each individual case may be some idiosyncratic factor that is not even represented by the generic variables used in research [. . .] thus it can be questioned whether broadly based generalizations about the antecedents of growth can *ever* be precise enough to be of much immediate value for managers' (p. 181). However, on a more optimistic note, we find reason to speculate that there may be more commonality across cases in the managerial challenges that growth leads to, and therefore in this chapter we emphasise the need for research into the consequences of growth. This review reinforces the need for research focusing on particular forms or modes of growth. It also highlights that related literatures actually inform questions of growth even if growth is not regarded as a 'keyword' in the research. In particular, we discuss the potential in integration with research on internationalisation, but we also mention the integration potential in literatures on diversification and on mergers and acquisitions. In combination, the three chapters in this part point out a multitude of research opportunities to be seized by future research.

## PART III – A CRITICAL LOOK AT THE GROWTH–PROFIT RELATIONSHIP

The 'integrative framework' excerpt commented on immediately above concludes 'future studies should either make a strong case for why firm growth is interesting in its own right, or explicitly include in the design those outcomes that growth is otherwise only assumed to lead to' (p. 182). In line with this advice, the chapters in this part investigate how growth relates to profitability. In the first chapter, 'Growing profitable or growing from profits: putting the horse in front of the cart?' we ask the questions: 'How do some firms manage to combine high growth with high profitability? Do they become profitable as a result of their growth, or do they attain high profitability before embarking on a high growth trajectory?'

Several theories suggest growth leads to high profitability. In a separate work (Davidsson et al., 2008) we also established that there is a pro-growth bias – a tendency to use growth as the sole outcome measure when what the researchers really are after is 'good performance' – in empirical research, and that this tendency is particularly pronounced in entrepreneurship research compared with research in management and strategy. In the chapter, we question whether the positive growth–profit relationship postulated in theories and assumed in much prior research generally holds up to scrutiny. Using the resource-based view as our theoretical frame, we argue that if firms try to grow without having unique resources (converted to market offerings that stand out), they would have to do so through price cuts and/or increased marketing, both of which would hurt profits. Instead, we argue, it is firms that first develop high profitability – reflecting having developed an attractive market offering – that can grow with sustained profitability. Empirical testing using two large data sets from different countries supports these ideas: firms in the enviable 'high growth/high profitability' category are much more likely to originate from the pool of firms that first show high profitability at low growth than from those showing high growth at low profitability. Firms in the latter category instead often retract to a 'low growth/low profitability' situation. This pattern shows considerable robustness across different time spans and categories of firm grouped by industry, size and age. This gave us reason to conclude that '[o]ur findings are a strong reason for practitioners and researchers alike to question a universal and uncritical growth ideology' (p. 214). However, we do not regard our results as the final word and therefore suggest a research agenda (p. 210–13) outlining how to seek further corroboration, rejection or boundary conditions for our tentative conclusions.

The second chapter, 'Performance configurations over time: implications for growth- and profit-oriented strategies', expands on the themes of the previous chapter. Conceptually, it offers an integrated model of growth–profit dynamics, where the superior 'exploitation ability' of large established firms and the (sometimes) superior 'discovery ability' of small, young and independent organisations are important components. Empirically, the chapter extends the analysis of growth–profitability relationships as related to firm age, testing hypotheses regarding where younger and older firms are over- and under-represented in terms of position as well as movements within the two-dimensional growth–profitability performance space.

## PART IV – THEORY-DRIVEN RESEARCH ON SPECIFIC FORMS OF GROWTH

The chapters in this final part represent what – based on the critical reviews discussed above – we believe to be one of the most important routes forward for research on firm growth: theory-driven research into the antecedents, interrelationships and effects of particular forms or modes of growth. The first chapter is titled 'Asset specificity and behavioral uncertainty as moderators of the sales growth–employment growth relationship in emerging ventures'. As we noted in Chapter 4, different indicators of growth represent different facets of the overall growth phenomenon. It also calls for future research to examine how different indicators might be conceptually linked to each other. The current chapter heeds this call and links employment growth and sales growth – the most popular growth indicators – conceptually and empirically. The research illuminates the suitability and limitations of using either as the sole indicator of a general construct of 'firm growth' in different contexts. Specifically, we use transaction cost economics (TCE) reasoning to derive and test hypotheses regarding when growth in sales and employment are and are not likely to be highly correlated. Technically, we hypothesise and model this as indicators of asset specificity and behavioural uncertainty acting as positive moderators of the relationship between sales growth and employment growth. The analysis yields consistent support for these ideas. Perhaps most interestingly, however, while the results hold up for the full sample and for a subsample of firms operating in resource-scarce environments, the hypotheses are not supported in a breakdown analysis of resource-abundant environments. This arguably speaks to the boundary conditions of TCE and similar theories.

The title of the final chapter in our collection, 'Organic and acquisitive growth: re-examining, testing and extending Penrose's growth theory', specifies both the theoretical vantage point and the modes of growth addressed in the chapter. Some reflection suggests that organic and acquisitive growth are likely to pose very different management challenges, both as regards to how growth is achieved and what organisational and performance-related consequences expansion brings. It is therefore surprising how little theoretical and empirical attention has been paid to this important distinction in previous research on firm growth. Chapter 5 represents one of the few attempts to bring conceptual clarity to the issue. Further, Penrose (1959) discussed the two modes at some length and depth. However, while some of her ideas and concepts were useful for developing hypotheses for this chapter, she did not work out in detail how the two modes relate to each other.

In the chapter we use the concepts of productive opportunity set (POS) and adjustment costs (AC) to predict how organic and acquisitive growth, respectively, in one period affect the firm's ability to grow organically in the following period. In short, we hypothesise that both forms of growth are associated with ACs. However, while organic growth adds little to the firm's POS, acquisitive growth has the potential of making additions to POS that dominate the negative effect of ACs. Thus, the amount of organic growth in the first period would have a negative effect on organic growth in the following period, while acquisitive growth brings new opportunities for organic growth in the following period. The carefully conducted econometric analysis of a large, ten-year panel data set supports these ideas. An important managerial implication of this research is that acquisitions may be an underused route to growth among small- and medium-sized firms. Inspired by the apparent usefulness of the Penrosean theoretical frame, we also offer in this chapter some ideas about future extensions of Penrose's work.

## REFLECTIONS ON THE FUTURE OF FIRM GROWTH RESEARCH

Each chapter contains recommendations for future research, many of them quite detailed. We will not repeat those recommendations here. Instead, we would like to take the opportunity to make some broad reflections about what we would like to see in the future. In essence, we advocate a redirection of firm growth research.

We would like to see less of research that attempts to test hypotheses related to explaining variance in growth rates across firms. Even if such research is theory-driven and uses the most appropriate statistical methods, we simply don't see that it will address or provide interesting answers to the most central questions related to understanding firm growth. For reasons discussed in this introductory chapter and detailed throughout the volume, we don't regard additional or more fine-grained explanations of how much firms grow as having the capacity to address the most pressing questions related to firm growth.

Instead we would like to see research that further develops firm growth theory. More precisely, we believe that much more work can be done in terms of extending and developing Penrose's theory. As some of the chapters discuss, research addressing 'how' firms grow in terms of growth modes or patterns is likely to lead to findings that are more exciting and radical theoretically, and more relevant and valid empirically, than is research related to explaining variance in growth rates across firms. Penrose's theory as it now stands is informative to this research, not least in terms of related and non-related diversification. However, there are certainly additional issues related to growth modes that her theory does not address or does not pursue in detail, which deserve theoretical attention. Extension of Penrose's theory into these areas should certainly be possible and feasible. We foresee that purely conceptual work, qualitative theory-developing work and quantitative theory-testing work all will play important roles in advancing such theory.

In a related manner, it appears that Penrose's theory has been tested and validated to a very little extent. In Chapter 10 we take an important step in this direction, but we believe that much more can be done. One option is to use the same approach as we do in Chapter 10 – to identify arguments in Penrose's theory that lend themselves to hypothesis formulation and explicit empirical testing. A careful reading of her works shows that it contains the substance for several testable hypotheses. Alternatively, it would seem highly fruitful to examine the extensive existing empirical body of firm growth research and to reinterpret it from a Penrosean perspective. Reinterpretation of existing results, re-analysis of resisting samples and cross-study meta-analyses seem like feasible routes for providing important insights into the validity of the Penrosean approach to firm growth.

## REFERENCES

Ajzen, I. (1991), 'The theory of planned behavior', *Organizational Behavior and Human Decision Processes*, **50**, 179–211.

Davidsson, P., F. Delmar and J. Wiklund (2006), *Entrepreneurship and the Growth of Firms*, Cheltenham, UK and Northampton, MA: Edward Elgar.

Davidsson, P. and S.R. Gordon (2012), 'Panel studies of venture creation: a methods-focused review and suggestions for future research', *Small Business Economics*, **39** (4), 853–876.

Davidsson, P., P.R. Steffens and J.R. Fitzsimmons (2008), *Performance Assessment in Entrepreneurship and Management Research: Is There a Pro-growth Bias?* Unpublished manuscript, Brisbane: Queensland University of Technology. http://eprints.qut.edu.au/12040/

Davidsson, P. and J. Wiklund (2000), 'Conceptual and empirical challenges in the study of firm growth', in D. Sexton and H. Landström (eds), *The Blackwell Handbook of Entrepreneurship*, Oxford, MA: Blackwell Business, pp. 26–44.

Delmar, F. and P. Davidsson (1999), 'Firm size expectations of nascent entrepreneurs', in P.D. Reynolds, W.D. Bygrave, S. Manigart, C. Mason, G.D. Meyer, H.J. Sapienza and K.G. Shaver (eds), *Frontiers of Entrepreneurship Research 1999*, Wellesley, MA: Babson College, Vol. 19, pp. 90–104.

Levie, J. and B.B. Lichtenstein (2010), 'A terminal assessment of stages theory: introducing a dynamic states approach to entrepreneurship', *Entrepreneurship Theory and Practice*, **34** (2), 317–50.

Lumpkin, G.T. and G.G. Dess (1996), 'Clarifying the entrepreneurial orientation construct and linking it to performance', *Academy of Management Review*, **21** (1), 135–72.

Penrose, E. (1959), *The Theory of the Growth of the Firm*, Oxford: Oxford University Press.

Unger, J.M., A. Rauch, M. Frese and N. Rosenbusch (2009), 'Human capital and entrepreneurial success: a meta-analytical review', *Journal of Business Venturing*, **26** (3), 341–58.

Wiklund, J. (1999), 'The sustainability of the entrepreneurial orientation–performance relationship', *Entrepreneurship Theory and Practice*, **24** (1), 37–48.

Wiklund, J., P. Davidsson, D.B. Audretsch and C. Karlsson (2011), 'The future of entrepreneurship research', *Entrepreneurship Theory and Practice*, **35** (1), 1–9.

Wiklund, J., P. Davidsson and F. Delmar (2003), 'What do they think and feel about growth? An expectancy-value approach to small business managers' attitudes towards growth', *Entrepreneurship Theory and Practice*, **27** (3), 247–69.

# PART I

# Explaining why and how much firms grow

# 1. Building an integrative model of small business growth*

**Johan Wiklund, Holger Patzelt and Dean A. Shepherd[1]**

## 1 INTRODUCTION

Small firm growth is a research area that has attracted considerable attention in recent years. Despite substantial increase in research volume, recent reviews of the literature on small firm growth suggest that little is still known about the phenomenon, and conceptual development has been limited (see Davidsson and Wiklund 2000, for an extensive discussion of the reviews and shortcomings in the field). A major reason for these shortcomings, it is argued, is that this literature is highly fragmented – several theoretical perspectives have been developed, but there is little conversation between these perspectives. For example, a striking feature of reviews of studies of firm growth is that each study only covers a fraction of the variables considered important in other studies (Storey 1994; Wiklund 1998).

Most of the growth studies explicitly or implicitly relate to one of a number of theoretical perspectives to derive hypotheses for empirical testing. While this approach may contribute substantially to our in-depth understanding of aspects of small business growth, it is often left to the reviewer of this literature to attempt to bring together the pieces, in order to 'see' the big picture. This is a difficult task, as evidenced by the lack of overarching models of growth (Davidsson and Wiklund 2000), yet important. In this chapter, we empirically combine five primary perspectives to develop a 'big picture' model of small firm growth – a model that is integrative, and both broad in scope and parsimonious in nature. This requires a focus on theoretical constructs at a high level of abstraction taken from the theoretical perspectives in the field, simultaneously allowing the investigation of the structural relations of many endogenous variables.

There are a number of benefits arising from an integrative model. First, it helps us understand how previous research fits within a broader model of small business growth. Thus, it provides an opportunity to gauge how much we really know about small business growth when we simultaneously consider the constructs from the dominant perspectives. Second, we are able to investigate the relationship of constructs and small business growth, while controlling for possible redundancies. This provides the opportunity of better assessing the contribution of each perspective to our understanding of small business growth. Third, we not only investigate the relationships proposed within a perspective, but also relationships that only exist across perspectives, which further increases explanatory ability. That is, we examine the indirect effects that some constructs might have on small business growth, which have not been adequately considered to date. Fourth, to some extent, we consider different levels of analysis. We look at the individual (human capital and attitudes), the firm (resources, entrepreneurial orientation (EO), and growth), and the environment (industry, task environment, and changes of task environment). This creates some challenges, but opens up considerable opportunities for future research.

The chapter proceeds as follows. First, we introduce five dominant perspectives by exploring the major constructs of each, and their relationship with small business growth. Second, we describe the research method used to integrate the five perspectives to build an overall model of small business growth. Third, we build the model, and detail the results. Fourth, we discuss the results by proposing a number of relationships, and challenging scholars to empirically test them. Finally, we offer some concluding comments.

## 2 THEORETICAL PERSPECTIVES OF SMALL BUSINESS GROWTH

Our purpose is to create an integrative 'big picture' model of small business growth. In order to develop and test an integrative model, we start out by reviewing previous research. In doing so, we focus on three aspects of this literature. First, we identify the underlying theoretical perspectives. This term refers to conceptual assumptions made, which guides what is observed and included in theoretical models. Second, we examine the theoretical constructs that are salient within each of the theoretical perspectives. These constructs are theoretical aggregates of manifest variables studied. For example, human capital is a theoretical construct harboring manifest variables such as education or management experience. Therefore, we classify studies focusing on experience and education, as dealing with the theoretical construct human capital. Third, we causally link these theoretical constructs to each other and to growth. Given our purpose, it is not possible, nor is it necessary, to review all the relationships between the many endogenous variables provided within each of the perspectives, and their relationship with small business growth. Rather, the following review distills each perspective into its underlying constructs, and the relationship between those constructs and small business growth. Finally, we discuss potential conflicts between perspectives, and develop an integrative approach.

## 2.1 Ontology of Small Businesses and Identification of Theoretical Perspectives

In order to identify important theoretical perspectives within the small business growth literature, it appears helpful to have a closer look at the ontology of small businesses, that is, the specification of their conceptualization (Gruber 1993). This is a difficult task, since small businesses, as all organizations, can undergo a variety of complex changes during their growth processes that make it difficult to determine the identity of the organization and observe organizational growth over time. For example, during their growth processes, small businesses can split up into more or less independent, separate legal units, and these units may not necessarily be controlled and owned by the same individuals to the same extent as the original entity did, yielding the question, which units should be considered when the growth of the original business is analyzed (Davidsson and Wiklund 2000). As Davidsson and Wiklund (2000) illustrate, different growth properties of the small business may be observed depending on whether a small business is viewed as all business activities controlled by an individual (group of individuals), as a particular business activity (set of business activities), or as a governance structure (coherently administered and controlled decision-making unit). Moreover, research has emphasized that small businesses are part of complex networks of economic actors, and are dependent on the existence of other entities (Lewin and Regine 1999), which raises additional difficulties for defining their organizational boundaries. In order to cover this variety of possibilities to conceptualize a small business, Fuller and Moran (2001) advocated a complexity theory approach, and view small businesses as complex adaptive systems that can be understood to exist simultaneously at six hierarchical ontological layers, where each layer is an emergent property of the layer below.

As our purpose is to build an integrative model of business growth, the perspectives that we use as the basis of this model should – besides being prevalent in the literature – reflect the ontological layers introduced by Fuller and Moran (2001). The two fundamental layers of Fuller and Moran's model refer to the mental models and individual capabilities (bottom layer), and attitudes of small business owners. Our model relates to these two layers in that we include an attitude perspective (e.g., Bellu and Sherman 1995; Kolvereid and Bullvåg 1996; Miner et al. 1994) and a resource-based perspective (e.g., Cooper et al. 1995; Davidsson and Honig 2003; Birley and Westhead 1990) including the human capital of the business owner as one important resource. The next higher ontological layer defines internal functional activities and relationships. The resource-based perspective covers this layer by referring to financial resources, which facilitate the development of internal functional activities, and network resources, including the relationship of the business owner to employees. The next higher ontological layer describes the business model (concept/strategy/vision) of the small business, which we address by drawing on the EO (a strategic orientation, e.g., Wiklund 1999; Zahra 1991; Zahra and Covin 1995) and the strategic 'fit' perspectives (e.g., Covin and Slevin 1989; Namen and Slevin 1993). Finally, the second highest and highest layer refer to the business-to-business relationships and external networks, respectively. Again, these are included in the network resources that are treated as part of the resource-based perspective in our model. Thus, the EO, strategic fit, resource-based, and attitude perspective are, consistent with Davidsson and Wiklund (2000), well-suited for building the basis to develop an integrated growth model since they reflect the different ontology of a small business, as identified by Fuller and Moran (2001). In addition, a prominent stream of the existing literature suggests that the environment, in which a small business operates, has a major impact on its growth opportunities (e.g., Kolvereid 1992; Pelham and Wilson 1996). We now introduce each perspective, and discuss the relationship between its constructs and small business growth.

## 2.2 Perspective 1: Entrepreneurial Orientation and Small Business Growth

There is a longstanding tradition of attributing the growth of small businesses to their entrepreneurial activities (cf. Davidsson 1989a, b and his references). However, the exact association between the two has been unclear (Davidsson et al. 2002), largely because of definitional problems with the concept of entrepreneurial activities. Miller (1983) noted that firms and individuals can be entrepreneurial, and subsequent research has found that a small firm's degree of entrepreneurial activity, or EO, is linked to its growth and performance (e.g., Covin and Slevin 1989; Wiklund 1999). Miller summarizes the characteristics of an entrepreneurial firm as: '[O]ne that engages in product-market innovation, undertakes somewhat risky ventures, and is first to come up with 'proactive' innovations, beating competitors to the punch' (Miller 1983: 771). Based on this characterization, several researchers have agreed that EO is a relevant conceptualization of entrepreneurship in existing firms. EO refers to a firm's strategic orientation, capturing specific entrepreneurial aspects of decision-making styles, methods, and practices. As such, it reflects how a firm operates rather than what it does (Lumpkin and Dess 1996).

Entrepreneurial orientation involves a willingness to innovate in order to rejuvenate market offerings, take risks in order to try out new and uncertain products, services and markets, and to be more proactive than competitors toward new marketplace opportunities (e.g., Covin and Slevin 1989, 1990, 1991; Miller 1983; Namen and Slevin 1993; Wiklund 1999; Zahra and Covin 1995; Zahra 1993). Concerning the individual dimensions of EO, previous research suggests that each can have a universal positive influence on growth. Innovative companies, creating and introducing new products and technologies, can generate extraordinary economic performance (McGrath et al. 1996), and have even been seen as the engines of economic growth (Schumpeter 1934; Brown and Eisenhardt 1995). Proactive companies can create first-mover advantage, target premium market segments, charge high prices, and 'skim' the market ahead of competitors (Zahra and Covin 1995). They can control the market by dominating distribution channels, and establish brand recognition. The link between risk taking and performance is less obvious. However, there is research to suggest that, while tried-and-true strategies may lead to high mean performance, risky strategies that lead to performance variation – because some projects fail, while others succeed – may generate more growth in the long term (March 1991; McGrath 2001).

Furthermore, there is reason to believe that EO as an overarching construct can have universally positive performance implications. A general tendency in today's business environment is the shortening of product and business model life cycles (Hamel 2000). Consequently, the future profit streams from existing operations are uncertain, and businesses need to constantly seek out new opportunities. An EO can assist companies in such a process. Several empirical studies find support for EO's positive impact on performance (cf. Wiklund 1999; Zahra 1991; Zahra and Covin 1995), and that it is important for firms to sustain or enhance their EO over time to outperform competitors and experience high growth rates (Madsen 2007).

## 2.3 Perspective 2: The Environment and Small Business Growth

The environment provides the small firm with growth opportunities that can be exploited (Davidsson 1989a, b; Stevenson and Jarillo 1986; 1990).

For example, a number of studies assess the environmental influence of location, industry, and market on performance. Specifically, work by Audretsch and coauthors has shown that the degree of scale economies (see Audretsch 1995) and unionization of workers within an industry (Acs and Audretsch 1990), and the possibility to introduce innovations (Vivarelli and Audretsch 1998) impact the growth of small businesses. Moreover, it is known that small business growth depends on the industry growth rate (Audretsch and Mahmood 1994) and market maturity (Baldwin and Gellatly 2003). All these studies describe the objective environment of a firm, the hard facts, and implicitly assume that there are inherent performance advantages for small firms in particular industries, markets, or locations (Cooper et al. 1994). The environment is analyzed at an aggregate level, that is, the environment is assumed to have the same effect on all firms in a particular industry, market, or location.

However, research has found that small firms that grow, tend to develop profitable and expanding market niches (Storey 1996, 1997) that are often quite narrow and appear difficult to describe by objective, industry- or market-wide variables. To address this issue, researchers have suggested that it may be advantageous to describe the environment of small businesses by a number of dimensions reflecting subjective perceptions of small business owners. These dimensions of the small firm's task environment have been investigated including the environment's munificence, turbulence, heterogeneity, hostility, dynamics, customer structure, and competition (Covin and Covin 1990; Kolvereid 1992; Pelham and Wilson 1996). First, *dynamic environments* are characterized by instability and continuous change. Windows of opportunity for growth arise from social, political, technological, and economic changes. Second, *hostile environments* create threats to the firm, either through increased rivalry or decreased demand for the firm's products, which can seriously reduce the growth opportunities for a small firm. Third, *environmental heterogeneity* captures the complexity of an environment, e.g., there may be many different market segments with varied characteristics and needs to be served by those operating in that industry. In heterogeneous markets, it is relatively easier for small firms to find and develop specific market niches than in markets where demand is homogeneous.

## 2.4 Perspective 3: Strategic Fit and Small Business Growth

Having identified the EO and environmental perspectives as important to explaining growth, it should be noted that the idea of EO being universally beneficial may be overly simplistic, as is the idea that an industry's attractiveness is universally beneficial for all firms. Scholars have long argued for the need for firms to achieve a fit between the characteristics of the firm and the environment in which it competes (Andrews 1987). It is likely that the effectiveness of any one strategic orientation depends on the nature of the environment. For example, one empirical study found that EO was associated with high performance among small firms operating in hostile environments, but not among those operating in benign environments (Covin and Slevin 1989).

Lumpkin and Dess (1996) suggest that the performance implications of EO are context specific, so that the relationship between EO and performance depends on the characteristics of the external environment. Therefore, increased understanding of the association between EO and growth is likely to be achieved by the concomitant consideration of strategic orientation and environment. Empirical research supports the proposition that the effect of EO on performance varies across different types of external environments (Covin and Slevin 1989; Namen and Slevin 1993).

## 2.5 Perspective 4: Resources and Small Business Growth

The resource perspective on small business growth harbors three distinct theoretical constructs. The first is related to the resource-based view in strategy, which has its focus on the resources of the firm. This perspective is focused on the combination and deployment of a firm's resources in order to achieve a competitive advantage (Conner 1991). The basic premise is that heterogeneous resources that are difficult to transfer or copy could be a source of sustainable competitive advantage. It has been suggested that resource-based theory can be important to understanding entrepreneurial phenomena (Alvarez and Busenitz 2001; Conner 1991), such as firm growth. The resource-based view, as defined in this literature, has started to be reflected in empirical entrepreneurship research (Alvarez and Busenitz 2001; Wiklund and Shepherd 2003a), and it has now been recognized that the link between the resources controlled by the firm and its effect on growth and performance is an important area for research.

One important extension of the resource-based view is the dynamic capabilities perspective (Teece et al. 1997). Dynamic capabilities refer to 'the firm's processes that use resources – specifically the processes to integrate, reconfigure, gain and release resources – to match and even create market change' (Eisenhardt and Martin 2000: 1107). These processes are important for small firms to create, discover, and successfully exploit new opportunities (Zahra et al. 2006), and may, therefore, be a prerequisite for pursuing an EO strategy. For example, resource-integrating capabilities with respect to selecting and combining risk-taking R&D employees, and equip them with appropriate financial and physical resources (e.g., sophisticated devices) facilitate the innovative efforts of the small business, and thereby its EO. Since there is still debate in the literature about which general dynamic capabilities contribute to the discovery and exploitation of new opportunities (Davidsson 2004), we focus on the underlying resources.

Certain strands of resources have received particular attention in the small business growth literature. Small firms have limited access to financial capital, which limits their growth (e.g., Hartarska and Gonzalez-Vega 2006). Financial capital is the most general type of resource, and can be relatively easily converted into other types of resources, and access to more financial capital can help firms expand more and perform better (Bamford et al. 1997). Research on liquidity constraints posits that financial capital is essential for the activities necessary to achieve growth. Financial capital provides resource slack, allowing experimentation with new strategies and innovative projects that might not be possible in a more resource-constrained environment (Cyert and March 1963; Cooper et al. 1994), which increases the willingness to innovate and pursue new opportunities (Castrogiovianni 1996; Zahra 1991).

A second construct in the resource-oriented literature on growth relates to the human capital of entrepreneurs running their businesses (e.g., Cressy 2006; Koeller and Lechler 2006). The theory on human capital posits that individuals with more, or higher quality, human capital achieve higher performance in executing relevant tasks (Becker 1975). In the growth context, human capital refers to the knowledge, skills, and experience that assist in successfully growing the business. Human capital provides the entrepreneur with knowledge that assists them in identifying opportunities and knowledge of ways to more effectively and efficiently pursue growth opportunities (cf. Alvarez and Busenitz 2001). The human resources of a small firm reach beyond those of the entrepreneur – the total resources of the workforce are important factors in determining the overall resources of the firm (Chandler and Hanks 1994a, b; Birley and Westhead 1990).

The third construct associated with the resource perspective relates to network resources. Entrepreneurial networks can be divided into inter-organizational, intra-organizational, and inter-personal networks. First, inter-organizational networks denote the strategic alliances the small firm has with other organizations. For example, small firms can use alliances with universities (e.g., Powell et al. 1996; Zucker et al. 2002), other small firms (e.g., Higgins and Gulati 2006), or large corporations (e.g., Rothaermel and Deeds 2004; Lerner and Merges 1998) to acquire important knowledge (Zahra and Bogner 2000), financial capital (DeCarolis and Deeds 1999), and manufacturing and marketing capabilities (Audretsch and Feldman 2003). Several studies have confirmed the notion that inter-organizational alliances can foster the growth of small businesses (e.g., Powell et al. 1996; Baum et al. 2000).

Second, intra-organizational networks can be understood as the relationships the small business owner has to other members of the management team. The nature of these relationships is crucial for the growth of young ventures because it determines team processes such as conflict and politics (Eisenhardt and Bourgeois 1988; Eisenhardt and Schoonhoven 1990) that can be detrimental to the growth of small businesses (Ensley et al. 2002). An important prerequisite to counteract these processes is that the intra-organizational networks are characterized by high levels of cohesion, shared leadership, and a common vision of the management team, which facilitate the development of small firms (Ensley et al. 2003). Existing literature suggests that shared team-specific experience can support these processes, thereby leading to higher growth rates (Kor 2003).

Third, inter-personal networks refer to inter-personal relationships of the small business owner, which form the basis of her/his social capital (Granovetter 1985; Brüderl and Preisendörfer 1998; Bosna et al. 2004). Social capital is particularly important for accessing, and reducing the costs of, resources (Cromie et al. 1994), such as those necessary to achieve growth. For example, social capital can enhance an individual's access to information about new opportunities and the equipment, financial capital, advice, information, and reassurance necessary to exploit such growth opportunities (Birley 1985; Johannisson 2000).

## 2.6 Perspective 5: Growth Attitude and Small Business Growth

In most economic literature, growth attitude is taken for granted – people act in ways to maximize their profits. Psychologists, concerned with all aspects of human behavior, have a more diverse view of the motives and attitudes underlying economic behavior. In the small business context, this diverse view may be of particular importance. In the entrepreneurship literature, Sexton and Bowman-Upton (1991) criticize growth models that do not consider the role of small business managers' attitudes, and argue that the growth attitudes of small business managers set limits to the growth a business will achieve. We know that people start and operate their own firms for a variety of reasons other than maximizing economic returns (Davidsson 1989a, b; Delmar 1996; Kolvereid 1992; Roper 1999; Storey 1994).

The causal direction between growth attitude and growth has been questioned. Growth may be an 'acquired taste,' as suggested by some authors (e.g., Davidsson et al. 2002). That is, small business managers who successfully manage their firms through a growth process (independent of their own previous attitude) may become and build up a more positive growth attitude as a result of the successful completion of growth. However, studies of growth using appropriate longitudinal designs have found support for a positive effect of attitude on growth (e.g., Bellu and Sherman 1995; Kolvereid and Bullvåg 1996; Miner et al. 1994; Wiklund and Shepherd 2003b).

The fulfillment of noneconomic personal goals, such as gaining independence or developing ideas, are stated as primary reasons for operating one's own firm (Douglas and Shepherd 2000). Whether or not running a small firm actually leads to the fulfillment of personal goals is an open question. It depends on whether there is a strong link between other aspects of attitude and the small business manager's goals to grow the business. For example, not all small business managers have, as a goal, to grow their business (Wiklund et al. 2003). Growth implies radical changes to the characteristics of the business. These changes may run counter to the founder's initial goals of, for instance, personal independence. Indeed, previous research indicates that expectations of changed working conditions arising from business growth are a primary concern for small business managers, which, in turn, affects their attitudes toward expanding their businesses (Wiklund et al. 2003). For example, as the business grows, the tasks required of the small business manager will likely also change. If the small business manager is favorably disposed to performing the new tasks that firm growth requires, then s/he will likely have a more positive attitude toward growth (holding the other factors of growth constant).

## 2.7 Conflicting Views and Integration of the Perspectives

Above we have identified five theoretical approaches and their accompanying theoretical constructs that are prevalent in the existing literature to explain small business growth. It is important to note, however, that these perspectives are not necessarily independent of each other, and that they may lead to conflicting hypotheses about growth under certain circumstances.

In the resource-based perspective, for example, the environment provides few restrictions to the growth of the small business. Although the expansion for particular resources and products may be limited by increasing resource costs and declining revenues for individual products, the firm can use other resources and create new markets in order to grow. As long as the managers are able to manage and deploy the resources available (Grant 1991), the environment does not limit the firm to a fixed set of growth opportunities. The firm can always grow to the extent that it has the resources to identify and exploit growth opportunities. In contrast, the environmental perspective states that growth opportunities are provided by the context, in which the firm operates, and that the small business can only grow when it exploits the opportunities offered by the environment (Davidsson 1989a, b; Stevenson and Jarillo 1986, 1990).

Moreover, there may exist interdependencies between the environment of the small business and the growth attitudes of the business owner, since the nature of the growth opportunities offered by the environment specifies the tasks the business owner has to perform to achieve growth. Since individuals favor different work-tasks (Miner 1990; Delmar 1996), the growth attitude of business owners may be determined, in part, by the environmental conditions in which small businesses operate.

One way to partially resolve the above issues and integrate the perspectives is to view the strategic orientation – here, the EO – of the small business as a central construct mediating the impact of resources, environment, and attitude on growth. For example, the availability of resources has been described as a prerequisite to engage in experimentation, risk-taking, and innovation (March 1991), and is, therefore, necessary for small businesses to develop an EO (Miller 1983; Covin and Slevin 1989; 1990). Moreover, it is known that firms are more likely to develop an EO under certain environmental conditions, specifically in dynamic and hostile environments (Miller 1983). Finally, scholars have highlighted the central role of the leader's attitude for strategic choices of firms (Kets de Vries et al. 1993). Thus, EO may serve as a central construct that partially takes into account and integrates conflicting and complementary implications that individual theoretical perspectives have on small business growth.

Even though EO may mediate the effect of resources, environment, and attitude on growth, however, it is likely that the EO-growth relationship itself is dependent on these constructs, specifically the environment of the small business. This is highlighted by the strategic fit perspective, which states that the strategic posture of the firm must match environmental conditions. Indeed, research has shown that EO does not have a uniformly positive effect on growth, but that under certain conditions, there may even be a 'dark side' of EO. For example, it appears that an EO can be inferior to a more conservative strategic orientation, and even detrimenal to growth under benign environmental conditions because in the latter case risky, innovative, and resource-consuming endeavors are unnecessary to achive high performance (Covin and Slevin 1989).

# 3 BUILDING AN INTEGRATED MODEL OF SMALL BUSINESS GROWTH

## 3.1 Analytical Approach

The next task of our analysis is to develop an empirical model that links the theoretical perspectives to growth and to each other in order to reflect the relationships that we have discussed above. In doing so empirically, we need an analytical approach that allows measurement of theoretical constructs consisting of a number of individually measured indicators (such as EO or attitude, see below), the possibility to include multiple links between these constructs in the model, and the potential to revise the model in light of empirical findings. That is, our first goal is to analyze the direct effect of EO on growth, and the effect of resources, environment, and attitude on EO. In a second step, we aim to relax the boundary conditions of this model by allowing for additional direct effects of resources, environment, and attitude on growth. Comparing the quality (explained variance) of both models allows us to assess the importance of individual relationships. To realize this two-step approach empirically, we rely on partial least square (PLS) analysis. Central to PLS is that theoretical constructs are incorporated directly in the model as latent variables consisting of a number of manifest indicators. For example, this allows us to include constructs such as EO and attitude that are measured by 8 and 14 individual indicators, respectively (see below). The analysis then reveals structural relationships between the constructs. Therefore, PLS is a suitable analytical approach for our study. PLS has been used in management research (Hulland 1999), in particular, for explaining complex relationships (Fornell and Bookstein 1982), such as those for explaining growth.

## 3.2 Sample and Design

The sampling frame was taken from the CD-ROM database UC-Select, which includes all incorporated Swedish companies. We randomly sampled independent firms from four sectors – knowledge-intensive manufacturing, labor-intensive manufacturing, professional services, and retail. A total of 808 small business managers from the sampling frame were contacted, of which 465 first responded to a telephone interview, and then to a mail questionnaire. Half of the sample had between 10 and 19 employees, and half between 20 and 49 employees, as stated in their latest annual report. These business sizes correspond to the European Union definition of a small business. We believe that this definition of a

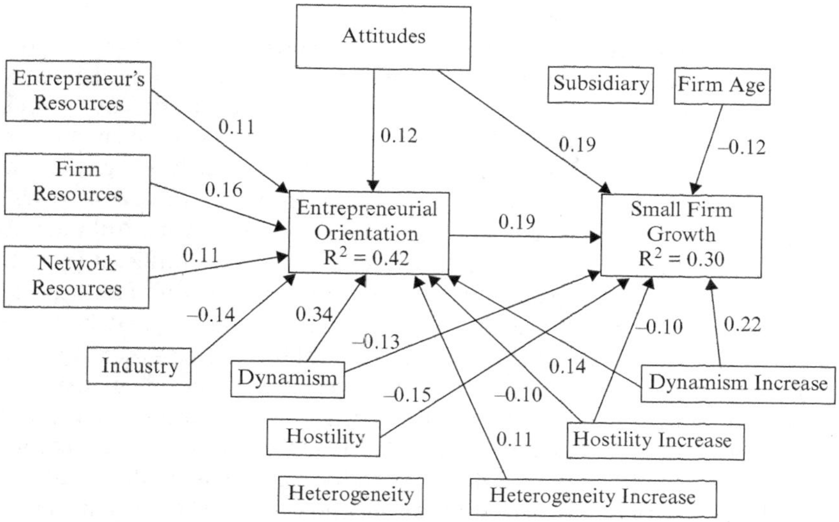


*Note:* Only relationships with path coefficients above or equal 0.10 are depicted as arrows

*Figure 1.1 Diagram of the results for the revised model of small business growth*

small business makes sense for our study, which takes place in a European setting; however, it is important to note that other studies, particularly those in non-European countries, have chosen other definitions. This may limit the comparability of our results to these other studies.

Data were collected on the independent and control variables. One year later, these 465 small business managers were again asked to complete a telephone interview, this time concerning only the dependent variable. Eighteen failed to do so, of which five had gone out of business, and 34 managing directors had been replaced during the period and were therefore excluded from the analyses. The final sample, therefore, consists of 413 small business managers (overall response rate of 51 per cent).

### 3.3 Variables and Measures

The theoretical constructs in the model are based on the review of literatures above. The large number of low-level variables in previous research can be abstracted into a small number of theoretical constructs – EO, environment, resources, and attitude – and the resulting model is illustrated in Figure 1.1.

### 3.3.1 Small business growth

There is little agreement in the existing literature on how to measure growth, and scholars have used a variety of different measures. These measures include, for example, growth of sales, employees, assets, profit, equity, and others (for a discussion see Davidsson and Wiklund 2000; Weinzimmer et al. 1998). Moreover, the time span, over which growth is analyzed in the literature, varies considerably, and ranges from one to several years. Also, growth has been measured in absolute or relative terms. Although it is not the purpose of this study to provide an analysis of different growth measures and their comparability, we point out that the different aspects embedded in each of the measures and combinations thereof may limit the comparability of our results to other studies and their generalizability.

To ensure some comparability with a maximum amount of existing growth studies, we decided to use four measures to capture small business growth. These measures capture the two most often used indicators (sales and employee growth). Moreover, it has been claimed that multiple growth indicators give richer information, and thus, are better than single indicators (Birley and Westhead 1990; Weinzimmer et al. 1998). Growth in terms of sales and employment was calculated as the relative change in size from 1996 to 1999 in all businesses controlled by the respondent. When assessing performance, comparisons with competing businesses in the market reveal important additional information (Birley and Westhead 1994). Therefore, respondents were asked to rate their sales and employment growth compared with competitors on five-point scales. Each of the variables were standardized, and summed to an index. The Cronbach's Alpha value of the scale was .91.

### 3.3.2 Entrepreneurial orientation

Miller's (1983) original scale for EO consisting of eight items was used. Two of these items describe the risk-taking behavior, three describe the proactiveness, and three refer to the innovativeness of the firm. A large number of studies have used this scale (e.g., Zahra and Covin 1995) or modifications thereof (e.g., Covin and Slevin 1989, 1990) to measure EO. Later, Lumpkin and Dess (1996) conceptually introduced autonomy and competitive agressiveness as potential additional components of the EO construct; however, even in recent EO studies scholars have decided to use the well-validated scale of Miller (e.g., Wiklund and Shepherd 2005). We follow these studies and refer to the original 8-item scale with risk-taking, proactiveness, and innovativeness as its underlying dimensions.

The items of Miller's (1983) EO scale are of the forced choice type, with pairs of opposite statements. A seven-point scale divides the two statements. In order to avoid response set contamination, the questions were arranged so that the entrepreneurial and nonentrepreneurial statements appeared on both the right and left sides. The theoretical construct is reflected in the indicators, i.e., each indicator brings unique information to the construct (cf. Fornell et al. 1990).

### 3.3.3 Environment

A total of six dimensions of the task environment are included. The scales for measuring environmental dynamism, heterogeneity, and hostility were taken from Miller and Friesen (1982). Changes over the past three years along these three environmental dimensions have their origin in Miller (1987). All items were measured on seven-point opposite statement scales. Each dimension consists of a number of items to reduce the complexity of the overall model. Association with one of four broad industry categories was taken from the data register. Specific questions were also asked about other industry characteristics, i.e., customer concentration, supplier concentration, and exports. The theoretical construct of industry is formed by these indicators.

### 3.3.4 Resources

All theoretical constructs pertaining to resources are formative, i.e., each indicator provides a unique aspect of resources. Resources of the firm consists of size in terms of employee sales, management team size, number of employees having university degrees, board size, and investment by external owner. In order to capture a relative measure of size and financial slack, we asked respondents to compare the firm's size and capital availability with that of its competitors. Miller's (1987) items were used to operationalize the perceived use of employees and the board in the decision-making process. The human capital of the manager was operationalized by various measures of experience and knowledge. Indicators included the type and length of education and training, experience with managing different types of firms (i.e., management, same industry, rapid-growth firm, and maximum number of subordinates), and tenure in present position. We also collected information on age, ethnicity, and gender, as well as whether the respondent started, inherited, bought, or is employed by the firm. These measures used to operationalize human capital are taken from Davidsson (1989a, b). In order to operationalize social capital, we asked respondents how important was a particular contact in providing advice on important decisions from a list of nine types of contacts (Davidsson 1989a, b, and one original item). These nine items were factor analyzed resulting in three factors, and corresponding indices were constructed. Respondents also indicated the firm's number of external board members.

### 3.3.5 Attitude

The work-task of managing a small business is likely to involve taking moderate risks, assuming personal responsibility for performance, paying close attention to feedback in terms of costs and profits, and finding new or innovative ways to make a new product, or provide a new service (e.g., Miner 1990; Miner et al. 1994). Since individual motivation consists of several related constructs that affect behavior (see Locke (1991) for a review), we relied on a number of concepts associated with the small business manager work-tasks. The different motives are viewed as attitude objects, and the strengths of the motives are tapped by the respondent's attitude toward the object. We build on the tripartite view, according to which attitudes can be broken down into three different classes of evaluative responses (Eagly and Chaiken 1993): (1) cognitive responses, also known as beliefs, are thoughts that people have about the attitude object; (2) affective responses consist of feelings, moods, or emotions that people have in relation to the attitude object; and (3) behavioral responses are the overt actions or intentions exhibited by people in relation to the attitude object. The goals of the respondent are viewed as affective responses, since they have to do with their feelings regarding a number of possible goals (8 items original, 10 from Davidsson 1989a, b). These 18 items were factor analyzed, resulting in six factors, and corresponding indices were constructed. *Favored work-tasks* are also seen as affective responses for the same reason (15 items from Delmar 1996). These items were factor analyzed resulting in four factors and corresponding indices were constructed. Expectations of changes that will occur in the firm as a result of growth refer to the beliefs held by respondents. Thus, *expected consequences of growth* are classified as cognitive responses (2 items original, 8 from Davidsson 1989a, b). These items were factor analyzed resulting in two factors and corresponding indices were constructed. The final set of variables concern *growth intentions* over the next five years. These variables are viewed as behavioral responses and were calculated based on present size and ideal size five years into the future in terms of employment and sales (2 items from Davidsson 1989a, b). This leads to a total of 14 variables. The theoretical construct of attitude is formed by these 14 variables, i.e., each variable brings some unique information to the construct (cf. Fornell et al. 1990).

## 3.4 Analysis

One of the important aspects of the research presented here is how the theoretical constructs utilized under different theoretical perspectives are linked to each other. In order to empirically assess this, there are two steps to the analysis. The first step tests the explanatory ability of a parsimonious integrated model. In this model, limited assumptions are made concerning structural relationships between constructs. Step 2 utilizes the information provided by the first step to revise the model in an attempt to increase its explanatory ability. One feature of PLS analysis is that it computes the correlation between all constructs, which can be used as a cue for adding structural relationships in the model. The model is generated by predicting EO and small business growth simultaneously. The simultaneous exploration of these relationships provides a big picture model of small business growth and allows for a series of propositions for empirical testing by future research.

### 3.4.1 Step 1: predicting growth by using the full integrative model

In the parsimonious base model, there are two endogenous constructs: EO and growth. That is, the model includes the direct effect of EO on small business growth, the direct effects of resources, attitude, and environment on EO, and the indirect effect of resources, attitude, and environment on small business growth via their impact on EO. The logic behind this base model builds on the basic premises of human action theory (Greve 2001). It suggests that, while characteristics of the small business or its manager may affect growth, such characteristics only have an indirect effect. They must be transformed into some type of action and activity in order to affect growth. Merely having the goal of expanding the business does not create growth unless the appropriate actions are taken. EO is a variable that captures actions and activities. Therefore, the base model assumes that all other constructs have an affect on EO, while EO, in turn, is the only construct affecting growth. The main focus of this first step of the analysis is, therefore, to: (1) test the ability of the theoretical constructs in the model to predict growth, (2) test the ability of the theoretical constructs in the model to explain EO in a growth context, i.e., given that growth is the ultimate dependent variable: to what extent can the model explain EO? (3) determine the relative importance of different theoretical constructs in the explanation of growth and EO, and (4) detect relationships among theoretical constructs not previously anticipated, which could lead to model revisions.

Table 1.1 shows the results of the analysis. The explained variance of growth is 13 per cent. Approximately 42 per cent of EO is explained in the model, which implies that the environment (industry and task), resources, and attitude *do* provide an explanation, in part, of variance in EO, even when the ultimate dependent variable is small business growth. The magnitude of the path coefficient for each latent construct, when predicting EO, provides information on the relative importance of each construct, i.e., the

*Table 1.1 PLS results for the base model of EO on small business growth*

| Predictor construct | Predicted construct | Path coefficient |
|---|---|---|
| Attitudes | EO | .13 |
| Industry | EO | −.13 |
| Task environment | EO | .44 |
| Entrepreneur's resources | EO | .10 |
| Firm resources | EO | .16 |
| Network resources | EO | .10 |
| Firm age | Growth | −.16 |
| Subsidiary | Growth | .08 |
| Entrepreneurial orientation | Growth | .29 |
| *Explained variance and model fit* | | |
| $R^2$ EO | .42 | |
| $R^2$ Growth | .13 | |
| RMS Cov (E, U) | .06 | |

*Note:* Path coefficients are equal to standardized regression coefficients in multiple linear regression analysis. RMS Cov (E, U) measures model fit. The closer to zero, the better the model fits the data

greater the magnitude of the path coefficient, the greater the importance of that construct in predicting EO. The task environment stands out as the single most important correlate of EO, whereas the magnitudes of the other path coefficients are fairly similar. All path coefficients reach .10 or above (Falk and Miller 1992 suggest .10 as a suitable cutoff for when a path coefficient should be considered), which suggests that all constructs in the model make a contribution to the explanation of the EO.

### 3.4.2 Step 2: revising the model for predicting growth

The full model tested in step 1 above explained only 13 per cent of the variance in growth. This relatively low level of explained variance could indicate that the model is mis-specified to some extent. Given the purpose of this article, we use PLS in an interactive fashion so that we can 'build' an integrative model of small business growth. An assessment of the correlations among latent variables suggests some additional direct linkages from these constructs to growth. More precisely, it appears that aspects of the task environment and attitude have direct effects on growth.

Adding these direct effects, we find that explained variance increases substantially to 30 per cent. This increase in explained variance indicates a substantial model improvement. The total explained variance in growth is consistent with, or greater than, many models of small business growth

*Table 1.2 PLS results for the revised model of small business growth*

| Predictor construct | Predicted construct | Path coefficient |
|---|---|---|
| Attitudes | EO | .12 |
| Industry | EO | −.14 |
| Dynamism | EO | .34 |
| Heterogeneity | EO | .07 |
| Hostility | EO | −.07 |
| Dynamism increase | EO | .14 |
| Heterogeneity increase | EO | .11 |
| Hostility increase | EO | −.10 |
| Entrepreneur's resources | EO | .11 |
| Firm resources | EO | .16 |
| Network resources | EO | .11 |
| Firm age | Growth | −.12 |
| Subsidiary | Growth | −.01 |
| Attitudes | Growth | .19 |
| Dynamism | Growth | −.13 |
| Hostility | Growth | −.15 |
| Dynamism increase | Growth | .22 |
| Heterogeneity increase | Growth | .07 |
| Hostility increase | Growth | −.10 |
| Entrepreneurial orientation | Growth | .19 |
| *Explained variance and model fit* | | |
| $R^2$ EO | .41 | |
| $R^2$ Growth | .30 | |
| RMS Cov (E, U) | .06 | |

*Note:* Path coefficients are equal to standardized regression coefficients in multiple linear regression analysis. RMS Cov (E, U) measures model fit. The closer to zero, the better the model fits the data.

(see Delmar (1997) for a review of explained variance in growth models). The graphical representation of the model is displayed in Figure 1.1, and the results in Table 1.2. Due to space limitations, the regression weights and factor loadings for manifest indicators are reported in the Appendix. As could be anticipated, explained variance in EO decreases somewhat (from 0.42 to 0.41) in this revised model. However, 30 per cent of the growth variable and, on average, 36 per cent of the variance in the two endogenous variables is explained, which is a major model improvement (explained variance is the best estimation of model fit in PLS analysis, and goodness-of-fit indices are largely irrelevant (Hulland 1999)).

In sum, the model demonstrates that attitude and components of the task environment (dynamism, hostility, and dynamism increase) have a direct effect on small business growth. Components of resources (resources of the individual, network resources, and resources of the firm), attitude, industry, and components of the task environment (dynamism, dynamism increase, hostility increase, heterogeneity increase) have an indirect effect on small business growth through EO. Most path coefficients are larger in relation to EO than to small business growth (exceptions are attitude, increase in environmental dynamism, and environmental hostility). This highlights the importance of understanding the antecedents of EO, offers a solid basis for an exploration of the indirect effect of constructs on small business growth via EO, and, although EO explains an important amount of the variance in small business growth, there is still a need to explore the direct effect of other constructs on growth.

## 4 PROPOSITIONS

Next, we explore each perspective on growth in terms of the relationship between its relevant constructs and small business growth, while controlling for the impact of the major constructs from other perspectives. The results are specified in terms of propositions regarding the direct and indirect effects of these constructs on small business growth through EO. When we find that a construct does not provide a significant explanation of the variance in the dependent construct, we propose that the relationship does not exist in order to provide a challenge for subsequent research to refute the proposed nonrelationship. We will discuss our propositions in light of existing small business literature. However, we would like to emphasize again that not all studies referred to below draw on the same definition of small business and the same operationalization of growth, as we do. Nevertheless, we believe that comparison with these studies does provide some support for the propositions.

### 4.1 Entrepreneurial Orientation and Small Business Growth

*Proposition 1 Entrepreneurial orientation has a positive effect on small business growth.*

Proposition 1 suggests that strategy of a small business with respect to EO affects its growth to a substantial degree, even when other factors are taken into account. It is sometimes argued that small firms are subjected to strong environmental pressures forming their development and performance (Aldrich and Auster 1986). From an ecological or institutional standpoint, the future growth of the small firm is largely a function of previous growth due to inertia and path dependence. Once the firm has been launched in a particular environment, managers can do little to affect the future of the firm due to environmental pressures and internal inertia. Ecological research claims that the findings the researchers have reached about the influence of purposeful action on firm outcomes, can be largely attributed to methodological artifacts (Carroll and Hannan 2000). On the contrary, in our research, we find that the strategic choices made by management in developing an EO of their firm have a strong independent influence on growth. These results are consistent with a recent study by Madsen (2007), showing that SMEs maintaining or even increasing their EO over time experience a faster employment growth than SMEs with decreasing EO.

### 4.2 Environment, Strategic 'Fit,' and Small Business Growth

*Proposition 2 The current task environment has a direct effect on small business growth, and has an indirect effect on small business growth through EO. Specifically, **(a)** dynamism has a direct negative effect, and an indirect positive effect, on growth, **(b)** hostility has only a direct negative effect on growth, and **(c)** heterogeneity has neither a direct nor indirect effect on growth.*

In general, proposition 2 suggests that the different dimensions of the task environment construct have differential direct and indirect impacts on small business growth. Specifically, proposition 2a suggests that dynamism simultaneously has a positive and a negative impact on small business growth. Dynamism has a direct negative impact on small business growth, which suggests that firms in dynamic environments grow slower than those in more stable environments, if their levels of EO are held constant. However, the indirect positive effect of dynamism on growth through EO suggests that in dynamic environments, where market demand is constantly shifting, opportunities become abundant, and growth should be highest for those firms that have an orientation for pursuing new opportunities because they have a good fit between their strategic orientation and the environment. Firms more content with existing operations, however, are less likely to benefit from a dynamic environment, because market demand might shift away from the firm's products, negatively impacting growth.

Other empirical observations support this notion. Zahra (1993) found a strong positive relationship between EO and performance among firms in dynamic growth environments, whereas these relationships were largely negative among the firms present in static and impoverished environments. Similarly, Miller (1988) found that innovative strategies in uncertain (unpredictable and dynamic) environments were associated with higher performance.

Proposition 2b suggests that hostility has only a direct negative effect on small business growth, and no direct effect on growth through EO. Such a finding is consistent with, for example, deterministic perspectives of the environment and firm performance where the environment is all powerful, and there is little that the small business can do to recognize the hostility of the environment and change the firm's growth trajectory by changing its strategic orientation (e.g., Aldrich and Auster 1986). It is also consistent with the empirical finding that during recessions, when the environment is generally hostile, small firms are more likely than large firms to go out of business.

Proposition 2c suggests that heterogeneity has no direct or indirect effect on small business growth. It could be that this task environmental variable does not increase our understanding of firm growth, or it may be useful for explaining large firm growth, but for small businesses, it has no effect on growth, or, of course, there is an effect (direct and/or indirect), but we are unable to detect the relationship. Whether heterogeneity does, in fact, impact small business growth requires more empirical tests. It will be interesting if others can refute our proposition.

*Proposition 3* *The change in the task environment has a direct effect on small business growth and has an indirect effect on small business growth through EO. Specifically,* ***(a)*** *dynamism increase has a direct positive and an indirect positive effect on small business growth,* ***(b)*** *hostility increase has a direct negative and an indirect negative effect on growth, and* ***(c)*** *heterogeneity increase has only an indirect positive effect on growth.*

Proposition 3a suggests that dynamism increase has both a direct positive and an indirect positive effect on small business growth. That is, as the environment is perceived to be increasing in dynamism, then this not only directly provides growth opportunities for small businesses, but also encourages these businesses to undertake more EO in order to more effectively discover and exploit these opportunities for growth. It is interesting to compare the implications of propositions 2a and 3a. The direct negative effect of dynamism, in combination with the direct positive effect of dynamism increase, suggests an important difference between an assessment of the snapshot image of the environment and environmental changes over time. Our interpretation of this finding is that small businesses have the ability to move between different types of task environments. Once they find a profitable market niche, it is important that this opportunity is exploited before moving on to pursue other opportunities.

Proposition 3b suggests that a hostility increase has a direct and indirect negative effect on small business growth. As a small business environment becomes more hostile, small businesses are likely to become less entrepreneurial in their orientation, and the environment is likely to provide fewer resources and opportunities to grow the business.

Proposition 3c suggests that heterogeneity increase has a positive indirect, but no direct effect on small business growth. This means that an increase in the complexity of the environment encourages the small businesses to develop a more EO, possibly to find or create attractive niches arising from the additional heterogeneity. It might also be that the small business is able to grow with less threat of retaliation, given the increasing complexity in the environment (e.g., greater causal ambiguity (Rumelt 1987)).

*Proposition 4 Industry has a direct effect on small business growth, but does not have an indirect effect on small business growth through EO.*

Covin and Slevin (1991) suggest that industry technological sophistication and industry life cycle stage affect EO, e.g., a disproportionately high share of hi-tech firms have been found to be entrepreneurial due to environmental conditions (Covin and Slevin 1991). However, to the authors' knowledge, these relationships have not yet been empirically tested. Zahra (1993) proposes a rationale for not testing these relationships because technological sophistication and industry life cycle stage refer to one type of conceptualization of the environment, whereas environmental dynamism, heterogeneity, and hostility refer to another. Therefore, according to Zahra, the researcher should choose only one of the conceptualizations, since the other becomes redundant.

Proposition 4 suggests that industry has an effect on small business growth, but no indirect effect, whereas propositions 2 and 3 suggest that the task environment and changes in that environment have both a direct and an indirect effect on small business growth through EO. This suggests that a possible explanation for the lack of research on the relationship between industry and EO in explaining small business growth is that there is no relationship (or it is a difficult one to find), and research presenting nonfindings is less likely to be published. It also has implications for Zahra's rationale that to include both industry and task environment variables in a single model is redundant; our proposition suggests that the impact of industry and task environment variables differ in their relationship with small business growth. Relative to including task environmental variables in a model, using only industry variables would overlook the direct effects of the environment and understate the importance of the indirect influence of the environment on small business growth though EO.

In sum, rather than a perspective of reductionism targeted at the environmental variables, our propositions suggest that it is likely important to include measures of change in the task environment over and above simply using measures of the current task environment. It also appears important to investigate the direct and the indirect effects (through EO) of the environment on small business growth, at least the indirect effects of dynamism, dynamism increase, hostility increase, and heterogeneity increase. We also propose that the redundancy created by including both industry variables and task environment variables may be less than first expected, and including both the 'industry' and 'task environment' constructs might improve the explanatory ability of small business growth models.

## 4.3 Resources and Small Business Growth

*Proposition 5 Resources have an indirect positive effect on small business growth through EO, but do not have a direct effect on small business growth. Specifically,* ***(a)*** *the resources of the firm (financial and human) have only an indirect positive effect on growth,* ***(b)*** *human capital of the manager has only an indirect positive effect on growth, and* ***(c)*** *the manager's social network has only an indirect positive effect on growth.*

In proposition 5a, we suggest that firms with greater access to human and financial resources are more likely to undertake an EO, which, in turn, facilitates small business growth. Studies have found that access to more financial capital facilitates the pursuit of resource-intensive growth strategies (Cooper et al. 1994) because, it is argued, slack resources can be used for experimentation with new strategies and practices, allowing the business to pursue new growth opportunities (Penrose 1959). Our proposition is consistent with these findings in that financial capital encourages a change to a more EO, which in turn leads to higher growth.

In proposition 5b, we propose that managers with considerable human capital know where to look for opportunities (Shane 2000), can more accurately assess the value of potential opportunities (Venkataraman 1997), and have the ability to exploit these opportunities (Cressy 2006; Kim et al. 2006), which encourages an EO. It is this EO that then facilitates small business growth. We suggest that human capital has little to no direct influence on small business growth – such as producing higher quality decisions that have a positive influence on growth – rather, we propose, human capital has a positive impact on EO, which, in turn, has a positive impact on growth.

In proposition 5c, we address the manager's social network. Research on social capital suggests that network ties provide access to resources necessary for opportunity exploitation (Birley 1985; Johannisson 2000). We propose that these resources are important to achieve small business growth, but primarily because they encourage an EO, and it is the EO that drives the small business growth. Propositions 5b and 5c both suggest that sources of resources that have an indirect positive effect on small business growth extend beyond the organization, and reside in the small business manager (human capital) and the network of the small business manager, and are consistent with those advocating the importance of investigating the resources of the individual in entrepreneurship research (Alvarez and Busenitz 2001).

The implications for future research arising from proposition 5 is that when investigating the role of resources on small business growth, EO should be considered. EO could be controlled to refute our proposition that resources do not have a direct effect on small business growth. Alternatively, EO could be included in the model to test the nature of the indirect relationship that resources have with small business growth through EO. Our findings suggest that in a small firm, resources must be put to use in creative ways (i.e., through adopting an EO). Merely providing a small firm with more money does not automatically mean it will expand.

### 4.4 Attitude and Small Business Growth

*Proposition 6 The growth attitude of the manager has a direct positive effect on small business growth and has an indirect positive effect on small business growth through EO.*

There have been a few studies that have researched the link between attitude and small firm growth, and have found that attitude may provide an important explanation, at least in part, for why some firms grow, while others do not (cf. Kolvereid and Bullvåg 1996; Miner 1990; Miner et al. 1989; Wiklund and Shepherd 2003b). Our model further delineates this explanation by proposing that the relationship between attitude and growth is two-fold: (1) a direct relationship between growth attitude and growth and, (2) an indirect relationship where growth attitude encourages a more entrepreneurial strategic orientation, which, in turn positively impacts small business growth.

The direct relationship is consistent with motivation theories that posit that, those who are more motivated (have a more positive attitude toward growth) will perform better at a task (in this case growth) when they invest more time and energy into that task (e.g., Davidsson 1989a, b; Kolvereid 1992; Miner et al. 1989). Furthermore, we anticipate that certain attitudinal patterns of the small business manager, in terms of goals, work-tasks, growth aspirations, and expected consequences of growth can be expected to generate a more EO and thus choose a strategy facilitating growth.

The goals of the small business manager are likely to influence the firm's strategic orientation. It appears that the personal goals of the entrepreneur have an influence on the strategy of the firm, mediated through the decision to behave entrepreneurially (Naffziger et al. 1994). For example, those individuals who have goals to be creative are more likely to be innovative and strive to develop new products (Amabile 1988), which is anticipated to have a positive influence on EO (see Khan (1986), who found that creativity was the most important variable in determining new venture success).

The small business manager's favored work-tasks are also likely to influence the firm's EO. Miner (1990) found that high growth entrepreneurs scored higher on the motivational construct of 'a desire to think about the future and anticipate future possibilities' than did other entrepreneurs. An interest in developing strategies for the future and working in marketing appears to be related to growth, while those who favor work-tasks associated with operations and accounting appear to operate small businesses that experience less growth.

Finally, the small business manager's expected consequences of growth are likely to influence the firm's EO. People's images of the future influence their current decisions by determining their goals and the procedures they select for achieving them. A connection between the present and the future is typically forged by people imagining various futures, considering the advantages and disadvantages of each, selecting their preferred end states, and then developing plans to achieve their desired goals, while avoiding negative outcomes (Locke and Latham 1990). Therefore, managers' images of the future outcomes arising from growth likely influence their strategic orientation.

## 5 DISCUSSION AND LIMITATIONS

In this chapter, we set out to develop a broad integrative model of small firm growth building on the theoretical perspectives utilized in previous research. Our model also gave us the opportunity to evaluate the relative importance of different perspectives and constructs.

One particularly interesting finding is that resources only had indirect effects on growth. That is, the effects were fully mediated by the EO construct. This finding is consistent with the spirit of the resource-based view of strategy. Eisenhardt and Martin (2000) note that in addition to the resources themselves, the organizational and strategic processes of firms are important because they facilitate the manipulation of resources into value-creating strategies. Empirical studies have mainly focused on the direct link between individual strands or configurations of resources and performance, while less attention has been devoted to how management can utilize these resources more effectively (Helfat 2000). Therefore, future research should focus not only on the resources (as has been done in the past), but also on how they are utilized. EO appears to be a useful construct for this purpose.

The environment appears to have complex relationships with small business growth. To some extent, this can explain inconsistencies in previous research. Among the environmental constructs examined, dynamism appears to be, by far, the most important both in terms of the current state and changes over time. Some of the complexity of the relationship between the environment and growth is captured through the strategic fit perspective. Based on our findings, it appears more relevant to consider EO and environmental dynamism simultaneously rather than separately. Furthermore, attitude in terms of goals, favored work-tasks, expected consequences of growth, and growth intentions appears important to small business growth.

EO appears to be a very useful construct in understanding small business growth. A strong direct effect of EO on growth is consistent with previous findings. However, in addition to the direct effect, we also find that EO works as a conduit for other variables. All constructs included in the model are valuable in explaining EO. This suggests that the effect on growth of, for instance, certain attitudes is further fueled, if also combined with an entrepreneurial strategic orientation. Therefore, it appears particularly important to include EO in models striving to explain small business growth.

Examining the results at a more detailed level, the three constructs that have the strongest influence on growth are the growth attitude of the small business manager, the EO of the firm, and the dynamism of the task environment where the firm operates. Interestingly, these constructs are related to the individual, the firm, and the environment respectively. Thus, although growth is studied at the firm level, in order to explain these firm-level outcomes, it is necessary to include explanatory variables from multiple levels.

One limitation of our study is the potential of reverse causality. For example, it may be that small businesses with high levels of EO mobilize resources differently than small businesses with low levels of EO, that is, EO effects the acquisition and utilization of resources. Managers of small businesses pursuing an EO strategy may put more emphasis on developing networks with other organizations in order to acquire information and source growth opportunities (Birley 1985; Johannisson 2000). These managers may also be more active in acquiring the substantial financial resources required for innovative efforts of their firm (Fildes 1990). Moreover, there is also the possibility that not only does an EO stimulate small business growth, but that growth in turn fosters the EO of a small business. For instance, growing sales lead to an increased inflow of cash for the small business, which the firm can use to pursue more innovative efforts, thereby stimulating EO. We believe that investigating these potential 'feedback' effects would be a valuable extension of the model presented in this study.

Another limitation is that we included only a limited number of constructs in the model, and that these constructs were analyzed at an aggregate level. It was not the purpose of our study to subdivide them into their underlying components. However, some of these constructs have been elaborated on more fine-grained in the literature. For example, with respect to network resources, our literature review shows that this construct can be divided into inter-organizational, intra-organizational, and inter-personal networks. Moreover, the literature review also demonstrates that scholars have used more dimensions to describe the industrial and competitive environment of organizations, as we included in our model. One possible avenue for going forward is to extend our model by taking a more fine-grained approach to (some of) the constructs we use in this study.

## NOTES

* Previously published as: Johan Wiklund, Holger Patzelt and Dean A. Shepherd (2009), 'Building an integrative model of small business growth', *Small Business Economics*, **32** (4), 351–74.

1. The authors would like to thank two anonymous reviewers for their helpful comments.

## REFERENCES

Acs, Z.J., & Audretsch, D.B. (1990). The determinants of small firm growth in US manufacturing. *Applied Economics, 22*, 143–153.

Aldrich, H.E., & Auster, E R. (1986). Even dwarfs started small: Liabilities of age and size and their strategic implications. *Research in Organizational Behavior, 8*, 165–198.

Alvarez, S.A., & Busenitz, L.W. (2001). The entrepreneurship of resource-based theory. *Journal of Management, 27*, 755–775.
Amabile, T.M. (1988). A model of creativity and innovation in organizations. *Research in Organizational Behavior, 10*, 123–169.
Andrews, K.R. (1987). *The concept of corporate strategy*. Burr Ridge, IL: Irwin.
Audretsch, D.B. (1995). *Innovation and industry evolution*. Cambridge, MA: MIT Press.
Audretsch, D.B., & Feldman, M.P. (2003). Small firm strategic research partnerships: The case of biotechnology. *Technology Analysis & Strategic Management, 15*, 273–288.
Audretsch, D.B., & Mahmood, T. (1994). Firm selection and industry evolution: The post-entry performance of new firms. *Journal of Evolutionary Economics, 4*, 243–260.
Baldwin, J., & Gellatly, G. (2003). *Innovation strategies and performance in small firms*. Cheltenham, UK and Northampton, MA, USA: Edward Elgar.
Bamford, C.E., Dean, T.J., & McDougall, P.P. (1997). *Initial strategies and new venture growth: An examination of the effectiveness of broad vs. narrow breadth strategies. Frontiers of Entrepreneurship Research*. Wellesley, MA: Babson College.
Baum, J.A., Calabrese, T., & Silverman, B.S. (2000). Don't go it alone: Alliance network composition and startup's performance in Canadian biotechnology. *Strategic Management Journal, 21*, 267–294.
Becker, G.S. (1975). *Human Capital* (2 ed.). Chicago: Chicago University Press.
Bellu, R.R., & Sherman H. (1995). Predicting firm success from task motivation and attributional style. A longitudinal study. *Entrepreneurship & Regional Development, 7*, 349–363.
Birley, S. (1985). The role of networks in the entrepreneurial process. *Journal of Business Venturing, 3*, 107–117.
Birley, S., & Westhead, P. (1990). Growth and performance contrasts between 'types' of small firms. *Strategic Management Journal, 2*, 535–557.
Birley, S., & Westhead, P. (1994). A taxonomy of business start-up reasons and their impact on firm growth and size. *Journal of Business Venturing, 9*, 7–31.
Bosna, N., van Praag, M., Thurik, R., & de Wit, G. (2004). The value of human and social capital investments for the business performance of startups. *Small Business Economics, 23*, 227–236.
Brown, S.L., & Eisenhardt, K.M. (1995). Product development: Past research, present findings, and future directions. *Academy of Management Review, 20*, 342–378.
Brüderl, J., & Preisendörfer, P. (1998). Network support and the success of newly founded businesses. *Small Business Economics, 10*, 213–225.
Carroll, G.R., & Hannan, M.T. (2000). *The demography of corporations and industries*. Princeton, New Jersey: Princeton University Press.
Castrogiovianni, G.J. (1996). Pre-start-up planning and the survival of new small firms. *Journal of Management, 22*, 801–823.
Chandler, G.N., & Hanks, S.H. (1994a). Founder competence, the environment, and venture performance. *Entrepreneurship Theory and Practice, 18*, 77–89.
Chandler, G.N., & Hanks, S.H. (1994b). Market attractiveness, resource-based capabilities, venture strategies, and venture performance. *Journal of Business Venturing, 9*, 331–349.
Conner, K. (1991). A historical comparison of resource-based theory and five

schools of thought within industrial organization economics. *Journal of Management, 17*, 121–154.
Cooper, A.C., Gimeno-Gascon, F.J., & Woo, C.Y. (1994). Initial human and financial capital as predictors of new venture performance. *Journal of Business Venturing, 9*, 371–395.
Cooper, A.C., Folta, T.B., & Woo, C.Y. (1995). Entrepreneurial information search. *Journal of Business Venturing, 10*, 107–120.
Covin, J.G., & Covin, T.J. (1990). Competitive aggressiveness, environmental context, and small firm performance. *Entrepreneurship Theory and Practice, 13*, 35–50.
Covin, J.G., & Slevin, D.P. (1989). Strategic management of small firms in hostile and benign environments. *Strategic Management Journal, 10*, 75–87.
Covin, J.G., & Slevin, D.P. (1990). New venture strategic posture, structure, and performance: an industry life cycle analysis. *Journal of Business Venturing, 5*, 123–135.
Covin, J.G., & Slevin, D.P. (1991). A conceptual model of entrepreneurship as firm behavior. *Entrepreneurship Theory and Practice, 16*, 7–25.
Cressy, R. (2006). Why do most firms die young? *Small Business Economics, 26*, 103–116.
Cromie, S., Birley, S., & Callaghan, I. (1994). Community brokers: Their role in the formation and development of business ventures. In: J.M. Veciana (Ed.), *SMEs: Internationalization, networks and strategy*. Hampshire, U.K: Avebury.
Cyert, R.M., & March, J.G. (1963). *A behavioral theory of the firm*. Englewood Cliffs, NJ: Prentice-Hall.
Davidsson, P. (1989a). *Continued entrepreneurship and small firm growth*. Stockholm: Stockholm School of Economics.
Davidsson, P. (1989b). Entrepreneurship – and after? A study of growth willingness in small firms. *Journal of Business Venturing, 4*, 211–226.
Davidsson, P. (2004). *Researching entrepreneurship*. Boston, MA: Springer.
Davidsson, P., & Honig, B. (2003). The role of social and human capital among nascent entrepreneurs. *Journal of Business Venturing, 18*, 301–331.
Davidsson, P., & Wiklund, J. (2000). Conceptual and empirical challenges in the study of firm growth. In: D. Sexton & H. Landström (Eds.), *The Blackwell handbook of entrepreneurship* (pp. 26–44). Oxford, MA: Blackwell.
Davidsson, P., Delmar, F., & Wiklund, J. (2002). Entrepreneurship as growth; growth as entrepreneurship. In: M.A. Hitt, R.D. Ireland, S.M. Camp, & D.L. Sexton (Eds.), *Strategic entrepreneurship: Creating a new mindset*. Oxford: Blackwell Publishing.
DeCarolis, D.M., & Deeds, D.L. (1999). The impact of stocks and flows of organizational knowledge on firm performance. An empirical investigation of the biotechnology industry. *Strategic Management Journal, 20*, 953–968.
Delmar, F. (1996). *Entrepreneurial behavior and business performance*. Stockholm: Stockholm School of Economics.
Delmar, F. (1997). Measuring growth: Methodological considerations and empirical results. In: R. Donckels & A. Miettinen (Eds.), *Entrepreneurship and SME research: On its way to the next millenium* (pp. 190–216). Aldershot, VA: Avebury.
Douglas, E., & Shepherd, D.A. (2000). Entrepreneurship as a utility maximizing response. *Journal of Business Venturing, 15*, 393–410.

Eagly, A.H., & Chaiken, S. (1993). *The psychology of attitudes.* Orlando, FLA: Harcourt Brace Jonanovich, Inc.
Eisenhardt, K.M., & Bourgeois, L.J. (1988). Politics of strategic decision making in high-velocity environments: Toward a midrange theory. *Academy of Management Journal, 31*, 737–770.
Eisenhardt, K.M., & Schoonhoven, C.B. (1990). Organizational growth: Linking founding team, strategy, environment, and growth among US semiconductor ventures. *Administrative Science Quarterly, 35*, 504–529.
Eisenhardt, K.M., & Martin, J.A. (2000). Dynamic capabilities: What are they? *Strategic Management Journal, 21*, 1105–1121.
Ensley, M.D., Pearson, A.W., & Amason, A.C. (2002). Understanding the dynamics of new venture top management teams: Cohesion, conflict, and new venture performance. *Journal of Business Venturing, 17*, 365–386.
Ensley, M.D., Pearson, A.W., & Pierce, C.L. (2003). Top management team process, shared leadership, and new venture performance: A theoretical model and research agenda. *Human Resource Management Review, 13*, 329–346.
Falk, R.F., & Miller, N.B. (1992). *A primer for soft modeling.* Akron, Ohio: University of Akron.
Fildes, R.A. (1990). Strategic challenges in commercializing biotechnology. *California Management Review, 32*, 63–72.
Fornell, C., & Bookstein, F.L. (1982). Two structural equation models: Lisrel and pls applied to consumer exit-voice theory. *Journal of Marketing Research, XIX*, 440–452.
Fornell, C., Lorange, P., & Roos, J. (1990). The cooperative venture formation process: A latent variable structural modeling approach. *Management Science, 36*, 1246– 1255.
Fuller, T., & Moran, P. (2001). Small entreprises as complex adaptive systems: A methodological question? *Entrepreneurship and Regional Development, 13*, 47–63.
Granovetter, M. (1985). Economic action and social structure: The problem of embeddedness. *American Journal of Sociology, 91*, 481–510.
Grant, R.M. (1991). The resource-based theory of competitive advantage: Implications for strategy formulation. *California Management Review, 33*, 114–135.
Greve, W. (2001). Traps and gaps in action explanation: Theoretical problems of a psychology of human action. *Psychological Review, 108*, 435–451.
Gruber, T.R. (1993). A translation approach to portable ontologies. *Knowledge Acquisition, 5*, 199–220.
Hamel, G. (2000). *Leading the revolution.* Cambridge, MA: Harvard University Press.
Hartarska, V., & Gonzalez-Vega, C. (2006). What affects new and established firms' expansion? Evidence from small firms in Russia. *Small Business Economics, 27*, 195–206.
Helfat, C.E. (2000). Guest editor's introduction to the special issue: The evolution of firm capabilities. *Strategic Management Journal, 21*, 955–959.
Higgins, M.C., & Gulati, R. (2006). Stacking the deck: The effect of top management team backgrounds on investor decisions. *Strategic Management Journal, 27*, 1–25.
Hulland, J. (1999). Use of partial least squares (PLS) in strategic management

research: A review of four recent studies. *Strategic Management Journal, 20*, 195–204.

Johannisson, B. (2000). Networking and entrepreneurial growth. In: D. Sexton & H. Landström (Eds.), *The Blackwell handbook of entrepreneurship* (pp. 26–44). Oxford, MA: Blackwell.

Kets de Vries, M.F.R., Miller, D., & Noel, A. (1993). Understanding the leader-strategy interface: Application of the strategic relationship interview model. *Human Relations*, 46, 5–22.

Kim, P.A., Aldrich, H.E., & Keister, L.A. (2006) Access (not) denied: The impact of financial, human, and cultural capital on entrepreneurial entry in the United States. *Small Business Economics, 27*, 5–22.

Khan, A.M. (1986). Entrepreneur characteristics and the prediction of new venture success. *Omega, 14*, 365–372.

Koeller, C.T., & Lechler, T.G. (2006). Economic and managerial perspectives on new venture growth: An integrated analysis. *Small Business Economics, 26*, 427–437.

Kolvereid, L. (1992). Growth aspirations among Norwegian entrepreneurs. *Journal of Business Venturing, 7*, 209–222.

Kolvereid, L., & Bullvåg, E. (1996). Growth intentions and actual growth: The impact of entrepreneurial choice. *Journal of Enterprising Culture, 4*, 1–17.

Kor, Y.Y. (2003). Experience-based top management team competence and sustained growth. *Organization Science, 14*, 707–719.

Lerner, J., & Merges, R.P. (1998). The control of technology alliances: An empirical analysis of the biotechnology industry. *Journal of Industrial Economics, 46*, 125–156.

Lewin, R., & Regine, B. (1999). *The soul at work: Unleasing the power of complexity science for business success*. London: Orion Business.

Locke, E.A. (1991). The motivation sequence, the motivation hub, and the motivation core. *Organizational Behavior and Human Decision Processes, 50*, 288–299.

Locke, E.A., & Latham, G.P. (1990). Work motivation and satisfaction: Light at the end of the tunnel. *Psychological Science, 1*, 240–247.

Lumpkin, G.T., & Dess, G.G. (1996). Clarifying the entrepreneurial orientation construct and linking it to performance. *Academy of Management Review, 21*, 135–172.

Madsen, E.L. (2007). The significance of sustained entrepreneurial orientation on performance of firms – A longitudinal analysis. *Entrepreneurship and Regional Development, 19*, 185–204.

March, J.G. (1991). Exploration and exploitation in organizational learning. *Organization Science, 2*, 71–87.

McGrath, R.G. (2001). Exploratory learning, innovative capacity, and managerial oversight. *Academy of Management Journal, 44*, 118–131.

McGrath, R., Tsai, M., Venkataraman, S., & MacMillan, I. (1996). Innovation, competitive advantage and rent: A model and test. *Management Science, 42*, 389–403.

Miller, D. (1983). The correlates of entrepreneurship in three types of firms. *Management Science, 29*, 770–791.

Miller, D. (1987). Strategy making and structure: Analysis and implication for performance. *Academy of Management Journal, 30*, 7–32.

Miller, D. (1988). Relating Porter's business strategies to environment and

structure: Analysis and performance implications. *Academy of Management Journal, 31*, 280–308.
Miller, D., & Friesen, P. H. (1982). Innovation in conservative and entrepreneurial firms: Two models of strategic momentum. *Strategic Management Journal, 3*, 1–25.
Miner, J.B. (1990). Entrepreneurs, high growth entrepreneurs, and managers: contrasting and overlapping motivational patterns. *Journal of Business Venturing, 5*, 221–234.
Miner, J.B., Smith, N.R., & Bracker, J.S. (1989). Role of entrepreneurial task motivation in the growth of technologically innovative firms. *Journal of Applied Psychology, 74*, 554–560.
Miner, J.B., Smith, N.R, & Bracker, J.S. (1994). Role of entrepreneurial task motivation in the growth of technologically Innovative firms: interpretations from follow-up data. *Journal of Applied Psychology, 79*, 627–630.
Naffziger, D.W., Hornsby, J.S., & Kuratko, D.S. (1994). A proposed research model of entrepreneurial motivation. *Entrepreneurship Theory and Practice, 18*, 29–42.
Namen, J.L., & Slevin, D.P. (1993). Entrepreneurship and the concept of fit: A model and empirical tests. *Strategic Management Journal, 14*, 137–153.
Pelham, A.M., & Wilson, D.T. (1996). A longitudinal study of the impact of market structure, firm structure, strategy, and market orientation culture on dimensions of small-firm performance. *Journal of the Academy of Marketing Science, 24*, 27.
Penrose, E. (1959). *The theory of the growth of the firm*. Oxford: Oxford University Press.
Powell, W.W., Koput, K.W., & Smith-Doerr, L. (1996). Interorganizational collaboration and the locus of innovation: Networks of learning in biotechnology, *Administrative Science Quarterly, 41*, 116–145.
Roper, S. (1999). Modeling small business growth and profitablity. *Small Business Economics, 13*, 235–252.
Rothaermel, F.T., & Deeds, D.L. (2004). Exploration and exploitation alliances in biotechnology: A system of new product development. *Strategic Management Journal, 25*, 201–221.
Rumelt, R.P. (1987). Theory, strategy, and entrepreneurship. In: D.J. Teece (Ed.), *The competitive challenge* (pp. 137– 158). Cambridge, MA: Ballinger.
Schumpeter, J. (1934). *The theory of economic development*. Cambridge, MA: Harvard University Press.
Sexton, D., & Bowman-Upton, N. (1991). *Entrepreneurship: creativity and growth*. New York: Macmillan.
Shane, S. (2000). Prior knowledge and the discovery of entrepreneurial opportunities. *Organization Science, 11*, 448–469.
Stevenson, H.H., & Jarillo, J.C. (1986). Preserving entrepreneurship as companies grow. *Journal of Business Strategy, 6*, 10–23.
Stevenson, H.H., & Jarillo, J.C. (1990). A paradigm of entrepreneurship: Entrepreneurial management. *Strategic Management Journal, 11*, 17–27.
Storey, D.J. (1994). *Understanding the small business sector*. London: Routledge.
Storey, D.J. (1996). *The ten percenters*. London: Deloitte & Touche.
Storey, D.J. (1997). *The ten percenters second report*. London: Deloitte & Touche.
Teece, D.J., Pisano, G., & Shuen, A. (1997). Dynamic capabilities and strategic management. *Strategic Management Journal, 18*, 509–533.

Venkataraman, S. (1997). The distinctive domain of entrepreneurship research: An editor's perspective. In: J. Katz & R. Brockhaus (Eds.), *Advances in entrepreneurship, firm emergence, and growth, vol. 3* (pp. 119–138). Greenwich, CT: JAI Press.

Vivarelli, M., & Audretsch, D.B. (1998). The link between the entry decision and post-entry performance: Evidence from Italy. *Industrial and Corporate Change, 7*, 485–500.

Weinzimmer, L.G., Nystrom P.C., & Freeman, S.J. (1998). Measuring organizational growth: Issues, consequences, and guidelines. *Journal of Management, 24*, 235–262.

Wiklund, J. (1998). *Small firm growth and performance: Entrepreneurship and beyond*. Jönköping: Jönköping International Business School.

Wiklund, J. (1999). The sustainability of the entrepreneurial orientation – performance relationship. *Entrepreneurship Theory and Practice, 24*, 37–48.

Wiklund, J., & Shepherd, D.A. (2003a). Knowledge-based resources, entrepreneurial orientation, and the performance of small and medium sized businesses. *Strategic Management Journal, 24*, 1307–1314.

Wiklund, J., & Shepherd, D.A. (2003b) Aspiring for, and achieving growth: The moderating role of resources and opportunities. *Journal of Management Studies, 40*, 1919–1942.

Wiklund, J., & Shepherd, D.A. (2005). Entrepreneurial orientation and small business performance: A configurational approach. *Journal of Business Venturing, 20*, 71–91.

Wiklund, J., Davidsson, P., & Delmar, F. (2003). What do they think and feel about growth: An expectancy-value approach to small business managers' attitudes toward growth. *Entrepreneurship Theory and Practice, 20*, 247–270.

Zahra, S. (1991). Predictors and financial outcomes of corporate entrepreneurship: An explorative study. *Journal of Business Venturing, 6*, 259–285.

Zahra, S. (1993). Environment, corporate entrepreneurship, and financial performance: A taxonomic approach. *Journal of Business Venturing, 8*, 319–340.

Zahra, S., & Covin, J. (1995). Contextual influence on the corporate entrepreneurship-performance relationship: A longitudinal analysis. *Journal of Business Venturing, 10*, 43–58.

Zahra, S., & Bogner, W.C. (2000). Technology strategy and software new ventures' performance: Exploring the moderating effect of the competitive environment. *Journal of Business Venturing, 15*, 135–173.

Zahra, S., Sapienza, H.J., & Davidsson, P. (2006). Entrepreneurship and dynamic capabilities: A review, model, and research agenda. *Journal of Management Studies, 43*, 917–955.

Zucker, L.G., Darby, M.R., & Armstrong, J.S. (2002). Commercializing knowledge: University science, knowledge capture, and firm performance in biotechnology. *Management Science, 48*, 138–153.

# APPENDIX: CONSTRUCTS AND MEASURES

*Table 1.A.1 Measures of small business growth*

| Dimension | Questions | Factor Loadings |
|---|---|---|
| Employment growth | Current number of FTEs over number of FTEs previous year. | 70 |
| Sales growth | This year's sales over last year's sales | 61 |
| Sales growth compared to competitors | Has your sales development been more positive or negative than that of your competitors over the past 12 months? Measured on 5-point scale | 76 |
| Value growth compared to competitors | Has the market value of your firm increased or decreased relative to your competitors over the past 12 months? Measured on 5-point scale Measures of entrepreneurial orientation | 77 |

*Table 1.A.2 Measure of entrepreneurial orientation*

| Dimension | Opinions about two statements anchoring seven-point scale | Factor Loadings |
|---|---|---|
| Risk-taking 1 | Owing to the nature of the environment it is best to explore it gradually via timid, incremental behavior versus Owing to the nature of the environment bold ranging acts are viewed as useful and common practice | 21 |
| Risk-taking 2 | Our firm has a strong proclivity for low-risk projects (with normal and certain rates of return) versus Our firm has a strong proclivity for high-risk projects (with chances of very high returns) | 45 |
| Proactiveness 1 | In our firm there is a strong tendency to follow competitors in introducing new things and ideas versus In our firm we always try to be ahead of competitors in product novelty or speed of innovation and usually succeed | 55 |
| Proactiveness 2 | Our firm is characterized by the fact that we favor the tried and true versus Our firm is characterized by the fact that we are growth, innovation, and development oriented | 71 |
| Proactiveness 3 | Our relationship to our competitors is characterized by the fact that we try to cooperate and coexist with competitors versus Our relationship to our competitors is characterized by the fact that we pursue a tough "undo-the-competitors" philosophy | 35 |
| Innovativeness 1 | In our firm there is a strong emphasis on R&D, technological leadership and innovation versus In our firm there is a strong emphasis on the marketing of true and tried products or services | 50 |
| Innovativeness 2 | During the past 3 years our firm has marketed, excluding mere minor variations, no new lines of products or services versus During the past 3 years our firm has marketed, excluding mere minor variations, a very large number of new lines of products or services | 65 |
| Innovativeness 3 | During the past 3 years, changes in product lines have been dramatic (e.g., changing from mechanical to electric circulators) versus During the past 3 years, changes in product lines have been of a minor nature (e.g., putting in towel with the soap) | 63 |

*Table 1.A.3 Measures of environment*

| Dimension | Questions for Task Environment | Factor Loadings |
|---|---|---|
| Dynamism (5 items; $\alpha = 60$) | To keep up with the markets and competitors at what rate must your firm change its marketing practices? At what rate are products/services becoming obsolete in your industry? To what extent is it difficult to predict the actions of competitors? Consumer demand and tastes? To what extent have there been changes in product/ service technology? Collected on seven-point scales. | 100 |
| Hostility (4 items; $\alpha = 60$) | How threatening is the environment? Is price competition? Is competition in product innovations? Is dwindling price competition? Collected on seven-point scales. | 100 |
| Heterogeneity (1 item) | To what extent is the nature of competition the same for our products? Collected on seven-point scales. | 100 |
| Change in dynamism (3 items; $\alpha = 60$) | Over the last 3 years, in your principal industry, to what degree has there been change in growth opportunities in the environment? In the innovation of new operating processes and new products and services? In research and development? | 100 |
| Change in hostility (2 items; $\alpha = 61$) | Over the last 3 years, in your principal industry, to what degree has there been change in the predictability of competitors' market activities? Change in the aggressiveness of competitors' market activities? | 100 |
| Change in heterogeneity (1 item) | Over the last 3 years, in your principal industry, to what degree has there been change in the needed diversity for production processes and marketing tactics to cater for different customers? | 100 |
| | *Questions for Industry* | |
| | Percentage of turnover generated by three largest customers | 56 |
| | Percentage of purchases from three largest suppliers | 26 |
| | Percentage of sales from exports | 50 |
| | Knowledge-intensive manufacturing | 43 |
| | Labor-intensive manufacturing | 73 |
| | Professional service sector | 31 |

*Table 1.A.4 Measures of resources*

| Dimension | Items | Regression weights |
|---|---|---|
| *Firm resources* | | |
| | How many full-time equivalent employees does the firm have today? | 25 |
| | How large do you expect your sales to be this year? | 40 |
| | How many persons are in the management team? | 31 |
| | How many people in the firm have tertiary degrees? | 9 |
| | How many people are on the board? | −35 |
| | What percentage of the firm has been sold to new owners over the past 3 years? | −33 |
| | The size of our firm (on a seven-point scale) is larger than most of our competitors or smaller than most of our competitors. | 9 |
| | The availability of capital during the past 3 years has been (on a seven-point scale) insufficient and a great impediment for our development or fully satisfactory for the firm's development. | −39 |
| | Important decisions that can be made by me or an employee are usually made by (on a seven-point scale) employee or myself. | 16 |
| | How many external members are there on your board of directors? | 8 |
| *Human capital* | | |
| | What is your highest level of completed education? | 63 |
| | How many business or management courses have you taken? | 36 |
| | Education in management or engineering | 12 |
| | How many different firms have you worked for as a manager for longer than a year? | 36 |
| | Approximately how many persons have you managed at one point in time? | 10 |
| | Have you ever worked as a manager in a rapid growth firm (annual sales growth of at least 20%)? | 26 |
| | What year did you become managing director of the firm? | 13 |
| | What year were you born? | −8 |
| | Were you born in Sweden? | 12 |

| | | |
|---|---|---|
| | Gender (male) | 35 |
| | Has anyone in your family ever started and then managed a firm? | 36 |
| | Did you start the firm where you are currently CEO? | 39 |
| | Have you ever started any other firm? | 1 |
| | Before becoming CEO did you have experience from the same industry? | −23 |
| | Are you at present associated with any other firm that you do *not* personally run? | −15 |
| *Network resources* | | |
| Formal professional advisors (3 items; α = 67) | How important, as a source of ideas and advice when making important decisions, are consultants? Lawyers? Regional development fund and similar government support agencies? | 67 |
| Day-to-day advisors (3 items; α = 61) | How important, as a source of ideas and advice when making important decisions, is your chartered accountant? Bank contact? Spouse and family? | −83 |
| Value chain advisors (3 items; α = 69) | How important, as a source of ideas and advice when making important decisions, are your customers? Suppliers? Employees? | 49 |
| Number of external board members | | −16 |

*Table 1.A.5 Measures of attitude*

| Dimension | Items | Regression weights |
|---|---|---|
| *Goals* | | |
| Creativity (α = 70) | How important is it to you that the firm makes possible that you have an outlet for your creativity? that you have the possibility for self-fulfillment? | 39 |
| Personal benefits (α = 52) | How important is it to you that the firm makes possible a high standard of living for you and your family in financial terms? that you have enough time left for family and leisure activities? that you reap the benefits from your own work? | −17 |
| Stability (α = 70) | How important is it to you that the firm yields high profits? that you can control and survey the firm's operations? that the firm is not overly dependent upon a small number of customers, suppliers, or lenders? that the firm is able to survive a crisis? that the firm's products and services are of high quality? | −2 |
| Power (α = 50) | How important is it to you that the firm makes possible that you gain a position in society? that you work independently and be independent from bosses? that you manage other people? | −4 |
| Sales growth | How important is it to you that the firm's sales increase? | 48 |
| Employment growth | How important is it to you that the firm's number of employees increases? | 9 |
| *Favored work tasks* | | |
| Strategy (α = 67) | How much time would you like to spend on: Board work? Market plans? Development of strategies? | 32 |
| Marketing (α = 79) | How much time would you like to spend on: Contacts with existing customers? Sales? Development of new customers? | 3 |
| Operations (α = 58) | How much time would you like to spend on: Calculating bids? Production? Purchasing? | −50 |

| | | |
|---|---|---|
| Accounting ($\alpha = 62$) | How much time would you like to spend on: Administration and finance? Performance auditing? Bank relations? | 8 |
| *Expected consequences of growth* | | |
| Work conditions ($\alpha = 61$) | What do you think your situation would be like if the firm was twice as big as it is today? Answered on a five-point scale from considerably easier to considerably more difficult. In terms of devoting time at work to the work-tasks you like the best? Managing the firm? Surveying and controlling the firm? | −18 |
| Firm characteristics ($\alpha = 70$) | What do you think your situation would be like if the firm was twice as big as it is today? Answered on a five-point scale from considerably easier to considerably more difficult. In terms of level of work required? In terms of employee well-being at work? In terms of the amount of your personal "income" and other economic benefits? In terms of independence in your relations with customers, suppliers, and lenders? In terms of the firm's ability to survive a crisis? In terms of high quality products and services? Do you think the firm would be worth more or less if sold? Five-point scale from considerably more to considerably less. | 21 |
| *Growth intentions* | | |
| Sales growth | If the firm develops the way you would like it to, how large would you like sales to be for the firm in 5 years' time? | 30 |
| Employment growth | If the firm develops the way you would like it to, how many employees would you like to have in 5 years' time? | −15 |

# 2. Aspiring for, and achieving growth: the moderating role of resources and opportunities*[1]

**Johan Wiklund and Dean A. Shepherd**

## INTRODUCTION

In most economic literature, the economic motive is taken for granted; people act in ways to maximize their profits. Psychologists, concerned with all aspects of human behaviour, have a more diverse view of the motives underlying economic behaviour. In the small business context, this diverse view may be of particular importance. We know that people start and operate their own firms for a variety of reasons other than maximizing economic returns (Davidsson, 1989a; Delmar, 1996; Kolvereid, 1992; Storey, 1994). The fulfilment of non-economic personal goals, such as gaining independence or developing own ideas, are stated as primary reasons for operating one's own firm (Douglas and Shepherd, 2000). Whether or not running a small firm actually leads to the fulfilment of personal goals is an open question. It depends on whether there is a strong link between the small business manager's goals and motivations on the one hand and business outcomes on the other, i.e., the extent to which business outcomes are under volitional control.

Small firm growth may be an area where volitional control is of particular interest. On the one hand, there is reason to believe that the personal motivation of the small business manager is linked to growth outcomes. Growth implies radical changes of the business characteristics. These changes may run counter to the founder's initial goals of, for instance, personal independence. Indeed, previous research indicates that expectations of changed work conditions is a primary concern for small business managers, which in turn affects their motivation to expand their businesses (Wiklund et al., 1997). This suggests that motivational differences may be an explanation as to why there are such large differences in small firm outcomes. On the other hand, there is reason to believe that small business growth is a function of the small business manager's personal abilities.

Concerning small firms, the ability of top management is regarded as one of the key capabilities ( Jennings and Beaver, 1997). In order to expand his or her business, the small business manager must have the ability to secure the resources needed for growth as well as the capability of developing the organization (Covin and Slevin, 1997; Sexton and Bowman-Upton, 1991). Thus, it would appear that personal ability plays an important role in small firm growth.

Relatively few studies have empirically investigated the link between motivation on the one hand, and small firm growth on the other. The relative scarcity of such studies may be attributed to research design requirements, as temporal separation of motivation and growth outcomes is necessary. Firm growth is not instantaneous. The motivations and behaviours of today will affect size changes into the future. Therefore, it is important to assess motivation at one point of time and size changes from that point onwards. We found only four published studies investigating the relationship between motivation and growth using such a design (i.e., Bellu and Sherman, 1995; Kolvereid and Bullvåg, 1996; Miner et al., 1994; Mok and van den Tillaart, 1990). Each finds some support for a positive relationship between motivation and growth, although these relationships are generally not very strong.

While these studies make significant contributions in this important area, they share two limitations. First, they rely on bi-variate analyses of motivation and growth and do not consider the possible direct or moderating influence of other variables. As mentioned above, small firm growth may be under some volitional control, but it is unlikely to be under total volitional control. In other words, a range of factors in addition to motivation, probably affect growth outcomes. Macro-economic development, market conditions, access to resources, as well as the skills and knowledge of the small business manager constitute some such factors (Covin and Slevin, 1997; Sexton and Bowman-Upton, 1991).

Several psychological theories deal with behaviour that is under limited volitional control. They share the common feature that behavioural outcome is modelled as a joint function of motivation and individual ability (Ajzen, 1991). There is strong theoretical reason to believe that individual ability (i.e., access to the resources and opportunities necessary to exert the behaviour) affects the relationship between motivation and outcomes (Ajzen, 1991). More specifically, the theory of planned behaviour has been successful in predicting other behaviours under limited volitional control (Ajzen, 1991; Bagozzi and Warshaw, 1992; Doll and Ajzen, 1992). Thus, a deeper understanding of the effect that motivation has on growth may benefit from the simultaneous consideration of both resources and the availability of opportunities for growth. In this chapter, we take an important step in this direction by developing a model of the relationship between motivation and growth, based on the theory of planned behaviour.

Second, previous studies of motivation and growth have used the single business entity as the unit of analysis. Recent research has shown that many individuals start and operate more than one business in parallel (Scott and Rosa, 1996; Westhead and Wright, 1998). Several avenues to expansion are open to growth-motivated individuals who can choose to build, merge with, and/or acquire other businesses. Davidsson and Wiklund (2000) argue that it is particularly important to examine the expansion of an individual's entire business activities when individual-oriented variables such as motivation are used to explain growth. Therefore, in this chapter we examine the effect of motivation on subsequent business growth by considering the expansion of all business activities that the individual controls.

The chapter proceeds as follows. First, we present the theory of planned behaviour, which leads to hypotheses concerning how growth aspirations, and variables pertaining to resources and opportunities interact with these aspirations, in explaining small business growth. Second, we describe the research method, including the sample and data collection using a longitudinal design. Third, we analyse the data and present results. Finally, we discuss the results and implications of the research for both scholars and practitioners.

## THE THEORY OF PLANNED BEHAVIOUR AND SMALL BUSINESS GROWTH

The theory of planned behaviour developed by Icek Ajzen (Ajzen, 1988, 1991) is a well-established (Olson and Zana, 1993; Petty et al., 1997) and validated (Locke, 1991) psychological theory purporting to explain and predict specific actions in specific contexts. The theory of planned behaviour is an extension of the theory of reasoned action (Ajzen and Fishbein, 1977), adding aspects of individual ability (Ajzen, 1991). This extension incorporates behaviours over which people have incomplete volitional control. Ajzen expresses the ability of an individual of exerting a specific behaviour in terms of their control over that specific behaviour. Behavioural control, in turn, consists of the individual's access to resources and opportunities relevant to the behaviour of interest. Access to time and money, and relevant skills and knowledge, for example, could be important in determining the resources and opportunities of performing a behaviour.

Central to this theory is the role of intentions: 'Intentions are assumed to capture the motivational factors that influence a behaviour; they are indications of how hard people are willing to try, of how much of an effort they are planning to exert in order to perform the behaviour. As a general rule, the stronger the intention to engage in a behaviour, the more likely should be its performance' (Ajzen, 1991, p. 181). Intentions have together with the individual's perception of behavioural control successfully predicted a range of behaviours including election participation, voting choice, weight loss and performance on cognitive tasks (Ajzen, 1991). Relevant to our study, drawing on the theory of planned behaviour, Kolvereid and Bullvåg (1996) generally found small positive relationships between growth intentions and achieved growth. However, these authors did not consider the direct influence of behavioural control on behaviour.

Ajzen's (1988) original model consists of the constructs: attitude towards the behaviour, subjective norm, intention, perceived behavioural control and behaviour. Attitude towards the behaviour, subjective norms, and perceived behavioural control explain intentions, whereas perceived behavioural control and intention predict behaviour. We focus on the variables of growth aspirations (which reflects attitudes towards growth and subjective norms) and perceived behavioural control – we do not directly measure the construct of intentions.

The theory of planned behaviour is a 'pure' psychological theory in the sense that it relates a number of psychological constructs to each other. Therefore, perceived behavioural control rather than actual behavioural control is included in the theory. Ajzen argues: 'The resources and opportunities available to a person must to some extent dictate the likelihood of behavioural achievement. Of greater psychological interest than actual control, however, is the *perception* of behavioural control and its impact on intentions and actions' (1991, p. 183, emphasis original). He then recognizes that: 'prediction of behaviour from perceived behaviour control should improve to the extent that perceptions of behavioural control realistically reflect actual control' (p. 185). As our intention is the explanation of growth and there is reason to believe that actual behavioural control plays a role in firm growth (cf. Ajzen's logic and the introduction), we model the influence of actual behavioural control on growth. Behavioural control is likely to moderate the relationship between growth aspirations and the achievement of growth. As Ajzen (1991, p. 188) notes, 'past theory as well as intuition would lead us to expect an interaction between motivation and control'.

In the entrepreneurship literature, Sexton and Bowman-Upton (1991) criticize growth models that do not consider the motivation of the

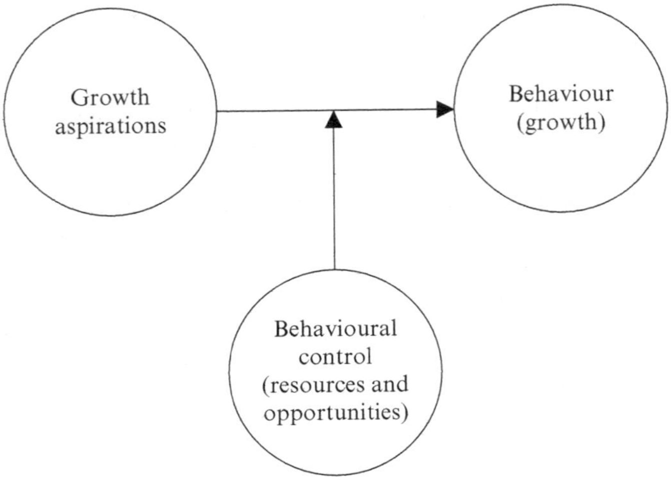


*Figure 2.1 Adapted version of the theory of planned behaviour for studying how growth aspirations influence actual growth*

individuals making the strategic decisions in a small business and argue that the growth aspirations of the small business manager set limits to the growth a business will achieve. Limits are also imposed by the growth opportunities available in the environment, the skills of the entrepreneur and the resources that the entrepreneur has access to. Refining this argument, Covin and Slevin (1997) suggest a model where growth is a function of growth aspirations, moderated by market constraints, entrepreneurial capability and organizational resources. Based on the theory of planned behaviour and acknowledging the contribution of these entrepreneurship scholars we propose and empirically test a motivation-based model of growth shown, in Figure 2.1.

**Growth Aspirations and Growth Realized**

Previous empirical research has found a direct positive relationship between motivation and growth (Bellu and Sherman, 1995; Kolvereid and Bullvåg, 1996; Miner et al., 1994; Mok and van den Tillaart, 1990). We therefore first test the hypothesis that growth aspirations directly influence subsequent growth. Thus:

*Hypothesis 1: Businesses controlled by small business managers with higher growth aspirations achieve greater growth.*

## The Moderating Effect of Resources and Opportunities

The effect of aspirations on behaviour is a function of (a) the extent to which the individual can decide at will to attempt to perform the behaviour and (b) the probability that attempting to perform the behaviour will lead to a successful outcome. In other words, the individual's control over the behaviour affects the strength of the aspiration–behaviour relationship (Ajzen, 1991; Bagozzi and Warshaw, 1992) by working as a moderator. Behavioural control, in turn, is influenced by the individual's access to resources and opportunities to exert the behaviour (cf. above for a definition and discussion of such factors). Therefore, we now turn to behavioural control factors that are of particular importance in a small business growth context and are likely to moderate the aspiration–growth relationship. The fact that the theory of planned behaviour is context specific means that aspirations and behavioural control must correspond to the particular behaviour in focus. Therefore, in predicting small business growth it is important to assess the specific resources and opportunities that may affect growth.

The growth of a small business is dependent upon the small business manager's capacity to manage growth (Sexton and Bowman-Upton, 1991). This involves the ability to conduct internal reorganizations in response to the increased size of the business as well as the ability to discover and exploit new growth opportunities (Covin and Slevin, 1997). The human capital of a small business manager gives him or her the ability of taking the measures necessary to achieve growth. That is, human capital provides the individual with the resources necessary to exert the behaviour (Ajzen, 1991). The cognitive science literature suggests that experience translates into expertise in strategic decision-making (e.g., Chase and Simon, 1973; Choo and Trotman, 1991). We know that the amount of experience people have affects the strategic choices they make and the models they use to make those decisions (Hitt and Barr, 1989; Hitt and Tyler, 1991). Greater human capital of the small business founder is likely to enhance organizational performance as it increases the chance that the small business manager makes correct decisions and conducts proper activities (Boone et al., 1996).

The human capital of a small business manager consists of skills and knowledge that assist in running the business successfully (Snell and Dean, 1992). Such skills and knowledge can be obtained through education and experience. A distinction can be made between general and specific human capital (Becker, 1975). General human capital is not related to the ability of conducting a specific job and typically refers to years of education or years of work experience (Rauch and Frese, 2000). A consistent finding for general human capital is that educated individuals are more likely to run faster-growing small businesses than those who are less educated (Sapienza and Grimm, 1997; Storey, 1994). But previous research has not found that general work experience affects small business growth. Specific human capital is specific to the domain of operating a small business and consists of skills and knowledge of conditions, internal and external to the small business, that help organize the business successfully, thus facilitating growth (Rauch and Frese, 2000). Specific human capital, such as start-up experience, management experience, and experience of working in rapidly growing organizations, has been found to explain, in part, the growth of small firms (Birley and Westhead, 1994; Macrae, 1992; Van de Ven et al., 1984). Thus:

*Hypothesis 2: The level of human capital will moderate the relationship between a small business manager's growth aspirations and the level of growth achieved. Growth will increase with growth aspirations but at a faster rate for those with (a) more education, and (b) more related experience (experience with start-up, management, and rapidly growing organizations).*

The growth of a small firm also depends on the type and amount of resources controlled by, or made available to it (Covin and Slevin, 1997). Securing funding may be particularly important in achieving the growth objectives of the firm (Sexton and Bowman-Upton, 1991). It is probable that lack of financial capital would restrict a small business manager's opportunities to take action. Many small business managers experience shortages of financial capital that limit their ability to pursue various initiatives (McGrath, 2006). Financial capital can relatively easily be converted into other types of resources (Dollinger, 1999). Access to more financial capital facilitates the pursuit of resource-intensive growth strategies (Cooper et al., 1994) because slack resources can be used for experimentation with new strategies and practices, allowing the business to pursue new growth opportunities (Penrose, 1959). A recent review of the literature indicated that several studies have found that access to financial capital affects small business growth (Storey, 1994). In a longitudinal study, Cooper et al. (1994) confirmed that access to financial capital predicted growth. Thus:

*Hypothesis 3: The level of access to financial capital will moderate the relationship between a small business manager's growth aspirations and level of growth achieved. Growth will increase with growth aspirations but at a faster rate for those with greater access to financial capital.*

While the access to financial capital can provide the small business manager with the means to conduct a range of activities, the growth of the firm will to some extent be determined by the growth opportunities in the firm's market niche. For any given product in any given niche, factors such as competition, the growth of overall demand, and changes in customer preferences, set limits to growth (Covin and Slevin, 1997; Sexton and Bowman-Upton, 1991). However, changes in the business environment can also offer new growth opportunities for small and new firms (Drucker, 1985). These changes create dynamics in demand, opening up growth opportunities for firms, which can deliver products and services attuned to the changing demand. Such opportunities described above can be expressed as environmental dynamism. More specifically, dynamic environments are associated with high unpredictability of customers and competitors, and high rates of change in market trends and industry innovation (Miller, 1987). The shifts in demand and conditions typical of a dynamic environment are likely to generate opportunities from which the growth-oriented business can take advantage (Chandler and Hanks, 1994; Covin and Slevin, 1991; Zahra, 1993). The less growth-oriented businesses, however, are less alert to opportunities in the dynamic environment and will therefore benefit less, and even face negative growth in such environments. Thus:

*Hypothesis 4: The degree of environmental dynamism will moderate the relationship between a small business manager's growth aspirations and level of growth achieved. Growth will increase with growth aspirations but at a faster rate with greater environmental dynamism.*

In sum, we hypothesize that small business managers with higher aspirations for growth achieve higher levels of growth but more human capital (higher educational level and greater specific experience), access to financial capital, and environmental dynamism enhance the effect of a small business manager's growth aspirations on the level of growth achieved.

## METHODS

### Sample and Design

The sample frame was constructed from the CD-ROM database UC-Select, which contains information on the annual reports of all limited businesses registered in Sweden. We randomly selected more than 200 independent small businesses from each of four sectors: knowledge-intensive manufacturing, labour-intensive manufacturing, professional services and retailing. Half of the sample had between 10 and 19 employees and half between 20 and 49 employees as stated in their latest annual report. These size brackets correspond to the European Union definition of small businesses.

In 1996, 808 small business managers (Chief Executive Officers) were contacted, and 630 of them agreed to participate in the survey. In 1999, those that participated in the study in 1996 were contacted again, of which 552 responded. Due to internal non-response, the effective sample size is somewhat lower in some of the analyses. In order to check for non-response bias, we compared the 552 who responded to all the questionnaires to those 256 who did not. Chi-squared and Student's t-tests were conducted concerning industry, size and previous growth. No statistically significant differences were found.

It is important to track the individual and not the small business given that our unit of analysis is the individual's growth aspirations. Therefore, 123 firms were removed from the study because the original CEO had been replaced. It is also important to include only those small business managers that have control over their strategic decisions (e.g., that the manager is not subservient to directions from the head office of a parent company). Another 103 CEOs were removed for this reason. The final sample is 326 (552 – 123 – 103) CEOs of small businesses, corresponding to 40 per cent of the original sample.

## Variables and Measures

### Growth

Four measures were used to capture small business growth. Growth in terms of sales and employment was calculated as the relative change in size from 1996 to 1999 in all businesses controlled by the respondent. When assessing performance, comparisons with competing businesses in the market reveal important additional information (Birley and Westhead, 1994). Therefore, respondents were asked to rate their sales and employment growth compared to competitors on five-point scales. Each of the variables were standardized and summed to an index. The Cronbach's Alpha value of the scale was 0.91.

### Growth aspirations

The scale measuring growth aspirations consisted of four questions that had been successfully used in two previous studies (cf. Davidsson, 1989a; Delmar, 1996). Respondents were asked whether a 25 per cent increase in the number of employees in five years would be mainly negative or mainly positive.[2] A seven-point scale ranging from very negative to very positive was used to measure this item. A similar question was then asked where a 100 per cent employee increase replaced the 25 per cent of the previous question. At the extreme level of growth aspiration individuals would score higher on the 100 per cent than the 25 per cent increase item (9.2 per cent of the sample). These individuals' responses were manually recoded to the highest value (seven) on the 25 per cent scale. Two open-ended questions were also posed. Respondents were asked to report the ideal size of the business in five years in terms of both sales and the number of employees. These responses and the 1996 size figures were used to calculate ideal growth rates of both sales and employees and converted to two seven-point scales. The two items from the 25 per cent and the 100 per cent scale were summed with the two items created from the open-ended questions to form a global growth aspiration index. The Cronbach's Alpha value of the index is 0.72 and corrected item-total correlations range from 0.47 to 0.55 indicating that the index has acceptable reliability (Nunnally, 1967) and that all items share sufficient variance with the index (Nunnally and Bernstein, 1994).

In order to establish construct validity further, we followed the guidelines provided by Robinson et al. (1991). Convergent validity was established by correlating our index with another index aimed at measuring expected consequences of growth consisting of ten items with a Cronbach's Alpha value of 0.78 (the measures were derived from expectancy theory). The correlation between the two indices was 0.62, suggesting that the correlation between the two underlying theoretical constructs, corrected for measurement error, is 0.81 (Cohen and Cohen, 1983). To establish discriminant validity, we correlated the growth aspirations index with previous three-year growth rate in terms of employees and sales. None of these correlations were above 0.10. These analyses taken together warrant the construct's convergent and discriminant validity according to Robinson's et al. (1991) criteria.

**General human capital (education level)**

Respondents were asked to state their highest level of completed education. This variable was then recoded into years of education.

**Specific human capital (experience)**

To measure experience, three variables deemed to be important to growth in previous research were utilized – start-up experience, management experience and experience of working in rapidly growing organizations. As these three variables all represent different ways of gaining experience (i.e., specific human capital) they all measure a common experience construct. Hence, they were summed to an index. It should be noted, however, that these indicators are formative, meaning that the construct is an effect of its indicators as opposed to reflective indicators where the underlying construct causes the empirical observations (Wold and Jöreskog, 1982). Therefore, reliability analysis, which is suitable for reflective indicators, conveys no relevant information.

Respondents were asked if they had started any other business. This variable was coded zero for those who had no start-up experience and one for those that did. The respondents were then asked if they had ever worked as a manager in another business or organization for more than a year. This variable was coded zero if they had no such experience and one if they did. If the respondent had worked as a manager in a rapid-growth business (annual sales growth of at least 20 per cent) the rapid-growth experience variable was coded one, if not it was coded zero. The respondents' total score on these three variables was summed into the experience index.

**Access to financial capital**

A subjective measure of 'access to capital' was utilized and captured on a seven-point scale anchored by 'insufficient and a great impediment for our development' and 'fully satisfactory for the business's development'.

**Environmental dynamism**

The construct 'environmental dynamism' captures industry growth rates as well as other dimensions of increased environmental dynamism. We used Miller's (1987) scale consisting of four items to capture this variable. The Cronbach's Alpha value of the scale is 0.69.

**Control variables**

As business size, business age, industry (i.e., manufacturing, service and retail), and the age of the small business manager have been frequently investigated in previous research and may influence growth (see Delmar (1997) for a review of predictors of growth), they were included as control variables. Initial analyses suggested that the Swedish equivalents of ISIC codes we used for stratification were not always updated or relevant. The interview included a question about the respondents' main line of business (manufacturing, retail or service). Cross-referencing these with the ISIC codes showed some deviations. We chose to rely on the respondents' self-report of main activity as a better indicator of their main industry.

The correlations and descriptive statistics for the non-categorical variables are presented in Table 2.1. To ensure that multicollinearity was not

*Table 2.1 Descriptive statistics and Spearman correlations for relevant variables*

| | Mean | S.D. | 1 | 2 | 3 | 4 | 5 | 6 | 7 | 8 | 9 | 10 | 11 | 12 |
|---|---|---|---|---|---|---|---|---|---|---|---|---|---|---|
| 1. Growth | –0.03 | 3.39 | | | | | | | | | | | | |
| 2. Business size | 22.03 | 11.42 | –0.07 | | | | | | | | | | | |
| 3. Business age | 30.28 | 28.64 | –0.19** | –0.05 | | | | | | | | | | |
| 4. Respondent's age | 48.04 | 8.39 | 0.04 | –0.08 | 0.12 | | | | | | | | | |
| 5. Growth aspiration | 16.99 | 5.67 | 0.02 | –0.05 | 0.10 | 0.07 | | | | | | | | |
| 6. Education | 12.13 | 2.39 | 0.06 | 0.11 | –0.01 | –0.20 | 0.03 | | | | | | | |
| 7. Experience | 1.53 | 1.74 | 0.04 | 0.14* | –0.34** | 0.10 | 0.19** | 0.12 | | | | | | |
| 8. Financial capital | 4.73 | 1.92 | 0.11 | 0.10 | 0.00 | 0.00 | –0.15* | –0.05 | –0.07 | | | | | |
| 9. Environ-mental dynamism | 16.89 | 3.52 | 0.16* | 0.17* | –0.27** | 0.04 | 0.12 | 0.03 | 0.15* | –0.00 | | | | |
| 10. Aspiration *education | 205.90 | 83.01 | –0.01 | –0.01 | –0.11 | –0.16* | 0.87** | 0.47** | 0.22** | –0.16* | 0.11 | | | |
| 11. Aspiration *experience | 26.97 | 34.53 | 0.04 | 0.13 | –0.35** | 0.07 | 0.38** | 0.09 | 0.97** | –0.10 | 0.18** | 0.37** | | |
| 12. Aspiration *financial capital | 76.96 | 40.76 | 0.11 | 0.05 | –0.08 | –0.04 | 0.46** | –0.04 | 0.05 | 0.74** | 0.06 | 0.37** | 0.14* | |
| 13. Aspiration *dynamism | 284.29 | 119.51 | 0.11 | 0.03 | –0.22** | –0.04 | 0.82** | 0.04 | 0.23** | –0.07 | 0.59** | 0.73** | 0.39** | 0.46** |

*Note:* n = 326.

an issue, multicollinearity diagnosis was applied. Due to space limitations, individual figures are not reported, but a calculation of the variance inflation factor (VIF) finds that the values of all first order terms are below 2.2, which is well below critical values (cf. Hair et al., 1998).

## ANALYSIS AND RESULTS

### Independent (Main) Effects Only Model

The hypotheses were tested using hierarchical regression analysis. The results are displayed in Table 2.2. The control variables of business size, business age, manufacturing, and service were first entered in a base model reported in column 2. This model fails to explain a statistically significant

*Table 2.2 Hierarchical regression analysis: independent and interaction effects on actual growth*

| | Base model | Independent effects only | Interaction effects |
|---|---|---|---|
| Manufacturing | –0.08 | –0.06 | 0.04 |
| Service | 0.00 | 0.00 | 0.16 |
| Business size | 0.06 | 0.03 | 0.01 |
| Business age | –0.08 | –0.06 | –0.03 |
| Age of respondent | –0.15* | –0.13 | –0.09 |
| Growth aspiration | | 0.15* | 1.55***[a] |
| Education | | 0.04 | –0.36[a] |
| Experience | | –0.06 | 0.45*[a] |
| Financial capital | | 0.17* | 0.32[a] |
| Environmental dynamism | | 0.13 | 1.36***[a] |
| Aspiration *education | | | 0.85* |
| Aspiration *experience | | | 0.45* |
| Aspiration *financial capital | | | –0.18 |
| Aspiration *environmental dynamism | | | 2.35*** |
| $R^2$ | 0.04 | 0.11* | 0.24*** |
| Adj. $R^2$ | 0.02 | 0.06* | 0.19*** |
| $\Delta R^2$ | | 0.06* | 0.13*** |

*Notes:*
Standardized regression coefficients are displayed in the table.
a. In the presence of interactions, the coefficients for independent terms making up the interactions convey no meaningful, but possibly misleading information (Cohen and Cohen, 1983).
$*p < 0.05$; $**p < 0.01$; $***p < 0.001$; n = 326.

share of the variance of the growth-dependent variable. In the next step, the independent (main) effects were entered. The results are reported in column 3 of the table. The main effects model makes a significant contribution over and above the base model ($\Delta R^2 = 0.09$, $p < 0.05$). Within the main effects model, the findings suggest that access to financial capital, and growth aspirations have a statistically significant influence on growth. The positive sign of the regression coefficients suggests that growth was higher for those individuals that had greater access to financial capital, and for those with a greater growth aspiration. The latter finding provides support for the hypothesis that greater growth aspiration is associated with higher business growth (Hypothesis 1). There was no evidence that experience, education or environmental dynamism had a main effect relationship with growth.

**Full Model Including Interaction Effects**

The hierarchical approach is necessary since an interaction effect exists if, and only if, the interaction term gives a significant contribution over and above the main effects only model (Cohen and Cohen, 1983).[3] As displayed in the right column of the table, the addition of the interaction terms gives an explanatory contribution over and above that of the main effects only model. Explained variance increases by 0.15 to 0.27 and the increase is statistically significant at $p < 0.001$. This suggests that interaction effects are indeed present. Examining the regression coefficients of the interaction terms, it is evident that education, experience and environmental dynamism moderate the relationship between growth aspirations and growth.

To determine the nature of these interactions, each relationship was plotted on a y-axis of growth and an x-axis of growth aspirations for high and low levels of the moderator terms (plus and minus one standard deviation from their mean, cf. Baker and Cullen (1993) and Cohen and Cohen (1983)). These plots are displayed in Figures 2.2a–c. Figure 2.2a indicates that growth increases with aspiration but at a greater rate for those with higher education. This finding provides support for Hypothesis 2a. Figure 2.2b indicates that growth increases with aspiration but at a greater rate for those with more experience, supporting Hypothesis 2b. Figure 2.2c indicates that growth increases with aspiration but at a greater rate for those in more dynamic environments. This latter finding provides support for Hypothesis 4. The interaction with access to capital was not statistically significant and therefore Hypothesis 3 is not supported.

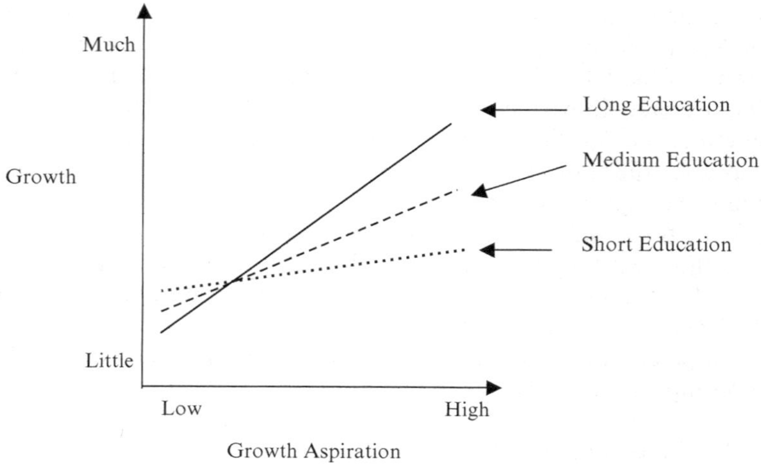


*Figure 2.2a* *Interaction of aspiration and education on growth*

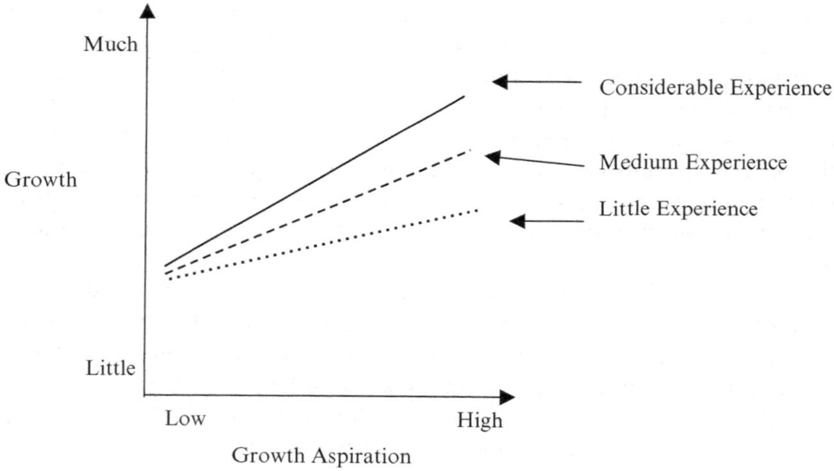


*Figure 2.2b* *Interaction of aspiration and experience on growth*

# DISCUSSION

In this chapter, we used the theory of planned behaviour to develop a model of small business managers' growth aspirations and the level of growth achieved. Consistent with previous findings and others' assump-

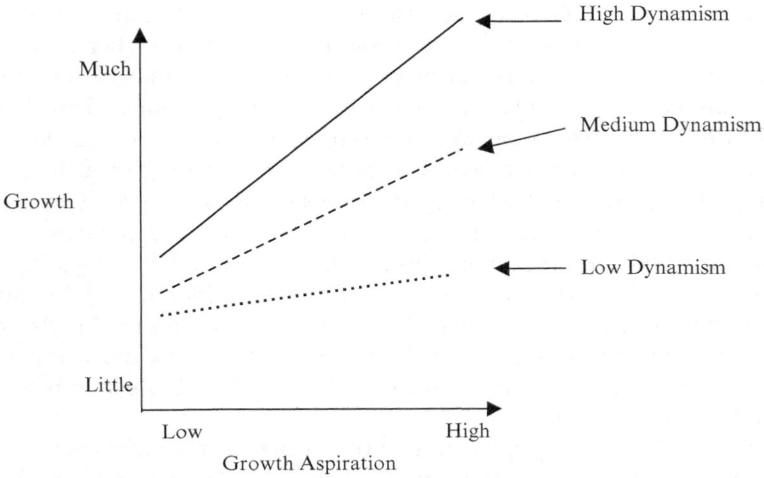


*Figure 2.2c Interaction of aspiration and dynamism on growth*

tions, we found that small business managers' aspirations to expand their business activities is positively related to actual growth. However, the relationship between aspirations and growth appears more complex than stated. It depends on the level of education and experience of the small business manager as well as the dynamism of the environment in which the business(es) operates.

These findings are largely consistent with our model and the theory of planned behaviour. In addition, they provide empirical support to the propositions made by Sexton and Bowman-Upton (1991) and Covin and Slevin (1997). As suggested by Sexton and Bowman-Upton (1991), models that fail to take growth motivation into account fail to explain why so many firms experience no, or just marginal, growth. Small business managers must have the ability to manage a growing organization and to spot new opportunities. They must also secure the resources necessary for expansion, and the environment must offer suitable growth opportunities. However, the effect that all these factors have on growth will be contingent upon the aspirations of the small business manager (Covin and Slevin, 1997). Unless the small business manager has a propensity for growth, the firm is unlikely to expand.

One of the interesting findings from this study is that when only the independent effects were investigated, education level did not have a significant relationship with growth. We found, as hypothesized, that it requires simultaneous consideration of the small business manager's growth aspirations. Growth increases with aspiration but at a faster rate for those with higher levels of education. It appears that higher education represents an important aspect of human capital, one that better equips the small business manager to achieve his or her aspirations. Growth, for those with higher education, appears to be more under volitional control, i.e., education facilitates growth for those who want their firms to grow. Storey (1994) finds that growing small businesses are more likely to be managed by more highly educated individuals. Our comparison of the main effect and contingent relationships involving education suggests that the effect of education on growth might remain hidden if only the main effect relationships are investigated. We argue, based on this study's findings, that simultaneous consideration of an individual's growth aspirations provides an even deeper understanding of the relationship between education and growth.

Based on the literature, we argued that a manager's experience is also an important aspect of human capital. The results concerning experience were very similar to that of education. No direct relationship between experience and growth was found. Experience affected growth only when accompanied by growth aspirations. Although experience may give the small business manager the relevant expertise in how to manage the business and achieve growth, it has limited effect on growth unless he or she actually intends to expand the business.

Interpreted from the viewpoint of the theory of planned behaviour, our findings suggest that a small business manager constrained by a shortage of human capital, such as education and experience, is unlikely to achieve substantial growth regardless of their motivational level. In this respect, our findings reinforce the notion from the theory of planned behaviour concerning behaviour under limited volitional control. Not only aspirations, but also resources are necessary for behavioural performance (at least, in this case, the education level and the experience of the small business manager). Research that fails to investigate interaction effects similar to the ones we have revealed here may lead to the premature conclusion that growth aspirations have a very limited influence on subsequent growth.

Another interesting finding of this study is that the independent effects model infers that growth is not significantly related to environmental dynamism. However, the lack of significance is due to insufficient acknowledgement of the complexity of the relationship. When we jointly consider growth aspirations, environmental dynamism, and growth, we find that environmental dynamism does indeed play a role – it magnifies the influence that aspirations have on growth. Given that dynamic environments provide greater opportunities, our findings reinforce the notion from the theory of planned behaviour that not only is motivation necessary for behaviour but so are opportunities. Our findings of a contingent relationship are also consistent with contemporary theorizing on entrepreneurship which suggests that entrepreneurship research should not be concerned solely with the individual but rather with the interaction of the individual and the quality of the opportunity (Shane and Venkataraman, 2000; Venkataraman, 1997). If individuals and opportunities are studied separately, results may be seriously confounded.

The only hypothesis not supported by the data concerns the interaction of access to financial capital and growth aspirations. Instead we found that access to financial capital had a direct effect on growth. This suggests that small businesses with access to more financial capital grow more, aspirations aside. A plausible interpretation of this finding is that access to slack financial resources allows experimentation within the firm, allowing it to pursue new opportunities (March and Simon, 1963, p. 146) regardless of the small business manager's aspirations.

**Limitations**

While we believe that the results are likely to be generalizable to small businesses outside Sweden, care must be taken in assessing country effects such as culture. Although evidence from several countries suggests that only a small fraction of all small businesses grow to substantial size, there are national differences suggesting that a larger share of businesses become larger in, for example, the UK (Storey, 1994) and the USA (Birch, 1977) than in Sweden (Davidsson et al., 1994). Such differences may stem from individual differences in growth aspirations, perceived opportunity, resource structures or some combination of these.

We must point out that the measurement of resources and opportunities are relatively course-grained in the present study. A more fine-grained assessment including direct measurement of the entrepreneur's ability to access resources and the actual opportunities available to the individual business rather than the general dynamics of the industry would probably strengthen the relationship between these variables and actual outcomes (cf. Shane and Venkataraman, 2000). More specifically, experience in management, start-ups, and with growing businesses is better captured as a continuous variable (i.e., number of years). While experience is often used as a proxy for expertise, operationalizations that consider both the number of years of experience and the quality of that experience would likely produce stronger and more significant results. The measurement of 'access to financial capital' should also be strengthened by a multi-item operationalization. However, this being said, we should also note that it is not possible to establish predictive validity unless a measure is reliable (Nunnally and Bernstein, 1994). The fact that our variables largely had a significant influence on growth in the hypothesized direction would suggest that they are (predictively) valid (cf. Nunnally and Bernstein, 1994).

We have argued that growth aspiration is an individual-level construct and can be achieved through internal (organic) growth or by alternative methods that may not be integrated into the original business entity. While it is possible that an individual might have different aspirations for different businesses under their control, the results support our argument that individuals have a generalized aspiration for growth that is reflected in realized growth across their businesses. This suggests that when investigating the relationship between an individual's aspirations and growth, scholars may need to expand their growth measures beyond a single business unit – care must be taken in the choice of both the measure of growth and the unit of analysis.

Finally, there is a possibility of survivor bias. Six firms in the sample had gone out of business before the first survey, and another 31 went out of business during the three years of the study. Many more had failed, of course, before the sampling frame was constructed. Therefore, we can only generalize our findings to *surviving* small businesses. It is possible that higher growth aspiration is also associated with greater risk-taking propensity. Risk-taking, in turn, may be associated with higher chances of failure. Due to high failure rates among new and small firms, future research needs to address whether those characteristics that lead to higher growth among surviving businesses are also associated with a higher risk of failure.

## Future Research and Implications

This study uses a longitudinal design and focuses on small businesses in Sweden. According to recent reviews, a lack of longitudinal designs in the field of entrepreneurship research is a major methodological shortcoming hampering further theoretical development (cf. Aldrich and Baker, 1997; Chandler and Lyon, 2001; Davidsson et al., 2001; Sexton, 1997). This is particularly important in growth studies, since growth itself is a change process. Therefore, measuring independent variables at the end of the growth period can severely bias results. We have taken an important step by temporally separating independent and dependent variables to investigate the relationship between aspirations and growth while considering the role of resources and opportunities.

A natural extension of this study is to investigate heterogeneity of growth aspirations among small business managers. Why do some small business managers aspire to grow their businesses rapidly while others do not? The theory of planned behaviour offers a theoretical framework for such an empirical investigation. It should be possible to build on previous work on the antecedents of growth motivation (e.g., Davidsson, 1989b; Kolvereid, 1992; Wiklund et al., 1997) in assessing how attitudes towards the behaviour and social norms influence growth aspirations and, in turn, how growth aspirations and perceived behavioural control influence intention.

A more detailed examination of the interplay between growth and growth aspirations may be particularly interesting. Ajzen (1991) admits that feedback loops probably are present in his model. Feedback from growth to growth aspirations is likely. Growth may be an 'acquired taste', i.e., managers of expanding firms may experience the benefits of expansion and larger size and thus become more motivated to grow their firm(s). In other words, it appears plausible that the experience of realized growth affects future growth aspirations.

These issues are beyond the scope of the chapter but highlight the importance of research into the antecedents of growth aspirations. Within the scope of this research was the relationship between a small business manager's growth aspirations and realized growth. Care must be taken however in generalizing these results to managers of new and large businesses. There may be important differences in the aspiration–growth relationship for these different types of managers. Theoretical and empirical exploration of such differences could make an important contribution to the literature.

The practical implications of this chapter's findings are numerous. First, small business managers with greater growth aspirations are more likely to realize growth. This suggests that there is an opportunity for economic growth if small business managers' growth aspirations can be increased. Second, education plays an important role in enabling growth aspirations to be realized. Governments and others wishing to grow an economy need to emphasize the importance of education. Finer-grained research that investigates which aspects of education are most important to growth would be valuable for educators. Third, the aspirations of small business managers are important but so is the macro environment. Environments that produce or allow the pursuit of opportunities enable growth aspirations to be realized. Therefore, governments need to focus on both the education of individuals and vibrant markets.

This chapter has made a number of contributions to the literature. First, we empirically assess the relationship between growth motivation and actual growth, an area which has received little attention in the past.

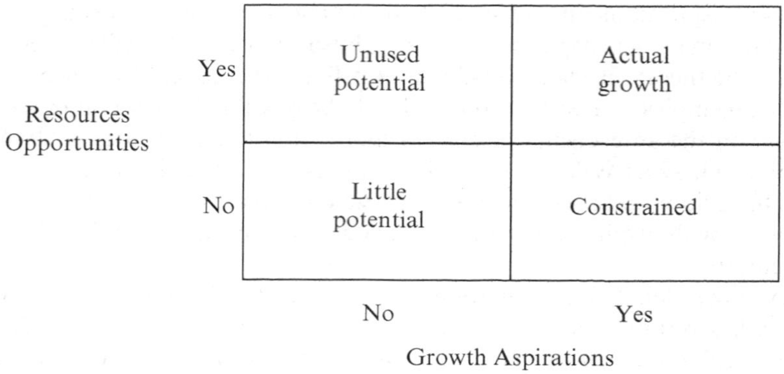


*Source:* Adapted from Sexton and Bowman-Upton (1991) and Wiklund (1998).

*Figure 2.3 Four types of firms in terms of resources and opportunities for growth and growth aspirations*

Second, we explicitly assess the influence of personal ability on growth, something that previous growth motivation studies have not addressed. We used the theory of planned behaviour as a framework from which we empirically investigated the moderating role of resources and opportunities. Growth aspirations are important to small firm growth, but unless the small business manager has access to relevant resources and opportunities, growth will be constrained. Third, we used the growth of the small business manager's total business activities as the dependent variable. Given that growth aspirations are an individual-level construct, we captured realized growth of all that individual's businesses. Finally, reviews of entrepreneurship research suggest problems with cross-sectional studies and advise the use of longitudinal designs (e.g., Aldrich and Baker, 1997). Our use of a longitudinal design better captured the temporal relationship of growth aspirations and realized growth.

Based on our findings, Figure 2.3 categorizes small firms along two dimensions; resources and opportunities for growth provides one dimension, and growth aspirations the other. Depending on their position along these two dimensions, four types of small firms are identified.

(1) Starting with the firms in the upper right quadrant, which both possess the necessary opportunities and resources, *and* the aspiration to grow, those are the ones that exhibit *actual growth*.
(2) In the upper left quadrant are the firms which have an *unused potential* since they, if they were motivated, have the ability, resources and

opportunity to expand. A relatively large proportion of all small firms are probably in this situation.

(3) Firms which strive for growth but lack certain skills, capital, or other abilities, resources and opportunities, we call *constrained*. These firms are situated in the lower right quadrant.

(4) Firms in the fourth category have neither motivation nor abilities or resources for growth, and thus have *little potential* for growth. All firms are not suited for expansion. Due to limited management abilities, these firms may actually perform better if they remain at a smaller scale. This group still has an important role in society for creating employment etc.

## CONCLUSIONS

This study takes an important step towards an increased understanding of a small business manager's growth aspirations and realized growth. While there is a relationship between the aspiration for, and actual growth, the relationship is more complex – it depends on the educational level and experience of the small business manager as well as the level of environmental dynamism. Education, experience and environmental dynamism appear to magnify the effect that growth aspirations have on growth. This is consistent with the theory of planned behaviour and the importance of resources and access to opportunities in realizing aspirations. We have taken an important step, but there is considerably more to learn about small business managers' aspirations and growth. Given the importance of small businesses to most economies, such research has important practical implications.

## NOTES

* Previously published as: Johan Wiklund and Dean A. Shepherd (2003), 'Aspiring for, and achieving growth: the moderating role of resources and opportunities', *Journal of Management Studies*, **40** (8), December, 1919–41.

1. We would like to express our gratitude to the Stockholm School of Entrepreneurship, the Knut & Alice Wallenberg Foundation and the Swedish Foundation for International Cooperation in Research and Higher Education for financial support. Per Davidsson, Scott Shane and Tomas Åstebro provided valuable comments on earlier versions of the chapter.
2. While it is unlikely to impact the results, it should be noted that a five-year time horizon was used to operationalize growth aspirations yet there is a three-year time difference from when aspirations and growth were measured.
3. The alternative approach is to have the control variables, main effect variables, and interaction variables in one model and use the significance of the interactions' regression

coefficients to test one's hypotheses. Correlation between main effect variables and corresponding interaction terms might inflate the effect size of the interaction term. The hierachical approach tests the interaction terms contribution over and above the main-effect model and therefore represents a more conservative test of moderation.

## REFERENCES


Ajzen, I. (1988). *Attitudes, Personality, and Behavior*. Chicago, IL: Dorsey Press.

Ajzen, J. (1991). 'The theory of planned behavior'. *Organizational Behavior and Human Decision Processes*, **50**, 179–211.

Ajzen, I. and Fishbein, M. (1977). 'Attitude-behavior relations: a theoretical analysis and review of empirical research'. *Psychological Bulletin*, **84**, 888–918.

Aldrich, H. and Baker, T. (1997). 'Blinded by the cites? Has there been progress in the entrepreneurship field?.' In Sexton, D. and Smilor, R. (Eds), *Entrepreneurship 2000*. Chicago, IL: Upstart Publishing Company.

Bagozzi, R. and Warshaw, P.R. (1992). 'An examination of the etiology of the attitude-behavior relation for goal-directed behaviors'. *Multivariate Behavioral Research*, **27**, 4, 601–34.

Baker, D.D. and Cullen, J.B. (1993). 'Administrative reorganization and configurational context; the contingent effects of age, size and change in size'. *Academy of Management Journal*, **36**, 1251–77.

Becker, G. S. (1975). *Human Capital*, 2nd ed. Chicago: Chicago University Press.

Bellu, R.R. and Sherman, H. (1995). 'Predicting business success from task motivation and attributional style: a longitudinal study'. *Entrepreneurship and Regional Development*, 349–63.

Birch, D. (1977). *The Job Generating Process*. Cambridge, MA: MIT Program on Neighborhood and Regional Change.

Birley, S. and Westhead, P. (1994). 'A comparison of new businesses established by "novice" and "habitual" founders in Great Britain'. *International Small Business Journal*, **12**, 1, 38–60.

Boone, C., de Brabander, B. and van Witteloostuijn, A. (1996). 'CEO locus of control and small firm performance: an integrative framework and empirical test'. *Journal of Management Studies*, **33**, 5, 667–99.

Chandler, G.N. and Hanks, S.H. (1994). 'Founder competence, the environment, and venture performance'. *Entrepreneurship Theory and Practice*, **18**, 3, 77–89.

Chandler, G.N. and Lyon, D.W. (2001). 'Issues of research design and construct measurement in entrepreneurship research: the past decade'. *Entrepreneurship Theory and Practice*, **25**, 4, 101–13.

Chase, W. and Simon, H. (1973). 'Perception in chess'. *Cognitive Psychology*, 55–81.

Choo, F. and Trotman, K. (1991). 'The relationship between knowledge structure and judgments for experienced and inexperienced auditors'. *The Accounting Review*, July, 464–85.

Cohen, J. and Cohen, P. (1983). *Applied Multiple Regression/Correlation Analysis for the Behavioral Sciences*, 2nd ed. Hillsdale, NJ: Lawrence Erlbaum Associates.

Cooper, A.C., Gimeno-Gascon, F.J. and Woo, C.Y. (1994). 'Initial human and financial capital as predictors of new venture performance'. *Journal of Business Venturing*, **9**, 5, 371–95.

Covin, J.G. and Slevin, D.P. (1991). 'A conceptual model of entrepreneurship as business behavior'. *Entrepreneurship Theory and Practice*, Fall, 7–25.
Covin, J.G. and Slevin, D.P. (1997). 'High growth transitions: theoretical perspectives and suggested directions'. In Sexton, D. and Smilor, R. (Eds), *Entrepreneurship 2000*. Chicago, IL: Upstart Publishing Company.
Davidsson, P. (1989a). *Continued Entrepreneurship and Small Firm Growth*. Stockholm: Stockholm School of Economics.
Davidsson, P. (1989b). 'Entrepreneurship – and after? A study of growth willingness in small businesses'. *Journal of Business Venturing*, **4**, 211–26.
Davidsson, P. and Wiklund, J. (2000). 'Conceptual and empirical challenges in the study of business growth'. In Sexton, D. and Landström, H. (Eds), *The Blackwell Handbook of Entrepreneurship*. Oxford: Blackwell.
Davidsson, P., Lindmark, L. and Olofsson, C. (1994). *Dynamiken i svenskt näringsliv (Business Dynamics in Sweden)*. Lund, Sweden: Studentlitteratur.
Davidsson, P., Low, M. and Wright, M. (2001). 'Editors' Introduction: Low and MacMillan ten years on: achievements and future directions for entrepreneurship research'. *Entrepreneurship Theory and Practice*, **25**, 3.
Delmar, F. (1996). *Entrepreneurial Behavior and Business Performance*. Stockholm: Stockholm School of Economics.
Delmar, F. (1997). 'Measuring growth: methodological considerations and empirical results'. In Donckels, R. and Miettinen, A. (Eds), *Entrepreneurship and SME Research: On its Way to the Next Millennium*. Aldershot, VA: Avebury, 190–216.
Doll, J. and Ajzen, I. (1992). 'Accessibility and stability of predictors in theory of planned behavior'. *Journal of Personality and Social Psychology*, **63**, 5, 754–6.
Dollinger, M.J. (1999). *Entrepreneurship: Strategies and Resources*. Upper Saddle River, NJ: Prentice Hall.
Douglas, E. and Shepherd, D.A. (2000). 'Entrepreneurship as a utility maximizing response'. *Journal of Business Venturing*, **15**, 5, 393–410.
Drucker, P. (1985). *Innovation and Entrepreneurship*. New York: Harper and Row.
Hair, J.F., Anderson, R.E., Tathum, R.L. and Black, W.C. (1998). *Multivariate Data Analysis with Readings*. New York: Macmillan.
Hitt, M.A. and Barr, S.H. (1989). 'Managerial selection decision models: examination of configural cue processing'. *Journal of Applied Psychology*, **74**, 1, 53–61.
Hitt, M.A. and Tyler, B.B. (1991). 'Strategic decision models: integrating different perspectives'. *Strategic Management Journal*, **12**, 327–51.
Jennings, P. and Beaver, G. (1997). 'The performance and competitive advantage of small firms: a management perspective'. *International Small Business Journal*, **15**, 2, 63–75.
Kolvereid, L. (1992). 'Growth aspirations among Norwegian entrepreneurs'. *Journal of Business Venturing*, **7**, 209–22.
Kolvereid, L. and Bullvåg, E. (1996). 'Growth intentions and actual growth: the impact of entrepreneurial choice'. *Journal of Enterprising Culture*, **4**, 1, 1–17.
Locke, E.A. (1991). 'Introduction to special issue'. *Organizational Behavior and Human Decision Making*, **50**, 2, 151–3.
Macrae, D.J.R. (1992). 'Characteristics of high and low growth small and medium sized businesses'. *Management Research News*, **15**, 2, 11–17.
March, J.G and Simon, H. (1963). (Reprinted in 1993.) *Organizations*. New York: Wiley.
McGrath, R. (2006). 'Entrepreneurship, small firms, and wealth creation: a

framework using real options reasoning'. In Pettigrew, A. Thomas, H. and Whittington, R. (Eds), *Handbook of Strategy and Management*. London: Sage, 101–13.

Miller, D (1987). 'The structural and environmental correlates of business strategy'. *Strategic Management Journal*, **8**, 1, 55–76.

Miner, J.B., Smith, N.R. and Bracker, J.S. (1994). 'Role of entrepreneurial task motivation in the growth of technologically innovative businesses: interpretations from follow-up data'. *Journal of Applied Psychology*, **79**, 4, 627–30.

Mok, A.L. and van den Tillaart, H. (1990). 'Farmers and small businessmen: a comparative analysis of their careers and occupational orientation'. In Donckels, R. and Miettinen, A. (Eds), *New Findings and Perspectives in Entrepreneurship*. Aldershot, VA: Avebury.

Nunnally, J.C. (1967). *Psychometric Theory*. New York: McGraw-Hill.

Nunnally, J.C. and Bernstein, I.H. (1994). *Psychometric Theory*. New York: McGraw-Hill.

Olson, J.M. and Zana, M.P. (1993). 'Attitudes and attitude change'. *Annual Review of Psychology*, **44**, 117–54.

Penrose, E. (1959). *The Theory of the Growth of the Business*. Oxford: Oxford University Press.

Petty, R.E., Wegener, D.T. and Fabrigar, L.R. (1997). 'Attitudes and attitude change'. *Annual Review of Psychology*, **48**, 609–47.

Rauch, A. and Frese, M. (2000). 'Human Capital of Small Scale Business Owners and Business Success: A Longitudinal Study of Moderators and Mediators'. Paper presented at the ICSB World Conference 2000, Brisbane, Australia.

Robinson, J.P., Shaver, P.R. and Wrightsman, L.S. (1991). 'Criteria for scale selection and evaluation'. In Robinson, J.P., Shaver, P.R. and Wrightsman, L.S. (Eds), *Measures of Personality and Social Psychological Attitudes*. San Diego, CA: Academic Press, 1–16.

Sapienza, H.J. and Grimm, C.M. (1997). 'Founder characteristics, start-up process, and strategy/structure variables as predictors of shortline railroad performance'. *Entrepreneurship Theory and Practice*, **20**, Fall, 5–24.

Scott, M. and Rosa, P. (1996). 'Opinion: Has business level analysis reached its limits? Time for a rethink'. *International Small Business Journal*, **14**, 4, 81–9.

Sexton, D.L. (1997). 'Entrepreneurship research needs and issues'. In Sexton, D. and Smilor, R. (Eds), *Entrepreneurship 2000*. Chicago, IL: Upstart Publishing Company.

Sexton, D.L. and Bowman-Upton, N.B. (1991). *Entrepreneurship: Creativity and Growth*. New York: Macmillan.

Shane, S.A. and Venkataraman, S. (2000). 'The promise of entrepreneurship as a field of research'. *Academy of Management Review*, **25**, 217–26.

Snell, S.A. and Dean, J.W. (1992). 'Integrated manufacturing and human resource management: a human capital perspective'. *Academy of Management Journal*, **35**, 3, 467–504.

Storey, D.J. (1994). *Understanding the Small Business Sector*. London: Routledge.

Van de Ven, A.H., Hudson, R. and Schroeder, D. (1984). 'Designing new business startups: entrepreneurial, organizational, and ecological considerations'. *Journal of Management*, **10**, 1, 87–107.

Venkataraman, S. (1997). 'The distinctive domain of entrepreneurship research: an editor's perspective'. In Katz, J. and Brockhaus, J. (Eds), *Advances in Entrepreneurship, Business Emergence, and Growth*. Greenwich, CT: JAI Press.

Westhead, P. and Wright, M. (1998). 'Novice, portfolio, and serial founders: are they different?'. *Journal of Business Venturing*, **13**, 173–204.
Wiklund, J. (1998). 'Small Firm Growth and Performance: Entrepreneurship and Beyond'. Doctoral Dissertation. Jönköping: Jönköping International Business School.
Wiklund, J., Davidsson, P., Delmar, F. and Aronsson, M. (1997). 'Expected consequences of growth and their effect on growth willingness in different samples of small firms'. *Frontiers of Entrepreneurship Research*. Wellesley, MA: Babson College.
Wold, H. and Jöreskog, K.G. (1982). 'The ML and PLS techniques for modelling with latent variables: historical and comparative aspects'. *Systems Under Indirect Observation: Causality, Structure, Prediction*. Amsterdam: North-Holland, 263–70.
Zahra, S. (1993). 'A conceptual model of entrepreneurship as business behavior: a critique and extension'. *Entrepreneurship Theory and Practice*, **16**, 5–21.

# 3. The effect of small business managers' growth motivation on firm growth: a longitudinal study*

**Frédéric Delmar and Johan Wiklund[1]**

## INTRODUCTION

The psychological construct of motivation has an important role to play in entrepreneurship research. As stated by Shane, Locke, & Collins (2003, p. 257): 'We believe that the development of entrepreneurship theory requires consideration of the motivations of people making entrepreneurial decisions.' One of the areas in entrepreneurship where motivation is potentially of great importance relates to firm growth. There is research to suggest that growth is one of the most important outcomes of entrepreneurial efforts because it indicates the degree of success of that effort (Bhidé, 1999; Venkataraman, 1997), and effort exerted is closely related to the individual's motivation (Davidsson, Delmar, & Wiklund, 2002). Research examining the link between growth motivation and growth appears to support this view as it finds a positive relationship between growth motivation and growth (e.g., Baum, Locke, & Kirkpatrick, 1998; Baum, Locke, & Smith, 2001; Kolvereid & Bullvag, 1996; Miner, Smith, & Bracker, 1989).

Implicitly, the view underlying this research and the theories used is the assumption that growth motivation affects the future growth of the firm, i.e., that growth motivation has a causal effect on firm growth. However, in their review and test of leading theories on goal-directed behaviors, Bagozzi and Kimmel (1995) demonstrated that these theories are incomplete because they fail to consider the feedback from past behavior and behavioral outcomes. Drawing on these findings, later research has further elaborated on the relationship between motivation and behavior (see e.g., Conner, Sheeran, Norman, & Armitage, 2000; Ouellette & Wood, 1998; Perugini & Conner, 2000; Sheeran & Abraham, 2003; Triandis, 1977).

Specifically, the temporal stability of motives has been investigated, with results indicating that stable motives are good predictors of behavior (Sheeran & Abraham, 2003). These recent theoretical developments open up for the possibility that both motivation and future behavior represent reactions to past behavior and outcomes rather than being the result of the commitment to specific motives (e.g., Ouellette &Wood, 1998), thus challenging the causal structure of motivational models in entrepreneurship research.

To our knowledge, no research has considered how the outcomes of past behavior and the stability of motives affect the relationships between the motivations of small business managers and future outcomes. Such research is important because the failure to recognize the influence of past behavior and temporal stability of motives could lead to misinterpretations of the causal effects of motivations on outcomes. This has implications for how we model the relationship between motivation and outcomes in entrepreneurship research. Explicating and testing the causal structure of research models constitute an important step in theory development (see e.g., Whetten, 1989 for a discussion of theoretical contributions and Gartner, 1989 for a specific discussion on entrepreneurship theory and theory development).

Therefore, the purpose of this chapter is to examine the causal direction between growth motivation and firm growth. We test to what extent the motivation of small business managers affects growth accounting for the feedback from previous growth using longitudinal data and cross-lagged regression analyses.

The chapter continues as follows. Next we provide a short summary of the theoretical rationale for the study. We then review relevant motivation–outcome research and develop our hypotheses. This is followed by a section on methodology, which describes our sample and variables and analyses and results. Finally, we discuss the findings and draw the theoretical and empirical implications of the research.

## THEORY AND HYPOTHESES

### Temporal Stability of Growth Motivation

Motivation theories build on the premise that our motivations affect our behavior. Motivation affects the choice of behavior, the longevity of the behavior, and the level of effort (Kanfer, 1991). The growth motivation of a small business manager, defined as the aspiration to expand the business, reflecting attitudes and subjective norms in Ajzen's (1991) theory of planned behavior, affects his or her choice to expand the business, the willingness to sustain this choice over time, and at what level of effort. As opposed to many other behaviors and outcomes studied in the motivation literature, growth is not instantaneous but a process that unfolds over time (Penrose, 1959). Empirical studies of firm growth have typically assessed periods varying from 1 or 2 years up to 5 years (Wiklund & Shepherd, 2005). Over such relatively long time periods, there are multiple activities, actions, and decisions that affect the firm growth process. If the small business manager is motivated to expand his or her firm during a short period of time only but later prioritizes other goals and behaviors – for example because the efforts put into expanding the business did not lead to the desired outcomes (McCloy, Campbell, & Cudeck, 1994) – there is likely little effect of growth motivation on actual growth during extended periods of time. Unless motivation remains relatively constant over time until the behavior is performed, prediction will be weak (Ajzen, 1995). Empirically, research has found that stable motivations are good predictors of behavior while unstable motivations have no association with behavior (Sheeran, Orbell, & Trafimow, 1999). Therefore, an implicit assumption in the literature on growth motivation is that this motivation remains relatively stable over time.

The stability of growth motivation is central to theoretical development and to our subsequent hypotheses because the argument for the relationship between motivation and growth hinges on relative stability of growth motivation, but it has not been empirically assessed in the literature. Some indirect indications of stability may be inferred from previous research. A few studies have assessed the relationship between growth motivation and growth using a time lag between motivation and growth and have found support for a positive association (e.g., Baum et al., 2001; Kolvereid & Bullvag, 1996). Unless these findings are spurious, it suggests that growth motivation has some stability over time. This allows us to formulate our first hypothesis:

*Hypothesis 1: Growth motivation at time1 (T1) has a positive effect on growth motivation at time2 (T2).*

### The Effect of Growth Motivation on Growth

The effect of motivation on behavior is less obvious than may be assumed for two primary reasons. First, the strength of the relationship is affected by the individual's degree of volitional control, i.e., the ability to perform the behavior at will. Environmental constraints and insufficient ability or task comprehension (i.e., not understanding what to do) diminish the effect of motivation on behavior. For example, the greater an individual's ability, the greater is his or her tendency to choose to act (Kanfer, 1991; McCloy et al., 1994). Limited volitional control has been incorporated into goal-directed behavioral theories. The theory of planned behavior is an extension of the theory of reasoned action (Ajzen & Fishbein, 1977), adding aspects of individual ability (Ajzen, 1991), thus incorporating behaviors over which people have incomplete volitional control. As expected, this theory has been shown to outperform the theory of reasoned action in situations of limited volitional control (Netemeyer, Burton, & Johnston, 1991).

The expansion of a firm is an example of a behavior that is under limited volitional control. Unless the managers of the firm have the ability to develop suitable strategies and can spot growth opportunities, the firm will not grow irrespectively of the motivation to expand the business (Wiklund & Shepherd, 2003).

Second, the complexity of the behavior also affects its relationship with motivation. The expansion of a business is complex and can therefore be considered a fuzzy task (Campbell, 1988), characterized by multiple ways of attaining the desired outcome. It is also characterized by uncertainty and interdependencies. This means that small business managers can choose many different ways to achieve growth and the goal of growing the firm can be interdependent with other goals. For example, small business managers may want to expand their firms but can achieve this desired outcome in several different ways; they can acquire another firm or grow organically; grow by increasing sales while outsourcing the production, thus expanding sales but not employment. Furthermore, if the goal of expanding the business conflicts with other goals, the small business manager may choose actions that do not completely fulfill the expansion goal.

Therefore, motivation theories suggest that growth motivation should have a positive effect on growth, but the effect could not be expected to be very large given that the behavior is under limited volitional control and that the task of expanding a business could be regarded as complex and fuzzy. Previous empirical research tends to confirm this (e.g., Baum et al., 2001; Bellu & Sherman, 1995; Kolvereid & Bullvag, 1996; Mok & Van den Tillaart, 1990). These studies find some support for a positive relationship between motivation and growth, although these relationships are generally not very strong compared to what has been found for less complex behaviors under greater volitional control (see, e.g., Armitage & Conner, 2001 for a meta-analysis of the relationship between motivation and behavior in the theory of planned behavior). This leads us to anticipate a positive (but relatively weak) relationship between growth motivation and growth. Thus:

*Hypothesis 2: Growth motivation at T1 has a positive effect on growth at T2.*

## The Feedback of Past Growth on Growth Motivation

Bagozzi and Kimmel (1995) suggest that a shortcoming of theories of goal-directed behavior is their failure to properly consider the role of past behavior. The possible feedback of previous behaviors and outcomes on future motivation is an important aspect of motivation theories because it has consequences for the modeling of the causal order of the two constructs.

These authors suggest that past behavior affects the motivation to perform the behavior in the future. While it is true that past behavior is not emphasized by the theories, feedback from outcomes to motivation have been recognized by the theory of planned behavior (Ajzen, 1991), Bandura's (1986, 1991) social cognitive theory as well as attribution theory (Anderson, 1991; Thomas & Mathieu, 1994; Weiner, 1985). In general, if previous behavior is perceived as successful by an individual, we would expect that the future motivation of that individual to perform the task increases. On the other hand, if the previous behavior is perceived as a failure, we would expect the motivation to decrease for the task or to become directed toward another target (cf. Bagozzi & Warshaw, 1992).

In the context of this chapter, this means that a small business manager who has experienced firm growth and attributes that outcome to his or her own ability will get a higher growth motivation than another small business manager who has not experienced firm growth or does not attribute that outcome to his or her own ability. The actual growth outcome is an important indicator of the entrepreneur's ability to manage and expand the firm. If the outcome is positive, motivation will be reinforced. If the outcome is negative, the entrepreneur's motivation will be reduced (Orpen, 1980; Silver, Mitchell, & Gist, 1995; Thomas & Mathieu, 1994).[2] Thus, these theories suggest that to some extent, growth motivation can be seen as an 'acquired taste' (cf. Davidsson et al., 2002) resulting from past growth outcomes. This argument leads to the following hypothesis:

*Hypothesis 3: Growth at T1 has a positive effect on growth motivation at T2.*

## The Independent Impact of Motivation

As illustrated in previous discussions, it is fair to say that several different claims about the association between growth and growth motivation have been made in the literature. Calls for research that makes a more detailed examination of the interplay between growth and growth motivation have been made in the literature (Wiklund & Shepherd, 2003). Bagozzi and Kimmel (1995) noted that empirical applications of motivation theories often failed to take into account the effect of past behavior, which had profound effects on the relationship between motivation and behavior. Specifically, they showed that past behavior in some models was a much better predictor of future behavior than was motivation and that the inclusion of past behavior even potentially reduced the effect of motivation to zero. If these results hold up in the present context, past growth would be a better predictor of future growth than would growth motivation. If so, there is little reason to rely on motivation theories if the primary interest is to investigate factors that influence the growth of small firms. Moreover, the application of motivation theories to the context of small firm growth would seem superfluous. We, therefore, test which has a greater influence on growth – past growth or growth motivation. Motivation theories hold that the intentional behavior of individuals has a strong *independent* impact on the future development of their firms (Ajzen, 1995; Bandura, 1982; Weiner, 1992). Siding with these theories, we hypothesize that even if we include past growth in the model, the effect of growth motivation is stronger than the effect of past growth. Thus:

*Hypothesis 4:* *Growth motivation at T1 has a stronger impact on growth at T2 than has growth at T1.*

The relationships that we test and our hypotheses are summarized in Figure 3.1.

## METHOD

### Research Design and Samples

Two samples were combined to test the hypotheses. Both sample frames were taken from Statistics Sweden's data on incorporated companies in Sweden. By law, all incorporated companies have to report the data of this database. The samples were stratified over the Swedish equivalent of ISIC codes (high-technology manufacturing, low-technology manufacturing, services, and professional services), and standard Swedish size brackets: 5–9, 10–19, and 20–49 employees in the first study and 10–19 and 20–49 employees in the second study. The samples are detailed in Table 3.1.

The data were collected over the telephone from the managing director, who in most cases was also the majority owner. The managing director

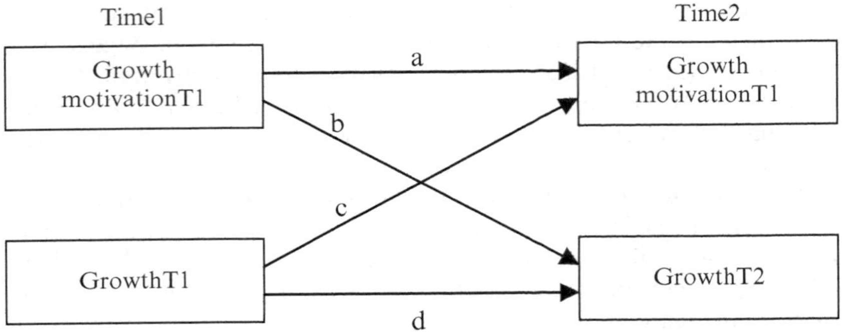


a > 0 = hypothesis 1
b > 0 = hypothesis 2
c > 0 = hypothesis 3
b > d = hypothesis 4

*Figure 3.1 Cross-lagged analysis of growth and growth motivation*

*Table 3.1 Development of the two samples across the period of observation*

| | First round | Second round |
|---|---|---|
| Sample 1 | | |
| Data collected year | 1994 | 1998 |
| Number sampled | 730 | 400 |
| Number interviewed | 400 (54.8%) | 314 (78.5%) |
| Number of known exits | | 29 |
| Sample 2 | | |
| Data collected year | 1996 | 1999 |
| Number sampled | 808 | 630 |
| Number interviewed | 630 (78.0%) | 549 (87.1%) |
| Number of known exits | | 52 |
| Combined | | |
| Total number of cases | 1030 | 863 |

was explicitly asked for at the beginning of the interview. The exact same questions were asked in all interviews. In both samples, data were collected twice, measuring growth and growth motivation at both points in time. In a few cases, the managing director had been replaced during the time between the two interviews. These cases were excluded from the analyses. In the first study, data were collected in 1994 and 1998; in the second study they were collected during 1996 and 1999. Thus, the first study had a time span of 4 years between the waves and the second study had a 3-year time span. Response rates were notably high (54.8– 87.1 per cent), which helps safeguard against nonresponse bias. The collection of data at two points in time reduces the problem of memory decay and cognitive bias as well as common method variance. It also allows for testing of causal order between the constructs using cross-lagged regressions. Granger causality holds that an effect in a prior period can lead to an effect in a subsequent period; however, an effect in a subsequent period cannot lead to an effect in a prior period.

As a result of the different size brackets included in the two studies, there are some significant differences between the two samples. Sample 1 includes firms that are significantly smaller (mean = 18.1 employees, standard deviation [SD] = 39.4 vs. mean = 23.0 employees, SD = 14.1) and younger (mean = 12.1 years, SD = 10.1 vs. mean = 29.4 years, SD = 27.7) than sample 2.

## Measures

Previous research suggests that growth in terms of employment and sales are important growth indicators that provide different and complementary information (Delmar, 1997; Delmar, Davidsson, & Gartner, 2003; Weinzimmer, Nystrom, & Freeman, 1998). Therefore, we relied on both these aspects concerning growth and growth motivation.

### Employment and sales growth

During all interviews we asked for present size in terms of employees (converted into full-time equivalents) and annual sales. We also asked for the corresponding figures 3 years ago. We explicitly tested these recall questions for potential recall bias. In the 1999 round of the second study, these '3 years ago' questions correspond to the 'present size' figures reported during the first round in 1996. We correlated these figures. The correlations of both sales and employment were above .95, which ensures that respondents were able to correctly recall the size of their firms 3 years ago. *GrowthT1* was calculated as the relative size change between the present size reported during the first round and the size 3 years prior. *GrowthT2* was calculated as the relative size change between the two rounds. Data were heavily skewed, containing several outliers. Several techniques exist to normalize data (e.g., logarithmic transformation). We relied on the Winsor technique (e.g., Kennedy, Lakonishok, & Shaw, 1992), where a fixed percentage (in our case 5 per cent) of the outlier cases at the tail of the distribution receive the same values as the observations at the truncation point (i.e., the 95 percentile). This transformation led to a distribution that was acceptable, with a minimum change in the data.

**Sales and employment growth motivation**

At each interview, we asked the respondents: 'If the firm develops the way you would like it to, how many employees and how many large sales would the firm have 5 years ahead? Disregard possible inflation.' Based on these responses, growth motivation was calculated as the relative difference between intended size and current size in terms of employment and sales. *Growth MotivationT1* was tapped during the first interview rounds and *Growth MotivationT2* was tapped during the second. Again, Winsorization was used to normalize the data. This measure is similar to what has been used in previous studies of growth motivation. Kolvereid & Bullvag (1996) refer to a similar variable as growth intention; Wiklund and Shepherd (2003) call it growth aspiration and Wiklund, Davidsson, and Delmar (2003) call it attitude toward growth. All these authors relate to Ajzen's (1995) theory of planned behavior. We argue that calling it an intention is overreaching, as the measure has no component of intended effort. Rather, we suggest that the concept represents a growth aspiration, which reflects attitudes and subjective norms in Ajzen's theory.

Two other possible measures of growth motivation were also available: (1) whether a 25 per cent increase in the number of employees in 5 years' time would be mainly negative or mainly positive and (2) whether a 100 per cent increase in the number of employees in 5 years' time would be mainly negative or mainly positive. While it would have been possible to utilize either of these alternative measures of the dependent variable or to compute a global growth motivation index, we prefer to rely on the question concerned with growth motivation in terms of growth rates because it makes the measurement scales for growth motivation and growth symmetrical (relative growth rates). This sort of symmetry in independent and dependent variables is deemed important by motivation theories (e.g., Ajzen & Fishbein, 1980; Eagly & Chaiken, 1993).

In order to validate the measure we created a global growth intention index consisting of our two growth motivation variables and these two items from the 25 per cent and the 100 per cent scales. The Cronbach's alpha value of the index was .72 and corrected item-total correlations ranged from .47 to .55, indicating that the index has acceptable reliability (Nunnally, 1967) and that all items share sufficient variance with the index (Nunnally & Bernstein, 1994). This index was also successfully used in predicting actual growth outcomes in another study (Wiklund & Shepherd, 2003). This suggests that our growth motivation variables measure is (1) sufficiently reliable and (2) predictively valid (Nunnally & Bernstein,

1994). We therefore feel confident in relying on the chosen measures for growth motivation.

### Control Variables

Previous research suggests that the individual characteristics of the small business manager, firm size and age, and industry affect growth (Davidsson, 1989; Delmar, 1996; Wiklund, 1998). We asked the respondent to state his or her highest completed education and constructed dummy variables for elementary school, trade school, high school, and university degree (university degree being the base category), which covers the vast majority of respondents. We also asked how the respondent became CEO of the firm and created dummy variables for the categories started, bought, inherited, or other. We asked what year the respondent was born, which was recoded into age at the time of the interviews. Based on the sampling frame, dummy variables were constructed for the four industries sampled (high-technology manufacturing, low-technology manufacturing, services, and professional services). The number of employees during the first survey round was included to measure size. Finally, we asked if the respondent knew which year the firm was founded. Their responses were recoded into firm age at the time of the interviews.

### Correcting for Selection Bias

Several of the small firms failed between the first and second survey rounds and others did not complete all survey rounds. Because the variables that have an effect on growth may also impact business failure, attrition may not be random but instead systematic in a fashion similar to self-selection (Heckman, 1979). Therefore, unless the results are corrected for attrition, results may have a survivor bias. We therefore used the Heckman-type correction models (cf. Heckman, 1979; Shaver, 1998).

Heckman-type correction models use a two-step process. First, based on theory, a model is developed for the probability of survival, which can predict this probability for each case. To develop the model for survival (selection model), we used research findings on factors contributing to small business survival and high performance (Wiklund, 1998). Specifically, firm age, firm size, and industry were used in the selection model (these variables also appear in the models for predicting the dependent variables). Second, a correction is made for self-selection (survival) by incorporating these predicted individual probabilities into the estimation model. A significant Rho suggests that if a correction had not been made then self-selection would have likely biased the results.

**Analysis**

First, the study's measures were investigated to assess the quality of the data. Second, we compared the Pearson correlations between growth motivation and growth with previous research. Third, the hypothesized relationships were investigated using cross-lagged regressions to embed the variables within the proposed research model as a means of gaining further insights regarding causal relationships.

Our hypotheses suggest relatively complex causal relationships between growth motivation and growth. Specifically, they state dual causality between growth motivation and growth, suggesting that motivation affects growth and that there is feedback from achieved growth on future growth motivation. In order to test these hypotheses, we relied on cross-lagged regression analysis. Cross-lagged regressions are used to determine the causal relationship between constructs that are measured at least twice (Cohen & Cohen, 1983). It has been used in several studies to untangle the causal relationship between constructs where correlations have been noted in past research. For example, studies have examined the causal relationship between employee satisfaction and organizational effectiveness (Koys, 2001), between communication effectiveness and innovativeness (Lind & Zmud, 1991), or if political talk shows influence the audience or whether the audience is merely selecting sources consistent with previous political attitudes (Yanovitzky & Capella, 2001).

The cross-lagged model we used is displayed in Figure 3.1 together with the hypotheses. As illustrated in the figure, two separate analyses were performed. First, growth at T2 (second survey) was regressed on growth at T1 and growth motivation at T1 (first survey). Second, growth motivation at T2 (second survey) was regressed on growth at T1 and growth motivation at T1 (first survey). In addition, a comparison of the size of the regression coefficients tells us which causal relationships were stronger. Since we measured growth and growth motivation in both employment and sales, this gave us a total of four different regression analyses.

## RESULTS

Table 3.2 reports means, SDs, and correlations between all variables. The low correlations provided initial evidence of discriminant validity. The correlation between growth motivation and actual growth was .27 for employment and .29 for sales. As a first assessment of our results, we compared these values to previous empirical studies investigating the relationship between growth motivation and growth using a longitudinal design. Mok and Van den Tillaart (1990) reported cross-tabulations of growth expectations and relative sales growth. Converting this to a correlation using the formula suggested by Rosenthal (1991) it became .42. Miner et al. (1994) reported a correlation of .48 for task motivation and absolute sales growth, and a correlation of .47 for task motivation and absolute employment growth. Bellu and Sherman (1995) found a correlation of .43 between task motivation and relative sales growth. Kolvereid and Bullvag (1996) reported mean differences between growth-oriented and not growth-oriented entrepreneurs. Converting the means to correlations (Rosenthal, 1991), they became .12 for sales and .16 for employment. Thus, our relationships between growth motivation and growth appeared to be of a similar magnitude compared to what has been found in previous research.

**Predicting Growth Motivation**

Tables 3.3 and 3.4 present the results from the hierarchical cross-lagged regressions performed for growth motivation and firm growth, respectively. The last rows in the models present the correlation of the error terms of the selection model and the prediction model (Rho). Then follows model fit ($\chi^2$ and log likelihood), the increase thanks to the addition of the research variables ($\Delta\chi^2$), and the number of cases included. Due to internal missing values the number of cases varied across the models. It could be noted in Table 3.3 that Rho was significant in the prediction of growth motivation, suggesting that results would have been biased had we not corrected for sample selection.

Model 1 is the base model including the control variables predicting sales growth motivationT2. The model was statistically significant ($\chi^2 = 51; p < .001$). The regression coefficients show that CEO age had a negative effect on growth motivation. The negative effect of all education dummy variables suggested that those with the longest education (university degree = base category) had the highest growth motivation. The 'Firm other' category, i.e., those who neither started, inherited nor bought the firm (e.g., employed CEOs) showed the lowest growth motivation. Higher growth motivation was also noted for respondents in the second sample (origin of sample) and firms that were subsidiaries within business groups.

The research variables were added in model 2. These additions improved significantly the model fit ($\Delta\chi^2 = 158; p < .001$). The effect of growth motivationT1 on growth motivationT2 was positive and statistically significant ($\beta = .301; p < .001$), providing partial support for hypothesis 1. The effect of growthT1 on growth motivationT2 was also positive and statistically significant ($\beta = .081$; $p < .05$), providing partial support for hypothesis 3.

*Table 3.2 Descriptive statistics*

| Variable | Mean | SD | 1) | 2) | 3) | 4) | 5) | 6) | 7) | 8) |
|---|---|---|---|---|---|---|---|---|---|---|
| 1) Emp growthT2 | 1.17 | .44 | 1.00 | | | | | | | |
| 2) Emp growth motT2 | 1.37 | .46 | .08 | 1.00 | | | | | | |
| 3) Sales growthT2 | 1.25 | .48 | .72 | .13 | 1.00 | | | | | |
| 4) Sales growth motT2 | 1.63 | .62 | .12 | .75 | .09 | 1.00 | | | | |
| 5) Emp growthT1 | 1.29 | .51 | .07 | .10 | .09 | .17 | 1.00 | | | |
| 6) Emp growth motT1 | 1.46 | .49 | .27 | .31 | .15 | .32 | .07 | 1.00 | | |
| 7) Sales growthT1 | 1.58 | .67 | .12 | .09 | .09 | .16 | .76 | .08 | 1.00 | |
| 8) Sales growth motT1 | 1.70 | .61 | .10 | .29 | .15 | .39 | .10 | .65 | .12 | 1.00 |
| 9) Age of CEO T1 | 47.73 | 8.79 | −.18 | −.11 | −.18 | −.11 | −.18 | −.15 | −.18 | −.12 |
| 10) Elementary school | .17 | .38 | −.09 | −.10 | −.09 | −.11 | −.01 | −.07 | −.02 | −.12 |
| 11) High school | | .10 | .30 | −.01 | −.06 | .00 | −.06 | .08 | −.02 | .06 |
| 12) Trading school | .36 | .48 | .09 | .01 | .05 | .01 | .00 | .01 | −.03 | −.02 |
| 13) Age of firm T1 | 25.50 | 25.58 | −.15 | −.05 | −.15 | −.02 | −.21 | −.19 | −.14 | −.15 |
| 14) Number of emp T1 | 19.89 | 11.37 | −.10 | .01 | −.06 | .04 | .27 | −.14 | .26 | −.12 |
| 15) Firm bought | .26 | .44 | −.07 | .03 | −.06 | .00 | −.10 | −.04 | −.09 | −.06 |
| 16) Firm heritage | .16 | .36 | −.08 | −.05 | −.09 | −.02 | −.15 | −.05 | −.10 | .00 |
| 17) Firm other | .20 | .40 | .02 | .04 | .03 | .00 | .02 | .01 | .03 | −.04 |
| 18) High tech | .28 | .45 | −.04 | −.04 | −.03 | .02 | .04 | −.07 | .05 | .01 |
| 19) Low tech | .26 | .44 | −.03 | −.03 | .00 | −.01 | .07 | .02 | .08 | .04 |
| 20) Prof serv | .24 | .43 | .01 | .00 | −.01 | −.05 | −.16 | .01 | −.15 | −.02 |
| 21) Origin of sample | 1.72 | .45 | −.13 | −.03 | −.19 | .00 | .13 | −.18 | .14 | −.21 |
| 22) Subsidiary T1 | .13 | .34 | .03 | .09 | .06 | .10 | .05 | .01 | .07 | .04 |

*Note:* N = 673, Correlations greater than .09 are significant at $p < .05$; those greater than .11 are significant at $p < .01$; and those greater than .13 are significant at $p < .001$.
SD, standard deviation.

| 9) | 10) | 11) | 12) | 13) | 14) | 15) | 16) | 17) | 18) | 19) | 20) | 21) | 22) |
|---|---|---|---|---|---|---|---|---|---|---|---|---|---|
| 1.00 | | | | | | | | | | | | | |
| .22 | 1.00 | | | | | | | | | | | | |
| −.04 | −.01 | −.15 | 1.00 | | | | | | | | | | |
| −.09 | −.35 | −.25 | 1.00 | | | | | | | | | | |
| .15 | .02 | −.02 | −.05 | 1.00 | | | | | | | | | |
| .00 | −.07 | −.05 | −.02 | .12 | 1.00 | | | | | | | | |
| .08 | −.04 | .00 | −.01 | .15 | .01 | 1.00 | | | | | | | |
| −.07 | .00 | .02 | .07 | .30 | −.04 | −.24 | 1.00 | | | | | | |
| −.14 | −.13 | −.03 | −.05 | .10 | .16 | −.18 | −.17 | 1.00 | | | | | |
| .05 | .03 | .08 | .05 | .03 | −.02 | .01 | .07 | −.16 | 1.00 | | | | |
| .06 | .08 | .03 | .08 | .01 | .07 | .05 | .03 | −.09 | −.37 | 1.00 | | | |
| −.03 | −.01 | −.07 | −.06 | .03 | −.04 | −.05 | −.02 | .07 | −.35 | −.33 | 1.00 | | |
| .08 | .06 | .12 | −.06 | .35 | .36 | −.07 | −.01 | .26 | −.01 | .02 | −.05 | 1.00 | |
| −.11 | −.11 | −.07 | −.04 | .01 | .20 | −.18 | −.12 | .50 | −.13 | −.07 | .16 | .24 | 1.00 |

*Table 3.3 Regression analysis with Heckman selection for sales growth motivationT2 and employment growth motivationT2*

| | Sales growth motivationT2 | | | | Employment growth motivation | | | |
|---|---|---|---|---|---|---|---|---|
| | Model 1 | | Model 2 | | Model 3 | | Model 4 | |
| | B | (SE) | B | (SE) | B | (SE) | B | (SE) |
| Age of CEO T1 | −.008 | (.002)** | −.004 | (.003)† | −.005 | (.002)* | −.002 | (.002) |
| Elementary school | −.146 | (.064)* | −.092 | (.064) | −.103 | (.049)* | −.088 | (.048)† |
| High school | −.200 | (.079)* | −.142 | (.078)† | −.125 | (.060)* | −.094 | (.060) |
| Trading school | −.121 | (.049)* | −.044 | (.050) | −.065 | (.039)† | −.039 | (.038) |
| Age of firm at T1 | .000 | (.001) | .001 | (.001) | .000 | (.001) | .001 | (.001) |
| Number of emp. T1 | .000 | (.002) | .000 | (.002) | −.001 | (.002) | −.001 | (.002) |
| Firm bought | .017 | (.052) | .058 | (.052) | .058 | (.040) | .085 | (.040)* |
| Firm heritage | −.011 | (.066) | −.007 | (.066) | −.004 | (.052) | .015 | (.051) |
| Firm other | −.164 | (.068)* | −.140 | (.067)* | −.046 | (.053) | −.043 | (.052) |
| High tech | .074 | (.074) | .028 | (.069) | −.015 | (.055) | −.019 | (.053) |
| Low tech | .089 | (.074) | −.006 | (.071) | .020 | (.055) | −.027 | (.053) |
| Prof services | −.088 | (.074) | −.075 | (.070) | −.038 | (.055) | −.033 | (.053) |
| Origin of sample | .212 | (.065)** | .221 | (.062)*** | .139 | (.048)** | .120 | (.047)* |

| | | | | | | | | |
|---|---|---|---|---|---|---|---|---|
| Subsidiary at T1 | .195 | (.074)** | .141 | (.075)† | .107 | (.059)† | .094 | (.058) |
| GrowthT1 | | | .081 | (.033)* | | | .094 | (.034)** |
| Growth motivationT1 | | | .301 | (.037)*** | | | .249 | (.033)*** |
| Constant | 1.526 | (.162)*** | .650 | (.188)*** | 1.286 | (.126)*** | .687 | (.145)*** |
| *Model* | | | | | | | | |
| Rho | .92*** | | .85*** | | .87*** | | .84*** | |
| log likelihood | 1060 | | 981 | | 895 | | 836 | |
| $\chi^2$ | 51*** | | 124*** | | 31** | | 97*** | |
| $\Delta\chi^2$ | | | 158*** | | | | 118*** | |
| Uncensored obs. | 735 | | 698 | | 757 | | 727 | |
| Censored obs. | 176 | | 176 | | 176 | | 176 | |

*Notes:* † $p < .10$; * $p < .05$; ** $p < .01$; *** $p < .001$

*Table 3.4 Regression analysis with Heckman selection for sales growthT2 and employment growthT2*

| | Sales growthT2 | | | | Employment growthT2 | | | |
|---|---|---|---|---|---|---|---|---|
| | Model 5 | | Model 6 | | Model 7 | | Model 8 | |
| | B | (SE) | B | (SE) | B | (SE) | B | (SE) |
| Age of CEO T1 | −.006 | (.002)** | −.005 | (.002)* | −.005 | (.002)** | −.004 | (.002)* |
| Elementary school | −.060 | (.051) | −.024 | (.053) | −.078 | (.046)† | −.053 | (.047) |
| High school | −.025 | (.060) | .002 | (.062) | −.056 | (.055) | −.037 | (.056) |
| Trading school | −.003 | (.040) | .032 | (.042) | .039 | (.037) | .056 | (.037) |
| Age of firm at T1 | .000 | (.001) | .000 | (.001) | −.001 | (.001) | .000 | (.001) |
| Number of emp. T1 | .000 | (.002) | −.001 | (.002) | −.003 | (.002)† | −.002 | (.002) |
| Firm bought | −.076 | (.041)† | −.057 | (.043) | −.071 | (.038)† | −.071 | (.038)† |
| Firm heritage | −.115 | (.054)* | −.109 | (.055)* | −.096 | (.049)† | −.088 | (.050)† |
| Firm other | .025 | (.054) | .031 | (.057) | −.013 | (.050) | −.018 | (.050) |
| High tech | −.002 | (.054) | −.018 | (.055) | −.008 | (.049) | −.001 | (.047) |
| Low tech | .057 | (.053) | .027 | (.055) | .034 | (.048) | .011 | (.048) |
| Prof services | −.045 | (.053) | −.034 | (.054) | −.021 | (.049) | −.004 | (.047) |
| Origin of sample | −.057 | (.048) | −.071 | (.052) | .075 | (.043)† | .047 | (.044) |

| | | | | | | | | |
|---|---|---|---|---|---|---|---|---|
| Subsidiary at T1 | .066 | (.060) | .057 | (.064) | .003 | (.056) | .006 | (.057) |
| GrowthT1 | | | .057 | (.029)* | | | .051 | (.033) |
| Growth motivationT1 | | | .072 | (.030)* | | | .197 | (.033)*** |
| Constant | 1.538 | (.132)*** | 1.310 | (.156)*** | 1.309 | (.119) | .922 | (.143)*** |
| *Model* | | | | | | | | |
| Rho | .78* | | .72 | | .77** | | .62 | |
| Log likelihood | 1003 | | 967 | | 947 | | 903 | |
| $\chi^2$ | 29** | | 34*** | | 37*** | | 72*** | |
| $\Delta\chi^2$ | | | 72*** | | | | 88*** | |
| Uncensored obs. | 824 | | 782 | | 838 | | 803 | |
| Censored obs. | 176 | | 176 | | 176 | | 176 | |

*Notes:* † $p < .10$; *$p < .05$; **$p < .01$; ***$p < .001$

Model 3 is the model for employment growth motivation with only the control variables. The results of the base model were quite similar to those obtained for sales growth motivation. The base model including the control variables was statistically significant ($\chi^2 = 31; p < .01$). The signs of the coefficients were typically the same. A negative statistically significant coefficient could be noted for CEO age. Again, those with the longest education (university degree) had the highest growth motivation. Higher growth motivation was again noted for respondents in the second sample (origin of sample).

In model 4 we entered the research variables. The addition gave a statistically significant improvement to the model fit ($\Delta\chi^2 = 118; p < .001$). The effect of growth motivationT1 on growth motivationT2 was positive and statistically significant ($\beta = .249; p < .001$), providing additional support for hypothesis 1.[3] The effect of growthT1 on growth motivationT2 was also positive and statistically significant ($\beta = .094; p < .01$), providing additional support for hypothesis 3. Thus, hypotheses 1 and 3 were supported by both analyses.

**Predicting Firm Growth**

We now turn to the analysis of firm growth. The results are shown in Table 3.4. Model 5 was statistically significant ($\chi^2 = 29; p < .01$). It is the base model with the control variables included that predict sales growth. The regression coefficients show that CEO age had a negative effect on sales growth. Similarly, a negative effect was noted for those who have inherited their firm. In model 6, we added the research variables to the model and we noted a statistically significant improvement in model fit ($\Delta\chi^2 = 72; p < .001$). The effect of growth motivationT1 on growthT2 was positive and statistically significant ($\beta = .072; p < .05$), providing partial support for hypothesis 2. The effect of growthT1 on growthT2 was also positive and statistically significant ($\beta = .057; p < .05$).

The results of model 7 for employment growth were quite similar to those obtained for sales growth. This base model including the control variables was statistically significant ($\chi^2 = 37; p < .001$). The only statistically significant coefficient was the negative effect of CEO age. Adding the research variables in model 8 made a statistically significant improvement to model fit ($\Delta\chi^2 = 88; p < .001$). The effect of growth motivationT1 on growthT2 was positive and statistically significant ($\beta = .197; p < .001$), providing additional support for hypothesis 2. Thus, hypothesis 2 was supported by both analyses. The effect of growthT1 on growthT2 was positive but not statistically significant ($\beta = .051$).

### Comparing Size Effects

The three first hypotheses were supported by our data concerning employment as well as sales. These findings suggest that there are mutual causal relationships between growth motivation and growth. Hypothesis 4 stated that growth motivation at T1 has a stronger impact on growth at T2 than has growth at T1. We tested this hypothesis by comparing the size of the regression coefficients of growth motivationT1 vs. growthT1 in model 6 concerning sales growth and in model 8 concerning employment growth.

We found support for hypothesis 4 when employment was examined. In model 8, growth motivationT1 had a significantly larger effect than growthT1 on growthT2 ($\chi^2 = 9.11; p < .003$). However, we did not find support for our hypothesis when sales was examined. For sales, growth motivationT1 had a larger coefficient than growthT1 on growthT2, but the difference was not statistically significant ($\chi^2 = .14$).

### Summary of Results

We find temporal stability of growth motivation, which is a prerequisite for growth motivation being a relevant predictor of growth. Our results also suggest an effect of growth motivation on growth. However, we also noted that past growth affected growth motivation, suggesting mutual relationships between growth motivation and growth. All these results apply to sales as well as employment growth. In order to further test the relevance of growth motivation in studies of growth, we compared the size effect of growth motivation vs. past growth in the prediction of growth. The hypothesis that motivation has a stronger effect on firm growth than has past growth was supported for employment growth but not for sales growth. In sum, these findings suggest that growth motivation is a relevant predictor of growth and an important variable to include in studies of small firm growth.

## DISCUSSION

In this study, we have addressed the relationship between growth motivation and actual growth in small firms. The incentive for conducting this research is that recent research suggests that the relationship between the two concepts is more complex than previous empirical research suggest, calling for this type of research (Wiklund & Shepherd, 2003). Further, recent development of motivation theories indicates that the temporal stability of motives and the effect of previous behavior on motives affect the appropriate modeling of the relationship between motivation and behavior. The neglect to incorporate such constructs undermines our ability to more fully understand how motives affect our behavior and subsequent performance. More specifically, including notions of feedback loops and stability in motives over time is likely to lead to better models. By consecutively collecting data on both growth motivation and growth, correcting for sample selection and applying cross-lagged regression analysis, we have tried to test such a model of growth motivation and firm growth. Consequently, we were able to establish some important and interesting relationships between the constructs.

We find that growth motivation has a unique impact on the growth of the firm, but that there are important feedback loops from growth to motivation. This provides support for the idea that the motivations of managers affect important firm outcomes such as growth. In other words, earlier research on the effect of motivation on firm growth appears valid, but it underestimated the importance of past growth in this process. Managers vary in their motivations to grow their firms, and those motivations affect growth achieved. Growth motivation, in turn, is partly affected by previous outcomes but remains relatively stable over time. This is an important result, as motivations have to be stable to be good predictors of behavior. Hence, growth motives are effective predictors of firm growth when they are stable over time.

**Theoretical Implications**

One important implication of these findings is that it makes sense to study motivation in the context of small firm growth. Small business managers do affect the growth of their firms by their intentional behavior. Another important implication is that while the bulk of previous research has relied on cross-sectional designs, the conclusions drawn – that motivation affects growth – were supported by our more careful analyses. It should be noted, however, that in the case of sales growth, past growth was an equally good predictor as was growth motivation. This suggests that at the least, past growth should be included as a control variable in models predicting growth in order not to overestimate the effect of growth motivation.

This finding also leads us to speculate that there are some substantive differences between sales and employment growth. Sales growth reflects increases in output and is often used as a proxy for performance, while employment growth relates to increases in the stock of resources of the firm (cf. Penrose, 1959). The processes leading to sales and employment growth are quite different. Sales growth does not just happen because management wants it, but is determined by the market. Many different strategic choices can lead to sales growth, such as productivity increases, new product development, or new market entry. It is likely that such strategic considerations have long-lasting effects (if successful) and only gradually disappear in the face of competition. It also suggests that growth motivation only indirectly influences sales growth because relevant strategies have to be implemented to create sales growth. This explains our finding that sales growth in previous periods had a strong effect on future growth – just as strong as growth motivation. Conversely, employment growth is directly affected by the motivation of management. Small business managers have discretion to choose to add new employees or not and employees can be added to the firm more or less instantaneously. This would explain our strong effect of employment growth motivation and the nonsignificant effect of previous employment growth.

Without doubt, the vast majority of studies of the relationship between growth motivation and growth has been concerned with how motivation affects growth. Our findings of feedback from growth on motivation suggest that there is ample opportunity to make a contribution to the literature by instead focusing on the reverse relationship, i.e., how outcomes affect future motivations and how these motivations change over time depending on whether intended outcomes materialize or not.

For example, a natural extension of this study is to investigate heterogeneity of growth intentions among small business managers. How do previous outcomes affect the intentions of small business managers to grow their businesses in the future? The theory of planned behavior, modified in accordance with the findings of Bagozzi and Kimmel (1995), offers a theoretical framework for such an empirical investigation. It should be possible to incorporate previous work on the antecedents of growth motivation (Davidsson, 1989; Kolvereid, 1992; Wiklund et al., 2003) in assessing how attitude toward the behavior, perceived behavioral control, and social norms are influenced by past outcomes and how it affects intention.

Our findings also add to the debate on the extent to which top managers influence the performance of their firms (see Bowman & Helfat [2001], and Carroll & Hannan [2000], for opposing views on the topic). Based on our findings, it appears that managers indeed do contribute to performance, at least in small firms. It appears that their aspirations to expand the firm affect subsequent growth. This suggests that motivation theories can be valuable in understanding the relationship between management and outcomes if feedback loops are accounted for.

We also contribute to the literature on goal-directed behavior by testing the importance of motivation in a natural setting where the task is complex and the individual has limited control over outcomes. Most research in this domain examines simpler behaviors where individuals can more easily exert behaviors at will (e.g., driver compliance with speed limits [Elliott, Armitage, & Baughan, 2003] or choice of travel [Bamberg, Ajzen, & Schmidt, 2003]). Moreover, we use as dependent variable a relatively distal outcome (firm growth) rather than the actual behavior or a proximal outcome, such as the ability to solve a specific problem. This is an advantage when studying complex tasks where there are multiple ways of attaining the desired outcome (Campbell, 1988). The reliance of a narrow set of behaviors or proximal outcomes would probably have left out several possibilities of attaining the goal. Firm growth also has the advantage of being a measure of success or failure. The attainment of such outcomes has stronger effects on the individual's subsequent motivation and learning than has the performance of specific behaviors (Silver et al., 1995; VandeWalle & Cummings, 1997). While we realize that the study of complex behaviors under limited volitional control and distal outcomes introduces noise, our results suggest that it is possible to study such relationships in a meaningful way. We hope these findings will spur others to examine other relationships between the motivations of managers and firm-level outcomes.

## PRACTICAL IMPLICATIONS

The practical implications of this chapter's findings are numerous. Small business managers with greater growth motivation are more likely to realize growth. This suggests that there is an opportunity for economic growth if small business managers' growth intentions can be increased. Small businesses employ the majority of the workforce in most developed countries (e.g., Davidsson, Lindmark, & Olofsson, 1994; Storey, 1994), and small firms are of great importance to the development of these economies and the creation of new jobs (Carree & Thurik, 1998; Robbins, Pantuosco, Parker, & Fuller, 2000). Governments and others wishing to grow an economy need to understand that motivation plays an important role for the development and growth of small firms, and that measures to encourage the growth motivation of small business managers can have positive economic consequences. The importance of motivation has largely been overlooked in policy programs. So far there has been an overemphasis on implementing support programs that provide small businesses with resources that aim at increasing the ability for small businesses to grow, including training programs for small business managers and tax cuts. Implicit in most supportive programs is the assumption that if only small businesses had these resources and abilities they would grow. It may instead be possible for government to make growth a more attractive option for small business managers. For example, tax reliefs currently in place for very small businesses may make it less attractive for small business managers to expand their businesses beyond the point of receiving these relief.

Our results indicate that there are long-term effects of growth motivation because of feedback from previous outcomes. Growth motivation affects growth, which in turn has a positive effect on future growth motivation. This suggests that once a small business manager is motivated to try to expand the firm and is successful in doing so, his or her commitment to expansion will be reinforced. More generally, this finding suggests that the early outcomes of new firms operated by growth-motivated managers are of great importance. If they are able to achieve their growth targets, their motivation to further expand their businesses will be reinforced, leading to virtuous circles, with increased motivation and growth. Conversely, negative early outcomes are likely to lead to reduced growth motivation. Given that growth motivation is relatively stable over time but influenced by previous outcomes, the effects of such early outcomes are likely to be relatively long lasting.

As noted earlier, however, motivation is not the only factor influencing the growth of small businesses. It is important that growth-oriented small businesses can access the resources they need at reasonable costs, and that growth opportunities are abundant in the economy. Furthermore, it is vital that they understand how to manage the firm through a growth process and understand the consequence of expanding a firm, most of which are positive.

Furthermore, these results support the notion that intentional behavior has an impact on firm development, as suggested by psychological and strategy research, even if the impact is relatively small. Firm growth is not only the result of initial conditions, or follows an initial path. Both the behavior of the small business manager and the ongoing process of growth itself affect outcomes.

**Limitations**

Our data were composed of two different samples collected during different phases of the economic cycle. We find significant differences between the samples when modeling growth motivation. This suggests that to some extent, results might shift across samples, culture, and economic trends. However, our results hold in both samples, which we interpret as an indication of robustness. We have also taken into consideration that sales growth and employment growth are not equivalent processes, and that they need to be studied separately. The similarities of results across these two measures further indicate robustness. However, there are important limitations to this study. While we believe that the results are likely to be generalizable to small businesses outside of Sweden, care must be taken in assessing country effects such as culture because growth motivation may, to some extent, have cultural roots.

We relied on the CEO as the single informant. In cases where there are several owner-managers, this could lead to measurement error of growth motivation. Given that we used repeated measures, common method variance should not be a problem. Reliance on single informants should therefore not lead to spurious results because random measurement error attenuates rather than overestimates true relationships.

In this chapter, we have only measured growth motivation and growth. However, owner-managers can have multiple goals that are interrelated. The specific mix of goals and how they relate to firm outcomes still needs more research. Although motives seem to be quite stable over time, some owner-managers will change motives depending on feedback and other information. For example, how will a growth-oriented owner-manager react to a major setback in the firm's development, or how will an owner-manager motivated to remain at the same size react to a profitable opportunity that involves expansion in order to be exploited? Those are interesting areas for future research that are not covered in this chapter.

The fact that we only measure growth motivation and growth also means that we cannot totally rule out effects of third variables and of intermediate variables such as strategy or behavior. We have tried to minimize the possibility of a third variable problem by adding a number of important control variables. Intermediate variables such as strategy and actual behavior would have been an important addition to our model because they are more proximal to the entrepreneur's or small business manager's motives and abilities than are firm outcomes that *a priori* depend on a number of factors that the entrepreneur cannot control. However, firm outcome probably represents the most important form of feedback about the values of the strategies and behaviors initiated by the entrepreneurs, which leads us to conclude that our interpretation of results is valid.

**Future Research**

A better understanding of growth motivation and small firm growth could serve to more closely integrate current work in entrepreneurship and firm behavior. Future research should investigate in more details the interplay among motivation, strategy, firm operations, and firm performance. Studying these factors will give us a better understanding of how motives translate into behavior and how behavior affects performance and firm growth. This study has shown that small firm managers do affect the growth of their firm by their motivation, but how does this motivation translate into behavior, and which behaviors are more effective than others?

## NOTES

Financial support was provided from Jan Wallander's foundation, Knut and Alice Wallenberg's foundation, Ruben Rausing's Foundation and Sparbankernas Research Foundation. We thank Michael Frese, Gerard George, and Dean Shepherd for their comments on earlier drafts of this chapter.

* Previously published as: Frédéric Delmar and Johan Wiklund (2008), 'The effect of small business managers' growth motivation on firm growth: a longitudinal study', *Entrepreneurship Theory and Practice*, **32** (3), May, 437–57.

1. Both authors contributed equally and are listed alphabetically.
2. The escalation of commitment literature suggests that the opposite is also possible, i.e., that people may be enticed to commit even further resources to a failed course of action (e.g., Brockner, 1992). However, we follow the major line of reasoning in the motivation literature in stating our hypothesis.
3. As an additional test of the stability of growth motivation, we compared the mean values at T1 and T2. Employment growth motivation decreased by .17 SD and sales growth motivation decreased by .13 SD. Differences smaller than .25 SD are considered as very small and could be disregarded (Cohen, 1969). Thus, this test corroborates our previous findings.

## REFERENCES

Ajzen, I. (1991). The theory of planned behavior. *Organizational Behavior and Human Decision Processes, 50*, 179–211.

Ajzen, I. (1995). Attitudes and behavior. In A.S.R. Manstead & M. Hewstone (Eds.), *The Blackwell encyclopedia of social psychology* (pp. 52–57). Oxford: Blackwell Publishing Ltd.

Ajzen, I. & Fishbein, M. (1977). Attitude–behavior relations: A theoretical analysis and review of empirical research. *Psychological Bulletin, 84*, 888–918.

Ajzen, I. & Fishbein, M. (1980). *Understanding attitudes and predicting social behavior*. Englewood Cliffs, NJ: Prentice-Hall.

Anderson, G.A. (1991). How people think about causes: Examination of the typical phenomenal organization of attributions for success and failure. *Social Cognition, 9*(4), 295–329.

Armitage, C.J. & Conner, M. (2001). Efficacy of the theory of planned behaviour: A meta-analytic review. *British Journal of Social Psychology, 40*, 471–499.

Bagozzi, R.P. & Kimmel, S.K. (1995). A comparison of leading theories for prediction of goal-directed behaviours. *British Journal of Social Psychology, 34*, 437–461.

Bagozzi, R.P. & Warshaw, P.R. (1992). An examination of the etiology of the attitude–behavior relation for goal-directed behaviors. *Multivariate Behavioral Research, 27*, 601–634.

Bamberg, S., Ajzen, I., & Schmidt, P. (2003). Choice of travel mode in the theory of planned behavior: The roles of past behavior, habit, and reasoned action. *Basic and Applied Social Psychology, 25*, 175–187.

Bandura, A. (1982). The psychology of chance encounters and life paths. *American Psychologist, 37*(7), 747–755.

Bandura, A. (1986). *Social foundations of thought and action: A social cognitive theory*. Englewood Cliffs, NJ: Prentice-Hall.

Bandura, A. (1991). Social cognitive theory of self-regulation. *Organizational Behavior and Human Decision Processes, 50*, 248–287.

Baum, R.J., Locke, E.A., & Kirkpatrick, S.A. (1998). A longitudinal study of the relation of vision and vision communication to venture growth in entrepreneurial firms. *Journal of Applied Psychology, 83*(1), 43–54.

Baum, R.J., Locke, E.A., & Smith, K.G. (2001). A multidimensional model of venture growth. *Academy of Management Journal, 44*(2), 292–303.

Bellu, R.R. & Sherman, H. (1995). Predicting firm success from task motivation and attributional style. A longitudinal study. *Entrepreneurship and Regional Development, 7*(4), 349–363.

Bhidé, A.V. (1999). *The origins and evolution of new businesses*. New York: Oxford University Press.

Bowman, E. & Helfat, C.E. (2001). Does corporate strategy matter? *Strategic Management Journal, 22*(1), 1–23.

Brockner, J. (1992). The escalation of commitment to a failing course of action: Toward theoretical progress. *Academy of Management Review, 17*(1), 39–61.

Campbell, D.J. (1988). Task complexity: A review and analysis. *Academy of Management Review, 13*(1), 40–52.

Carree, M.A. & Thurik, A.R. (1998). Small firms and economic growth in Europe. *Atlantic Economic Journal, 26*, 137–146.

Carroll, G.R. & Hannan, M.T. (2000). *The demography of corporations and industries*. Princeton, NJ: Princeton University Press.

Cohen, J. (1969). The statistical power of abnormal-social psychological research: A review. *Journal of Abnormal and Social Psychology, 65*, 95–121.

Cohen, J. & Cohen, P. (1983). *Applied multiple regression/correlation analysis for the behavioral sciences* (2nd ed.). Hillsdale, NJ: Lawrence Erlbaum Associates.

Conner, M., Sheeran, P., Norman, P., & Armitage, C.J. (2000). Temporal stability as a moderator of relationships in the Theory of Planned Behaviour. *British Journal of Social Psychology, 39*, 469–493.

Davidsson, P. (1989). *Continued entrepreneurship and small firm growth*. Stockholm: Stockholm School of Economics, The Economic Research Institute.

Davidsson, P., Delmar, F., & Wiklund, J. (2002). Entrepreneurship as growth; growth as entrepreneurship. In M.A. Hitt, R.D. Ireland, S.M. Camp, & D.L. Sexton (Eds.), *Strategic entrepreneurship: Creating a new mindset* (pp. 328–342). Oxford: Blackwell Publishers.

Davidsson, P., Lindmark, L., & Olofsson, C. (1994). *Dynamiken i svenskt näringsliv (Business dynamics in Sweden)*. Lund, Sweden: Studentlitteratur.

Delmar, F. (1996). *Entrepreneurial behavior and business performance*. Stockholm: Stockholm School of Economics, The Economic Research Institute.

Delmar, F. (1997). Measuring growth: Methodological considerations and empirical results. In R. Donckels & A. Miettinen (Eds.), *Entrepreneurship and SME research: On its way to the next millennium* (pp. 199–216). Aldershot, U.K.: Ashgate.

Delmar, F., Davidsson, P., & Gartner, W.B. (2003). Arriving at the high growth firm. *Journal of Business Venturing*, *18*(2), 189–216.

Eagly, A.H. & Chaiken, S. (1993). *The psychology of attitudes* (1st ed.). Fort Worth, TX: Harcourt Brace Jovanovich, Inc.

Elliott, M.A., Armitage, C.J., & Baughan, C.J. (2003). Drivers' compliance with speed limits: An application of the theory of planned behavior. *Journal of Applied Psychology*, *88*, 964–972.

Gartner, W.B. (1989). Some suggestions for research on entrepreneurial traits and characteristics. *Entrepreneurship Theory and Practice*, *14*(Fall), 27–37.

Heckman, J.J. (1979). Sample selection bias as a specification error. *Econometrica*, *47*(1), 153–162.

Kanfer, R. (1991). Motivation theory and industrial and organizational psychology. In M.D. Dunnette & L.M. Hough (Eds.), *Handbook of industrial and organizational psychology* (2nd ed., Vol. 1, pp. 75–170). Palo Alto, CA: Consulting Psychologists Press Inc.

Kennedy, D., Lakonishok, J. & Shaw, W.H. (1992). Accomodating outliers and nonlinearity in decision models. *Journal of Accounting, Auditing and Finance*, *7*(2), 161–193.

Kolvereid, L. (1992). Growth aspirations among Norwegian entrepreneurs. *Journal of Business Venturing*, *7*, 209–222.

Kolvereid, L. & Bullvag, E. (1996). Growth intentions and actual growth: The impact of entrepreneurial choice. *Journal of Enterprising Culture*, *4*(1), 1–17.

Koys, D.J. (2001). The effects of employees satisfaction, organizational citizenship behavior, and turnover on organizational effectiveness: A unit-level, longitudinal study. *Personnel Psychology*, *54*, 101–114.

Lind, M.L. & Zmud, R.W. (1991). The influence of a convergence in understanding between technology providers and users on information technology innovativeness. *Organization Science*, *2*(2), 195–217.

McCloy, R.A., Campbell, J.P., & Cudeck, R. (1994). A confirmatory test of a model of performance determinants. *Journal of Applied Psychology*, *79*(4), 493–505.

Miner, J.B., Smith, N.R., & Bracker, J.S. (1989). Role of entrepreneurial task motivation in the growth of technologically innovative firms. *Journal of Applied Psychology*, *74*(4), 554–560.

Miner, J.B., Smith, N.R., & Bracker, J.S. (1994). Role of entrepreneurial task motivation in the growth of technologically innovative firms: Interpretations from follow-up data. *Journal of Applied Psychology*, *79*(4), 627–630.

Mok, A.L. & Van den Tillaart, H. (1990). Farmers and small businessmen: A comparative analysis of their careers and occupational orientation. In R. Donckels & A. Miettinen (Eds.), *New findings and perspectives in entrepreneurship* (pp. 203–230). Aldershot, U.K.: Avebury.

Netemeyer, R.G., Burton, S., & Johnston, M. (1991). A comparison of two models for the prediction of volitional and goal-directed behavior: A confirmatory analysis approach. *Social Psychology Quarterly*, *54*, 87–100.

Nunnally, J.C. (1967). *Psychometric theory*. New York: McGraw-Hill.

Nunnally, J.C. & Bernstein, I.H. (1994). *Psychometric theory*. New York: McGraw-Hill.

Orpen, C. (1980). The relationship between expected job performance and causal attributions of past success or failure. *Journal of Social Psychology*, *112*, 151–152.

Ouellette, J.A. & Wood, W. (1998). Habit and intention in everyday life:

The multiple processes by which past behavior predicts future behavior. *Psychological Bulletin*, *214*(1), 54.

Penrose, E. (1959). *The theory of the growth of the firm*. Oxford: Oxford University Press.

Perugini, M. & Conner, R. (2000). Predicting and understanding behavioral volitions: The interplay between goals and behaviors. *European Journal of Social Psychology*, *30*(5), 705–731.

Robbins, D.K., Pantuosco, L.J., Parker, D.F., & Fuller, B.K. (2000). An empirical assessment of the contribution of small business employment to U.S. state economic performance. *Small Business Economics*, *15*, 293–302.

Rosenthal, R. (1991). *Meta-analytic procedures for social research* (Rev. ed., Vol. 6). Newbury Park, CA: Sage Publications, Inc.

Shane, S., Locke, E.A., & Collins, C.J. (2003). Entrepreneurial motivation. *Human Resource Management Review*, *13*(2), 257–279.

Shaver, J.M. (1998). Accounting for endogeneity when assessing strategy performance: Does entry mode choice affect FDI survival? *Management Science*, *44*, 571–585.

Sheeran, P. & Abraham, C. (2003). Mediator of moderators: Temporal stability of intention and the intention–behavior relation. *Personality and Social Psychology Bulletin*, *29*(2), 205–215.

Sheeran, P., Orbell, S., & Trafimow, D. (1999). Does the temporal stability of behavioral intentions moderate intention–behavior and past behavior–future behavior relations? *Personality and Social Psychology Bulletin*, *25*(6), 721–730.

Silver, W.S., Mitchell, T.R., & Gist, M.E. (1995). Responses to successful and unsuccessful performance: The moderating effect of self-efficacy on the relationship between performance and attributions. *Organizational Behavior and Human Decision Processes*, *62*(3), 286.

Storey, D.J. (1994). *Understanding the small business sector*. London: Routledge.

Thomas, K.M. & Mathieu, J.E. (1994). Role of causal attributions in dynamic self-regulation and goal processes. *Journal of Applied Psychology*, *79*(6), 812–818.

Triandis, H.C. (1977). *Interpersonal behaviour*. Monterey, CA: Brooks/Cole.

VandeWalle, D. & Cummings, L.L. (1997). A test of the influence of goal orientation on the feedback-seeking process. *Journal of Applied Psychology*, *82*(3), 390–400.

Venkataraman, S. (1997). The distinctive domain of entrepreneurship research: An editor's perspective. In J. Katz & R.H.S. Brockhaus (Eds.), *Advances in entrepreneurship, firm emergence, and growth* (Vol. 3, pp. 119–138). Greenwich, CT: JAI Press.

Weiner, B. (1985). An attributional theory of achievement motivation and emotion. *Psychological Review*, *92*(4), 548–573.

Weiner, B. (1992). *Human motivation: Metaphors, theories, and research*. Newbury Park, CA: Sage Publications, Inc.

Weinzimmer, L.G., Nystrom, P.C., & Freeman, S.J. (1998). Measuring organizational growth: Issues, consequences and guidelines. *Journal of Management*, *24*(2), 235–262.

Whetten, D.A. (1989). What constitutes a theoretical contribution. *Academy of Management Review*, *14*(4), 490–495.

Wiklund, J. (1998). *Small firm growth and performance*. Jönköping, Sweden: Jönköping International Business School.

Wiklund, J., Davidsson, P., & Delmar, F. (2003). What do they think and feel about growth? An expectancy-value approach to small business managers' attitudes toward growth. *Entrepreneurship Theory and Practice*, *27*(Spring), 247–270.

Wiklund, J. & Shepherd, D.A. (2003). Aspiring for and achieving growth: The moderating role of resources and opportunities. *Journal of Management Studies*, *40*(8), 1919–1942.

Wiklund, J. & Shepherd, D.A. (2005). *Knowledge accumulation in growth studies: The consequences of methodological choices*. Paper presented at the ERIM 29 Expert Workshop 'Perspectives on the Longitudinal Analysis of New Firm Growth,' Rotterdam, NL.

Yanovitzky, I. & Capella, J.N. (2001). Effect of call-in political talk radio shows on their audiences: Evidence from a multi-wave panel analysis. *Journal of Public Opinion Research*, *13*(4), 377–397.

# PART II

# Changing the firm growth research agenda

# 4. Are we comparing apples with apples or apples with oranges? Appropriateness of knowledge accumulation across growth studies*

**Dean A. Shepherd and Johan Wiklund**[1]

## INTRODUCTION

Firm growth has long been a topic of interest to scholars. By investigating the causes of firm growth, researchers gain insights into the drivers of this key dimension of firm performance (Wennekers & Thurik, 1999) and the key drivers of economies (Birch, 1977). Although we have undoubtedly made progress in our understanding of firm growth, mixed results cast a shadow of uncertainty over this collection of works (Davidsson & Wiklund, 2000; Weinzimmer, Nystrom, & Freeman, 1998). Although Davidsson and Wiklund and Weinzimmer et al. have proposed that methodological differences across studies have contributed, at least in part, to these mixed results, there has been insufficient investigation of which methodological differences produce mixed results and when results are robust across methodological differences.

Weinzimmer et al. (1998) made a substantial contribution to the growth literature by taking a number of steps toward empirically investigating these issues. First, they find that there is a weak correlation between different indicators of growth (sales, employment, or assets) and between different formulae for computing growth (absolute, relative, and regression line). Second, they show that the type of indicator and formula used for measuring growth has an impact on the nature of the relationship between a number of independent variables and firm growth. Like Weinzimmer et al., we investigate researchers' methodological choices in growth studies and the impact that these choices should have on how knowledge is accumulated. For example, when investigating absolute employee growth, is it appropriate for researchers to refer to empirical findings on relative employee growth (e.g., Davidsson, Kirchhoff, Hatemi–J, & Gustavsson, 2002; Davila, Foster, & Gupta, 2003; Wing & Yiu, 1996), absolute sales growth (e.g., Autio, Sapienza, & Almeida, 2000; Florin, Lubatkin, & Schulze, 2003; McDougall, Covin, Robinson, & Herron, 1994), and/or absolute asset growth (e.g., Hopkins & Hopkins, 1997; Lee, Lee, & Lee, 2003)? Is it appropriate to accumulate knowledge across studies that investigate absolute sales growth using a 1-year time span (e.g., Collins & Clark, 2003) with those that use a 3-year time span (e.g., Covin & Slevin, 2000)? Is it appropriate to accumulate knowledge across studies investigating relative assets growth using a 1-year time span with studies investigating relative sales growth using a 3-year time span?

Knowledge accumulation is dependent upon relationships among constructs being robust across different operationalizations of those constructs (Eden, 2002). To the extent that differences in growth measures lead to different relationships among constructs, there is a reduction in the appropriateness of accumulating knowledge across these studies. To investigate the appropriateness of knowledge accumulation across studies using different measures of growth, we conduct analyses on all Swedish firms incorporated during the 1994 to 1998 period (68,830 firms) and track their growth over their first 6 years of existence. Our unique panel data allows us to build on the initial steps taken by Weinzimmer et al. (1998) to investigate the concurrent validity between different growth measures.

We use measurement theory and a philosophy of science perspective to investigate the appropriateness of knowledge accumulation across growth studies (for new firms). In doing so, we make a number of important contributions. First, we conduct extensive analyses to show which measures have concurrent validity and which do not. Thus, we are able to give recommendations on which measures scholars can use interchangeably in research and which cannot. Second, our findings provide an explanation for the limited progress of general growth theories and help establish appropriate boundary conditions for growth theories. Our empirical findings of instances of low concurrent validity between measures and heterogeneity in concurrent validity across measures play 'an appropriate role in theory development' (Tsang & Kwan, 1999, p. 776); a contribution to theory is made by improving 'the present state of knowledge accumulation' (Tsang & Kwan, p. 771) and providing multiple avenues for future theoretical and empirical work (detailed in the discussion).

This chapter proceeds as follows. First, we discuss measurement decisions and the importance of knowledge accumulation. Second, we review the empirical literature on growth to reveal their methodological choices. Third, we describe our method and present the findings. Finally, we discuss the findings and their implications for accumulating knowledge from previous studies and conducting future research.

## MEASUREMENT CHOICES OF GROWTH STUDIES AND THEIR CONSEQUENCES

One important aspect of strategy research relates to firm growth (Penrose, 1959; Rugman & Verbeke, 2002), but theory development in firm growth has been notably slow (Davidsson & Wiklund, 2000; Storey, 1994; Weinzimmer et al., 1998). Davidsson and Wiklund proposed that lack of theoretical advancement is due to mixed results and lack of comparability across studies. Although not directly addressed in terms of concurrent validity, scholars of firm growth have noted mixed results, difficulties in accumulating knowledge across growth studies, and attributed blame to the use of different measures and/or the use of samples from different populations (Davidsson & Wiklund; Delmar, 1997; Weinzimmer et al.). These issues of consistency related to researchers' decisions about measurement and generalizability of samples raises the important question of whether, and to what extent, the knowledge gained from firm growth research can be accumulated across different methodological choices.

In this chapter, we explore to what extent variations in measurement choices have likely retarded the advancement of growth theory. We do so by focusing on the measurement of growth – the dependent variable of growth theories. Although researchers must make choices between different growth measures, there is little guidance on which choices are most appropriate (Weinzimmer et al., 1998).

To determine variations in measurement choices reflected in growth studies, we extend the review offered by Weinzimmer et al. (1998) by examining papers published from 1992 up to and including 2006 in the same management journals, namely: *Academy of Management Journal*, *Administrative Science Quarterly*, *American Sociological Review*, *Entrepreneurship Theory and Practice*, *Journal of Business Venturing*, *Journal of Management*, *Journal of Management Studies*, *Journal of Small Business Management*, *Management Science*, *Organization Science*, and *Strategic Management Journal*. We used 'EBSCO's Business Source Premier' search engine and database to find papers with the key word 'growth' (default field), published from 1992 up to and including 2006, and published in one of the journals listed earlier. This search produced 295 papers. The purpose of this selective review is to indicate the types of measurement decisions made in empirical growth studies. Given this purpose, we included only papers that were empirical, that had growth

*Table 4.1 Growth studies' use of indicators, formulae, and time spans*

| | 82 studies |
|---|---|
| Indicator | |
| Sales | 61 |
| Employees | 13 |
| Profit | 9 |
| Equity/assets | 6 |
| Other | 15 |
| Formula | |
| Relative | 37 |
| Absolute | 32 |
| Other | 6 |
| Not reported | 7 |
| Time span | |
| 1 year | 14 |
| 2 years | 11 |
| 3 years | 5 |
| 4 years | 5 |
| 5 years | 13 |
| Other | 19 |
| Not reported | 8 |

as their dependent variable, and that had the firm as the unit of analysis. Eighty-two out of the 293 papers fulfilled all these criteria.

Among the 82 studies reviewed, we classified measurement decisions by: (1) the use of growth indicator(s), (2) the formula used to calculate growth, and (3) the length of the time span over which growth is studied (time span). We present this information in Table 4.1.

First, although sales growth was a popular indicator, these studies accounted for just over 60 per cent of all reviewed papers. The balance of studies used employee growth (12.5 per cent), profit (8.7 per cent), equity/assets (5.8 per cent), and other measures (14.4 per cent). The 'other' category included various indicators of growth such as growth in the number of franchising outlets (Shane, 1996) and in geography covered (Julian & Castrogiovanni, 1995). Interestingly, only 22 studies (26.8 per cent) used two or more growth indicators. The choice of indicator is important, because different indicators will capture different aspects of the growth construct, depending on firms' strategic choices. For example, because Nike outsources production, it can expand sales (high sales growth) with minimal increases in employment or assets (low growth in employment and in assets). Researchers are free to choose among a range of indicators to explore firm growth, and we investigate the implications of those choices for how we should accumulate knowledge on firm growth.

Second, there were two equally dominant formulae used to calculate growth – relative (45 per cent) and absolute (39 per cent) – and two relatively unique formulae, one of which calculated growth using regression analysis, estimating the slope of the growth line (growth was represented by the regression coefficient of the slope) and the other using self-reported growth measured on Likert-type scales. We focus on absolute and relative measures. Following convention, we measured absolute growth as the difference in size at two different time points and measured relative growth as the percentage change in size, typically by dividing absolute growth by initial size. Initial size will influence the measured level of growth differently, depending on whether an absolute or relative measure is used. For example, let us compare two firms – Alpha and Beta – started at the same time and at the same size. Alpha grows sales twice as much as Beta before data collection begins, and then increases the number of units sold by the same amount as Beta during a later period as data are collected. Using an absolute measure of growth over the data collection period, Alpha and Beta had the same growth, but using a relative measure Alpha grew less than Beta because of Alpha's greater growth in the period prior to data collection. Researchers are free to choose between absolute and relative formulae for calculating growth, and we investigate the implications of that choice.

Third, time spans vary considerably but are generally short. Most of the studies calculated growth using a time span of between 1 and 5 years. Rarely did a study use two or more time spans for calculating growth. If the growth of individual firms is not linear but varies over time, the results obtained will differ depending on the chosen time span. For example, compare a firm (which we will call Delta) that grows rapidly over a 2-year period and then stops growing for the next 3 years with another firm (which we will call Gamma) that grows moderately and consistently over the 5-year period. The researcher's choice of a 2-year time span could indicate that Delta had higher growth than Gamma, but if the choice was to use a 5-year period, then the reverse could be the case – Gamma had higher growth than Delta. Researchers are free to explore firm growth by choosing one of many different time spans, and we investigate the implications of that choice.

Fourth, we examined if certain combinations of indicator, formula, and time span were common across studies. It appears that researchers' methodological choices of indicator, formulae for calculating growth, and time span are independent such that researchers did not use any one combination consistently. For example, of the 61 studies, 60 per cent used relative formulae and 52 per cent used absolute formulae (a small number of studies used both), and with each of these studies, the time spans varied considerably.

Fifth, we assessed whether 'theories in use' affected methodological choices. While this assessment is highly subjective, we found little evidence of such a relationship. It appears that researchers make their theoretical and methodological choices independently of each other. For example, studies that investigated the relationship between specific strategies and sales growth would typically cite other growth studies to develop hypotheses (even though those growth studies reflected different methodological choices – different indicators, formulae, and time spans) and generalize the findings to growth in general (rather than to a specific operationalization of growth). Although there is some evidence that such an approach is likely inappropriate (Weinzimmer et al., 1998), in this chapter, we investigate to which it is more or less appropriate. That is, based on our analysis that follows, we can make tentative conclusions on which measures demonstrate high concurrent validity such that knowledge accumulation is appropriate, which demonstrate moderate concurrent validity such that knowledge accumulation is possible, and which demonstrate low concurrent validity such that knowledge accumulation is inappropriate.

In sum, this literature review illustrates that there is great variability on the indicators, formulae, and time spans used by researchers in their empirical studies and that much research assumes concurrent validity of the selected growth measure with other growth measures. That is, in developing hypotheses and referencing the empirical findings of other growth studies, many do not distinguish between studies that use different growth measures. There appears to be an implicit assumption that these choices are of subordinate importance and that results are robust to choices over indicator, formula, and time span. In other words, the assumption is made that the concurrent validity (correlation) among growth measures is high. We empirically test these implicit assumptions.

## RESEARCH METHOD

### Population/Sample

The sample consists of the population of incorporated companies registered in Sweden during the period 1994 to 1998 (i.e., excluded from the sample are sole proprietorships and partnerships). By law, incorporated companies must register with the Swedish patent office before commencing operations, and must file annual reports (certified by a chartered accountant). We accessed all annual reports for their first 8 years of existence. There was a total of 68,830 companies registered, but some of these companies did not file any subsequent reports (i.e., typically, they were 'shelf' companies that did not have operations and were therefore not required to file an annual report). Of the companies registered during the 1994 to 1998 period, 58,304 provided complete annual statements for their first year of existence. During the 6 years covered in this study, close to half the population of new firms did not survive (30,556 companies dropped out of the sample); some firms were absorbed by other companies through mergers, while others went bankrupt.

### Growth Measures

Based on the literature review, we identified five common growth indicators: growth in (1) sales, (2) employees, (3) profit, (4) assets, and (5) equity. We used size information from annual reports of sales, number of employees, profit after depreciation and financial expenses, total assets, and total equity, respectively. Absolute growth was simply computed as the size at 1 year minus the size of the previous year, and for a relative measure, we divided the absolute measure of growth by the size at the initial year. Such calculations require the choice of a time span over which to capture growth. We calculated all time spans given the seven time periods represented by the annual reports (although given the consistency of results across time spans, we report a subset of these results later). It is important to note that because we analyze variance and do not use compound formulae to calculate growth, it is unnecessary to make adjustments for inflation.

### Analysis

We address the potential for concurrent validity in terms of the extent of agreement among measures of growth. Although the consistency among different measures is typically tested using Pearson product moment correlations (Loo, 2002), it is difficult to specify a single threshold upon which two measures can be considered to support concurrent validity. For correlations in general, Cohen (1988) argues that .1 is a small correlation, .3 a moderate, and .5 a large correlation. Specifically addressing concurrent validity, Burke, Joyner, Czech, & Wilson (2000) noted that a correlation of above .7 is needed for constructs to share

50 per cent of the variance. Based on this (i.e., Burke et al.; Cohen; Loo), we use the following classification scheme for levels of concurrent validity:

**High concurrent validity**: when two measures have a correlation coefficient of .5 or greater.
**Moderate concurrent validity**: when two measures have a correlation coefficient between .3 and .5.
**Low concurrent validity**: when two measures have a correlation coefficient between .1 and .3.
**No concurrent validity**: when two measures have a correlation coefficient below .1.

Suggesting that a pair of growth measures has high concurrent validity does not mean that they provide exactly the same information about the underlying construct; rather, they share a sufficient amount of variance that enables these different measures to provide a similar picture of the underlying construct. It allows us to have some faith that we are comparing apples with apples to accumulate knowledge. Low or no concurrent validity indicates that we are comparing apples with oranges and that we should not be accumulating knowledge; rather, new knowledge should progress around each independently, and/or we should develop theories that explain (link) these two streams of research.

Rather than providing a distinct cutoff for when two measures demonstrate concurrent validity, we examine tendencies and indicate which pairs of measures have more in common than other pairs. Further, we do not provide levels of statistical significance because we study the whole population rather than a sample. Presenting the results for all growth indicators, using both absolute and relative formulae for their calculations and considering every possible time span, would require a matrix of unwieldy size. Given the exploratory nature of our study and space limitation, we report the results for the most common combinations, and also those that are likely to be the most informative.

Specifically, we use a 1-year time span to investigate the concurrent validity between the absolute and relative measures of each growth indicator (Table 4.2), a 1-year time span to investigate the concurrent validity between each absolute growth measure (Table 4.3), and a 1-year time span to investigate the concurrent validity between each relative growth measure (Table 4.4). We then investigate the concurrent validity of each absolute measure using a 1-year time span with the same absolute measure using a 3-year time span (Table 4.5, top). We then repeat these analyses for relative measures (Table 4.5, bottom). It would have been possible to

*Table 4.2 Correlations of absolute and relative measures of growth as firms age using a 1-year time span*

| Age | Employee growth | Sales growth | Profit growth | Asset growth | Equity growth |
|---|---|---|---|---|---|
| 1 | .440 | .109 | .045 | .979 | .813 |
| 2 | .515 | .118 | –.055 | .034 | 1 |
| 3 | .383 | .035 | –.087 | .161 | .289 |
| 4 | .448 | .050 | –.005 | .351 | .063 |
| 5 | .509 | .286 | .130 | .061 | .055 |
| 6 | .459 | .035 | .028 | .020 | .023 |
| 7 | .394 | .031 | –.004 | .027 | .010 |
| Mean | .450 | .095 | .007 | .233 | .322 |

compare measures across combined methodological choices (for example, absolute sales growth using a 1-year time span with relative equity growth using a 3-year time span). Because such comparisons are less informative and less likely to generate high correlations they were deemed less valuable and not included.

## RESULTS

### Concurrent Validity Between Absolute and Relative Growth Measures

Table 4.2 presents, in a condensed format, the results of our analysis for absolute and relative measures of each indicator of growth using a 1-year time span for the firms' first 7 years. The first column indicates the age of the firms (growth for their first 7 years). The remaining columns present the results of the correlation analyses. Column 2 represents the correlation for employee growth between absolute and relative measures (using a 1-year time span). The remaining columns represent the correlations between absolute and relative measures for sales growth (column 3), profit growth (column 4), assets growth (column 5), and equity growth (column 6).

We first examine the results for the relationship between relative and absolute employment growth presented in column 2. On average, over the seven time periods of observation, relative employee growth and absolute employee growth have a correlation coefficient of .450, which approaches the threshold for high concurrent validity. The correlation coefficient for absolute and relative measures of equity growth was .322, which indicates

*Table 4.3 Correlations of absolute measures of growth as firms age using a 1-year time span*

| Employee growth | Age | Employee growth | Sales growth | Profit growth | Asset growth | Equity growth |
|---|---|---|---|---|---|---|
| | 1 | 1 | .352 | .030 | .019 | .032 |
| | 2 | 1 | .213 | .080 | –.060 | –.066 |
| | 3 | 1 | .419 | –.220 | .090 | .003 |
| | 4 | 1 | .394 | –.229 | .069 | .047 |
| | 5 | 1 | .372 | .096 | .093 | .062 |
| | 6 | 1 | .343 | .037 | .007 | –.012 |
| | 7 | 1 | .287 | –.082 | .086 | .068 |
| Mean | | 1.000 | .340 | –.041 | .043 | .019 |
| **Sales growth** | **Age** | **Employee growth** | **Sales growth** | **Profit growth** | **Asset growth** | **Equity growth** |
| | 1 | | 1 | .530 | 0 | .128 |
| | 2 | | 1 | 0 | 0 | –.006 |
| | 3 | | 1 | .029 | .138 | .082 |
| | 4 | | 1 | .075 | .128 | .085 |
| | 5 | | 1 | –.055 | .148 | –.027 |
| | 6 | | 1 | .248 | .265 | .135 |
| | 7 | | 1 | .005 | .452 | .160 |
| Mean | | | 1.000 | .119 | .162 | .080 |
| **Profit growth** | **Age** | **Employee growth** | **Sales growth** | **Profit growth** | **Asset growth** | **Equity growth** |
| | 1 | | | 1 | –.227 | .006 |
| | 2 | | | 1 | –.308 | –.325 |
| | 3 | | | 1 | –.425 | –.069 |
| | 4 | | | 1 | –.117 | –.473 |
| | 5 | | | 1 | .434 | .843 |
| | 6 | | | 1 | .234 | .749 |
| | 7 | | | 1 | –.269 | –.284 |
| Mean | | | | 1.000 | –.097 | .064 |
| **Asset growth** | **Age** | **Employee growth** | **Sales growth** | **Profit growth** | **Asset growth** | **Equity growth** |
| | 1 | | | | 1 | .969 |
| | 2 | | | | 1 | .986 |
| | 3 | | | | 1 | .612 |
| | 4 | | | | 1 | .117 |
| | 5 | | | | 1 | .709 |
| | 6 | | | | 1 | .550 |
| | 7 | | | | 1 | .383 |
| Mean | | | | | 1.000 | .618 |

*Table 4.4 Correlations of relative measures of growth as firms age using a 1-year time span*

| Employee growth | Age | Employee growth | Sales growth | Profit growth | Asset growth | Equity growth |
|---|---|---|---|---|---|---|
| | 1 | 1 | .336 | –.013 | .163 | .037 |
| | 2 | 1 | .024 | .024 | .012 | .004 |
| | 3 | 1 | .064 | .021 | –.006 | –.018 |
| | 4 | 1 | .062 | –.050 | .121 | .019 |
| | 5 | 1 | .309 | .261 | .344 | .216 |
| | 6 | 1 | .019 | .027 | .363 | .018 |
| | 7 | 1 | .072 | .013 | .201 | –.018 |
| Mean | | 1.000 | .127 | .040 | .171 | .037 |
| **Sales growth** | **Age** | **Employee growth** | **Sales growth** | **Profit growth** | **Asset growth** | **Equity growth** |
| | 1 | | 1 | .021 | .064 | –.003 |
| | 2 | | 1 | .014 | .085 | .084 |
| | 3 | | 1 | –.007 | .036 | .011 |
| | 4 | | 1 | .001 | .068 | .008 |
| | 5 | | 1 | .683 | .717 | .506 |
| | 6 | | 1 | .030 | .469 | –.022 |
| | 7 | | 1 | .183 | .392 | .006 |
| Mean | | | 1.000 | .132 | .262 | .084 |
| **Profit growth** | **Age** | **Employee growth** | **Sales growth** | **Profit growth** | **Asset growth** | **Equity growth** |
| | 1 | | | 1 | –.026 | .012 |
| | 2 | | | 1 | .172 | .186 |
| | 3 | | | 1 | –.766 | –.951 |
| | 4 | | | 1 | –.064 | –.005 |
| | 5 | | | 1 | .040 | .685 |
| | 6 | | | 1 | .012 | .005 |
| | 7 | | | 1 | –.035 | –.008 |
| Mean | | | | 1.000 | –.095 | –.011 |
| **Asset growth** | **Age** | **Employee growth** | **Sales growth** | **Profit growth** | **Asset growth** | **Equity growth** |
| | 1 | | | | 1 | .869 |
| | 2 | | | | 1 | .775 |
| | 3 | | | | 1 | .782 |
| | 4 | | | | 1 | .036 |
| | 5 | | | | 1 | –.008 |
| | 6 | | | | 1 | .045 |
| | 7 | | | | 1 | .016 |
| Mean | | | | | 1.000 | .359 |

*Table 4.5 Correlations of growth measures at 1-year time span and at 3-year time span*

| Age | Employee growth | Sales growth | Profit growth | Asset growth | Equity growth |
|---|---|---|---|---|---|
| **Absolute growth measures** | | | | | |
| 3 | .659 | .677 | .205 | .018 | .040 |
| 4 | .502 | .619 | .604 | .983 | .973 |
| 5 | .558 | .495 | .910 | .410 | .770 |
| 6 | .607 | .428 | .358 | .796 | .648 |
| 7 | .586 | .682 | .268 | .955 | .819 |
| Mean | .582 | .580 | .469 | .632 | .650 |
| **Relative growth measures** | | | | | |
| 3 | .732 | .278 | .130 | .104 | .042 |
| 4 | .552 | .974 | .275 | .477 | .736 |
| 5 | .415 | .645 | .018 | .022 | 504 |
| 6 | .531 | .980 | .086 | .111 | 668 |
| 7 | .548 | .515 | .224 | .083 | .511 |
| Mean | .556 | .678 | .147 | .159 | .492 |

moderate concurrent validity. The concurrent validity for absolute and relative measures for sales growth (r = .095), profit growth (r = .007), and asset growth (r = .233) were all low.

**Concurrent Validity Between Different Absolute Growth Measures**

Table 4.3 presents the results of our analysis for absolute measures of growth with each other absolute measure of growth using a 1-year time span for the firms' first 7 years. The first column indicates the absolute measure of growth to be correlated with the other absolute growth measures. The second column indicates the age of the firms. The next five columns represent the five absolute measures of growth: absolute employee growth (column 3), absolute sales growth (column 4), absolute profit growth (column 5), absolute asset growth (column 6), and absolute equity growth (column 7). On average, over the seven time periods of observation, one pair of measures reached high concurrent validity and one pair reached moderate concurrent validity. The correlation coefficient for absolute asset growth and absolute equity growth is

.618, which indicates high concurrent validity. The correlation coefficient for absolute employee growth and absolute sales growth is .340, which indicates moderate concurrent validity. All other combination pairs of absolute measures of growth demonstrate low concurrent validity.

### Concurrent Validity Between Different Relative Growth Measures

Table 4.4 presents the results of our analysis for relative measures of growth with each other relative measure of growth using a 1-year time span for the firms' first 7 years. The first column indicates the relative measure of growth to be correlated with the other relative growth measures. The second column indicates the age of the firms. The next five columns represent the five relative measures of growth: relative employee growth (column 3), relative sales growth (column 4), relative profit growth (column 5), relative asset growth (column 6), and relative equity growth (column 7). On average, over the seven time periods of observation, no pairs of measures reached high concurrent validity. The correlation coefficient for relative asset growth and relative equity growth is .359, which indicates moderate concurrent validity. The correlation coefficient for relative sales growth and relative equity growth is .262, which approaches moderate concurrent validity. Both indicate moderate concurrent validity. All other combination pairs of relative measures of growth demonstrate low concurrent validity.

### Concurrent Validity for the Same Growth Measures With Different Time Spans

The upper portion of Table 4.5 is similar to that of Table 4.2, but instead presents the results of our analysis for absolute measures of growth with a 1-year time span and the same absolute measure using a 3-year time span for years 3 to 7. Years 1 and 2 were not included because it is not possible to compute growth using a 3-year time span for these years. The concurrent validity was high (or approaching high) for all pairs of 1- and 3-year time spans for absolute growth measure. Specifically, the correlation coefficient for absolute employee growth (1-year time span) and absolute employee growth (3-year time span) is .582; sales growth across time spans is .580, asset growth across time spans is .632, and equity growth across time spans is .650. These all indicate high concurrent validity. While not meeting the threshold of high concurrent validity, absolute profit growth across time spans approaches this threshold ($r = .469$).

The lower portion of Table 4.5 is similar to the upper portion, although the results are for relative measures of growth using 1- and 3-year time spans. The correlation coefficient for relative employee growth over a 1- and 3-year time span is .556, and sales growth across time spans is .678, both of which indicate high concurrent validity. Concurrent validity for relative equity growth across the two time spans approaches the threshold for high (r = .492). Concurrent validity for relative profit growth across times spans (r = .147) and relative asset growth across time spans (r = .159) is low.

### Robustness of Results for an Older Cohort of Firms

In this chapter, because of the likelihood of sample attrition, we followed firms from their inception for 6 consecutive years. It is possible that allowing for firms to mature and more firms to drop out of the population would produce different results. In order to test if this is the case, we conducted identical analyses for firms that were 25 years of age. That is, we selected a cohort of firms that were 25 years old and followed their growth for 6 consecutive years. Due to space limitations, it is not possible to report these results here. However, these analyses produced similar results in terms of measures showing larger or smaller concurrent validity. The major difference was that, overall, the correlations were smaller. Thus, if anything, there appears to be less concurrent validity among older than among younger firms for the measures examined here.

## DISCUSSION

### A General Comment on Concurrent Validity and Knowledge Accumulation

The management literature has offered several critical accounts of the limited theoretical development in growth studies. Notwithstanding the possibilities for additional causes, methodological issues are likely to be a major reason for limited progress. In this chapter, we first point out that scholars make different choices regarding growth indicators, formulae, and time spans in their development and use of growth measures. There were few studies in the literature that used the exact same combinations along these three dimensions. We then examined the extent to which it is appropriate to accumulate knowledge across different measurement choices, that is, the extent to which there is concurrent validity. If concurrent validity is low, then this could explain why theoretical progress has been slow, because knowledge accumulation is dependent upon relationships among constructs being robust across different operationalizations (Eden, 2002). Table 4.6 summarizes our

Table 4.6 *Measures of growth that have concurrent validity*

| Measure | Measure | Mean concurrent validity |
|---|---|---|
| Absolute and relative formulae, same indicator | | |
| Relative employee growth (1-year time span) | Absolute employee growth (1-year time span) | Moderate to High |
| Relative equity growth (1-year time span) | Absolute equity growth (1-year time span) | Moderate |
| Absolute growth, different indicators | | |
| Absolute employee growth (1-year time span) | Absolute sales growth (1-year time span) | Moderate |
| Absolute asset growth (1-year time span) | Absolute equity growth (1-year time span) | High |
| Relative growth, different indicators | | |
| Relative sales growth (1-year time span) | Relative asset growth (1-year time span) | Low to Moderate |
| Relative asset growth (1-year time span) | Relative equity growth (1-year time span) | Moderate |
| Absolute growth, different time spans | | |
| Absolute employee growth (1-year time span) | Absolute employee growth (3-year time span) | High |
| Absolute sales growth (1-year time span) | Absolute sales growth (3-year time span) | High |
| Absolute profit growth (1-year time span) | Absolute profit growth (3-year time span) | Approaching High |
| Absolute asset growth (1-year time span) | Absolute asset growth (3-year time span) | High |
| Absolute equity growth (1-year time span) | Absolute equity growth (3-year time span) | High |
| Relative growth, different time spans | | |
| Relative employee growth (1-year time span) | Relative employee growth (3-year time span) | High |
| Relative sales growth (1-year time span) | Relative sales growth (3-year time span) | High |
| Relative equity growth (1-year time span) | Relative equity growth (3-year time span) | Approaching High |

*Notes:* All other combinations have low or no concurrent validity.

results of those measures that demonstrate moderate, moderate to high, and high concurrent validity. Pairs of growth measures not listed in Table 4.6 represent low or no concurrent validity. We now examine in more detail when knowledge accumulation is appropriate and when it may be inappropriate.

**Concurrent Validity Across Absolute and Relative Measures of Growth**

As indicated in Table 4.6, we only found evidence of acceptable concurrent validity between two indicators of growth across their absolute and relative measures for employee growth. Employee growth demonstrated moderate to high concurrent validity across its absolute and relative measures. This level of concurrent validity was relatively consistent as firms aged. Equity growth demonstrated moderate concurrent validity across its absolute and relative measures. Relative and absolute measures of all other growth indicators – sales growth, asset growth, and profit growth – demonstrated low concurrent validity.

These findings suggest that for studies that investigate absolute employee growth, their results are likely to be somewhat comparable with, and can build upon, studies that use relative measures of employee growth (and vice versa) – together, they contribute to an accumulation of knowledge on an aspect of firm growth. Although such an accumulation of knowledge also appears appropriate across absolute and relative measures of equity growth, our results suggest that it is not (or at least less) appropriate across absolute and relative measures of sales, asset, and profit growth. How serious a problem is this for knowledge accumulation?

One probable outcome is that it is difficult to attain convergence for the findings of relative measures in studies using absolute measures (and vice versa) for indicators other than employee growth or equity growth. The influence of independent variables likely differs in replications of growth studies depending on whether studies use absolute or relative measures of growth because of low concurrent validity. Support for this notion is provided by the analyses carried out by Weinzimmer et al. (1998), who used a sample of large and old firms to estimate regression equations for absolute and relative employee, assets, and sales growth over a 4-year time span for a specific set of independent variables. Seven independent variables were significant in explaining employee growth, five appearing in both relative and absolute growth. Nine independent variables significantly explained asset growth, but only two appeared in both relative and absolute growth. Similarly, eight independent variables significantly explained sales growth, but only two appeared in both relative and absolute growth. In sum, their findings indicated that similar variables explained relative and absolute employment growth, but this was not the case for the other analyzed growth measures.

Therefore, with the possible exceptions of employee growth and equity growth, we would recommend that researchers not develop hypotheses for absolute growth based on previous empirical findings using relative measures (and vice versa), because they likely (should) represent two distinct bodies of literature. It is possible that we need to use different theories to explain absolute and relative growth for sales, assets, and profits.

Interestingly, the concurrent validity was high across absolute and relative equity measures in the firms' first 2 years, moderate over the next year, and low in the remaining 4 years (aged 4 to 7). Future research can theoretically and empirically investigate whether concurrent validity between equity growth's absolute and relative measures significantly declines over time. It might be that for studies investigating absolute equity growth of firms that are less than 5 years old, their results are highly comparable with, and can build upon, studies that investigated relative equity growth, but this may not be the case for more established firms (over 5 years old).

## Concurrent Validity Across Different Indicators of Growth

### Absolute employee growth and absolute sales growth

Table 4.3 illustrates that absolute employee growth has moderate concurrent validity with absolute sales growth, and this concurrent validity appears relatively consistent as firms age. Evidence of concurrent validity for absolute sales growth and absolute employee growth has important implications for further research (within the boundary conditions of this study). First, for studies that investigate absolute sales growth, their results are likely to be somewhat comparable with, and can build upon, studies that use absolute employee growth (and vice versa). This is important, particularly for theories that are most interested in empirically investigating absolute employee growth because the empirical growth literature is primarily based on measures of sales growth (a substantial portion of which have measured sales using absolute growth). Second, it might be possible to test a theory of sales growth collecting data on employee growth or a theory of employee growth collecting data on sales growth. This is not to imply that such a situation is preferable – clearly, it is not; these do not measure the same thing but the findings of this study suggest that they do share a moderate level of variance such that their concurrent validity provides the opportunity to accumulate knowledge across these two measures.

**Absolute asset growth and absolute equity growth**

Table 4.3 illustrates that absolute asset growth has high concurrent validity with absolute equity growth. With 1 year as an exception, the level of concurrent validity is relatively consistent as firms age. Therefore, it appears appropriate to accumulate knowledge across growth studies that use absolute asset growth and absolute equity growth. The implications are that theories developed based on one of the measures transcend to the other, and theory tests should be robust across these two indicators. Studies interested in explaining growth in terms of the accumulation of resources need not be overly concerned about which of these indicators to choose, but can rely on the indicator that is easier to access.

**Relative asset growth and relative equity growth**

Overall, there is moderate concurrent validity for relative asset growth and relative equity growth; however, there is high variability in that concurrent validity across firm ages (see Table 4.4). Specifically, there is high concurrent validity for the firms' first 3 years and low concurrent validity for the next 4 years. Therefore, we qualify the implication by stating that for studies that investigate the relative assets growth of new firms that are less than 4 years old, their results are likely highly comparable with, and can build upon, studies that investigated the relative equity growth of new ventures that are less than 4 years old. The same cannot be said for 4 years and older. Future research can investigate how and why there is a change in concurrent validity. Does concurrent validity consistently decrease as firms age, or is there some form of threshold at year 4 that fundamentally (and rapidly) changes the relationship between relative asset and equity growth (as appears to be the case in our data)? We believe that investigating the change in the nature of these growth measures may provide an important contribution to our understanding of a firm's transition from new to established.

**Relative sales growth and relative asset growth**

Table 4.4 illustrates that relative sales growth has moderate concurrent validity with relative asset growth. In contrast with the pattern of results for relative asset and equity growth measures, concurrent validity is low for the firms' first 4 years but high for the next 3 years. Again, this offers an important research opportunity: if concurrent validity is low and then increases with age (continuously or as a step), what does this relationship between relative measures of sales and assets tell us about the firm maturation process? Is it that once internal routines have become more established that sales and assets 'get in sync' in the way that they grow? Is legitimacy the mechanism for this synchronicity? Although there is a multitude of potential answers, future theoretical and empirical work can make an important contribution in addressing these questions.

**Concurrent Validity Across Different Time Spans**

For all indicators of absolute growth (absolute employee, sales, profit, asset, and equity growth), there is high concurrent validity (approaching high concurrent validity for absolute profit growth) between when these measures are calculated using a 1-year time span and using a 3-year time span. These high levels of concurrent validity are consistent as firms age. Relative employee, sales, and equity growth also show evidence of high concurrent validity (approaching high concurrent validity for relative equity growth), which is consistent as firms age. In contrast, relative profit and relative asset growth have low concurrent validity between when they are calculated using a 1-year and a 3-year time span. These findings indicate that researchers can have confidence in accumulating knowledge across absolute measures that use a 1-year time span and a 3-year time span. Similarly, it appears appropriate to accumulate knowledge across time spans for relative employee, sales, and equity. However, it appears inappropriate to accumulate knowledge across time spans for the relative measures of growth in assets and profit.

**Implications for Future Research**

In this study, we found evidence that there is concurrent validity between some of the different growth measures and across 1- and 3-year time spans as summarized in Table 4.6. This provides the opportunity for knowledge accumulation across specific studies. *Employment growth* shows concurrent validity across its relative and absolute measures, and its absolute measure with absolute sales growth. *Equity growth* demonstrates concurrent validity across its absolute and relative measures, its absolute measure with absolute asset growth, and its relative measure with relative asset growth. *Sales growth* demonstrates concurrent validity with its absolute measure and absolute employee growth, and its relative measure with relative assets. *Asset growth* demonstrates concurrent validity with its absolute measure and absolute equity growth, and its relative measure with both relative sales growth and relative equity growth. With the exception of across time spans (which we will discuss next), *profit growth* demonstrates little concurrent validity with other indicators or measures.

We also found evidence that there is low concurrent validity for a number of different growth measures. Some sets of measures that demonstrate a mean level of concurrent validity show considerable variability over time, so that for some periods, concurrent validity is low. Although the finding of low concurrent validity may appear to be bad news because it points to limitations in the ability to accumulate knowledge across types of studies, we believe that it represents good news because it points to where researchers need to create new knowledge. Thus, our empirical findings have the following contributions to further theoretical work.

First, perhaps our theories are too broad, and by narrowing the boundary conditions, we are able to build richer theories that, when empirically tested, better describe a particular aspect of the growth. This will have implications for practice and education. Given our results, we would recommend that future research clearly specify the theory's domain (specify the relevant dimensions of growth), and whether results apply to young or established firms. If explicitly delineating their theoretical approaches, we believe that researchers have many opportunities to make significant contributions to the literature and overcome field fragmentation. For example, given the generally low shared variance among many growth measures, we question if general theories of growth are meaningful. If a theory is able to explain some measures of growth but not others, is it then really a general theory of growth? Instead, we urge researchers to acknowledge the context specificity of measures, and thus, the context specificity of theories.

Second, when building theories of growth based on previous empirical findings, it is important to be careful in which studies to include and aggregate and which studies to exclude. We recommended a more narrow scope for theory development, and the same applies to theory testing. Different measures of growth often tap into different dimensions of the growth construct. Consequently, growth theories should not be refuted based on non-findings for one or a few operationalizations of growth. If the theory has not been specified to apply to those specific measures tested, such a finding only suggests that the theory does not hold within that particular domain. It may still be valid within other domains. For example, whether or not Penrose's theory extends into other domains, such as absolute sales growth of service firms, is an empirical question. Even if it does not, it may still be highly relevant in the context for which it was originally developed.

The third recommendation flows naturally from those mentioned earlier, which is to replicate previous studies. These replications should closely follow previous studies concerning growth indicators, formulae for computing growth, and time spans, because findings appear specific to these methodological choices. Some scholars may view replications as less innovative and exciting. However, we believe that the field needs more replication research, and there appears to be acceptance among scientists and journal editors that replication is an important vehicle for accumulating knowledge. For example, in a recent note from Dov Eden, as an editor of the *Academy of Management Journal*, he argues that: 'replication research is an indispensable ingredient in the scientific progress' (2002, p. 842).

Fourth, knowing which growth measures have low concurrent validity provide researchers opportunities to develop theories that link these growth measures. In doing so, such research will provide a bridge that allows knowledge to be accumulated across studies that use these different growth measures. For example, perhaps there are temporal aspects that can help define the relationship between two growth measures. Such theories and empirical testing will provide further opportunities for knowledge accumulation.

Finally, in a similar vein to the previous point, situations where there is a mix of high and low concurrent validity may provide important opportunities for the creation of new knowledge. For example, a pair of growth measures may have mean moderate concurrent validity over the first 7 years of the firm's life; however, investigation of each year reveals that concurrent validity changes as firms age. Can a theory be developed to explain the ebb and flow of concurrent validity between different growth measures? We have a better understanding of the interrelationships between financial aspects of the firm using financial ratios, but the relationship between these different growth measures remains a mystery.

Based on the chapter's empirical evidence and the earlier discussion, we hope that we have demonstrated the need for more theoretical work and productive avenues for it.

## Limitations

Despite studying the whole population of a cohort of firms and relying on archival data underwritten by chartered accountants rather than self-reported numbers, this study, like all studies, has limitations. First, this chapter is limited to cohorts of firms in one specific country. It is possible that other populations would produce different results. To ensure that our findings are generally applicable, future research needs to examine cohorts from other countries. Such tests of empirical generalization (Tsang & Kwan, 1999) would be valuable in determining the generality of our findings.

Second, we did not utilize composite growth measures consisting of several different indicators of growth. It is possible that such combinations would produce results that are more consistent. However, given the weak correlations among measures, it is difficult to find indicators that would meet conventional criteria for being combined into indices (i.e., reliability

[Cronbach's alpha] is likely to be very low). More generally, we did not consider any variable manipulations. Some studies use log-transform variables, Winsor techniques, or other manipulations that alter the distribution of the growth measures. It is possible that such manipulations produce correlations of greater magnitude among measures. However, analysis of manipulated measures is beyond the scope of the current chapter.

Finally, we chose to study cohorts of firms during their first years of existence, thereby minimizing survivor bias and limiting unobserved heterogeneity arising from the effect of growth in previous unobserved periods. Delimiting instead the sample to specific industries or size groups could possibly lead to stronger correlations. This is precisely the point we raise – that theories and their tests may be context specific.

## CONCLUSION

The spirit of this chapter is not to discredit previous research on firm growth. On the contrary, our review showed that over the past 12 years, research on growth has proliferated, which has led to several valuable insights into the phenomenon. Instead, we wish to provide an explanation for the limited knowledge accumulation noted by scholars. Our review shows that there is great variability in researchers' use of indicators, formulae, and time spans. Empirically, we find low concurrent validity among many of the different measures of growth, but do find high and moderate concurrent validity among a select few growth measures. We conclude that researchers' choices among measures of growth and samples are important because they have the potential of influencing findings, and thus, these methodological choices have direct implications for knowledge accumulation. We can enhance progress in knowledge accumulation when future research makes deliberate and informed choices about their use of indicators, formulae, and time spans.

We conclude this chapter by revisiting the questions of the introduction. To the first set of questions – 'When investigating absolute employee growth, is it appropriate for researchers to refer to empirical findings on relative employee growth, absolute sales growth, and/or absolute asset growth?' – this chapter suggests that the answers are YES, YES, and NO. To the second and third questions – 'Is it appropriate to accumulate knowledge across studies that investigate absolute sales growth using a 1-year time span (e.g., Collins & Clark, 2003) with those that use a 3-year time span (e.g., Covin & Slevin, 2000)?' and 'What about relative asset growth using different time spans?' – this chapter suggests that the answers are YES and NO. We recognize that we should only tentatively hold this chapter's recommendations, but these recommendations are important as they represent a comprehensive attempt at investigating the appropriateness of knowledge accumulation in the growth literature.

## NOTES

* Previously published as: Dean A. Shepherd and Johan Wiklund (2009), 'Are we comparing apples with apples or apples with oranges? Appropriateness of knowledge accumulation across growth studies', *Entrepreneurship Theory and Practice*, **33** (1), January, 105–23.

1. We would like to thank Denis Gregoire for his help in categorizing growth studies.

## REFERENCES

Autio, E., Sapienza, H.J., & Almeida, J.G. (2000). Effects of age at entry, knowledge intensity, and imitability on international growth. *Academy of Management Journal*, *43*(5), 909–925.

Birch, D. (1977). *The job generating process, final report on economic development administration*. Cambridge, MA: MIT Program on Neighborhood and Regional Change.

Burke, K.L., Joyner, A.B., Czech, D.R., & Wilson, M.J. (2000). An investigation of concurrent validity between two optimism/pessimism questionnaires: The life orientation test-revised and the optimism/ pessimism scale. *Current Psychology*, *19*, 129–137.

Cohen, J. (1988). *Statistical power analysis for the behavioral sciences* (2nd ed.). Mahwah, NJ: Lawrence Erlbaum.

Collins, C.J. & Clark, K.D. (2003). Strategic human resource practices, top management team social networks, and firm performance: The role of human resource practices in creating organizational competitive advantage. *Academy of Management Journal*, *46*(6), 740–752.

Covin, J.G. & Slevin, D.P. (2000). Pioneers and followers: Competitive tactics, environment, and firm growth. *Journal of Business Venturing*, *15*(2), 175–211.

Davidsson, P., Kirchhoff, B., Hatemi–J, A., & Gustavsson, H. (2002). Empirical analysis of business growth factors using Swedish data. *Journal of Small Business Management*, *40*(4), 332–350.

Davidsson, P. & Wiklund, J. (2000). Conceptual and empirical challenges in the study of firm growth. In D. Sexton, H. Landström (Eds.), *The Blackwell handbook of entrepreneurship* (pp. 26–44). Oxford, MA: Blackwell.

Davila, A., Foster, G., & Gupta, M. (2003). Venture capital financing and the growth of startup firms. *Journal of Business Venturing*, *18*, 689–709.

Delmar, F. (1997). Measuring growth: Methodological considerations and empirical results. In R. Donckels, A. Miettinen (Eds.), *Entrepreneurship and SME research: On its way to the next millennium* (pp. 190–216). Aldershot, VA: Avebury.

Eden, D. (2002). Replication, meta-analysis, scientific progress, and AMJ's publication process. *Academy of Management Journal*, *45*, 841–847.

Florin, J., Lubatkin, M., & Schulze, W. (2003). A social capital model of high-growth ventures. *Academy of Management Journal*, *46*(3), 374–385.

Hopkins, W.E. & Hopkins, S.A. (1997). Strategic planning-financial performance relationships in banks: A causal examination. *Strategic Management Journal*, *18*(8), 635–653.

Julian, S.D. & Castrogiovanni, G.J. (1995). Franchisor geographic expansion. *Journal of Small Business Management*, *33*, 1–11.

Lee, J., Lee, J., & Lee, H. (2003). Exploration and exploitation in the presence of network externalities. *Management Science*, *49*(4), 553–571.

Loo, R. (2002). A psychometric and cross-national examination of a belief in a just world scale. *Journal of Applied Social Psychology*, *32*, 1396–1406.

McDougall, P.P., Covin, J.G., Robinson, R.B., & Herron, L. (1994). The effects of industry growth and strategic breadth on new venture performance and strategy content. *Strategic Management Journal*, *15*(7), 537–555.

Penrose, E.T. (1959). *The theory of the growth of the firm*. Oxford: Oxford University Press.

Rugman, A.M. & Verbeke, A. (2002). Edith Penrose's contribution to the Resource-Based View of strategic management. *Strategic Management Journal*, *23*, 769–779.

Shane, S.A. (1996). Hybrid organizational arrangements and their implications for firm growth and survival: A study of new franchisors. *Academy of Management Journal*, *39*, 216–234.

Storey, D.J. (1994). *Understanding the small business sector*. London: Routledge.

Tsang, E.W. & Kwan, K.M. (1999). Replication and theory development in organizational science: A critical realist perspective. *Academy of Management Review*, *24*, 759–782.

Weinzimmer, L.G., Nystrom, P.C., & Freeman, S.J. (1998). Measuring organizational growth: Issues, consequences and guidelines. *Journal of Management*, *24*, 235–263.

Wennekers, S. & Thurik, R. (1999). Linking entrepreneurship and economic growth. *Small Business Economics*, *13*(1), 27–56.

Wing, C.C.K. & Yiu, M.F.K. (1996). Firm dynamics and industrialization in the Chinese economy in transition: Implications for small business. *Journal of Business Venturing*, *11*(6), 489–506.

# 5. Advancing firm growth research: a focus on growth mode instead of growth rate*

**Alexander McKelvie and Johan Wiklund**

## INTRODUCTION

Firm growth constitutes one of the central topics of entrepreneurship research. Despite substantial interest and massive empirical research, theoretical development in the field has been notably slow (e.g., Davidsson & Wiklund, 2000; Delmar, Davidsson, & Gartner, 2003; Shepherd & Wiklund, 2009). A telling illustration is that the most comprehensive, adequate, and popular theory on growth was developed some 50 years ago with Penrose's (1959) publication of *The Theory of the Growth of the Firm*. In this chapter, we explain that a major reason for this lack of development is the impatience of researchers to prematurely address the question of 'how much?' before adequately providing answers to the question 'how?' In other words, the vast majority of the research has been occupied with explaining differences in growth across firms, not acknowledging that there may be substantially qualitative differences in terms of how firms go about achieving this growth. A recent review (Shepherd & Wiklund) found over 80 empirical studies in our leading management and entrepreneurship journals published over the past 15 years attempting to explain differences in growth, not considering potentially qualitative differences in firms' growth paths.

We argue that the 'how' aspect of growth is a necessary and fundamental question that needs to be better understood before we can turn our attention to how much a firm grows. Specifically, this chapter identifies three conceptually distinct streams of growth research, and briefly reviews the contribution and limitations of each stream. As part of this review, we discuss different modes of growth, namely organic growth, growth by acquisition, and hybrid models. We show, based on a discussion of the extant literature, that to date, the literature has paid insufficient attention to the issue of mode of growth. We then propose a new research agenda illustrating how mode of growth can be examined within each of these three research streams identified, suitable research questions and approaches that can help further our understanding of business growth. This suggested re-focusing of growth research efforts allows us to offer a way forward for better understanding the 'how' of business growth and embracing the heterogeneous nature of the phenomenon. This, in turn, leads to valuable insights into addressing the subsequent question of 'how much' growth. We also provide some methodological considerations that enable researchers to overcome many of the common pitfalls of the 'how much' stream of literature.

This study thus offers three main contributions to the literature. First, this chapter brings to light many of the challenges that come about with the study of firm growth within the three streams of growth research identified. In particular, these problems occur when examining firm growth in a quantitative manner. The discussion of these challenges provides important insights into why the study of firm growth has resulted in limited cumulative knowledge, despite the large number of studies into the subject. Second, we argue and present evidence that insufficient attention has been paid to the notion of the mode of growth that firms use for their expansion. We identify three distinct growth modes – organic, acquisition, and hybrid mode. Notably, our inclusion of hybrid models of growth denotes an extension to the literature that, at the best of times, only *mentions* potential differences between organic growth and growth via acquisition. Third, on the basis of the modes of growth identified, we develop a research agenda that suggests relevant research questions and approaches within the three research streams. It is our hope that this research agenda can assist in redirecting growth research onto a path where greater contributions can be achieved.

The chapter proceeds as follows: Next we review the growth literature, sorting it into three different streams: Growth as an Outcome, The Outcome of Growth, and The Growth Process. We then turn to discuss hybrid modes of growth – an area that has received limited attention. The next section develops a research agenda, with specific suggestions for each of the research streams. The chapter ends with conclusions.

## THREE STREAMS OF GROWTH RESEARCH

Reviews of the growth literature tend to result in a relatively negative account of the state of affairs (Coad, 2007; Davidsson & Wiklund, 2000; Macpherson & Holt, 2007; Phelps, Adams, & Bessant, 2007; Shepherd & Wiklund, 2009; Storey, 1994; Weinzimmer, Nystrom, & Freeman,

1998). In particular, it seems that attempts to classify the literature into coherent streams of literature have been difficult, not to say impossible. For example, examining 113 studies concerned with small firm growth, Macpherson & Holt (p. 186) conclude:

> We should also note that, given that the impetus behind using systematic reviews is the provision of sound evidence bases upon which future research can be directed, it is somewhat ironic that our findings suggest such a base to reveal a myriad of often asymmetric relationships between entrepreneurs, customers, advisors, technologies that cannot be confined by a single set of classifications or recommendations.

Examining an extensive number of different approaches to studying growth, Coad (p. 59) ends up with equally bleak results. He reaches the conclusion that theories purporting to explain growth are inadequate and recommends that theorizing should give way to empirical work, although recognizing that empirical work has also been disappointing because growth rates seem to be largely random:

> We have observed that theoretical predictions have been of limited use in understanding the growth of firms, if not downright misleading. It appears to us that the way forward is through empirical analysis. We recommend a Simonian methodology (Simon, 1968) whereby facts are first pursued through empirical investigations, and in a second stage theories are formulated as attempts to explain the "stylised facts" that emerge. Empirical research into firm growth has nonetheless come up against some major obstacles. The main message that seems to emerge is that growth is largely a random process.

With these accounts in mind, we conducted an extensive review of the literature. Note that our main purpose with this chapter is not to provide an exhaustive review of the literature. The importance of the subject of growth to the field of entrepreneurship and other related fields such as economics and management make an exhaustive review impractical for one chapter. For instance, over the past few years alone, there have been a number of high-quality reviews of different parts of the growth literature, such as new venture growth (Gilbert, McDougall, & Audretsch, 2006), knowledge and learning in growth (Macpherson & Holt, 2007; Phelps et al., 2007), small business growth (Dobbs & Hamilton, 2007), measurement constructs in growth (Shepherd & Wiklund, 2009), and a more economics-oriented perspective on growth (Coad, 2007). We refer scholars to these works for more broad-scale reviews of each part of the literature. Nevertheless, we follow the lead of Shepherd and Wiklund and focus our attention on the 82 articles they identified published in the leading management and entrepreneurship journals (*Academy of Management*

*Journal, Administrative Science Quarterly, American Sociological Review, Entrepreneurship Theory and Practice, Journal of Business Venturing, Journal of Management, Journal of Management Studies, Journal of Small Business Management, Management Science, Organization Science*, and *Strategic Management Journal*) between the years 1992 and 2006. In addition to this, we searched the Google Scholar search engine for highly cited works using 'firm growth' and 'business growth' as search terms. This led to the identification of several additional and more recent works, as well as some highly cited books (e.g., Bhide, 2000; Storey, 1994) and some book chapters that provide more provocative pieces that speak to our central theme.

In the works that we thus identified, we examined theories and research designs used. We started by limiting ourselves to studies interested in the growth of individual businesses. Thus, we excluded studies dealing with the growth of aggregates of businesses. Similar to Macpherson & Holt (2007), our first finding was that the approaches used for studying firm growth are extremely vast and it is virtually impossible to arrive at a classification scheme that allows us to succinctly summarize the literature in a meaningful way. The types of theories and data used to understand firm growth vary substantially. Consequently, and similar to Macpherson and Holt, we concluded that it would not be feasible to summarize and classify the empirical results of these studies. However, rather than concluding that it was too difficult or not meaningful to assess the state of affairs of the growth literature, we looked for other feasible ways of classifying the literature. We noted that there were qualitative differences between the papers reviewed in terms of the role played by growth in the theories used and developed and/or in the analyses applied. We feel that these differences were suitable for identifying different streams of research. This represents a highly aggregated mechanism for classifying the literature into broad streams.

Specifically, we found that some studies empirically or conceptually viewed growth as a dependent variable and used a set of independent variables to explain variance in this growth outcome. We labeled this stream of research *Growth as an Outcome*. A second stream of literature instead dealt with how growth (or increased size) leads to organizational consequences, such as a need for change or certain decision making or competencies. In a way, this literature treats growth as a variable that influences other variables. We, therefore, refer to this as *The Outcome of Growth* stream of research. Finally, we also identified literature that treated growth neither as an independent variable, nor as a dependent variable, but instead was interested in the actual growth process. Accordingly, we label this stream of research *The Growth Process*. Note that these three literature streams that we have identified may be considered 'ideal' types. Although we present them as being clear-cut and independent of each other, the reality is that there are a number of overlaps between these streams of research.

## GROWTH AS AN OUTCOME

The first stream, and conceivably the largest, examines growth as an outcome. For the most part, this stream of literature uses growth as the dependent variable and essentially has as its primary goal to explain varying growth rates and/or increments of growth. The different theoretical lenses used to explain this variance have been many, ranging from population density approaches (Barron, 1999) to firms' human resource practices (Batt, 2002) to individual traits and motivations (Baum, Locke, & Smith, 2001). In a recent review of the literature, Gilbert et al. (2006) find that the most commonly used predictor measures are the personal characteristics of the entrepreneur, the resources available to the firm, the strategy of the firm, the geographic location of the firm, and its industry context. In a well-cited study that essentially summarizes into one paper many of the major previous findings spread out in the literature, Baum et al. use multiple levels (i.e., individual, firm, and industry) to try to explain growth differences. In his review of the literature of the growth specifically of small firms, Storey (1994) reviews the most common variables used to predict differences in growth rates and notes that few, if any, variables have a similar influence on growth across the different studies included in his review. Despite hundreds of studies into explaining firm-level growth differences, the main finding in this stream of literature is that researchers have been unable to isolate variables that have a consistent effect on growth across studies (cf. Shepherd & Wiklund, 2009; Weinzimmer et al., 1998). Moreover, despite efforts to integrate multiple theoretical perspectives and levels of analysis, models are typically only able to explain a limited portion of the differences in growth among firms. We argue that there are a number of potential empirical and theoretical explanations for why these limitations occur.

### Unit of Analysis

A first challenge of this stream of research lies in its unit of analysis. It goes without saying that the study of firm growth involves examining individual firms. Indeed, at any singular point in time, empirically capturing 'a firm' can be done rather simply, based on either the name of the firm or a particular identifying organizational number. However, the task of identifying the specific organizational unit that expands becomes more difficult as one tries to trace a firm over time. Growth is a process, and 'growth' is the differential outcome between (at least) two points in time (Delmar et al., 2003; Penrose, 1959). For instance, many growth studies use questionnaires where there are lagged dependent variables or where firms are asked to measure/account for their growth over a certain number of years (see Shepherd & Wiklund, 2009, for a review). Different time periods are used, with many of the most common ones being 1-, 3-, or 5-year periods (Delmar et al.).

Nevertheless, while it may be possible to use the same distinguishing feature (i.e., firm name, contact individual, organizational number) to follow 'the firm' over time, the actual existing firm itself may not be something that is comparable with the firm that was first studied in the previous temporal period. There are a number of reasons for this. First, firms change legal form and parental/subsidiary status. For instance, one step in the development of a firm may be to become incorporated. As part of this process, the legal name of the firm may remain the same, but its organizational number may change. This legal change may also be that the firm becomes a subsidiary of another firm or develops a subsidiary or holding firm. Levie (1997), e.g., found that a significant number of growing firms in Scotland, Ireland, and France spawned de novo subsidiary firms, i.e., had new firms under one ownership umbrella that were not acquisitions of previously existing firms. As these subsidiaries are considered new firms, their characteristics (i.e., sales, number of employees) may not be included into the parent company's financial record. These legal changes, including changing legal form or spawning subsidiaries, provide challenges for identifying the actual firm under analysis and how growth – within the unit of analysis – may be difficult to capture. As an example of the magnitude of this problem, Davidsson and Wiklund (2000) look at the changes to all firms in Sweden with 20+ employees over a 10-year time period. They find that each year, many firms undergo some legal change, with some firms moving from being entirely independent to becoming parent companies, whereas others are spun-off or bought out. As a whole, over a 10-year period, over 50 per cent of the firms in their data set (4,779 out of 8,562 firms) underwent some change that would challenge whether the unit of analysis (i.e., the firm) was indeed the same unit as previously.

Furthermore, the intentions and goals of the firm may change over time. Many firms bring in new managers or acquire external funding. As a consequence, the expectations for growth may vary substantially over time (e.g., Delmar & Wiklund, 2008). The demands placed on firms that bring in new owners oftentimes differ from those of previous owners. Two examples are the demands placed on firms that acquire venture capital (e.g., Davila, Foster, & Gupta, 2003) and how, based on the goals of the venture capitalists, the firm attempts to grow as much as possible in order to provide returns to the venture capitalists. Similarly, firms that undergo an initial public offering also tend to have higher demands placed upon growth in order to offer return to their new owners (Arthurs & Busenitz, 2006; Florin, 2005). While this may seem to primarily be relevant for a certain type of growth-oriented firm, new and small firms also may have some variance in their willingness to grow. For instance, in their study of growth willingness over time, Delmar and Wiklund find that willingness to grow, as measured in an earlier time period, was able to largely predict subsequent growth willingness. However, this was not a complete predictor. Rather, actually achieving growth during the time gap between the first measurement and the subsequent measurement also helped predict the firm's eagerness to grow. The conclusion is that achieving growth can help spur on future growth, similar to an entrepreneur getting a taste of success and being enticed into future growth. This could also be the case of an entrepreneur being forced into working for the firm full time after being laid off of a regular employment or believing confidently in the potentially increased levels of 'success' for the firm. This finding may be especially germane for studies of new and small firms when one key actor (e.g., the entrepreneur or CEO) has a central impact on the firm (Bowman & Helfat, 2001; Hambrick & Mason, 1984). However, we suggest that the changing nature of the goals of the firm provides a setback for a consistent understanding of growth.

Similarly, as firms develop and grow, they may simply change their activities, the markets they serve, the products they offer, and anything else they might do. Bamford, Dean, & Douglas (2004) criticize the new venture growth literature as attempting to explain the initial resource conditions of firms and their effect on subsequent growth. Yet, the practicalities are that the empirical measurement of these 'initial resources' actually takes place at a much later temporal period. The result is that the independent variables when actually measured may be very different from what they initially were. Moreover, the resource and decision choices that firms make are not stable over time (Bamford et al.). For new and small firms in particular, the effect of time is important for understanding how firms change and grow over time. Lichtenstein and Brush (2001) examine the temporal changes that take place when building a resource base and McKelvie and Davidsson (2009) find, in a 3-year time-lagged study, that the later-stage resource bases have much higher explanatory power for innovation than earlier measures. Their findings suggest that firms change so much over that period (i.e., 3 years) that earlier measures have little – if any – explanatory power. Further, some studies of new firm growth would need to decide at what stage a firm is actually a firm. Empirical evidence suggests that many new firms start small (i.e., one to three employees) and remain that way throughout their existence (e.g., Birley & Westhead, 1990; Davidsson, Lindmark, & Olofsson, 1998; Garnsey, Stam, & Hefferman, 2006). However, many growth studies are not interested in that type or size of firm; rather, they wait until a firm has achieved a certain 'normal' or 'average' size of a start-up or accomplished one of many important stages of development, such as achieving first sales. This may be too restrictive as it excludes many different types of firms and early gestation periods where the firms try to acquire first customers, etc. In any case, there are a number of reasons that provide some challenge to the unit of analysis defined as the 'firm' that may provide a hurdle from accurately being captured during growth studies.

**Differences in Modes of Growth**

A second problem with looking at growth as an outcome is growth seems to be treated in an over-simplistic phenomenon (cf. Davidsson & Wiklund, 2000). In general, studies have inherently assumed internal ('organic') growth, whereas many firms do not grow organically. Gilbert et al. (2006), in their review, even described themselves as 'surprised' by the lack of distinction between organic and other growth modes in the literature. However, there is some evidence that there are important distinctions to be made here. The diversification literature holds that different modes of growth (internal, acquisitive, or mixed) may be related to the product market strategy of the firm, i.e., whether firms continue operating within familiar domains or diversify their activities into unrelated fields (e.g., Busija, O'Neill, & Zeithaml, 1997). In examining growth patterns among high-growth ventures, Delmar et al. (2003) find that 10 per cent of the firms in their sample grew primarily via acquisition. Furthermore, they found that it was the acquisitions that these firms engaged in (and not their internal organic growth) that were the primary sources of their employment growth. Hambrick and Crozier (1985) also note that many successful high-growth firms achieve this based on their acquisition activity.

Furthermore, there is evidence that the size of the firm may predict differences between organic growth and growth by acquisition. Levie (1997) asserts that the choice to grow organically or via acquisition may be a function of the age of the firm. McKelvie, Wiklund, & Davidsson (2006) also find that for smaller firms, almost all of their growth comes from organic growth, while the converse is true for the largest firms. That is, large firms primarily grow via acquiring others, whereas small firms grow organically. In fact, firms that were considered high growth in terms of employment actually shrink quite markedly in terms of their organically created new jobs. In other words, the creation of new jobs for society is negative for large firms as they simply 'add' jobs via acquisitions instead of creating them internally (McKelvie et al.). Building on Penrose's (1959) distinction between entrepreneurial and managerial services, these authors conclude that organic and acquisition growth might be different processes, requiring different explanations in terms of the entrepreneurial and managerial resources and services.

### Variation in Growth Rates Over Time

A third problem with this 'Growth as an Outcome' stream of research is that it typically relies on analysis methods that assume linear relationships among variables, most often regression analysis. Such analysis methods are poorly suited to account for the fact that few firms are able to engage in consistent, linear growth over time. There are two issues with this. Studies that look at growth over a longer temporal period – say 3 or 5 years – may ignore the ups and downs that occur within that time frame. Simply by looking at the mean growth rate, or the size differences between the starting year and the ending year, ignores the naturally occurring variations that come about in the growth of a firm. Numerous studies have found that the size of firms varies in a non-linear fashion over time (e.g., Delmar et al., 2003; Zook & Allen, 1999). Such erratic growth patterns also include the most rapidly growing firms (Markman & Gartner, 2002). One empirical example of this is Garnsey et al.'s (2006) study of a sample of British, German, and Dutch start-up firms. They find that the growth of these firms is anything but linear and stable. The rate of firm growth for each of these firms increases, plateaus, and even decreases over time. Variation in growth rates can also represent important events that occur within the firm, such as earning a major new contract or the launch of a new product. Only relatively few firms are able to engage in linear, stable growth (e.g., Garnsey et al.), which suggests that these important events are more likely discontinuous than monotonically smooth (Gersick, 1994).

As part of this, there may be some limitations to linear growth that would suggest that growth is not sustainable or undeviating over time. In many industries, physical limitations exist that may be difficult to overcome. For some firms, overcoming these limitations may require substantial capital outlays needed to increase capacity, or involve adding large numbers of managers or employees, which might imply excessive work and the potential hazard costs of bringing in many new individuals into the firm. In any case, these limitations may create discontinuous expansion trajectories of firms. The existence of capacity constraints limiting the ability of firms to grow in a linear manner has been studied in a few contexts, such as the ability of hotels to survive in New York based on the number of rooms actually available for rent (Baum & Mezias, 1992), organizational change in the wine industry due to actual storage capacity of a wine cellar (Delacroix & Swaminathan, 1991), production capacity in breweries (Carroll & Swaminathan, 1992), and the licensing capacity governing the number of children at a day care (Baum & Oliver, 1991).

Moreover, the mode of growth may provide limitations to the consistent nature of growth. For instance, few firms can realistically be expected to consistently engage in growth by acquisition over a prolonged period of time. While acquiring other firms may be an appropriate strategy in some cases, the limitations to financial capital and integrating the acquired firm into the acquiring firm may suggest that this strategy is best followed on a discontinuous basis.

## Indicators of Growth

A major hurdle that needs to be overcome is to determine the appropriate growth indicator to apply (Weinzimmer et al., 1998). This essentially involves determining the appropriate dependent variable to employ to effectively capture growth. Many different measures of growth have been used, including sales levels, profitability, number of employees, and market share (Gilbert et al., 2006; Shepherd & Wiklund, 2009; Storey, 1994). The choice of growth measure represents a different type of growth that may or may not reflect growth in terms of other metrics. In other words, these different measures are not interchangeable.

Delmar et al. (2003) find that growing firms tend to grow in certain manners. However, many firms classified as high-growth firms using one metric are not high-growth firms using other metrics. Murphy, Trailer, & Hill (1996) find that one positive predictor of growth may actually be a negative predictor of another type of growth. For example, engaging in a major advertising campaign may increase sales growth but decrease growth in profitability (Bamford et al., 2004). Recently, Shepherd & Wiklund (2009) examined the relationship between the most commonly used measures of growth. They found that there is low concurrent validity for a number of growth measures and high variability among these over time. There is some discussion that the use of sales growth is the most effective growth variable as it translates easily across countries and industry contexts, and apparently also is the metric of choice for entrepreneurs (Delmar et al.; Hoy, McDougall, & Dsouza, 1992). However, Shepherd and Wiklund find that employment growth seems to be the metric that shows best concurrent validity. Further, they suggest that this finding helps to bring the accumulation of knowledge forward inasmuch as it points to the need to better pinpoint the particular aspect of growth that needs to be measured. As an extension of that, they argue that future research should clearly specify the domain of the theory to be used and whether it applies to young or established firms. This helps to overcome fragmentation within the field. For instance, Penrose's (1959) *The Theory of the Growth of the Firm* specifically focuses on growth rates concerning the expansion of assets and employment ('human and other resources') in the context of industrial firms (Penrose, p. xi).

There is a clear need to more appropriately link theories to growth measures in order to better explain these differences. This has prompted a new set of studies to test theoretical predictions between varying measures of growth. For instance, Chandler, McKelvie, & Davidsson (2009) successfully use Transaction Cost Economics predictions to explain the relationship between sales growth and employment growth over time. They find that these economic predictions hold in resource-constrained industries but are not supported in resource-munificent industries. Similarly, Davidsson, Steffens, & Fitzsimmons (2009) use Resource-Based View thinking to examine the relationship between profit and sales growth. Their findings challenge the commonly used assumption that growth is always a sign of success and that unprofitable growth may lead to future profits via increasing market share, etc. Together, these studies show that different aspects of growth are not necessarily related but can become related over time and that different theories can be used to explain how and why these differences may come about.

## Differences in the Willingness to Grow

It is important to point out that research on growth involves studying the exception rather than the rule. Numerous studies (e.g., Birley & Westhead, 1990; Gimeno, Folta, Cooper, & Woo, 1997) actually find that the majority of firms start small and remain small during their life spans. One aspect that has been brought forward and tested is the impact of willingness to grow on the subsequent growth of the firm. Empirical work has shown that many firms are not interested in growth (Wiklund, Davidsson, & Delmar, 2003). Reasons for not wanting to grow include potential drawbacks to the well-being of employees, independence from other stakeholders, the firm's ability to control growth, and the likelihood of survival (Wiklund et al.). As a consequence, part of the lack of solid knowledge in growth research is that there is such a wide variation across samples and in the types of firms that are examined. It is not particularly alarming that willingness to grow and the subsequent behavior of the firm are different between high-potential high-tech firms and small 'mom and pop' type service firms (Cooper, Gimeno-Gascon, & Woo, 1994). Gilbert et al. (2006) do point out that some of the literature that looks at 'how much' does take into account variance in the entrepreneur's/manager's actual willingness to grow to a certain level, one example being Baum et al. (2001). However, the 'more is better' halo effect assumption concerning growth does make this negligible (Barringer, Jones, & Neubaum, 2005). Growth is not always an indicator of success as the goals of different founders/managers may differ (Delmar & Wiklund, 2008).

## THE OUTCOME OF GROWTH

The second stream of growth literature focuses on the outcomes of growth. In other words, this stream of research uses growth as an independent variable and examines the changes that result within the organization as a consequence of growth, with a particular focus on the challenges associated with managing an increasingly larger organization. This line of research does not deal with explaining variance in growth rates but rather takes growth as a given and examines its consequences. While there is less empirical research investigating the implications of growth, the most prominent studies within this stream tend to use stages of development, life cycle, or stages models arguments (Phelps et al., 2007). Although there are a few differences between these terms (e.g., life cycle vs. stages), these terms are generally used interchangeably. For our purposes, it is sufficient to assess the life cycle models as a group, because their conceptual similarities are greater than their differences. In any case, this line of research adopts a biological metaphor to capture the entire life span of a firm and includes varying steps that occur along this span, including gestation, birth, growth, and death (e.g., Greiner, 1972). Here, within this stream of literature, firms grow through a number of predictable life-cycle stages:

> Organizations have lifecycles just like living organisms do; they go through the normal struggles and difficulties accompanying each stage of the Organizational Lifecycle and are faced with the transitional problems moving to the next phase of development (Adizes, 1989, p. xiii).

This type of research has borne the brunt of many criticisms. For instance, it has been accused of a lack of conceptualization and theoretical foundation (O'Farrell & Hitchens, 1988). However, the primary empirical criticism is that the models are deterministic. The biological metaphor assumes that all firms pass through all the stages of the life cycle. However, the empirical reality is that a substantial proportion of all firms do not grow, and a large portion of firms cease activities during their first few years of existence, and exit after passing through only one or two stages of development (depending on the definition of stages in that particular model) (Birley & Westhead, 1990). Further, many firms that do survive never grow beyond a very small size, as shown in any assessment of the size distribution of firms, and correlations of size and age (cf. Coad, 2007). The implication of this is that many firms, if not the majority of firms, never move beyond an early stage of development.

Although stages of development models do not necessarily have to be based on the biological metaphor, there is a basic assumption that for each stage of development, there is an optimal configuration.[1] A configuration relates to the relationships among environment, strategy, and structure (e.g., Ketchen, Thomas, & Snow, 1993; Short, Payne, & Ketchen, 2008) – elements of structure, strategy, and environment are aligned with each other and appear in a limited number of configurations. According to stages of development models, growth itself, or more accurately, the larger size that a growing firm reaches, is the contingency that puts the firm's configuration out of balance, and leads to problems (cf. Phelps et al., 2007). Thus, studies using this perspective define transitions between stages in terms of dominant problems that management needs to address. These problems and how management deals with them triggers the transformation of the firm into a new configuration or stage:

> An organization will face significant problems if its internal development is too far out of step with its size. The greater the degree of incongruity between an organization's size and the development of its operational systems, the greater the probability that the firm will experience the onset of growing pains (Flamholtz, 1986, pp. 44–45).

As this quotation illustrates, life cycle models are mainly concerned with the need for change that growth imposes on the firm, and how this growth affects other characteristics of the firm such as organizational structure and strategy. Growth creates organizational problems within the firm that need to be resolved (Fombrun & Wally, 1989). As a firm grows within a particular stage, the configuration becomes inappropriate and the firm needs to transform itself. After the transformation, the firm enters the next configuration and growth stage, where the process is repeated (e.g., Churchill & Lewis, 1983; Greiner, 1972). Different problems must be addressed during different stages of growth, resulting in the need for different management skills, priorities, and structural configurations over the development of the firm. Empirical studies have looked into managerial issues and the problems of firms of different sizes and growth rates (Flamholtz, 1986; Fombrun & Wally; Hanks, Watson, Jansen, & Chandler, 1993; Kazanjian, 1988; Kazanjian & Drazin, 1990). These studies find that small firms are not just scaled down versions of large firms, which is in itself a valuable contribution.

Nevertheless, research in *The Outcome of Growth* stream shows a limitation in that all these models assume that growth takes place using specific organizational arrangements. That is, these models assume that there is one organizational unit that grows organically. There is no room for acquisition growth, or for growth through diversification into a number of organizational units in these models. Thus, these models do not acknowledge that firms may use modes of growth other than organic, internal growth. In other words, these models typically do not account for potentially different patterns of development and growth. For instance, these models do not take into account growth via acquisition or that a firm may actually consist of several small, subsidiary units as opposed to one larger, more developed unit. In a sense, this is another and potentially equally important criticism against the determinism of this line of research.

## GROWTH AS A PROCESS

The previous two streams of research that we have discussed deal with growth as either an 'input' or an 'output.' To some extent, theories and models in these streams treat the growth process as a 'black box.' Far less research has dealt with the issue of *how* firms grow, i.e., the growth process. This stream of literature attempts to get at the internal nature of growth and specifically what goes on within the firm while it is *growing*. In other words, the studies that fit into this stream of literature usually have a temporal perspective and examine what goes on within the firm.

While this area of research appears to be more limited, there are a number of overlapping components between this stream of literature and the previous two. These overlaps, while not always explicitly dealt with in the literature, speak to the same problem: not truly understanding the heterogeneous nature of growth. For instance, consider the problem of 'what happens while a firm grows?' As we have discussed previously in the 'Growth as an Outcome' section, there are a number of potential dependent variables that have been used to measure growth. The implication is that researchers have tended to try to explain what leads to growth in that particular variable. However, the multitude of variables does not necessarily correlate well, suggesting that the process of growth may involve multiple, and not always temporally related, actions and indicators. In other words, the process of growth is different for different firms and, therefore, the internal actions vary substantially. For instance, one firm increasing its sales growth based on engaging in a major marketing campaign or hiring a new sales person may not necessarily experience profitability. At the same time, a firm that releases a radically new product may achieve the same sales growth rate as the firm engaging in a marketing campaign, but have substantially higher profitability. If one were to compare the firm releasing the new product and comparing its profitability with a firm that is laying off a number of employees, their profitability might be similar, yet the internal processes leading to that are certainly different. This may be one reason why firm growth tends to not be more erratic than linear (Garnsey et al., 2006).

In any case, there are relatively few studies examining the growth process. Two recent quantitative studies attempt to unpack the complicated nature of the potential relationships while employing theory. In one study, Chandler et al. (2009) use Transaction Cost Economics reasoning to see when firms experiencing sales growth will add employees. They find that there are two very diverging paths taken by these firms depending on the munificence of the environment. Thus, they suggest that the decisions going into growing the firm in terms of employees are very different depending on environmental characteristics. In the other study, the authors use the Resource-Based View to examine the relationship between profit and sales growth and find that growth can actually have very negative consequences for profitability (Davidsson et al., 2009). Together, these studies show that the 'how' is not an entirely predictable process and that firms can grow in many different ways.

One reason why these two examples stand out is that they are among the few that look at the growth process with a theoretical lens other than that of Penrose's theory. Indeed, many of the recently published studies in leading journals specifically examining growth have used Penrose's theory (e.g., Garnsey et al., 2006; Macpherson & Holt, 2007; Mishina, Pollock, & Porac, 2004; Pettus, 2001). Her work appears to be the main, or at least most highly used, theory of growth.

Penrose's theory can be traced back to her 1952 paper in *American Economic Review*. However, she is perhaps best known for her seminar piece *The Theory of the Growth of the Firm* (Penrose, 1959) and the associated case study of the Hercules Powder Corporation (Penrose, 1960). The main thrust of Penrose's theory is that firms are administrative entities made up of potentially valuable resources. The main function of managers is to decide what resources to deploy and what activities to carry out. Within this context, she identifies two types of firm-specific capabilities: entrepreneurial and managerial capabilities (Penrose, 1960). Entrepreneurial capabilities are a function of imagination, whereas managerial capabilities are based on the execution of ideas and are essentially practical in nature. Interestingly, Penrose notes that entrepreneurial capabilities are a necessary, but not sufficient condition, for growth and managerial capabilities need to be in place for growth to actually occur.

The ability of the firm to grow is thanks to its productive opportunity set. This set is determined by the myriad ways in which the firm can carry out any usage of its resources. The primary method is to search for novel uses of the existing resource bases of the firm. The premise here is that a firm's resources are never used at full capacity. This leaves some slack resources that can potentially be exploited. A second method revolves around using the entrepreneurial capabilities of managers. This requires that managers use their judgment (i.e., make predictions based on the perceptions of customer preferences and innovation) to decide the best manner of combining existing resources. In other words, the ability to expand a firm lies in the extent to which a manager perceives there to be opportunities and his/her willingness to act upon them using existing resources (Penrose, 1959, p. 84). The larger the opportunity set, the larger the growth potential.

However, growth requires managerial capabilities. A lack of managerial capabilities is a serious limitation to growth because firms need managerial oversight to make sure that all goes well. Any expansion requires new managers to be brought aboard and trained to make sure that they can do their jobs correctly. This may constitute a limiting factor to growth as any new manager needs to be integrated into how the firm works.

Aside from briefly summarizing the main ideas of Penrose's theory, it is important to note that Penrose makes a clear distinction between organic growth and growth by acquisition and that each provides unique opportunities and challenges for the firm. For instance, both modes of growth require entrepreneurial qualities in the firm and access to managerial resources (Penrose, 1959, p. 128). Her arguments suggest that there are limits to both organic and acquisitive growth, and that the use of one mode of growth may have consequences for the use of the other: '*The significance of merger [and acquisition] can best be appraised in the light of its effect on and limits to internal growth*' (Penrose, p. 5).

For organic growth, Penrose argues that as a firm expands, its potential resource combinations expand with it. Yet, firms are not able to continue their growth *ad infinitum*. There are specific limits as to the extent to which a firm can grow. One example of a limit is naturally the set of combinations that managers are able to see and willing to act upon. To both 'see' and 'act upon' requires the successful matching of perceived opportunities with a combination of resources. In other words, it is the matching that determines the scope of the productive opportunity set, not simply the amount of resources under control. The limit comes about as firms develop routines that begin to constrain the ability to recombine existing resources (e.g., Nelson & Winter, 1982). These routines and resources involved therein provide for potential limitations for learning in areas that fall beyond the scope in which the firm already possesses prior knowledge (Cohen & Levinthal, 1990; Teece, 1988). This prompts firms to become increasingly myopic and search 'close in' before moving to less familiar areas (Cyert & March, 1963). In order to develop new growth opportunities, especially as the 'low hanging fruit' of opportunities that lie closely at hand may become exhausted, firms' managers may find it difficult to sustain high levels of organic innovation over time. As a consequence, firms that have exhibited higher levels of organic growth in the past may be forced to look to more far-reaching terrains for their future growth. Organic growth will lead to the development of new resources that are similar, not complementary, to resources already existing in the firm's productive opportunity set. The literature on acquisitions attests that it is complementaries, not similarities, that create value (Harrison, Hitt, Hoskinsson, & Ireland, 2001). The net effect of this, over time, is that it is increasingly difficult for the firm to rely on organic growth for maintaining a current or stable growth.

While this creates a potential barrier to sustained organic growth over time, Penrose (1959) is careful not to argue that if a firm limits itself to organic growth, it runs the risk of exhausting the firm's set of growth opportunities. She therefore notes that acquisitions could allow firms to break away to new paths of development: '*Acquisitions can be a means of obtaining the productive services and knowledge that are necessary for a firm to establish itself in a new field*' (Penrose, p. 126). This would imply an expansion to the productive opportunity set of the firm. The opportunity set is shaped by the managers' ability to use any resources that are at their disposal, including managers' entrepreneurial capabilities. One important facet of Penrose's work is that new knowledge generated by organic growth, such as the release of a new product, is path dependent and generally closely intertwined with the firm's existing knowledge base. Acquiring a firm provides a novel diversity of resources and knowledge, and thus increases the opportunity set of the firm. The acquisition of resources and knowledge may enable the firm to break away from established resource combinations, paths of actions, and ways of thinking as indicated by exploratory learning (March, 1991). Furthermore, she argued that acquisitions may be best suited for those companies that lacked the ability to expand organically.

While this mode of growth appears to be an attractive option for Penrose, she does note that acquiring other firms creates new challenges for managers. For instance, their time and managerial capabilities would be required to be devoted to integrating resources from the acquired firm with the acquirer. This would create adjustment costs and also potential limited organic growth post-acquisition, as there would be insufficient managerial resources to simultaneously manage integration and organic growth. The earlier arguments suggest that, on the one hand, acquisitions may draw managerial resources and attention away from the resource combination needed to generate organic growth. Therefore, the adjustment costs associated with acquisitions will decrease the possibility of future organic growth. On the other hand, an acquisition may also enable the firm to discover radically new paths of resource combinations and thus open up new growth opportunities for the firm that are different from those previously pursued. In short, Penrose's careful study of the growth process leads to the conclusion that the choice between acquisition growth and organic growth is a strategic one and that the two processes are fundamentally different in many respects.

## HYBRID MODES OF GROWTH

In the above we have identified three distinct streams of growth research and the key characteristics of each. We have noted that the distinction between different modes of growth has been considered in the 'Growth as a Process' stream while the 'Growth as an Outcome' and the 'Outcome of Growth' streams have largely ignored this issue. We argue that this is a major shortcoming in these lines of research that hampers further conceptual development. Later, we identify important aspects of hybrid modes and suggest ways in which hybrid modes can be integrated into the three streams of research.

The major distinction made by Penrose (1959) and others is that between organic and acquisitive growth. To this, we add a hybrid mode of growth that is neither organic nor acquisitive but falls somewhere in between. Hybrid forms involve contractual organizational forms that, e.g., can allow firms to overcome issues related to limited managerial capacity (Shane, 1996). The term hybrid is used as this type of mode of growth lies somewhere in between the market and the hierarchy or combines elements of each (Williamson, 1991). Thus, hybrid forms of growth lie somewhere in between organic and acquisitive growth or combines elements of each. Hybrid modes consist of contractual relationships that bind external actors to the firm at the same time as the firm maintains a certain amount of ownership and control over how any assets are used. This type of mode can take a number of forms, including franchising, licensing, and joint ventures/strategic alliances. These all have important contributions to understanding how firms grow.

*Franchising* is an important mode of growth for many firms, and may be the mode of choice for many industries, such as restaurants, lodging, tax preparation, and printing/ copying. In fact, some reports state that franchises account for more than 40 per cent of retail sales (Combs, Ketchen, & Hoover, 2004). Franchising works by having a franchisee enter a legal agreement with a franchiser in exchange for using the franchiser's intellectual property. The franchiser receives compensation for using this asset; generally a lump-sum payment and a royalty fee based on an agreed-upon metric (Miller & Grossman, 1990). The franchisee also must adhere to the set out requirements of the franchiser, such as maintaining quality standards, operating procedures, and product mix (Combs et al.).

Franchising offers a number of benefits for growth that other internal modes do not provide. This method of growth allows firms to overcome limitations to managerial capacity and save time from hiring competent managers. As franchisees tend to own at least part of their own franchise, their goals are more likely to be in line with the franchiser (Shane, 1996). Related to the managerial capacity problem is the frequently mentioned agency (i.e., principal-agent) problem that may occur when principals (i.e., owners) and agents (i.e., managers) have diverging goals. Principals need to either monitor the behavior or offer strong incentives in order to keep the agent's interests in line with the principals' (e.g., Eisenhardt, 1989). This problem is circumvented for franchisors in the sense that new franchisees often will be part or full owners of their own franchises (Castrogiovanni & Justis, 2002). This reduces the likelihood for franchisees to act in their own best interests at the risk of damaging corporate reputations by, e.g., reducing the quality of the products offered for the sake of profitability.

A second major benefit of franchising is that it helps firms grow without any major resource outlays (Combs & Ketchen, 2003). As franchisees pay the capital necessary for investing in their own outlets, franchisers are able to actually acquire capital as opposed to diverting limited resources to that endeavor (Combs & Ketchen, 1999; Kaufman & Dant, 1996). This provides a valued source of income to the firm, as well as implies that new competent managers are brought into the firm (Oxenfeldt & Kelly, 1968). These new managers bring valuable local market knowledge, which allows firms to better identify appropriate locations and local market conditions in order to expand geographically (Minkler, 1992).

As with all modes of growth, there are drawbacks to franchising. To begin with, this mode of growth involves giving up some level of control over the firm and its growth. As franchisees are quasi-independent, they are responsible for the actions of their own franchises. Second, this mode implies a legal contract that must be monitored and maintained in order to ensure that franchisees remain committed to acting in the best interests of the franchise and not their own personal interests. Common problems associated with this mode involve franchisees damaging the reputation of the firm and free-riding. Third, the franchiser may need to transfer specific knowledge to the franchisee. The more specific the knowledge that needs to be transferred, the more difficult it becomes, especially if the portion of ownership retained by the franchiser is small (Darr, Argote, & Epple, 1995).

*Licensing* also is a hybrid mode of growth. It involves licensers selling the rights to a licensee to use a piece of intellectual property. Licensing out a firms' intellectual property provides an added revenue stream to the licenser via royalties paid to the firm based on usage. This mode also allows licensing firms to overcome any potential deficiencies in manufacturing, marketing, or distribution (Fosfuri, 2006). The licensee is generally responsible for all costs involved in selling or using the intellectual property, whereas the costs involved in developing the technology lie with the licenser. This licensing strategy is particularly useful for start-up firms so that they can quickly acquire positive cash flow, overcome a lack of complementary assets (Arora, Fosfuri, & Gambardella, 2001), and also work with more established firms that have experience, legitimacy, and knowledge concerning market entry and customer needs (Gans, Hsu, & Stern, 2002). However, there is evidence that even large established firms employ this mode of growth. Recent studies concerning licensing have shown that large, innovative firms such as IBM generate substantial sales growth thanks to the licensing of their technologies (Kline, 2003) and that worldwide revenues from licensing reach approximately $100 billion (*The Economist*, 2005). From the licensee perspective, firms are able to quickly make use of a tested technology without heavy investments in development costs (Arora et al.).

Similar to franchising, licensing intellectual property allows firms to overcome resource deficiencies and grow at a quicker pace than internal modes of growth. At the same time, contractual issues come into play. Teece (1988) identifies a number of these challenges, including having a contract that leaves the door open to opportunistic behavior and leakages of proprietary information concerning the intellectual property. Unfortunately, the growth literature examining the role of licensing is limited (Lichtentaler, 2008).

*Strategic alliances* and *joint ventures* are a further form of hybrid growth. These forms involve collaboration between two or more firms with the goal of being able to draw synergies or leverage the other's resource bases. Strategic alliances tend to be more informal in nature whereas joint ventures lead to pooling of resources into a newly created legal entity (Madhok, 2006). Despite this legal distinction between the two, we will treat them together in our discussion.

The main purpose of strategic alliances and joint ventures is to acquire resources and capabilities that the firms otherwise would need to develop on their own (Das & Teng, 2000). For many growing firms, the goal of entering into a strategic alliance is to access new technologies. Technological or research-based alliances essentially bring together the specific and oftentimes tacit skills to collaborate on developing new technologies. This saves other firms from investing time and resources into risky technology development. The alliance may also be between a highly knowledgeable technological firm and a firm with more complementary assets (Deeds & Hill, 1996). The result is oftentimes that firms are able to grow more quickly and less expensively based on leveraging the others' resource base. The role of alliances is established in the growth literature, and in particular with a focus on technology ventures (Park & Kim, 1997; Sarkar, Echambadi, & Harrison, 2001).

Similarly, joint ventures provide firms with the opportunity to grow by sharing risk and resources with a partner firm. The majority of joint venture research, in the context of growth, involves entering into joint ventures as a method for entering new foreign markets (Lu & Beamish, 2006; Zahra, Ireland, & Hitt, 2000). For the most part, one of the partners in the joint venture is a local firm that possesses valuable knowledge and a market presence. Together, both joint ventures and strategic alliances are less risky and less costly methods of growing compared to organic or acquisition growth (Pearce & Hatfield, 2002).

In the same sense as the other hybrid modes of growth, there are two key foci in this literature. First, the nature of resources, and in particular overcoming a lack of resources, is important in understanding the growth of firms. Many enter into alliances or joint ventures to overcome a lack of specific technological knowledge (Hagerdoorn & Schakenraad, 1994), to convert financial slack into less tangible capabilities (Patzelt, Shepherd, Deeds, & Bradley, 2008), or to overcome a lack of international/local knowledge (Lu & Beamish, 2006). Second, there is a focus on the nature of the agreements put into place that can help avoid agency problems. The research has focused on the nature of the specific contracts involved in creating these new organizational forms (Reuer, Ariño, & Mellewigt, 2006).

Hybrid modes offer firms methods of growing that would not necessarily be captured in traditional studies of firm growth. For instance, studies measuring growth in the number of employees may entirely miss out on the increase in size and capacity of the 'firm' that engages in franchising or alliances. It may also neglect the important role of licensing in understanding changes in profitable growth. Further, these modes do not fit into the espoused constructs and models that attempt to explain firm growth, such as Penrose's theory or life cycle models. Yet, the hybrid modes of growth are frequently used by firms as they help to avoid a number of problems concerning managerial capacity and a lack of resources. Also, while theories such as agency and resource scarcity can be used to explain the reasoning *why* firms may choose to grow via a hybrid method as opposed to an internal or external method, they certainly do not explain whether these same firms grow or not. In other words, these theories provide some evidence as to the choice of growth mode but say little about the causal mechanism of growth. They do not explain the reasoning as to why the firm can grow but rather provide input into understand *how* they grow.

## A RESEARCH AGENDA

We are not the first to make recommendations as to how future growth research should be conducted. We believe, however, that our recommendations are fundamentally different from previous ones in one important respect. Prior scholars have typically centered on suggestions that call for greater awareness among growth scholars about the potential limitations and pitfalls of previous growth research. Arguably, these suggestions make it more demanding to conduct growth research. For example, suggestions involve: the need for longitudinal data and more careful consideration and measurement of the unit that actually grows (Davidsson & Wiklund, 2000); more careful matching of the growth theory in use and the measurement of growth (Shepherd & Wiklund, 2009); reliance on methodologies that get close to practice, such as ethnography (Macpherson & Holt, 2007); or quite the opposite, namely increased use of sophisticated statistical methods (Coad, 2007).

We agree with these scholars that it would be beneficial if growth research developed in somewhat new directions. However, rather than suggesting greater methodological or conceptual sophistication, we suggest that research reverts to asking more basic questions. Specifically, we believe that the question of mode of growth should be of primary interest. The fact that firms can use different modes of growth has proven to be a challenge that existing theories and research designs have had problems dealing with. In the section below we develop recommendations about how this research question could be pursued within the three streams of literature that we have identified. Table 5.1 summarizes what has been currently done within each of the three research streams and what we believe is needed to move growth research forward within each stream.

*Table 5.1 Suggested research questions for three streams of growth research*

| Research stream | Traditional research | Suggested research |
|---|---|---|
| Growth as an outcome | A set of independent variables are used to predict differences in growth rates across firms | A set of independent variables are used to predict:<br>• The choice between modes of growth<br>• The parallel combination of growth modes |
| The outcome of growth | Managerial problems resulting from growth within a stage of development and/or during the transition between stages | • The sequencing of different growth modes<br>• Similarities and differences of the managerial implications of different modes of growth<br>• Performance implications of acquired vs. organic vs. hybrid growth |
| The growth process | Examines the internal "how" aspects of growth including different aspects of growth and limitations to growth | • Extension of Penrose's growth theory to account for (a) 50 years of changing corporate realities and theoretical development and (b) hybrid growth modes (building on the resource-based view)<br>• Longitudinal, real-time case studies of firms utilizing different growth modes |

## Growth as an Outcome

Irrespective of the theoretical perspectives applied and independent variables used, a main conclusion of empirical research attempting to predict growth rates is that the stochastic part of the variation by far outweighs the systematic part. In other words, explained variance in growth research is notably low. Based on the empirical evidence, it is hard to challenge the notion that growth rates of firms are nearly random (Geroski, 2005). We therefore feel that attempts to provide solutions to how explained variance can be improved, unfortunately, are largely futile. We instead suggest that research interested in Growth as an Outcome attempt to predict *mode* of growth. We believe that such efforts will be more successful and of great value, not least because an important reason why predictions of growth rates have been so unsuccessful is precisely because they have failed to account for the fact that firms can and do choose different modes of growth. McKelvie et al. (2006) conclude that there is systematic variation in the mode of growth pursued (i.e., old and large firms pursue acquired growth, whereas young and small firms grow organically).

A baseline research question would be to explain which mode of growth firms choose and why. It seems that such a research question could be fruitfully studied within a discrete choice framework. Relevant outcomes could be: no growth, acquired growth, organic growth, and hybrid growth. A set of independent variables could then be used to predict which of these growth modes firms choose. For example, a person operating a successful restaurant might reach the conclusion that there is room for an additional restaurant in the marketplace. The important decision for the entrepreneur, and also of interest for the researcher, would involve choosing the most feasible/lucrative alternative – to start a new restaurant from scratch, to buy an existing restaurant and potentially modify it, or to start franchising the restaurant concept. Approaching this from a growth willingness perspective might also uncover that an entrepreneur's willingness to grow might vary depending on the expectations of the work involved with the mode of growth (i.e., hiring and training new employees vs. acquiring a set of employees in another firm vs. engaging in legal contract with external partners/franchisees).

It would be premature to favor any particular theoretical frameworks for explaining the choice of growth mode. Previous reviews have revealed that there is no lack of candidate theories for explaining growth rates, ranging from individual levels to environmental models (e.g., Gilbert et al., 2006). We anticipate that these existing theoretical approaches could be equally well, or better, adapted to address the question of the choice of mode of growth. Among the few texts that explicitly address choice of growth mode, Coad (2007) notes that the nature of existing capabilities and of those needed for expansion likely influence the choice between organic and acquired growth, whereas McKelvie et al. (2006) show that firm size and other resource endowments are related to the choice between these modes. In addition, the M&A and joint venture literatures have identified reasons as to why firms enter into such agreements, but typically treat this as a choice between the use or non-use of the specific growth mechanism rather than as a choice between different ways of achieving growth. Other theories for choosing more hybrid models include agency theory and overcoming resource constraints (Michael, 1996). The literature on naturally occurring barriers to growth may also be useful in this decision, such as potentially engaging in hybrid or acquisitive modes to help overcome these barriers. The theories presented in all of these literatures can likely be expanded to instead address the choice between different modes of growth.

Another, and somewhat more sophisticated, research question would be to examine the relationship among the different growth modes. The discrete choice approach that we suggested in the above assumes that the different modes of growth are mutually exclusive. This need not be the case. Most obviously, firms can pursue different modes of growth in parallel. Firms with outstanding market potential or impatient management might pursue such combined growth strategies to maximize their expansion. One example of a firm that has blended different modes of growth is the fast-food giant McDonald's, which franchises the majority of its restaurants, but owns and operates 15 per cent of the outlets and runs others as joint ventures. However, it is also possible for firms to switch between modes and, e.g., sequentially start with one mode and then move to another. Building on real options logic, Kogut (1991) provides an interesting study of how a joint venture with a specific firm can be viewed as real options for later acquiring that firm. Thus, Kogut's research suggests that joint ventures can lead to acquisitions.

In our review, we identified several weaknesses in this stream of research (i.e., unit of analysis, variation of rates of growth over time, indicators of growth, etc.). By carefully examining the mode of growth used, it might be possible to better understand the hitherto unexplained fluctuation of growth rates exhibited by firms over time. For example, considering growth mode could provide an adequate explanation for why one firm can double its number of employees in one year (e.g., via acquisition) or achieve substantial sales increases without adding employees (e.g., via a hybrid model). On the whole, we argue that a re-focus onto the mode of growth will substantially improve our understanding of growth as an outcome.

## The Outcome of Growth

This literature has traditionally been concerned with how businesses grow organically through a number of stages and the managerial challenges associated with each stage and/or the transitions between them. Observing and discussing the shortcomings of this line of research, Phelps et al. (2007, p. 12) suggest a re-conceptualization consisting of a 'maturity model':

> By integrating absorptive capacity and tipping points into a maturity model, we propose a series of possible learning states that growing firms may occupy. The base state is ignorance; the firm does not realize that it is facing important key issues. This is followed by awareness of one or more key issues. Once it is aware of an issue, new knowledge can be actively sought or passively received. Finally, implementation of the action must follow to achieve real change.

We agree that this might be a valuable approach to better understand the challenges of organic growth and how to deal with them. It shares with previous stages of development models, however, the limitation that it overlooks the possibility for other modes of growth and the challenges that these growth modes present. For example, we imagine that the challenges faced by Fred De Luca when he started franchising the Subway concept must be quite different from those experienced by Steve Jobs in the early organic expansion of Apple.

There is a rich empirical literature dealing with the consequences of organic growth (e.g., Flamholtz, 1986; Kazanjian, 1988). Similarly, scholars have examined the consequences of acquiring and absorbing another firm (e.g., Graebner, 2004). A valuable contribution could be made by simply comparing the challenges identified in these respective research streams. Phelps et al. (2007) nicely summarize some of the major challenges identified in the stages of development literature. A similar review of the M&A literature and comparison could lead to the identification of similarities and differences between the consequences of utilizing these two modes of growth. For example, could an acquisition be a way of short-cutting and overcoming some of the problems associated with organic growth?

To date, this stream of literature has mainly been concerned with the managerial consequences of growth, but further investigation of other implications of growth would also appear valuable. One interesting research question pertains to the performance implications of the different modes of growth. It is a widely held opinion that most acquisitions fail and that, on average, there are no benefits of an acquisition to the acquirer firm (see King, Dalton, Daily, & Covin, 2004 for a review and meta-analysis). Similarly, there is a widely held view that organic growth has positive performance implications and growth is often even used as a direct proxy for financial performance when studying the growth of young and/or small firms, building on the assumption that these firms mainly grow organically. In other words, it appears that studies to date assume that the performance implications of organic growth are good, whereas the performance implications of acquisition growth are poor. A recent study by Davidsson et al. (2009), however, reveals that high organic growth[2] in one period was associated with poor financial performance in the next. Thus, this research suggests that just as with acquisitions, there might be negative performance implications also of organic growth. Indeed, a further examination and comparison of the financial performance implications of these two modes of growth appears to be of utmost value to the Outcome of Growth body of research.

**The Growth Process**

We have argued that to a large extent, it is the research focusing on the growth process that has revealed that firms use different modes of growth and that researchers need to separate between these different growth modes. Nevertheless, we believe that some of the most important contributions can be made within this research stream, provided that it deliberately examines different modes of growth. On the one hand, we feel that there is a need to update and develop the growth process theory that exists, i.e., primarily Penrose's (1959) theory, to include hybrid models of growth. In a recent paper, Lockett, Wiklund, Davidsson, & Girma (2010) suggest important extensions and modifications of Penrose's theory triggered by the insight that since the 1950s corporate realities have changed. In the foreword to the 1995 version of her book, Penrose notes an increase in inter-firm networking and formal alliances between firms. Consequently, firm boundaries blur, which calls for revised theories of the firm. By extension, such developments should also call for the revision of theories of firm growth so that they also incorporate joint ventures and other hybrid modes of growth. Similar to Lockett et al., we believe that the basic foundation and theoretical apparatus of Penrose's theory is sound with its focus on external productive opportunities, internal knowledge development, and adjustment costs. However, the main point is that additional modes of growth can and should be incorporated into this framework. Penrose's theory shares its emphasis on internal knowledge and bundling of resources with the resource-based view of the firm (e.g., Wernerfelt, 1984). Resource-Based Theory has now taken center stage in research into acquisitions, alliances, and many other related phenomena. Therefore, we feel that these ideas are coherent with Penrose's theory and that it should be possible to incorporate insights from such research into Penrose's theory.

On the empirical side, we foresee that in-depth longitudinal case studies of different types of growth processes would be particularly valuable in order to further develop growth process theory. Case studies are particularly important for building theory (Eisenhardt & Graebner, 2007), and it should be kept in mind that Penrose's growth theory is primarily based on the case study of the Hercules Powder Corporation (Penrose, 1960) and that Bhide's (2000) work on the growth of new firms also is based on case studies. Particular focus should be placed on real-time longitudinal case studies focusing on how expanding firms utilize and potentially combine different growth mechanisms. Recently, entrepreneurship scholars have called for a return to in-depth methods that look at process, such as narrative and case studies (e.g., Gartner, 2007; Van de Ven & Engleman, 2004), to better capture the in-depth thinking of entrepreneurs and decision makers. Such approaches are valuable for generating theoretical propositions concerning how firms choose and combine different growth modes that can then be tested using broad-based quantitative research designs.

## CONCLUSIONS

It is fair to say that progress in growth research has been limited in recent years. In this chapter we argue that a major reason for this is that growth is not one, but several different phenomena. Specifically, we have identified three research streams (Growth as an Outcome, The Outcome of Growth, and The Growth Process) and three basic modes of growth (organic, acquisitive, and hybrid). We suggest that researchers have prematurely tried to answer questions of 'how much' firms grow. We suggest that we first need to get a better grasp of the answer to the question 'how' firms grow, i.e., what mode of growth firms use and why. We note in Table 5.1 some important research questions that fundamentally change the most important research questions relating to 'how.' However, we feel more explicit implications of the new focus on growth mode are necessary. We argue that this altered focus has serious implications for understanding the phenomenon of growth, from a theoretical, empirical, and policy-making perspective.

### Theoretical Implications

There are a number of important theoretical implications of more clearly embracing different modes of growth. At a most basic level, we suggest that focusing on modes of growth may provide better insights into the causal mechanisms behind growth. A causal mechanism is the aspect of a theory that explains why a specific outcome occurs (Anderson et al., 2006; Davis & Marquis, 2005; Hedström & Swedberg, 1998). It explains *why* variables are related, probing beyond the observation that the variables are, in fact, related in one way or another (Kaplan, 1964). As we identified in our review of the literature, the majority of empirical studies have attempted to use predictor variables to explain some amount of (organic) growth. The causal mechanisms have covered individual-level factors, firm-based conditions and behaviors, industry development, and even more geographic factors. The limited cumulative knowledge from these studies suggests that this might not be a particularly fruitful endeavor. By embracing different modes of growth, researchers may be able to examine how different causal mechanisms lead to growth with much better accuracy. We suggest that the mechanisms that lead to organic growth may very well differ from those that lead to acquisitive and hybrid growth. Yet, without more concrete delineation of growth mode, researchers may be unnecessarily coagulating the causal mechanisms into common predictors. Isolating causal mechanisms and their effect on mode of growth implies better selecting theories a priori and even considering the development of new theories. Certain theories have a better fit with certain modes of growth because they are closely associated with the causal mechanisms underlying the particular mode of growth. Therefore, there should be a logical association between the mode of growth studies and theory used.

By doing this, researchers should be able to better understand why growth comes about, what each growth mode leads to, and how certain modes of growth entail facing different managerial and entrepreneurial challenges. We suggest that business growth may best be conceived of as a collective term for several rather different empirical phenomena, with different underlying causal mechanisms, requiring separate theoretical explanations (e.g., Davidsson & Wiklund, 2000).

**Methodological Implications**

More rigorous theorizing about the mode of growth also has natural implications for how to empirically study the heterogeneous nature of growth. A valuable first step, in collaboration with defining the mode of growth to be studied, is to find an appropriate sample of firms. Using a theoretically relevant sample, whether for a large-scale quantitative study or for a longitudinal qualitative study, is an obvious necessity to best understand the nature and outcome of mode of growth. From an empirical point of view, this may involve choosing to study firms in a relevant industry. For example, certain hybrid models of growth have strong associations with specific industries. Franchising is a common growth strategy among restaurants, copy centers, and hotels. Licensing strategies, on the other hand, typically occur in industries where intellectual protection is possible, useful, and actually occurs, such as in many high-tech markets. Furthermore, choosing an appropriate sample may also be a reflection of the type of firm studied. Previous empirical work has shown that small firms tend to grow organically whereas larger firms tend to grow via acquisition. Careful selection of an appropriate sample involves making a number of important choices as to what type of firm and *why* they are relevant to study that growth mode.

A further important empirical implication of our review is to also suggest more clear connection between the theory employed and the type of growth measure used. Certain theories also have a more or less natural fit with specific indicators of growth (i.e., sales, employees, profit). For instance, transaction cost economics may help to explain why a growing firm employs an employee or acquires further assets rather than obtaining them from the market. However, this theory does not help explain why a firm may increase its sales. On the contrary, theories of motivation and resource-based views may provide useful explanatory mechanisms for many growth measures. This may also be germane for understanding performance differences among different modes of growth.

Finally, there may also be some temporal effects of understanding the mode of growth. This is useful for understanding the sequence and timing of different modes of growth, the short- vs. long-term effects of mode of growth, and even some of the temporal impacts of one measure of growth on another. While some work has already been done in this regard, greater work embracing modes of growth may provide greater insights into how these mechanisms work together.

## Policy Implications

Policy makers tend to encourage firm growth as it is viewed as a vehicle for achieving higher employment, increased development of the economy, increased tax collection, and also a superior profile for its city, region, and country. However, there is evidence suggesting that the relationship between growth and positive effects for the economy are less straightforward than assumed. For example, at the macro level, growth by acquisition may simply 'transplant' jobs from a smaller firm into a larger acquiring firm, thus leading to a net zero employment gain. Yet, this same mode of growth may have greater long-term impact on the overall viability of the firm in the face of strong domestic and international competition, thus providing benefit to society. For hybrid growth, international actors may be the primary beneficiaries of any profitable growth if they own the intellectual property that is being licensed or are the franchiser.

From a policy perspective, focusing on the mode of growth has a number of implications. A first step is to understand and acknowledge that there are different modes of growth and that the societal implications of these modes differ. Second, policy makers should ensure that policies are in place to encourage and support the type of growth that they would like to see materialize. For instance, intellectual property rights and transaction costs have direct implications for the viability of licensing as a mode of growth. Similarly, acquisitions require access to well-functioning capital markets where firms and entrepreneurs can raise the necessary money. Organic growth is generally driven by increases in market demand. Therefore, overall economic conditions have direct implications for the number of firms that grow organically, but also for the choice between modes of growth. Delmaret al. (2003) showed that during economic recessions, acquisition growth became more common, whereas organic growth dominated in good times. Policies that dampen the negative implications for the entrepreneur associated with failure should also be valuable to stimulate entrepreneurs to pursue the bold actions associated with expanding a business.

**Final Thoughts**

On the basis of the three modes of growth that we identified, we outline a research agenda within each of the research streams. In doing so, we feel that the alternative approach that we propose, where the focus is firstly on 'how' firms grow instead of 'how much' primarily should result in invaluable insights into firm growth. This will help advance our understanding of this phenomenon that is so important to practitioners, policy makers, and researchers.

# NOTES

* Previously published as: Alexander McKelvie and Johan Wiklund (2010), 'Advancing firm growth research: a focus on growth mode instead of growth rate', *Enterpreneurship Theory and Practice*, **34** (2), March, 261–88.

1. Phelps et al. (2007) note that not all models are based on biological metaphors and refer to those alternative models as 'the Problems Perspective.' For the purpose of our chapter, although potentially less deterministic concerning the development stages, these models are essentially associated with the same limitations as biological metaphors.
2. These authors were unable to separate organic from acquisition growth but because the samples used included small firms, it is reasonable to assume that growth was organic.

# REFERENCES

Adizes, I. (1989). *Corporate lifecycles: How and why corporations grow and die and what to do about it*. Englewood Cliffs, NJ: Prentice Hall.

Anderson, P.J.J., Blatt, R., Christenson, M.K., Grant, A.M., Marquis, C., Neuman, E.J., et al. (2006). Understanding mechanisms in organizational research. *Journal of Management Inquiry*, *15*, 102–113.

Arora, A., Fosfuri, A., & Gambardella, A. (2001). *Markets for technology: Economics of innovation and corporate strategy*. Cambridge MA: MIT Press.

Arthurs, J.D. & Busenitz, L.W. (2006). Dynamic capabilities and venture performance: The effects of venture capitalists. *Journal of Business Venturing*, *21*, 195–215.

Bamford, C.E., Dean, T.J., & Douglas, T.J. (2004). The temporal nature of growth

determinants in new bank foundings: Implications for new venture research design. *Journal of Business Venturing*, *19*, 899–919.
Barringer, B.R., Jones, F.F., & Neubaum, D.O. (2005). A quantitative content analysis of the characteristics of rapid-growth firms and their founders. *Journal of Business Venturing*, *20*, 663–687.
Barron, D.N. (1999). The structuring of organizational populations. *American Sociological Review*, *64*, 421–445.
Batt, R. (2002). Managing customer services: Human resource practices, quit rates, and sales growth. *Academy of Management Journal*, *45*, 587–597.
Baum, R.J., Locke, E.A., & Smith, K.G. (2001). A multidimensional model of venture growth. *Academy of Management Journal*, *44*, 292–303.
Baum, J.A.C. & Mezias, S.J. (1992). Localized competition and organizational failure in the Manhattan hotel industry, 1989–1900. *Administrative Science Quarterly*, *37*, 580–604.
Baum, J.A.C. & Oliver, C. (1991). Institutional linkages and organizational mortality. *Administrative Science Quarterly*, *36*, 187–218.
Bhide, A. (2000). *The origin and evolution of new businesses*. New York: Oxford University Press.
Birley, S. & Westhead, P. (1990). Growth and performance contrasts between types of small firms. *Strategic Management Journal*, *11*, 535–557.
Bowman, E.H. & Helfat, C.E. (2001). Does corporate strategy matter? *Strategic Management Journal*, *22*, 1–23.
Busija, E.C., O'Neill, H.M., & Zeithaml, C.P. (1997). Diversification strategy, entry mode, and performance: Evidence of choices and constraints. *Strategic Management Journal*, *18*, 321–327.
Carroll, G.R. & Swaminathan, A. (1992). The organizational ecology of strategic groups in the American brewing industry from 1975 to 1990. *Industrial and Corporate Change*, *1*, 65–97.
Castrogiovanni, G.T. & Justis, R.T. (2002). Strategic and contextual influences on firm growth: An empirical study of franchisors. *Journal of Small Business Management*, *40*, 98–108.
Chandler, G.N., McKelvie, A., & Davidsson, P. (2009). Asset specificity and behavioral uncertainty as moderators of the sales growth-employment growth relationship in emerging ventures. *Journal of Business Venturing*, *24*, 373–387.
Churchill, C. & Lewis, V.L. (1983). The five stages of small business growth. *Harvard Business Review*, *61*, 30–50.
Coad, A. (2007). *Firm growth: A survey*. Papers on Economics and Evolution 2007–03, Max Planck Institute of Economics, Evolutionary Economics Group, Jena, Germany.
Cohen, W.M. & Levinthal, D.A. (1990). Absorptive capacity: A new perspective on learning and innovation. *Administrative Science Quarterly*, *35*, 128–152.
Combs, J.G. & Ketchen, D.J. (1999). Can capital scarcity help agency theory explain franchising? Revisiting the capital scarcity hypothesis. *Academy of Management Journal*, *42*, 196–207.
Combs, J.G. & Ketchen, D.J. (2003). Why do firms franchise as an entrepreneurial strategy? A meta-analysis. *Journal of Management*, *29*, 443–465.
Combs, J.G., Ketchen, D.J., & Hoover, V.L. (2004). A strategic groups approach to the franchising-performance relationship. *Journal of Business Venturing*, *19*, 877–897.
Cooper, A.C., Gimeno-Gascon, F.J., & Woo, C.Y. (1994). Initial human and

financial capital as predictors of new venture performance. *Journal of Business Venturing*, *9*, 371–395.
Cyert, R. & March, J. (1963). *A behavioral theory of the firm*. Englewood Cliffs, NJ: Prentice-Hall.
Darr, E.D., Argote, L., & Epple, D. (1995). The acquisition, transfer, and depreciation of knowledge in service organizations: Productivity in franchises. *Management Science*, *41*, 1750–1762.
Das, T.K. & Teng, B.S. (2000). A resource-based theory of strategic alliances. *Journal of Management*, *26*, 31–61.
Davidsson, P., Lindmark, L., & Olofsson, C. (1998). The extent of overestimation of small firm job creation: An empirical examination of the regression bias. *Small Business Economics*, *11*, 87–100.
Davidsson, P., Steffens, P., & Fitzsimmons, J. (2009). Growing profitable or growing from profits: Putting the horse in front of the cart? *Journal of Business Venturing*, *24*, 388–406.
Davidsson, P. & Wiklund, J. (2000). Conceptual and empirical challenges in the study of firm growth. In D. Sexton & H. Landström (Eds.), *The Blackwell handbook of entrepreneurship* (pp. 179–199). Oxford, MA: Blackwell.
Davila, A., Foster, G., & Gupta, M. (2003). Venture capital financing and the growth of startup firms. *Journal of Business Venturing*, *18*, 689–708.
Davis, C.F. & Marquis, C. (2005). Prospects for organization theory in the early twenty-first century: Institutional fields and mechanisms. *Organization Science*, *16*, 332–343.
Deeds, D.L. & Hill, C.W.L. (1996). Strategic alliances and the rate of new product development: An empirical study of entrepreneurial biotechnology firms. *Journal of Business Venturing*, *11*, 41–55.
Delacroix, J. & Swaminathan, A. (1991). Cosmetic, speculative, and adaptive organizational change in the wine industry. *Administrative Science Quarterly*, *28*, 274–291.
Delmar, F., Davidsson, P., & Gartner, W. (2003). Arriving at the high-growth firm. *Journal of Business Venturing*, *18*, 189–216.
Delmar, F. & Wiklund, J. (2008). The effect of small business managers' growth motivation on firm growth: A longitudinal study. *Entrepreneurship Theory and Practice*, *32*, 437–457.
Dobbs, M. & Hamilton, R.T. (2007). Small business growth: Recent evidence and new directions. *International Journal of Entrepreneurial Behavior & Research*, *13*, 296–322.
Eisenhardt, K.M. (1989). Agency theory: An assessment and review. *Academy of Management Review*, *14*, 57–74.
Eisenhardt, K.M. & Graebner, M.E. (2007). Theory building from cases: Opportunities and challenges. *Academy of Management Journal*, *50*, 25–32.
Flamholtz, E.G. (1986). *Managing the transition from an entrepreneurship to a professionally managed firm*. San Francisco, CA: Jossey-Bass.
Florin, J. (2005). Is venture capital worth it? Effects on firm performance and founder returns. *Journal of Business Venturing*, *20*, 113–135.
Fombrun, C.J. & Wally, S. (1989). Structuring small firms for rapid growth. *Journal of Business Venturing*, *4*, 107–122.
Fosfuri, A. (2006). The licensing dilemma: Understanding the determinants of the rate of technology licensing. *Strategic Management Journal*, *27*, 1141–1158.

Gans, J., Hsu, D., & Stern, S. (2002). When does start-up innovation spur the gale of creative destruction? *RAND Journal of Economics*, *33*, 571–586.
Garnsey, E., Stam, E., & Hefferman, P. (2006). New firm growth: Exploring processes and paths. *Industry and Innovation*, *13*, 1–20.
Gartner, W.B. (2007). Entrepreneurial narrative and a science of the imagination. *Journal of Business Venturing*, *22*, 613–627.
Geroski, P.A. (2005). Understanding the implications of empirical work on corporate growth rates. *Managerial and Decision Economics*, *26*, 129–138.
Gersick, C.J.G. (1994). Pacing strategic change: The case of a new venture. *Academy of Management Journal*, *37*, 9–45.
Gilbert, B.A., McDougall, P.P., & Audretsch, D.B. (2006). New venture growth: A review and extension. *Journal of Management*, *32*, 926–950.
Gimeno, J., Folta, T.B., Cooper, A.C., & Woo, C.Y. (1997). Survival of the fittest? Entrepreneurial human capital and the persistence of underperforming firms. *Administrative Science Quarterly*, *42*, 750–783.
Graebner, M.E. (2004). Momentum and serendipity: How acquired leaders create value in the integration of technology firms. *Strategic Management Journal*, *25*, 751–778.
Greiner, L.E. (1972). Evolutions and revolutions as organizations grow. *Harvard Business Review*, *50*, 37–46.
Hagerdoorn, J. & Schakenraad, J. (1994). The effect of strategic technology alliances on company performance. *Strategic Management Journal*, *15*, 291–309.
Hambrick, D.C. & Crozier, L.M. (1985). Stumblers and stars in the management of rapid growth. *Journal of Business Venturing*, *1*, 31–45.
Hambrick, D.C. & Mason, P.A. (1984). Upper echelons: The organization as a reflection of its top managers. *Academy of Management Review*, *9*, 193–207.
Hanks, S.H., Watson, C.J., Jansen, E., & Chandler, G.N. (1993). Tightening the life-cycle construct: A taxonomic study of growth stage configurations in high-technology organizations. *Entrepreneurship Theory and Practice*, *18*, 5–29.
Harrison, J.S., Hitt, M.A., Hoskinsson, R.E., & Ireland, R.D. (2001). Resource complementarity in business combinations: Extending the logic to organizational alliances. *Journal of Management*, *27*, 679–690.
Hedström, P. & Swedberg, R. (1998). Social mechanisms: An introductory essay. In P. Hedstrom & R. Swedberg (Eds.), *Social mechanisms: An analytical approach to social theory* (pp. 1–31). New York: Cambridge University Press.
Hoy, F., McDougall, P.P., & Dsouza, D.E. (1992). Strategies and environments of high growth firms. In D.L. Sexton & J.D. Kasarda (Eds.), *The state of the art of entrepreneurship* (pp. 341–357). Boston: PWS-Kent Publishing.
Kaplan, A. (1964). *The conduct of inquiry*. San Francisco, CA: Chandler Publishing.
Kaufman, P.J. & Dant, R.P. (1996). Multi-unit franchising: Growth and management issues. *Journal of Business Venturing*, *11*, 343–358.
Kazanjian, R.K. (1988). Relation of dominant problems to stages of growth in technology-based new ventures. *Academy of Management Journal*, *31*, 257–279.
Kazanjian, R.K. & Drazin, R. (1990). A stage-contingent model of design and growth for technology based new ventures. *Journal of Business Venturing*, *5*, 137–150.
Ketchen, D.J., Thomas, J.B., & Snow, C.C. (1993). Organizational configurations and performance: A comparison of theoretical approaches. *Academy of Management Journal*, *36*, 1278–1313.

King, D.R., Dalton, D.R., Daily, C.M., & Covin, J.G. (2004). Meta-analyses of post-acquisition performance: Indications of unidentified moderators. *Strategic Management Journal, 25*, 187–200.

Kline, D. (2003). Sharing the corporate crown jewels. *MIT Sloan Management Review, 44*, 89–93.

Kogut, B. (1991). Joint ventures and the option to expand and acquire. *Management Science, 37*, 19–33.

Levie, J. (1997). Patterns of growth and performance: An empirical study of young, growing ventures in France, Ireland and Scotland. In P.D. Reynolds, W. Bygrave, N.M. Carter, P. Davidsson, W.B. Gartner, C. Mason, et al. (Eds.), *Frontiers of entrepreneurship 1997* (pp. 419–443). Wellesley, MA: Babson College.

Lichtenstein, B.M.B. & Brush, C.G. (2001). How do "resource bundles" change in new ventures? A dynamic model and longitudinal exploration. *Entrepreneurship Theory and Practice, 25*, 37–58.

Lichtentaler, U. (2008). Externally commercializing technology assets: An examination of different process stages. *Journal of Business Venturing, 23*, 445–464.

Lockett, A., Wiklund, J., Davidsson, P., & Girma, S. (2010). Organic and acquisitive growth: Re-examining, testing, and extending Penrose's growth theory. *Journal of Management Studies*, doi: 10.1111/j.1467-6486.2009.00879.x.

Lu, J.W. & Beamish, P.W. (2006). Partnering strategies and performance of SMEs' international joint ventures. *Journal of Business Venturing, 21*, 461–486.

Macpherson, A. & Holt, R. (2007). Knowledge, learning and small firm growth: A systematic review of the evidence. *Research Policy, 36*, 172–192.

Madhok, A. (2006). How much does ownership really matter? Equity and trust relations in joint venture relationships. *Journal of International Business Studies, 37*, 4–11.

March, J. (1991). Exploration and exploitation in organizational learning. *Organization Science, 2*, 71–87.

Markman, G.D. & Gartner, W.B. (2002). Is extraordinary growth profitable? A study of Inc. 500 high-growth companies. *Entrepreneurship Theory and Practice, 27*, 65–75.

McKelvie, A. & Davidsson, P. (2009). From resource base to dynamic capability: An investigation of new firms. *British Journal of Management, 20*, 63–80.

McKelvie, A., Wiklund, J., & Davidsson, P. (2006). A resource-based view of organic and acquired growth. In J. Wiklund, D. Dimov, J. Katz, & D. Shepherd (Eds.), *Advances in entrepreneurship, firm emergence, and growth, Vol. 9, Entrepreneurship: Frameworks and empirical investigations from forthcoming leaders in European research* (pp. 179–199). Amsterdam: Elsevier.

Michael, S.E. (1996). To franchise or not to franchise: An analysis of decision rights and organizational form shares. *Journal of Business Venturing, 11*, 57–71.

Miller, A.R. & Grossman, T.L. (1990). *Business law*. Glenview, IL: Scott Foresman.

Minkler, A.P. (1992). Why firms franchise: A search cost theory. *Journal of Institutional and Theoretical Economics, 148*, 240–259.

Mishina, Y., Pollock, T.G., & Porac, J.F. (2004). Are more resources always better for growth? Resource stickiness in market and product expansion. *Strategic Management Journal, 25*, 1179–1197.

Murphy, G.B., Trailer, J.W., & Hill, R.C. (1996). Measuring performance in entrepreneurship research. *Journal of Business Research, 36*, 15–23.

Nelson, R.R. & Winter, S.G. (1982). *An evolutionary theory of economic change*. Cambridge, MA: Harvard University Press.

O'Farrell, P.N. & Hitchens, D.M.W.N. (1988). Alternative theories of small-firm growth: A critical review. *Environment and Planning*, *20*, 1365–1383.

Oxenfeldt, A.R. & Kelly, A.O. (1968). Will successful franchise systems ultimately become wholly-owned chains? *Journal of Retailing*, *44*, 69–83.

Park, S.H. & Kim, D. (1997). Market valuation of joint ventures: Joint venture characteristics. *Journal of Business Venturing*, *12*, 83–108.

Patzelt, H., Shepherd, D.A., Deeds, D., & Bradley, S.W. (2008). Financial clack and venture managers' decisions to seek a new alliance. *Journal of Business Venturing*, *23*, 465–481.

Pearce, J.A. & Hatfield, L. (2002). Performance effects of alternative joint venture resource responsibility structures. *Journal of Business Venturing*, *17*, 343–364.

Penrose, E. (1959). *The theory of the growth of the firm*. New York: Oxford University Press.

Penrose, E. (1960). The growth of the firm – A case study: Hercules Powder Corporation. *The Business History Review*, *34*, 1–23.

Pettus, M.L. (2001). The resource-based view as a development growth process: Evidence from the deregulated trucking industry. *Academy of Management Journal*, *44*, 878–896.

Phelps, R., Adams, R., & Bessant, J. (2007). Life cycles of growing organizations: A review with implications for knowledge and learning. *International Journal of Management Reviews*, *9*, 1–30.

Reuer, J.J., Ariño, A., & Mellewigt, T. (2006). Entrepreneurial alliances as contractual forms. *Journal of Business Venturing*, *21*, 306–325.

Sarkar, M.B., Echambadi, R.A.J., & Harrison, J.S. (2001). Alliance entrepreneurship and firm market performance. *Strategic Management Journal*, *22*, 701–712.

Shane, S.A. (1996). Hybrid organizational arrangements and their implications for firm growth and survival: A study of new franchisors. *Academy of Management Journal*, *39*, 216–234.

Shepherd, D. & Wiklund, J. (2009). Are we comparing apples with apples or apples with oranges? Appropriateness of knowledge accumulation across growth studies. *Entrepreneurship Theory and Practice*, *33*, 105–123.

Short, J.C., Payne, G.T., & Ketchen, D.J. (2008). Research on organizational configurations: Past accomplishments and future challenges. *Journal of Management*, *22*, 9–24.

Simon, H.A. (1968). On judging the plausibility of theories. In B. van Roostelaar & J.F. Staal (Eds.), *Logic, methodology and philosophy of science* III (pp. 439–459). Amsterdam: North-Holland Publishing.

Storey, D.J. (1994). *Understanding the small business sector*. London: Routledge.

Teece, D.J. (1988). Capturing value from technological innovation: Integration, strategic planning, and licensing decisions. *Interfaces*, *18*, 46–61.

The Economist. (2005). *A market for ideas*. 20 October: 48–51.

Van de Ven, A.H. & Engleman, R.M. (2004). Event- and outcome-driven explanations of entrepreneurship. *Journal of Business Venturing*, *19*, 343–358.

Weinzimmer, L.G., Nystrom, P.C., & Freeman, S.J. (1998). Measuring organizational growth: Issues, consequences and guidelines. *Journal of Management*, *24*, 235–262.

Wernerfelt, B. (1984). A resource-based view of the firm. *Strategic Management Journal*, *5*, 171–180.
Wiklund, J., Davidsson, P., & Delmar, F. (2003). What do they think and feel about growth? An expectancy-value approach to small business managers' attitudes toward growth. *Entrepreneurship Theory and Practice*, *24*, 37–48.
Williamson, O.E. (1991). Comparative economic organization: The analysis of discrete structural alternatives. *Administrative Science Quarterly*, *36*, 269–296.
Zahra, S.A., Ireland, R.D., & Hitt, M.A. (2000). International expansion by new venture firms: International diversity, mode of market entry, technological learning, and performance. *Academy of Management Journal*, *43*, 929–950.
Zook, C. & Allen, J. (1999). *The facts about growth*. New York: Bain and Company.

# 6. Towards an integrative framework for future research on small firm growth*

**Per Davidsson, Leona Achtenhagen and Lucia Naldi**

Our review has demonstrated that small firm growth is a complex phenomenon. The concept 'growth' denotes both a change in amount and the process by which that change is attained. Further, the growth can be achieved in different ways and with varying degrees of regularity, and it manifests itself along several different dimensions such as sales, employment, and accumulation of assets. This complexity has naturally led researchers to adopt different approaches to studying growth and to use different measures to assess it. Further, although our review shows that it can fruitfully be regarded as a growth issue, the research on small firms' internationalization has largely developed as a separate stream. Similarly, other relatively separate literatures have evolved, which effectively focus on different modes of growth although mostly without regarding the studies first and foremost as growth studies. This goes for topics such as mergers and acquisitions, diversification, and integration – research streams which have largely ignored the particularities of small firms and which in turn have been largely ignored among researchers focusing on small firm growth.

Despite this complexity and fragmentation, a considerable body of generalizable knowledge about small firm growth now exists, which is what we have tried to highlight in this book. One could easily emphasize the problems instead: weak conceptualization of the phenomenon of organizational growth; lack of integration of the different findings into a more comprehensive theory of growth; lack of high-quality in-depth studies; unwarranted uni-directional conceptualizations of growth; rather weak links between empirical findings and theory-building, etc. However, the luxury of seeing such deficiencies can only be enjoyed because many researchers put considerable effort into researching firm growth, thus little by little uncovering the true complexity of the phenomenon. What previ-

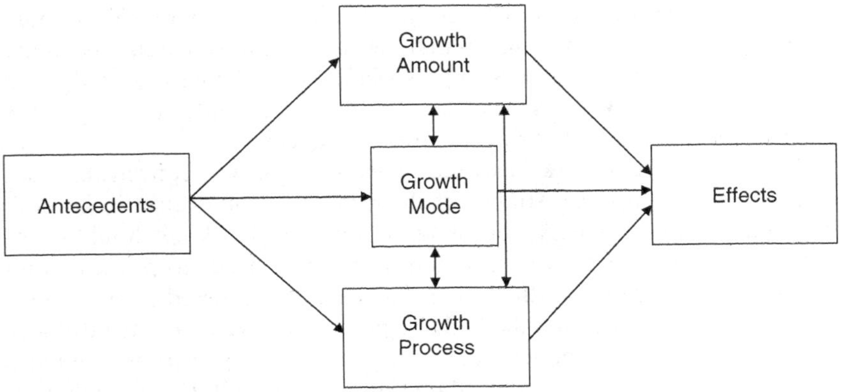


*Figure 6.1 Alternative foci for studies of small firm growth*

ous research – and taking stock of it – has achieved more than anything else is to clarify what aspects of this complex phenomenon has been relatively well researched, and which remain virgin ground, respectively. The remaining validity of some of the criticism of previous research only means that there are interesting research opportunities for followers to do better.

So what are these research opportunities? We choose to organize our discussion of future research needs around Figure 6.1.

Let us turn first to the question how *antecedents* relate to the *amount* of growth. This is the firm growth sub-topic which, consciously or not, has attracted the most interest in previous empirical research. We would hold that there is little need for further studies that try to identify factors that facilitate, predict, or hinder growth. A sufficient number of such factors have been identified in the literature already; the likelihood that any important ones would have been neglected is slim. Neither do we think it very meaningful to further explore the relative importance of different factors for the growth of 'small firms in general.' The population of small firms is too heterogeneous for this to be a very meaningful exercise, and the effects probably too specific to particular industries; geographic entities; cohorts and/or periods for such results to have much theoretical value. As revealed by Figure 6.1, the Antecedents → Growth Amount relationship is just one out of nine possible foci for scholarly analysis of small firm growth (not counting combinations of foci). Many of the other relationships are understudied and present interesting opportunities for researchers to make interesting contributions. At the very least we would think investing in new and comprehensive empirical studies of Antecedents → Growth Amount would have limited value until one has first taken more systematic stock of the knowledge that is already available. This could take the form of formal meta-analyses of extant research, including the assessment of moderators (e.g., specific growth measure used), and applying various theoretical tools to attain a deeper understanding of the meaning of the results that such an exercise unveils.

When this groundwork has been properly done it is conceivable that comprehensive empirical studies of the growth of 'small firm in general' would have great value. A well-designed study of that kind should probably apply a high level of abstraction. Further, it needs to pay attention to the interplay between different influences, as discussed in our above review. This said, we find it likely that a potentially even more fruitful way forward would be to conduct theory-driven studies of growth within more homogeneous samples of firms. Baum and Locke's (2004) psychological study is an exemplar in this regard. Eisenhardt and Schoonhoven (1990) likewise concentrated on a single industry, and also included interaction effects across levels of analysis. Using homogeneous samples is a way of controlling for the otherwise often confounding influence of variables one does not have a theoretical interest in (Kish, 1987). Moreover, the use of homogeneous samples allows one to use operationalizations that are maximally relevant for the one particular type of firm or industry. The issue of broader generalization, we would hold, is better dealt with through replication across several different samples, each of which is internally relatively homogeneous, than by trying to include all different types of small firms in the same study.

Turning now to studies of how the *amount* of growth relates to various *effects*, a general observation is that in studies of firm growth, positive 'ultimate' effects of growth are often implicitly or explicitly assumed without being tested. As implied by our above review of research on the effects of growth, we believe it is time for researchers to do better than just assuming that firm growth is an end in itself. When growth is the dependent variable used, researchers should explain why and for whom they believe firm-level growth to be important. Further, we need more studies that explicitly relate growth to important management-level goals such as profitability and firm value (cf. Cho and Pucic, 2005). The effects of growth in terms of management challenges that have to be dealt with are an issue we will return to shortly.

In policy-motivated research it is frequently assumed that head-counting on the micro level translates to corresponding employment effects on aggregate levels of analysis. Phenomena such as acquisition-based growth and one firm growing just to crowd out employment in another firm suggest that such an assumption is overly simplistic. For the purpose of policy as well as for testing industry- or region-level theory, the relationship between firm growth and economic development is better studied by letting the prevalence of high-growth organizations compete with other measures of economic dynamism for explaining aggregate-level economic development.

Different *modes* of growth are a clearly under-researched area in the small business literature. It is so under-researched, in fact, that studies that merely map out the phenomenon would have considerable value even if they say nothing about antecedents and effects. The question of modes would also benefit from increased integration of the knowledge that has been gained in already existing literatures that relate to growth. Internationalization is one such example, which we have here made an attempt to integrate with the growth literature. Other such areas of theorizing and empirical research, which clearly can inform our knowledge of growth whether framed in that way or not, are those dealing with diversification and integration. The fact that they so far have rarely dealt specifically with small firm issues does not mean that application in that area would not be fruitful. Research and theorizing concerning acquisitions have not typically focused on the problems of small firms, either; nor have they always portrayed the phenomenon as a growth issue to be compared with other modes of growth. However, the few empirical attempts that have been made to investigate issues of modes of small firm growth (other than internationalization) have yielded some very interesting results that certainly deserve being followed up. Studies are needed that can confirm or call in question, e.g., Davidsson and Delmar's (2006) result that there is a very strong relationship between (small) firm size and the tendency to grow organically; Lockett et al.'s (2011) finding regarding differential effects of organic and acquisitive growth on further organic growth; and Levie's (1997) observation that a distinct minority of rapidly growing firms display an array of different modes of achieving growth. Still more importantly, a theoretical understanding of what such relationships mean needs to be developed. For example, do small firms grow organically because they are more innovative or because they lack the resources to choose the (possibly safer and sounder) acquisition route to increased size?

We noted early in this book that Penrose (1959) pointed out that 'growth' does not only mean 'change in amount.' It sometimes also denotes the *process* by which this change comes into being. This is a sorely under-researched area and therefore another one where mere mapping of the phenomenon has value, although relationships with antecedents and effects are of the greatest interest. While the 'stages-of-development' or 'life cycle' literature can be rather elaborate on process issues, and while considerable commonalities exist across many such accounts, the empirical evidence is not impressive. The quantitative material, when existing at all, is typically cross-sectional and retrospective. To the extent concurrent process data underlie the theorizing it is often gathered rather unsystematically from the small, non-random sample of firms for which the theorist happens to have consulted.

What is needed here are case-based studies where the cases have been sampled on sound, theory-based criteria, as well as quantitative work on samples that are known to likely represent some relevant population of firms. These studies would need to avoid retrospection bias and the 'prediction of the past' of cross-sectional research by studying concurrent growth processes with a longitudinal design. They also ought to take on board Levie and Lichtenstein's (2010) criticism and suggestions regarding the fundamental assumptions that underlie the research. Preferably they should also be theory-based to the extent possible. The question is just what extent that is. The most recurring and/or intriguing themes from the 'stages-of-development' literature should, of course, be put to test. Strong *concepts* from various more-fundamental theories in economics and management undoubtedly have their place in a process context as well. However, most established theories arguably remain relatively silent on the process issues themselves, i.e., on how the realities represented by those concepts interrelate and develop over time. Therefore, the topic of growth processes is arguably an area where some exploration is not only excusable, but needed.

Are broadly based, quantitative studies of concurrent growth processes a feasible prospect? Maybe, and maybe not. One issue just mentioned is the (possible lack of) theoretical preparedness for such an exercise. In addition, it would undoubtedly be a type of project that requires significant financial resources as well as long-term commitment of the research team. Assuming sufficient theoretical preparedness has been secured for the systematic, large-scale study of growth processes – including their antecedents and/or effects – an interesting parallel and possible source of inspiration here is the *Panel Study of Entrepreneurial Dynamics* (PSED) and its international counterpart studies (Davidsson and Gordon, 2012; Gartner et al., 2004). This type of research has shown considerable promise as a means of studying firm start-up processes in large samples, especially with the help of a large number of time-stamped 'gestation activities'. In much the same manner, it is conceivable that growth processes could be studied through repeated surveys of a cohort reporting time-stamped, growth-related events, obstacles, achievements, etc. In comparison to the PSED research endeavor, a similar study of growth would have huge advantages in terms of cost and precision of sampling since the firms – unlike early-stage start-ups – are readily identifiable and their industry affiliation is known. This would make it possible to obtain a relatively homogeneous sample at reasonable cost. On the downside, it cannot be known which or how many of the firms in the sample will embark on significant growth trajectories during the studied period. This suggests that the sample would have to be fairly large to include a sufficient number of growth processes, and that either the focus of the study would have to be broadened to 'development' processes or large parts of the sample would be selected out by some screening mechanism at an early stage of each round of interviews.

We argued above that as regards *modes* and *process* the current state of knowledge is so under-developed that mere mapping out of the phenomenon would constitute worthwhile contributions. This said, publication in high-tier journals usually requires more than description. However, this may not necessarily imply a need to analyze antecedents and/or effects in terms of Figure 6.1. As indicated by the bidirectional arrows among the three aspects of growth, there are many theoretically and practically relevant questions to be asked and answered regarding these inter-relationships. For example, how does the use of alternative modes of growth relate to the total amount of growth that is achieved? Conversely, do aspirations for high amounts of growth entice entrepreneurs to employ other or more varied modes of growth, as hinted at by some prior studies? How and why does the mix of growth modes change in a firm's growth process over time? Do firms that demonstrate sustained growth over long periods of time achieve this through a process characterized by steady, continuous growth or one where growth spurts and periods of consolidation alternate? While not completely untouched by prior research, questions like these have not been pursued as the main focus by multiple studies of small firm growth.

It was argued above that the influence of antecedents on the amount of growth was the most thoroughly researched area of those implied by Figure 6.1. Our review also showed that quite a number of broad generalizations can be made regarding such relationships. Nevertheless, it can also be argued that this is not the type of results that best serves the needs of management practice. This is so in part because these 'growth factors' are often variables that the manager can do little about, and in part because the relationships represent probabilistic truths that may not bear much truth at all in most individual cases. That is, the most relevant 'growth factor' in each individual case may be some idiosyncratic factor that is not even represented by the generic variables used in research, or at least a much more concrete manifestation of such a factor, on which the research naturally stays silent. Thus, it can be questioned whether broadly based generalizations about the antecedents of growth can *ever* be precise enough to be of much immediate value for managers themselves, even if they should have some value as a diagnostic tool for management consultants.

It may be speculated that there should actually be more commonality across firms as regards what management challenges different forms of growth *lead* to (effects), regardless of what 'success factors' (antecedents) first led to that growth. If so, the type of study that holds most promise from the perspective of furthering management practice (and, hence, education) would be one that combines aspects of *amount, mode*, and *process*, and relates them to *effects* in terms of a range of management challenges such as acquiring and coordinating a growing resource base, adapting organizational structures and systems, and effectively dealing with recruiting, training, promotions, and other people issues in the growing firm. This no doubt partly coincides with what the literature on 'stages,' 'life cycles' and 'management transitions' have tried to address, although these literatures often postulate a singular process and allow for but a very narrow range of growth modes. It also represents an expanded version of the type of process study we advocated above, with all its research challenges – and more. It is a research task that would require a comprehensive, multi-year program under competent and dedicated leadership, but one which – if successfully undertaken – would really make a difference.

Most researchers will, of course, never get the opportunity to design and carry out such an effort. Perhaps they will never to be part of one, either. Fortunately, there is and will be room for more restricted contributions, for example on the growth effects of a couple of factors highlighted by some particular theory. Arguably, inclusion of interactions as well as consideration of mode and/or process will increase the value of such contributions. In explicitly starting from a well-articulated theory, such a study would already be an improvement relative to most of the predecessors. As our review has highlighted, the other ways in which there is opportunity for improvement largely concern the classical research virtues of making sure the sample and the measures match with the theory. It is thanks to previous research that we now can understand how we can do a better job in that regard. Finally, future studies should either make a strong case for why firm growth is interesting in its own right, or explicitly include in the design those outcomes that growth is otherwise only assumed to lead to.

## NOTE

* Previously published as: Per Davidsson, Leona Achtenhagen and Lucia Naldi (2010), 'Towards an integrative framework for future research on small firm growth', *Foundations and Trends in Entrepreneurship*, **6** (2), 135–43.

## REFERENCES

Baum, J.R. and E.A. Locke (2004), 'The relationship of entrepreneurial traits, skill, and motivation to subsequent venture growth'. *Journal of Applied Psychology* **89**(4), 587–598.

Cho, H.-J. and V. Pucic (2005), 'Relationship between innovation, quality, growth, profitability and market value'. *Strategic Management Journal* **26**, 555–575.

Davidsson, P. and F. Delmar (2006), 'High-growth firms and their contribution to employment: The case of Sweden 1987–96'. In: P. Davidsson, F. Delmar, and J.Wiklund (eds.): *Entrepreneurship and the Growth of Firms*. Cheltenham, UK and Northampton, MA, USA: Edward Elgar, pp. 156–178.

Davidsson, P. and S.R. Gordon (2012), 'Panel studies of new venture creation: a methods-focused review and suggestions for future research'. *Small Business Economics*, **39**(4), 853–876.

Eisenhardt, K.M. and C.B. Schoonhoven (1990), 'Organizational growth: Linking founding team, strategy, environment and growth among US semiconductor ventures, 1978–1988'. *Administrative Science Quarterly* **35**(3), 504–530.

Gartner, W.B., K.G. Shaver, N.M. Carter and P.D. Reynolds (2004), *Handbook of Entrepreneurial Dynamics: The Process of Business Creation*. Thousand Oaks, CA: Sage.

Kish, L. (1987), *Statistical Design for Research*. New York: Wiley.

Levie, J. (1997), 'Patterns of growth and performance: An empirical study of young, growing ventures in France, Ireland and Scotland'. In: P.D. Reynolds, W. Bygrave, N.M. Carter, P. Davidsson, W.B. Gartner, C. Mason, and P.P. McDougall (eds.): *Frontiers of Entrepreneurship 1997*. Wellesley: Babson College, pp. 419–443.

Levie, J. and B.B. Lichtenstein (2010), 'A terminal assessment of stages theory: Introducing a dynamic states approach to entrepreneurship'. *Entrepreneurship Theory and Practice* **34**(2), 317–350.

Lockett, A., J. Wiklund, P. Davidsson and S. Girma (2011), 'Organic and acquisitive growth: re-examining, testing and extending Penrose's growth theory'. *Journal of Management Studies* **48**(1), 48–74.

Penrose, E. (1959), *The Theory of the Growth of the Firm*. Oxford: Oxford University Press.

# PART III

# A critical look at the growth–profit relationship

# 7. Growing profitable or growing from profits: putting the horse in front of the cart?*

**Per Davidsson, Paul Steffens and Jason Fitzsimmons**

## 1. EXECUTIVE SUMMARY

Top lists of and praise for the economy's fastest growing firms abound in business media around the world. Similarly, in academic research there has been a tendency to equate firm growth with business success. This tendency appears to be particularly pronounced in – but not confined to – entrepreneurship research.

In this study we critically examine this tendency to portray firm growth as more or less universally favorable. While several theories suggest that growth drives profitability we first show that the available empirical evidence does not support the existence of a general, positive relationship between growth and profitability. Using the theoretical lens of the Resource-Based View (RBV) we then argue that *sound* growth *usually* starts with achieving sufficient levels of profitability. In summary, our theoretical argument is as follows: In a population of SMEs, superior profitability is likely to be indicative of having built a resource-based competitive advantage. Building such a valuable and hard-to-copy advantage may at first constrain growth. However, the underlying advantage itself and the financial resources generated through high profitability make it possible for firms in this situation to now achieve sound and sustainable growth – which may require building a series of temporary advantages – without having to sacrifice profitability. By contrast, when firms strive for high growth starting from low profitability, the latter often indicates lack of competitive advantage. Therefore growth must be achieved in head-to-head competition with equally attractive alternatives, leading to profitability deterioration rather than improvement. In addition, these low-profitability firms are unlikely to be able to finance strategies toward building valuable and difficult-to-imitate advantages while growing. Hence their growth would neither be sustainable nor lead to improved profitability. Based on these RBV arguments, we hold that although exceptions exist, it is advantageous in most situations to let profitability (and the competitive advantage it reflects) be the horse that pulls the growth cart, rather than the other way around. Consequently, we develop two hypotheses about growth–profit configurations over time.

*Hypothesis 1. Firms that show high profitability at low growth are more likely to reach a state of high growth and high profitability in subsequent periods than are firms that first show high growth at low profitability.*

*Hypothesis 2. Firms that show high growth at low profitability are more likely to reach a state of low growth and low profitability in subsequent periods than are firms that first show high profitability at low growth.*

We test these hypotheses using two longitudinal data sets of small- and medium-sized enterprises (SMEs) from Sweden and Australia. The results clearly support these hypotheses both for 1-year transitions and over the longest time span the data sets cover. The results also show a high degree of robustness across alternative, bivariate and multivariate testing techniques as well as across sub-categories by firm age, firm size and industry. All in all, the results suggest that 'profitability first' rather than 'growth first' is the preferable strategy for achieving high overall firm performance.

For *academics* these results suggest that positive theory should not portray SME growth in its own right as 'success' and that normative theory should attempt to better specify how and under which conditions firm growth contributes to outcomes that enhance company value. Further, empirical research aiming at explaining firm success ought not to rely solely on growth as the outcome variable. For business *practitioners* the results suggest they would often benefit from focusing on attaining high profitability before pursuing high growth. For those situations where growth may be considered necessary for attaining high profitability, we suggest that managers develop precise ideas about how growth can enhance the future profitability of their particular firm, rather than relying on growth automatically improving profitability. With respect to external *investors* the results suggest they should often resist the temptation to encourage rapid growth before securing a sound level of profitability. Finally, for *policy-makers* the results imply that policies should be developed that encourage firms to achieve the goal of being profitable rather than adopting policies that urge firms to grow as the primary goal. As firms that demonstrate high profitability often become growing firms that still enjoy above-average profits, policies that help firms become more profitable will also lead to more growth.

As with any empirical research this study is subject to certain limitations. Since our study did not include direct measures of the firms' resources it is possible that mechanisms other than the RBV-based ones used to develop our hypotheses may – at least in part – explain our results. However, given the strength and robustness of our findings we maintain that this research provides sound reasons to caution against both an uncritical view of 'growth' as a measure of 'success' and pursuing high growth before the firm has attained a sufficient level of profitability. Future research should test the generalizability of our results to longer time spans and other contexts. Future studies should also try to assess the resource-based mechanism in a more direct manner. This is a complicated matter that probably requires customized, longitudinal survey studies of relatively homogeneous samples of firms.

## 2. INTRODUCTION

Few things could be easier than growing the sales revenue of a firm. All one would have to do is to buy or produce the business's products or services at going market rates and sell them for significantly less. With the exception of a few, special cases, demand would soar and the firm would experience tremendous sales growth. However, this growth would obviously not reflect effective value creation and appropriation by the firm, and hence be neither profitable nor sustainable.

Despite this obvious fact, researchers, practitioners and policy-makers alike place a great deal of emphasis on firm growth *per se* as an indication of business success. Although the notion that growth can be harmful is not new (Ramezani et al., 2002:65; Markman and Gartner, 2002), adverse growth is usually treated as a relatively rare exception. In business media around the world, top lists and praise of the economy's fastest growing firms are ubiquitous (Nicholls-Nixon, 2005). Policy programs designed to stimulate and assist the growth of individual firms are common-place, presumably in the hope that this will result in increasing employment and tax revenue (Storey, 1994). Teaching cases and textbooks devote much space to the problem of how to achieve expansion for the firm (e.g., Hisrich et al., 2005; Wickham, 2004; Winn, 2004). Further, academics frequently use firm growth uncritically as an operationalization of business success; especially in entrepreneurship research (see Davidsson et al., 2007). Some researchers go so far as to make growth 'the very essence of entrepreneurship' (Sexton and Smilor,

1997:97) or include growth more or less as part of the definition of entrepreneurship (Stevenson and Jarillo, 1990:21, 25).

While we agree with Davidsson et al. (2002) that venture growth is an important topic for entrepreneurship research, we also agree with Alvarez and Barney (2004) that value creation (they use the term 'rent generation') and appropriation are the central tasks of entrepreneurial firms. As we emphasized with our opening 'high-growth recipe', growth is not direct evidence of effective value creation and appropriation. It is therefore an important task for entrepreneurship research to investigate the relationship between growth and profitability.

Through the theoretical lens of the Resource-Based View (RBV) we argue in this chapter that *sound* growth *usually* starts with achieving sufficient levels of profitability, i.e., that profitability is the 'horse' that should pull the growth 'cart' rather than the other way round. We also argue that firms which embark on a growth trajectory starting from low levels of profitability *usually* do not achieve high profitability as a result of their growth. Instead, as their growth is unlikely to be sustainable (Ramezani et al., 2002) they run an increased risk of becoming low performers on both dimensions. We test these hypotheses using two longitudinal data sets of small and medium enterprises (SMEs) from Sweden and Australia.

Although we use RBV logic to develop our hypotheses and interpret our results, it is important to point out that this study does not include direct measures of the firms' resources and hence we do not regard it a strong test of or contribution to resource-based theory (Arend, 2006). Our contribution concerns the understanding of the phenomenon of firm growth relative to how it has previously been conceived in the entrepreneurship literature. We employ a theory-driven *configuration* view of the interrelationship between profitability and growth. Rather than trying to explain as much of the variation in firms' growth or profitability as possible, we focus squarely on the following two questions. First, which firms are more likely to reach the preferred state of high growth combined with high profitability – is it high-growth firms with low initial profitability or high-profitability firms with low initial growth? Second, firms with which of these two original performance configurations are more likely to end up at the negative end of the performance spectrum, i.e., having low profitability and low growth?

In the following section we will briefly examine the theoretical arguments for firms becoming more profitable as a result of their growth. We then review the empirical literature to demonstrate the lack of general support for this notion. This is followed by the development of our RBV-based case for focusing on profitability before going for growth, which leads to two hypotheses that we test empirically. In the Method section we describe our samples and measures as well as our approach to the challenging problem of analyzing growth–profitability configurations over time. After presenting our results we discuss their implications. We suggest a research agenda for future studies, thereby also addressing the limitations of our study.

## 3. DOES GROWTH MAKE FIRMS PROFITABLE?

The assumption that sales growth is positively associated with profitability appears in a variety of literatures pertaining to *scale economies* (Besanko et al., 2004; Gupta, 1981), *experience effects* (Stern and Stalk, 1998), *first-mover-advantages* (FMAs) (Lieberman and Montgomery, 1988) and *network externalities* (Katz and Shapiro, 1985). These theories suggest growth will drive profitability either through the lowering of costs or by establishing a stronger market position. However, there is little empirical support for a strong and general growth–profitability relationship. For example, research in industrial economics have shown that scale economies are not much of a barrier to entry; that surviving new entrants operate for long times at sizes far smaller than the industry average; that *minimum efficient scale* is typically reached at a rather small size; that very limited cost advantages are usually gained beyond that minimum, and even that it is possible to operate significantly below it without severe cost disadvantage (Geroski, 1995; Hill, 1988; Siegfried and Evans, 1994).

In studies reporting association between growth and profitability measures the correlations range from relatively substantial positive (Cox et al., 2002; Chandler and Jansen, 1992; Mendelson, 2000), to those that are weakly positive yet statistically significant (Baum and Wally 2003; Cho and Pucic, 2005; Kim et al., 2004; Peng, 2004), to those finding no statistically or practically significant relationship (Roper, 1999; Sexton et al., 2000; both based on very sizable samples), to those showing a significant negative relationship (Markman and Gartner, 2002; Reid, 1995). The most comprehensive assessment of the issue is a meta-analysis by Capon et al. (1990). A close examination of their results reveals that a significant positive association between growth and financial performance is only found in across-industry studies. In within-industry studies, the effect is very small in magnitude and statistically non-significant (Capon et al., 1990:1154; Table 5). Thus, the results do not establish that firms that grow more than their direct competitors consequently become more profitable. Rather, the findings suggest that firms in growing industries benefit from the higher growth *and* profit rates of their industries; a theme well-known also from Product Life Cycle theory (Day, 1981). Similarly, studies of the relationship between market share or market share growth on the one hand, and profitability on the other, suggest that any positive relationship may be either industry-specific or spurious (Brush et al., 2000).

In summary, the empirical evidence on the relationship between firm growth and profitability is inconclusive. Despite the theoretical arguments there is little evidence of a general tendency for firms to become more profitable as a result of their growth. This indicates that although the two dimensions of performance sometimes move together there are frequent other instances when the growth–profitability relationship is neutral or negative.

## 4. THE RESOURCE-BASED VIEW AND PROFITABLE GROWTH

The Resource-Based View (RBV) is in its historical origin very closely connected to the core topic of our study, *profitable growth*. Penrose (1959) focused her entire study on firm growth. Similarly, Wernerfelt's (1984) seminal paper explicitly addresses the profitability of different routes to growth. Hence, it is with considerable justification that Kor and Mahoney (2004:190) claim that profitable growth is one of the 'cornerstones of a Resource-Based View of strategic management.'

Thus, we hold that RBV is a natural starting point in considering small firm growth and profitability. We use the label 'RBV' in a rather broad sense. We include in this notion extensions such as 'dynamic capabilities' (Teece et al., 1997), the 'knowledge-based view' (Kogut and Zander, 1992) or any other theoretical argument for efficiency-based, intra-industry performance advantages deriving from resource heterogeneity (Peteraf and Barney, 2003) whether or not the original contributors position their work as contributions to, critique of, or unrelated to original RBV formulations. Consistent with RBV, our focus is on growth and profitability comparisons of firms within industries (Peteraf and Barney, 2003).

The RBV attributes superior firm performance to competitive advantage. Barney (1991) presents the now-familiar argument that the sustainability of the advantage is contingent on the extent to which the firm's resources or resource bundles are *valuable, rare, hard-to-copy* and *non-substitutable* (VRHN). In a later, equally well-known reformulation the desirable resource qualities are specified as *valuable, rare, inimitable, and organized* (VRIO) (Barney, 1997). The 'O' in the latter formulation can be regarded an increased emphasis on the importance of having an effective *business model* in place – including an effective *revenue model* – thus assuring both value creation and value appropriation by the focal firm (Alvarez and Barney, 2004; Amit and Zott, 2001).

The RBV does not deny the existence of other sources of superior performance such as scale economies, FMAs, or behaviors like anti-competitive collusion; strategic ploys, and efforts to blunt competition (Peteraf and Barney, 2003). However, if based on scale *per se* a cost advantage is unlikely to be sustainable by Barney's (1991, 1997) criteria. Further, within a population of SMEs only a small proportion of firms would be recent entrants in emerging industries where FMAs are a major issue. When present, it is argued that FMAs become sources of sustained competitive advantage only when they are based on VRHN resources (Barney, 1991:105; cf. Wernerfelt, 1984:173). As regards 'strategic' behaviors that are not value-creating we hold that their successful pursuit is unlikely in a population of SMEs where each firm has very limited market power. Hence, we argue that in the context of SMEs, RBV provides a plausible explanation for why some firms show above-average profitability. With its focus on within-industry differences among firms competing in the same product markets RBV may actually be more applicable to SMEs than to large corporations (cf. Davidsson and Wiklund, 2000; Peteraf and Barney, 2003).

Therefore, our theoretical argument starts from the fundamental RBV-based premise that resource heterogeneity which has been successfully transformed into product market offerings with superior economic value is a major source of within-industry profitability differences for SMEs. Hence, without trying to explain the 'how' questions – a silence RBV has been criticized for (Barney and Arikan, 2001; Priem and Butler, 2001; Sirmon et al., 2007) – we accept the original RBV assumptions that resource heterogeneity exists (Barney, 1991) and that it is (often but not deterministically) transformed into product advantages (Wernerfelt, 1984) that create value to customers (Sirmon et al., 2007). However, we also consider the criticism that the original RBV employs a static view of competitive advantage (Priem and Butler, 2001) and embrace later developments suggesting it may be more realistic that firms need to develop a series of temporary advantages through valuable and hard-to-copy strategic moves in order to reach and maintain superior performance (Morrow et al., 2007; Sirmon et al., 2007; Zahra et al., 2006).

What implications does this have for firm growth? To facilitate our thinking, we sketch growth–profitability configurations in a simple 2×2 matrix (see Figure 7.1) where firms are positioned as either above or below their industry average on each dimension. This gives us four cases, which we label *Star* (high on both), *Profit* (high profitability/low growth), *Growth* (high growth/low profitability) and *Poor* (low on both). For

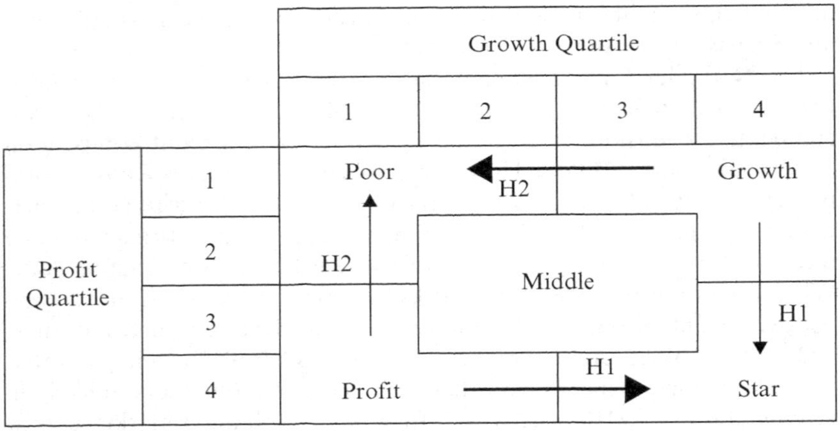


*Figure 7.1 Categorization schema of firms by growth and profitability*

the moment we can disregard the *Middle* category, which is created for empirical reasons in order to consider only substantive deviations from the average on either profitability or growth.

By the logic of RBV, firms should pursue growth opportunities that match their resource advantages. This would allow them to grow profitably, which is the essence of value creation (Sirmon et al., 2007). If they pursue other opportunities growth may destroy rather than create value (Kogut and Zander, 1992). Conversely, if they refrain from growth opportunities that match their resource advantages they may enjoy high levels of profitability based on a sub-optimally small volume of business, thus under utilizing opportunities for value creation and appropriation. Hence, from the perspective of RBV firms should strive to maximize *profitable growth*. Profitable growth in our scheme is reflected in the performance demonstrated by firms in the high growth, high profitability (*Star*) category in Figure 7.1.

In an interpretation relying on RBV *Star* firms have been able to establish a resource-based advantage to create superior value for customers (Peteraf and Barney, 2003; Sirmon et al., 2007). They are successfully exploiting this advantage through profitable growth. If maximization of value creation and value appropriation is the goal, achieving *Star* status is what firms in the other performance categories should be striving for.

Therefore, we now turn to the probability that firms in the *Profit* (high profitability/low growth) and *Growth* (high growth/low profitability) categories, respectively, can successfully make the transition to the desirable *Star* category. As regards *Profit* firms, by resource-based logic their above-average profitability suggests they have attained the ability to both create and appropriate value above the industry average. Developing this advantage may take its toll in terms of growth. For example, the study by Mishina et al. (2004) suggests that a product expansion logic – which Morrow et al. (2007) portray as exemplifying valuable and hard-to-copy strategic action – is negatively related to sales growth in the short term. Yet, Morrow et al. (2007) demonstrate that such strategies are positively associated with value creation as reflected in investors' expectations; a result consistent with Cho and Pucic's (2005) observation that profitability has a much stronger influence on company value than has growth.

This is presumably because first developing a resource-based advantage and translating it to superior market offerings at low growth sets the seed for sound, profitable growth in the future. Thus, we argue that *Profit* firms are in a good position to now expand while retaining their high profitability and thus transition to the *Star* category. Relative to low-profitability firms, the *Profit* firms are in a better position in at least two resource-related ways to make that transition. First, they have the underlying competitive advantage that enabled them to achieve above-average profitability. Unless the market potential for the current products is already exhausted these firms are likely to be able to grow organically through market penetration – the dominant form of SME growth, see Davidsson et al. (2006) – without the profitability-reducing tactics of price cutting and/or heavy promotion that would be needed to gain market share from firms with equal offerings (Peteraf and Barney, 2003). Second, the profitability of these firms creates greater cash flows and associated lower cost of the financial capital needed to enable growth (Marris, 1967; Scott and Pascoe, 1986). The cost-of-capital advantage holds for a comparison of retained earnings to external capital but likely extends to the cost of external capital itself, as a more profitable firm is likely to get external loans and equity on better terms than a less profitable firm with less financial slack (Bourgeois, 1981).

By contrast, we maintain that *Growth* firms (high growth and low profitability) are relatively unlikely to be able to exploit their growth to build resource advantages and subsequently attain superior profitability. We have noted above that there is no strong empirical support for firms gaining profitability advantages as a result of their growth. *Growth* firms' low level of profitability indicates that they are less likely than *Profit* firms to have established resource advantages that have been transformed into superior value creation for customers. Hence, assuming growth by organic market penetration, their expansion may require price cuts or costly marketing efforts to win over customers facing several equally appealing offerings (Peteraf and Barney, 2003). As regards product expansion, Mishina et al.'s (2004) findings make it appear unlikely that small firms would be able to grow at above-average rates based on such a strategy, not least because small firms are commonly constrained to basing their growth on internal finance (Carpenter and Petersen, 2002). If that constraint can be overcome, Mishina et al.'s (2004) results in combination with those obtained by Morrow et al. (2007) imply that infusion of external capital may help firms develop valuable and hard-to-copy strategies to create value through sales growth. However, if the development of a resource advantage is attempted concurrently with above-average expansion the firm is likely to face time-compression diseconomies, as discussed by Dierickx and Cool (1989). This may well be part of the reason why other research has found that while access to financial capital may facilitate growth it usually does it at the expense of profitability rather than helping the firm to achieve above-average profitability through growth (Florin et al., 2003).

All in all, our analysis suggests that while *Profit* firms are in a good position to achieve high growth without significant loss of profitability, *Growth* firms are not particularly likely to become more profitable as a result of their growth. On top of their apparent lack of a resource-based, superior market offering our reasoning suggests they also suffer from a cost-of-capital disadvantage compared with *Profit* firms. This suggests the following hypothesis:

**H1.** Firms that show high profitability at low growth (Profit firms) are more likely to reach a state of high growth and high profitability (become Star firms) in subsequent periods than are firms that first show high growth at low profitability (Growth firms).

Firms that are unable to reach *Star* status would at least want to avoid ending up in the *Poor* category, i.e., to perform below average on both dimensions in Figure 7.1 In order to avoid such development, *Growth* and *Profit* firms need to sustain above-average performance on one dimension; most likely the one on which they currently have high performance. We now turn to the probability that these two categories can avoid transition to the undesirable *Poor* category.

We have argued above that *Growth* firms are not particularly likely to become profitable as a result of their growth. If they lack resource-based competitive advantage – as our RBV arguments suggest many firms in this category do – the expansion would be gained in costly, head-to-head competition that, if anything, puts an additional downward pressure on profitability. The combination of high growth and low profitability puts the firm under financial strain that makes it difficult (and perhaps not desirable) for the firm to sustain its growth (Churchill and Mullins, 2001). Consequently the firm would slide into the *Poor* category. Infusion of external capital could make it possible to sustain the growth. However, when the firm does not show a promising development of profitability as result of earlier growth, external investors will become reluctant to plow money into further volume expansion. In all, *Growth* firms appear to face a relatively high risk of not being able to sustain their growth and instead at considerable risk of relapsing to the low growth and low-profitability (Poor) category. The well-established fact that the serial correlation of firm growth over time tends to be low (Coad, 2006) suggests this is a common phenomenon.

We have noted already that recent developments of RBV suggest that long-term sustainability of a given advantage is unlikely. Consequently, *Profit* firms face the risk of transitioning to *Poor* because the competitive advantage underlying their earlier high profit performance has eroded. However, they are in this regard no worse off than *Growth* firms, which we assume usually lack distinguishable, resource-based advantages. Further, because of the financial resources their earlier high profitability has provided them with, *Profit* firms are in a better position than *Growth* firms to invest in the development of the series or valuable and hard-to-copy strategic moves that may be required for sustained advantage (Morrow et al., 2007; Sirmon et al., 2007; Zahra et al., 2006) and hence high profitability. This seems particularly likely when the resources are not concurrently demanded for the financing of high growth. In all, compared to *Growth* firms, those in the *Profit* category appear to have better chances to avoid degenerating into showing low performance on both dimensions in subsequent periods. Hence our second hypothesis:

**H2.** Firms that show high growth at low profitability (Growth firms) are more likely to reach a state of low growth and low profitability (become Poor firms) in subsequent periods than are firms that first show high profitability at low growth (Profit firms).

In Figure 7.1 the hypotheses are represented graphically with thicker arrows denoting the transition our hypotheses suggest is relatively more likely. Note that our hypotheses are strictly probabilistic. We are thus not suggesting any route to high, combined growth/profit performance is inherently impossible. Some *Growth* firms may well be pursuing a sound strategy of maximizing value creation and appropriation over time by temporarily foregoing profits (Cowling, 2004; Florin et al., 2003). However, the popular assumption that this is the *norm* is the very notion that we challenge in this research. We hold that in a population of SMEs, only a very small proportion of cases are subject to true, potential performance advantages based on scale, market share, FMA or network externalities that are unrelated to RBV-type resource advantages and which require expansion at the expense of profitability in order to be realized.

# 5. METHOD

## 5.1 Data Sources

We use two separate data sources to examine our research questions. The data were originally collected by government statistical agencies in Australia and Sweden, over different 4-year periods. Both data sets contain a random sample of SMEs across many industries, though they stratify the population differently. In particular, the Australian sample contains a much larger number of firms in the smallest size class.

The Australian data is sourced from the Business Longitudinal Survey (BLS) conducted by the Australian Bureau of Statistics (ABS) over the period 1995 to 1998.[1] The sampling frame was all businesses on the ABS business register employing fewer than 200 employees, excluding primary industries other than mining, government enterprises, utilities and public services. A panel of 5031 businesses was established in the 1994–95 financial year. Each subsequent year, the panel consists of those businesses remaining alive, supplemented by a sample of new businesses added to the ABS business register in that year. Completed responses were collected between 84 per cent and 90 per cent of the panel for the surveys in 1995–96 to 1997–98. We use all cases that have complete data in any two subsequent years, or have complete data in the first year and cease business during the second. As a result, between 3488 and 3717 businesses are included in any one analysis.

The Swedish data originates from a longitudinal survey study undertaken in the years 1997–2000. The sample was drawn from Statistics Sweden's complete records of private limited liability companies with 10–250 employees, excluding agriculture, forestry and fishing as well as government enterprises, utilities and public services. The sampling frame was stratified as follows: two size groups of 10–49 and 50–250 employees; four industry sectors of manufacturing, retail/wholesale, professional services and other services; and the three corporate governance categories independent firms, member of company group of less than 250 employees, and member of company group larger than 250 employees. From each of the 24 strata 110 firms were randomly selected, except where the subpopulation was less than that number, resulting in a sample of 2455 firms.

Rather than representing items from the survey, the growth and profitability data we use are likewise data from Statistics Sweden's records. These data were originally collected as part of the statutory reporting required of businesses in Sweden, and were appended to the survey data set. Growth and profitability data was requested from Statistics Sweden only for firms that participated in at least the first survey round and for whom phone contact information could be obtained in 2000. This reduces the sample to 1917 cases. Missing data on growth and/or profitability in Statistics Sweden's files in addition to eliminating firms that merged or reorganized as part of a parent company further reduced the analyzable sample for this study to 1482 firms. As a result, our analysis of Swedish firms uses a minimum of 1470 businesses in any one analysis.

## 5.2 Measures

Sales growth was preferred over employment growth based on emerging consensus in the literature that for most purposes sales is the more relevant growth indicator (Davidsson and Wiklund, 2000; Delmar, 1997; Hoy et al., 1992; Weinzimmer et al., 1998). The specific formula used was the change in sales from Year 1 to Year *N* as a percentage of the sales in Year 1. For the Australian data, sales growth could be calculated in the first year (1995). For the Swedish data only current year sales are reported. Hence, growth can only be calculated from the second year (1998).

In line with Arend's (2006:410) recommendation we used return on assets (ROA) as our measure of profitability. Slightly different measures were used due to data availability. For the Australian sample, data on pretax ROA was available, calculated as the net profit (operating profit or loss before tax and extraordinary items) as a percentage of total assets in each year. After-tax ROA was available for the Swedish sample.

Since our theoretical foundation, RBV, is concerned with performance relative to competitors (Peteraf and Barney, 2003), both growth and profitability were calculated relative to other firms in the industry. Specifically, we divided by the industry median rather than the mean to reduce the impact of outliers.

## 5.3 Primary Analysis

Our research is concerned with the dual growth–profitability performance of firms over time. While the analysis problem entails aspects reminiscent of lagged and interaction effects in regression analysis (e.g., Cowling, 2004), this approach is not appropriate for our problem of predicting a multivariate outcome. Instead, we adopt a simple, intuitively appealing schema that allows us to follow a firm's trajectory in a two-dimensional growth–profitability performance space. We classify firms into five performance groups in any time period as shown in Figure 7.1. Firms are first separated into a 4×4 classification based on the two performance dimensions; sales growth and profitability. Specifically, firms are classified into quartiles for both sales growth and profitability. Both measures were calculated relative to other firms in their industry. They were then divided into the following five performance groups as displayed in Figure 7.1 above:[2]

- *Poor*: Low performance on both dimensions (below median on both and lowest quartile on at least one). This is the final state for hypothesis H2.
- *Middle*: Mid-performance (2nd or 3rd quartile) on both dimensions. This category is included to reduce the risk that minuscule movements have a large effect on results.
- *Growth*: High growth performance, but low profit performance (above median on the former and below on the latter, but not qualifying as *Middle*). This is the initial state presumed to lead to poorer outcomes for H1 and H2.
- *Profit*: High profit performance, but low growth performance (above median on the former and below on the latter, but not qualifying as *Middle*). This is the initial state presumed to lead to better outcomes in hypotheses H1 and H2.
- *Star*: High performance on both dimensions (above median on both and highest quartile on at least one). This is the final state for hypothesis H1.

Our interest is in how firms move in this growth–profit performance space over time. Similar to Markov chain analysis used in population dynamics we use state transition matrices as the starting point of our analysis. That is, for each performance group in one year, we calculate the proportion that moved to each group (or ceased business). As displayed in Figure 7.1, we are interested in comparing Growth to Star transitions with transitions from Profit to Star (H1). We are also interested in comparing *Growth* to *Poor* with *Profit* to *Poor* (H2). We test the differences between these specific transition proportions using standard z-tests.

In the transition matrices we also include transitions to 'Exit' as a separate category. This is an ambiguous category including not only financial failures but also voluntary closures and lucrative outright sales of firms to new owners (Gimeno et al., 1997; Headd, 2003). Consequently Exit should not be merged with the *Poor* category or be interpreted as a pure failure category. Also, this category is not directly comparable for Australia and Sweden as many of the Swedish exiting firms are not included in the available sample.[3] In addition to the separate analyses of the Australian and Swedish samples we will also examine the robustness of our findings by sub-categories based on industry, firm size, and firm age within each country. Thus we control for each of these variables one at a time.

We perform our growth and profitability calculations based on annual data. The theory on which our hypotheses are based does not suggest the ideal time period for which the transitions should be tested. Hence, we test our hypotheses over both a short time horizon (1-year transitions) and longest time horizon permitted by our data (2-year to 3-year transitions for Australia and Sweden respectively).

### 5.4 Supplementary Analysis

We did not use logistic regression as our primary method since the purpose of our research is not to predict which firms become *Star* or *Poor* but rather to compare whether *Profit* or *Growth* firms are more likely to end up in the *Star* or *Poor* categories. However, we supplement our primary analysis with a logistic regression approach to examine multivariate effects. In addition, since our analyses are based on variations in performance over time, we separately assess the possible influence of regression-to-the-mean (*r-t-m*) effects (Allen et al., 1979).

There is a risk that the longest time period we use for our main analysis is still on the short side if there is a strong tendency for 'investments in growth' to lower concurrent profitability while paying off in the long run. We therefore provide supplementary analyses using the survey-based part of the Swedish study. These data can address the same issues over longer time periods, both as regards the time period over which the initial and end states are assessed and the spacing between them.

## 6. RESULTS

### 6.1 Analysis of Entire Samples

The 1-year transition matrices as well as a complete transition matrix over the longest available period in each country are reported in Tables 7.A1a–7.A1b in the Appendix. In these analyses we have aggregated all the 1-year transitions provided by the data (three transitions for Australia and two for Sweden). These tables show that although a tendency to remain in one's category of origin is a major source of deviation from randomness, there are also many other deviations from statistical expectation in the tables that are of a large absolute magnitude. In what category

*Table 7.1 Hypothesis tests for whole sample.*

| | Final performance group | Star | | | Poor | | |
|---|---|---|---|---|---|---|---|
| | Initial performance group | Growth[a] | (H1) | Profit[a,b] | Growth[a] | (H2) | Profit[a,b] |
| Australia | 1-year transitions[c] | 11.6 | *** | 29.6 | 30.3 | *** | 11.0 |
| | 3-year transitions[d] | 10.2 | ** | 16.5 | 23.1 | *** | 12.1 |
| Sweden | 1-year transitions[e] | 5.4 | *** | 29.7 | 28.3 | *** | 17.7 |
| | 2-year transitions[f] | 11.5 | *** | 32.8 | 26.1 | * | 19.0 |

*Notes:*

a. The table reports percentage of specified initial performance group that transition to specified final performance group. Percentage signs are removed for readability.
b. Significance levels: *$p<0.05$; **$p<0.01$; ***$p<0.001$.
c. Aggregate of three 1-year transitions.
d. Aggregate of two 1-year transitions.
e. 1995–1998 transition.
f. 1998–2000 transition.

a particular firm is found in a particular year is clearly not random. The results indicate strong path dependence. As should be expected, this dependence is stronger for shorter-term transitions.

The transitions relating to our hypotheses are summarized in Table 7.1. The left half of this table provides very strong support for the hypothesis that *Profit* is more likely than *Growth* to transition to *Star* (H1). In the 1-year transitions the *Profit* firms are two to three times more likely to end up in the *Star* category. Although the tendency is even stronger in the 2-year transition based on Swedish data, the size of the category differences diminishes for the longer transitions in the Australian results. However, the difference is still substantial – an 'over representation' by 62 per cent (16.5/10.2) – and statistically significant in the 3-year Australian analysis.

Strong support is also provided, in the right hand side of the table, that firms in the *Profit* category are less likely than those originally being *Growth* firms to transition to *Poor* (H2). This result comes through relatively stronger in the Australian case, where *Growth* firms are two to three times more likely to end up among the firms that perform below average on both dimensions. Although not as strong, the difference is substantial and statistically significant also in the Swedish data, with a minimum 'over representation' of 37 per cent (26.1/19.0) for *Growth* firms making this transition, relative to firms originating in the *Profit* category. Thus, both hypotheses get strong support in the full sample analysis for both countries.

### 6.2 Analysis of Sub-samples

Tables 7.2a and 7.2b report the sub-group analyses that we perform in order to explore the robustness of our findings with variation in industry, firm size and firm age. These tests involve smaller sample sizes, and consequently lower power of the statistical tests, with average cell sizes ranging from 12 to 84.[4] Hence, differences of the same magnitude as reported for the full samples will not be associated with the same levels of statistical significance.

Table 7.2a demonstrates that H1 is supported across all sub-categories tested. Out of the 52 contrasts that could be made, 51 are in the expected direction and 41 are statistically significant (at $p = 0.05$ or better). The support is somewhat weak for the Retail industry, where the only reverse difference is found (for Australia in the 3-year analysis) and where the Swedish results include wholesale businesses as well. Similarly, Table 7.2b indicates that H2 holds up across sub-samples. Out of 52 contrasts, 51 are again in the expected direction and 30 reach statistical significance (at $p = 0.05$ or better). While the Retail industry again achieves only one statistically significant result out of four the reason seems to be lacking power; the estimated magnitude of the percentage difference is substantial in all four analyses. The one result that runs in the opposite direction concerns 1-year transitions for the 2–5-year-old firms in the Swedish data. In isolation this result would seem to indicate possible FMA effects. However, overall there is no obvious, general pattern across firm age groups so the reversal for the 2–5-year category in Sweden appears to be an idiosyncratic occurrence.

Within the boundaries of our empirical investigations, the effects hypothesized in both H1 and H2 appear to be robust. Across a range of industries, firm sizes and firm ages, firms that first achieve above-average profitability at low growth (*Profit*) are more likely to achieve the desirable state of high growth/high profitability (*Star*) than are firms that first go for above-average growth at low levels of profitability (*Growth*). Conversely, the latter category of firm is more likely than the former to transition to the low growth/low-profitability category (*Poor*).

### 6.3 Additional Observations

Table 7.1 can also be read as showing that *Growth* firms are two to three times more likely to transition to *Poor* than to *Star*. We note that if our results were entirely driven by costly 'investments in growth' that will eventually pay off we would expect to see this ratio diminish for longer transitions. Our results do not show any tendency in this direction. A

*Table 7.2a Sub-group tests of transitions to Star (H1).*

| Sub-group | Australia | | | | | | Sweden | | | | | |
|---|---|---|---|---|---|---|---|---|---|---|---|---|
| | 1-year transitions | | | 3-year transitions | | | 1-year transitions | | | 2-year transitions | | |
| | Initial year performance group | | | Initial year performance group | | | Initial year performance group | | | Initial year performance group | | |
| | Growth[a] | | Profit[a,b] | Growth[a] | | Profit[a,b] | Growth[a] | | Profit[a,b] | Growth[a] | | Profit[a,b] |
| Manufacturing | 9.8 | *** | 25.2 | 10.7 | n.s. | 13.4 | 15.0 | *** | 41.1 | 8.3 | *** | 44.6 |
| Prop./bus. serv | 10.6 | *** | 28.0 | 8.7 | ** | 22.6 | 13.7 | ** | 26.0 | 15.5 | n.s. | 25.8 |
| Retail[c] | 11.7 | ** | 23.1 | 13.3 | n.s. | 9.8 | 13.5 | n.s. | 21.1 | 8.3 | n.s. | 23.3 |
| Wholesale | 12.0 | *** | 23.8 | 8.0 | * | 17.2 | | N/A | | | N/A | |
| Other | 11.7 | *** | 28.9 | 10.7 | * | 19.6 | 19.1 | n.s. | 28.0 | 11.9 | ** | 34.0 |
| Size 1[d] | 14.6 | *** | 31.4 | 9.4 | ** | 19.6 | 13.0 | * | 26.0 | 5.7 | ** | 27.1 |
| Size 2[d] | 14.0 | *** | 29.4 | 13.6 | n.s. | 11.9 | 18.4 | * | 30.0 | 16.7 | ** | 35.4 |
| Size 3[d] | 11.3 | *** | 30.2 | 8.3 | * | 18.5 | 16.8 | ** | 30.3 | 13.7 | ** | 33.3 |
| Size 4[d] | 8.9 | *** | 27.5 | 9.9 | * | 16.2 | 10.6 | *** | 34.6 | 4.3 | *** | 35.7 |
| <2 years[e] | 13.3 | * | 24.0 | 6.5 | * | 21.7 | | N/A | | | N/A | |
| 2–5 years | 9.2 | *** | 36.4 | 9.1 | * | 18.1 | 20.4 | n.s. | 26.8 | 14.8 | n.s. | 19.0 |
| 5–10 years | 13.8 | *** | 28.8 | 14.5 | n.s. | 17.1 | 16.7 | ** | 30.2 | 9.8 | *** | 35.7 |
| 10–20 years | 13.9 | *** | 28.7 | 6.8 | ** | 16.6 | 16.0 | * | 27.6 | 18.0 | * | 33.3 |
| >20 years | 7.7 | *** | 30.1 | 11.5 | n.s. | 13.2 | 13.3 | *** | 31.6 | 8.1 | *** | 35.1 |

*Notes:*

a. The table reports percentage of specified initial performance group that transition to Star. Percentage signs are removed for readability.
b. Significance levels: *$p<0.05$; **$p<0.01$; ***$p<0.001$.
c. Retail and wholesale combined for Swedish sample.
d. Size classes for Australian sample based on revenue in Australian dollars: Size 1 <\$300K; Size 2 \$300K–\$1M; Size 3 \$1M–\$3M; Size 4 >\$3M. Size classes for Swedish sample based on revenue in Kronor: Size 1 <15M; Size 2 15M–\$50M; Size 3 \$50M–\$150M; Size 4 >\$150M.
e. The Swedish results are not reported as the sample included only 12 firms less than 2 years old.

*Table 7.2b Sub-group tests of transitions to Poor (H2).*

| Sub-sample | Australia | | | | | | Sweden | | | | | |
|---|---|---|---|---|---|---|---|---|---|---|---|---|
| | 1-year transitions | | | 3-year transitions | | | 1-year transitions | | | 2-year transitions | | |
| | Initial year performance group | | | Initial year performance group | | | Initial year performance group | | | Initial year performance group | | |
| | Growth[a] | | Profit[a,b] | Growth[a] | | Profit[a,b] | Growth[a] | | Profit[a,b] | Growth[a] | | Profit[a,b] |
| Manufacturing | 26.8 | *** | 12.5 | 18.1 | n.s. | 12.4 | 35.3 | *** | 15.2 | 30.6 | n.s. | 21.4 |
| Prop./bus.serv | 34.2 | *** | 10.4 | 32.0 | ** | 11.8 | 25.9 | n.s. | 20.6 | 25.4 | n.s. | 22.6 |
| Retail[c] | 22.8 | *** | 7.1 | 20.0 | n.s. | 9.8 | 28.8 | n.s. | 16.9 | 20.8 | n.s. | 10.0 |
| Wholesale | 24.0 | *** | 10.2 | 26.4 | * | 14.1 | | N/A | | | N/A | |
| Other | 29.7 | *** | 12.1 | 25.0 | ** | 12.0 | 22.7 | n.s. | 17.2 | 23.7 | n.s. | 17.0 |
| Size 1[d] | 27.9 | *** | 10.0 | 21.1 | ** | 10.1 | 31.2 | n.s. | 29.2 | 28.6 | n.s. | 25.0 |
| Size 2[d] | 32.6 | *** | 11.1 | 28.8 | *** | 7.9 | 26.2 | ** | 12.9 | 25.0 | n.s. | 21.5 |
| Size 3[d] | 29.8 | *** | 16.0 | 20.5 | n.s. | 15.2 | 28.2 | * | 17.6 | 24.7 | * | 11.1 |
| Size 4[d] | 30.6 | *** | 8.8 | 22.5 | n.s. | 16.2 | 29.4 | ** | 9.6 | 28.3 | n.s. | 17.9 |
| <2 years[e] | 26.0 | ** | 11.5 | 21.7 | n.s. | 13.0 | | N/A | | | N/A | |
| 2–5 years | 28.6 | *** | 9.1 | 24.5 | ** | 11.1 | 14.3 | n.s. | 19.5 | 29.6 | * | 9.5 |
| 5–10 years | 25.8 | *** | 12.3 | 18.6 | n.s. | 15.0 | 27.5 | n.s. | 23.6 | 23.0 | n.s. | 21.4 |
| 10–20 years | 33.9 | *** | 11.1 | 27.7 | *** | 11.0 | 37.2 | ** | 17.1 | 28.0 | n.s. | 20.5 |
| >20 years | 32.7 | *** | 11.6 | 22.9 | ** | 10.4 | 27.1 | *** | 14.1 | 25.6 | n.s. | 19.5 |

*Notes:*

a. The table reports percentage of specified initial performance group that transition to Poor. Percentage signs are removed for readability.

b. Significance levels: *$p<0.05$; **$p<0.01$; ***$p<0.001$.

c. Retail and wholesale combined for Swedish sample.

d. Size classes for Australian sample based on revenue in Australian dollars: Size 1 <$300K; Size 2 $300K–$1M; Size 3 $1M–$3M; Size 4 >$3M. Size classes for Swedish sample based on revenue in Kronor: Size 1 <15M; Size2 15M–$50M; Size3 $50M–$150M; Size 4 >$150M.

e. The Swedish results are not reported as the sample included only 12 firms less than 2 years old.

further inspection of Tables 7.A1a–b reveals that no other category is as likely as the *Growth* firms to end up in the *Poor* group, apart from the firms that were already in the latter category. Conversely, no other group is as likely as the *Profit* firms to end up as *Stars*, except those that were *Stars* already in the first period. Moreover, not only the *Profit* firms but also those in the *Middle* category 'outperform' the *Growth* firms in every analysis as judged by a higher frequency of transitions to *Star* and a lower frequency of transitions to *Poor*.

All in all, these additional observations suggest a quite strong superiority for 'profitability first' over 'growth first' as a strategy to achieve high overall firm performance. This conclusion would be moderated if there were a strong tendency for *Growth* firms to transition to *Profit*, indicating that the firm now enjoys above-average profits based on a larger volume of business. Tables 7.A1a–b show that such transitions are unusual and about equally likely for firms originating in the *Poor* or *Middle* categories. Hence, there is no support in this data for the general soundness of the idea of 'growing profitable'.

### 6.4 Supplementary Analysis

Our supplementary analyses using multiple logistic regressions uniformly support the results and conclusions reported above. As an example, for the 1-year Australian transition 1995–96 to *Star* group, the dummy variable for *Profit* coefficient, B, was 0.93, significant at >0.001. *Profit* firms were estimated as 2.6 times more likely than *Growth* firms (exp B) to become *Star*. In all analyses our hypotheses were supported at 0.01 level or better. The control variables showed little evidence of significance.

We tested regression-to-the-mean effects by taking multiple measurements to reduce random error as suggested by Yudkin and Stratton (1996). Specifically, we averaged each firm's growth and profitability in years 1 and 2 to establish the initial performance groups, and similarly average years 3 and 4 to determine final groups. The resulting transition percentages and patterns were extremely close to the 1-year transitions. The average difference in the transition matrix percentages was only 1.6 per cent, and our hypotheses remained strongly supported. Hence we are confident that our findings are not substantially confounded by *r-t-m* effects.

To provide further confidence in our results over longer time periods we conducted supplementary analyses using survey-based measures of net profitability and sales growth relative to other firms in the industry over the last 3 years, reported in both 1997 and 2000 in the Swedish data. These were self-reported on a five-point scale: much worse, worse, equal, better and much better. These data allow us to perform similar analyses referring to an initial growth–profitability configuration calculated over 3 years as related to a subsequent growth–profitability configuration calculated over the following, non-overlapping 3-year period. These analyses also support our hypotheses (H1 and H2). This additional analysis demonstrates that the most important aspects of our results hold up for longer periods and for both self-report and accounting-based performance measures.

## 7. DISCUSSION

Our results suggest that high profitability, low-growth firms are more likely to become high profitability, high-growth firms compared with firms that start from a position of high growth and low profitability. Firms that grow at low levels of profitability are not very likely to achieve high profitability as a result of their expansion. Instead, these firms are considerably more likely to transition to the sub-sample of firms that is below average on both growth and profitability. That is, our results suggest that attempting to 'grow profitable' is a dubious strategy that often backfires. The scope of our empirical examination is restricted to small and medium-sized firms and we do not aspire to generalize beyond that context. As we have pointed out repeatedly there may also be special cases within that general context where our main results do not apply.

We argue that the results are consistent with an RBV-based interpretation. Before going for significant growth, firms need to develop some kind of competitive advantage based on the identification and successful exploitation of the uniqueness of their resource bundles. We hold that in a population of SMEs, superior profitability is likely to be indicative of having developed such an advantage. The underlying advantage and the financial resources generated through high profitability make it possible for firms in this situation to subsequently achieve sound and sustainable growth without having to sacrifice profitability. By contrast, empirical evidence from previous research suggests firms do not generally achieve high profitability merely as a result of their growth. When firms pursue high growth starting from low profitability it often indicates the growth must be achieved in head-to-head competition with equally attractive alternatives, which would make profitability deteriorate rather than improve. In addition, these low-profitability firms are unlikely to be able to finance strategies toward building valuable and hard-to-copy advantages while growing. Hence their growth would neither be sustainable nor lead to improved profitability.

The resource-based mechanism underlying the configurative growth–profitability relationships that we have uncovered has been assumed rather than assessed in a more direct manner. We have not directly tested the existence or nature of resource heterogeneity among the firms in our samples; nor have we examined if and how such heterogeneity is transformed into differences in value creation in the market place. This also means there may be other explanations for our results. In support of a Porterian view of strategy (Porter, 1985) it can be noted that Capon et al.'s (1990) meta-analysis indicates firms can enjoy a high growth/high profitability position by being in the 'right industry'. However, while investors can freely move from industry to industry, firms usually cannot, and this across-industry perspective is not relevant to our within-industry analysis. A within-industry application of the Porterian perspective reveals that our results are consistent with such a view as well: firms have high profitability because of a favorable market position. This strong position, further fueled by the lower cost of financing growth (because of high retained earnings), allow them to grow successfully. To a considerable extent this is the same explanation as what we have offered. As noted by Porter (1991), emphasis on resources or market positions are (at least for within-industry analysis; *our remark*) complementary rather than being each other's substitutes. Porter (1991:108) argues that 'resources are only meaningful in the context of performing certain activities to achieve certain competitive advantage.' Conversely, the advantage gained by a favorable market position is usually contingent on possession and use of unique resources.

The Porterian perspective emphasizes the environment more than does the RBV but shares its belief in strategic choice. Evolutionary (Aldrich, 1999) and in particular so ecological perspectives (Hannan and Freeman, 1977) emphasize the role of the environment even more and have less faith in deliberate strategic action. Applying such perspectives, our results would be explained by firms being partly or totally selected by the environment for certain performance configurations, with limited ability to do much about it. As we have not investigated the strategic intent of our firms our empirical analysis does not allow us to rule out that environmental forces played a major role in their performance configurations and changes thereof over time.

Importantly, however, we hold that most feasible interpretations of the underlying mechanisms would lead to the same cautioning against SMEs in general seeking growth when starting from a weak profitability position. We have not been able to find or construe a compelling theoretical argument that is consistent with our results as well as the literature we have reviewed and yet arrives at the conclusion that going for growth before ascertaining high levels of profitability is *usually* a sound route to enhanced value creation among SMEs. This gives us confidence in the conclusion that in most situations it is advantageous to let profitability (and the competitive advantage it reflects) be the horse that pulls the growth cart, rather than the other way around.

## 7.1 Implications

### 7.1.1 Implications for academics

The implications for academics span theorizing, research design and teaching. For *positive theory* the primary implication is that it is descriptively wrong to portray SME growth as 'success'. The exceptions are too frequent to accept this proposition even as an approximation. *Normative theory*, in its turn, should be more precise in specifying how and under which conditions (what type of) firm growth contributes to more terminal outcomes like company value (or stakeholder utility), either directly or via increased profits. Further, growth and profitability are logically not symmetric components for building company value. Although high profitability at low growth may be sub-optimal it is difficult to see how high profitability could be value-destroying. Above-average growth, on the other hand, certainly can be value-destroying when it entails the expansion of loss-generating activities. For example, Ramezani et al. (2002:65) conclude that 'Our empirical results indicate that maximizing growth does not maximize corporate profitability or shareholder value.' These logical and empirical arguments suggest that normative theory should not portray growth and profitability as equally important and/or mutually compensating aspects of firm performance.

For *research design* our results strongly imply caution with the use and interpretation of growth as a measure of firm performance. In the absence of direct measures of company value examining growth and profitability– jointly but as separate outcome dimensions appears to be a better practice, allowing more detailed insights and sounder overall interpretation. When non-availability of data forces a heavy reliance on growth as performance indicator, increasing the time period assessed would be a step in the right direction, as unsound growth is less likely to be sustained. Finally, the implications of our results for academics in their role as *educators* are that we should show more respect for owner–managers' reluctance to grow and accept external financing (cf above) and be less eager to advocate a growth ideology without suitable qualifiers.

### 7.1.2 Implications for practitioners

Our interpretation of the results suggests that rather than being very eager to expand, SME (owner–) managers should be eager to build and identify the uniqueness of their resource endowments and transform them into product/market offerings that enable them to generate sufficient profits. When they have proven an above-average ability to create and appropriate value in the small scale they have the basis for attaining sound, profitable growth that will be easier to manage and less of a threat to the long-term well-being of the firm and its owners. Managers who believe that in their particular context growth is necessary to become profitable should develop precise ideas concerning how growth can enhance profitability of their particular firm, rather than relying on a belief that growth more or less automatically improves profitability.

For external investors, our results imply that high growth in a low-profitability situation is a warning signal rather than an unambiguous sign of positive development. However, we must caution that our results do not necessarily apply to the much more select group of high-potential firms that VCs invest in. First-mover-advantage (FMA) reasoning suggests radical innovators who create entirely new markets play under different rules from the average SMEs. This said, the lack of proof that size leads to eventual profitability is something that has concerned the very researchers who coined the FMA concept: (Lieberman and Montgomery, 1998:1122). Similarly, in the specific context of disruptive innovation, Christensen and Raynor (2003) have argued forcefully for *patience for growth but impatience for profit*, a notion directly in line with our 'profits first' arguments and findings for SMEs more generally. In combination with our results, this provides sound reason for external investors to put more emphasis on establishing profitability through VRIO resources within their portfolio of firms, and having more patience for the growth that can eventually realize the full value of opportunities developed and pursued by these firms.

For policy-makers the main implication is that rather than pushing firms to grow, policies should be geared toward helping firms become more profitable. Our results demonstrate that firms that show high profitability often become growing firms that still enjoy high profitability. Therefore, if policies can help more firms become highly profitable – arguably an objective better aligned with the small firm owner–managers' own goals (Sapienza et al., 2003; Wiklund et al., 2003) – the problem of growth will take care of itself.

## 7.2 A Research Agenda

In this section we use Whetten's (1989) well-known discussion of the 'What? How? Why? Who? Where? and When?' of theoretical contributions as a device to organize our suggestions regarding how future research can reach further – conceptually and empirically – employing the same general approach that we have used in this chapter. Regarding the *What*, our contribution was to focus on the interplay between two dimensions of performance; growth and profitability, rather than trying to maximize explained variance in one of them. According to Whetten (1989) the main consideration regarding what factors to include in a theoretical model is *comprehensiveness* vs. *parsimony*. Our argument has tended toward the latter, so inclusion of additional factors may be advisable. While empirically hard to come by, we would advise the explicit inclusion of *company value* in future work, as this is arguably a more terminal goal than either growth or profitability. The study by Cho and Pucic (2005) illustrates the value of making this extension.

Further, while our use of 'growth' as a uni-dimensional concept may be a useful initial simplification future work might benefit from relaxing this assumption as it is well-known that 'growth' is a complex phenomenon (Davidsson et al., 2006). For example, recent work by Lockett et al. (2007) suggests that previous organic growth acts as a constraint on future organic growth while acquisitive growth may act as a catalyst for future organic growth. Similarly, Mishina et al. (2004) develop and find some support for differential hypotheses regarding product vs. market expansion with regard to the speed of growth. Thus, conceptually and empirically incorporating distinctions by type of growth in these terms may be important.

Refinement of the theoretical and empirical notion of 'profitability' may also be an important route for further development. In particular, the distinction between effects of profitability and access to capital should preferably be explicitly modeled and measured. We suggest future research examine whether – after controlling for the cost-of-capital effect – the effect of having retained earnings is different from the effect of externally infused capital in ways that accord with our hypotheses. If so our RBV-based interpretation would gain currency over explanations based on scale, experience or network externalities.

As regards the *How* our contribution was the suggestion and empirical substantiation of a contingent relationship between the two performance dimensions 'growth' and 'profitability' over time, essentially suggesting that a 'profit first' approach is usually superior to a 'growth first' strategy. The most important extension we can see here is empirical in the first instance, namely to test our hypotheses over longer periods of time in order to rule out that the main patterns are reversed. The latter result, suggesting that in a majority of cases high growth starting from low profitability represents sound investments in future value creation, would have profound repercussions on our theoretical argument.

A theoretical refinement regarding the nature of the relationships would be to consider the possibility of non-linear effects by speed of growth, as implied by Dierickx and Cool's (1989) notion of 'time-compression diseconomies'. Differences in curvature depending on initial performance configuration would then be of particular interest. Our argument under *How* above suggests moderation by type of growth is also likely. For empirical testing this development would require the identification of an analysis technique – preferably allowing also for multivariate modeling including control variables – that is more ideally suited to the task than either of the approaches – transition matrices and logistic regression – that we have applied.

The *Why* dimension is arguably the one which Whetten (1989) maintains is the most important for theoretical development. Our contribution in terms of *Why* is the provision of a resource-based rationale for the empirical patterns we observe. We have mentioned already (under *What* and *How*) that further refinement of this theoretical explanation may include consideration of differential effects by type of growth as well as contingent non-linearity by starting configuration as well as by type and speed of growth. However, the most important development regarding the suggested resource-based mechanism would be to move it to the *What* domain; that is, to explicitly include it in the empirical design. Our study shares with most published research referring to RBV a lack of explicit assessment of key variables (Arend, 2006) and in this regard future studies must aim to reach further.

This is challenging because mere quantification of generic resource stocks clearly does not suffice for adequate testing of RBV-based hypotheses. Although RBV is inherently hard to operationalize and 'perfect' research design impossible to attain, we agree with Arend (2006) that a promising way forward would be longitudinal survey studies designed specifically for the purpose. A longitudinal design is essential for assessing the dependent variable and establishing whether observed competitive advantages are sustained. A survey approach is the only conceivable way in which the VRIO qualities of resources could be directly assessed and meaningfully compared. Because of the breadth of the notion of 'resource' in RBV and the innumerable ways in which resources can provide advantages on their own or in combination the assessment of resources and their VRIO qualities can never be complete. However, a focus on narrowly defined empirical contexts may make the task somewhat manageable. 'North American architectural woodwork firms' (Baum and Locke, 2004) and 'law firms created in the Greater Vancouver Regional District 1990–98' (Cliff et al., 2006) may serve as inspirational exemplars. A narrow empirical context restricts the range of relevant resources to assess and makes it feasible for the investigators to attain deep enough knowledge for developing and applying high-quality measures adapted to the specific context. This would make for a much stronger test of theory than the use of diluted, 'one-size-fits-all measures' applied to a heterogeneous population of firms.

Whetten's (1989) discussion of the *Who, Where* and *When* concerns the boundary conditions of the theory. We have argued that our resource-based rationale may be more applicable to SMEs, but empirical testing in a large firm context might suggest it can be generalized also to that domain. Our results showed considerable stability across broad industry groupings; however our theorizing suggests the main results should not hold up in contexts where economies of scale; experience effects; FMAs or network externalities are pronounced. This may vary by country as well as by industry. For example, one might theorize that trading off current profit for growth may have a higher potential payoff in the dynamic context of 'transition economies' (Peng and Heath, 1996) or where the domestic market is larger and the venture capital industry better developed (such as in the US) compared to the empirical contexts we have investigated.

Further, we have in this chapter not discussed or tested the accuracy of our hypotheses under differing business cycle conditions. It is conceivable that the relative soundness of going for 'profit first' or 'growth first' varies with business cycle dynamics, especially in combination with consideration of type of growth. For example, Davidsson and Delmar (2000) found that 'high-growth firms' change the composition of their growth in such a way that acquisitions make up a larger share in downturns while organic growth comes more to the fore in upturns.

In conclusion, as regards the *Who, When* and *Where* we would advise that future studies a) develop precise theoretical ideas concerning how the growth–profitability dynamics might vary by context, and b) carefully select empirical settings – industries, countries and time periods – that clearly represent the theoretically defined contextual conditions. To the extent such an approach led to theoretically expected differential results our theoretical understanding would gain refinement and the boundary conditions of our argument would be better defined. To the extent the results are more or less uniform across contexts and in line with the original findings we have presented our theoretical explanation would gain generalizability.

## 8. CONCLUSION

Growth is often portrayed as evidence of business success. This tendency is particularly pronounced in the entrepreneurship research literature.

Our findings are a strong reason for practitioners and researchers alike to question a universal and uncritical growth ideology. Our results show that firms in the desirable state of high growth/high profitability are much more likely to originate from profitable firms with low growth than from growing firms with low profitability. Firms in the latter category are instead more likely to retreat to a low growth/low-profitability state. Hence, seeing profitability as the horse that pulls the growth cart seems in most cases to be a sounder worldview than the opposite. Obviously, not all will be prepared to accept this conclusion based on the theoretical rationales and empirical evidence we have provided. We see our results as an invitation and hopefully an inspiration for other researchers to verify or challenge them, and to provide additional input into how they should be interpreted.

## ACKNOWLEDGMENT

This manuscript has benefited from constructive feedback on drafts from Evan Douglas, Duane Ireland, Belinda Luuk, J. Peter Murmann, Pramodita Sharma, Dean Shepherd, the anonymous reviewers and several other colleagues who participated at presentations at the Academy of Management Meeting 2005; ESBRI, Stockholm; Jonkoping International Business School; Schloss Ringberg, and the University of New South Wales.

## NOTES

* Previously published as: Per Davidsson, Paul Steffens and Jason Fitzsimmons (2009), 'Growing profitable or growing from profits: putting the horse in front of the cart', *Journal of Business Venturing*, **24** (4), 388–406.

1. Refers to financial years ending in July of nominated year.
2. We also used several other methods of categorizing firms to ensure our results were not an artifact of the categorization schema. We categorized firms into four groups (no middle category), each group representing a quarter of Figure 7.1. We also repeated the analysis for quartiles defined over the entire population, rather than relative to industry. For each categorization schema, the substantive results presented in this chapter were supported.
3. Differences are due to several factors. The Swedish sample does not include firms with less than ten employees (the size category most likely to exit). Further, the richer survey data allowed firms who continued trading but changed registration number (and would otherwise have been considered to have exited) to be included and those who have not exited but trading abnormally (in process of liquidation, merger or reorganization) to be excluded.
4. Sample size of entire sample/5 sub-groups/25 cells (5 × 5 transition matrix). 1-year results aggregate multiple years to increase sample of transitions.

## REFERENCES


Aldrich, H.E., 1999. Organizations Evolving. Sage Publications, Newbury Park, CA.

Allen, M.P., Panian, S.K., Lotz, R.E., 1979. Managerial succession and organizational performance: a recalcitrant problem revisited. Administrative Science Quarterly 24 (2), 167–180.

Alvarez, S.A., Barney, J.B., 2004. Organizing rent generation and appropriation: toward a theory of the entrepreneurial firm. Journal of Business Venturing 19 (5), 621–635.

Amit, R., Zott, C., 2001. Value drivers in e-business. Strategic Management Journal 22, 493–520.

Arend, R.J., 2006. Tests of the resource-based view: do the empirics have any clothes? Strategic Organization 4 (4), 409–422.

Barney, J.B., 1991. Firm resources and sustained competitive advantage. Journal of Management 17 (1), 99–120.

Barney, J.B., 1997. Gaining and Sustaining Competitive Advantage. Addison Wesley, Menlo Park, CA.

Barney, J.B., Arikan, A.M., 2001. The resource-based view: origins and implications. In: Hitt, M.A., Freeman, R.E., Harrison, J.S. (Eds.), Handbook of Strategic Management. Blackwell, Oxford, MA, pp. 124–188.

Baum, J.R., Locke, E.A., 2004. The relationship of entrepreneurial traits, skill, and motivation to subsequent venture growth. Journal of Applied Psychology 89 (4), 587–598.

Baum, J.R., Wally, S., 2003. Strategic decision speed and firm performance. Strategic Management Journal 24, 1107–1129.

Besanko, D., Dranove, D., Shanley, M., 2004. Economics of strategy, 3 ed. Wiley, New York, NY.

Bourgeois, L.J., 1981. On the measurement of organizational slack. Academy of Management Review 6 (1), 29–39.

Brush, T.H., Bromiley, P., Hendrickx, M., 2000. The free cash flow hypothesis for sales growth and firm performance. Strategic Management Journal 21, 455–472.

Capon, N., Farley, J.U., Hoenig, S., 1990. Determinants of financial performance: a meta-analysis. Management Science 36 (10), 1143–1159.

Carpenter, R.E., Petersen, B.C., 2002. Is the growth of small firms constrained by internal finance? The Review of Economics and Statistics 84 (2), 298–309.

Chandler, G.N., Jansen, E., 1992. The founder's self-assessed competence and venture performance. Journal of Business Venturing 7 (3), 223–236.

Cho, H.-J., Pucic, V., 2005. Relationship between innovation, quality, growth, profitability and market value. Strategic Management Journal 26, 555–575.

Christensen, C.M., Raynor, M.E., 2003. The Innovator's Solution. Harvard Business School Press, Boston, MA.

Churchill, N.C., Mullins, J.W., 2001. How fast can your company afford to grow. Harvard Business Review 135–142 (May).

Cliff, J.E., Jennings, P.D., Greenwood, R., 2006. New to the game and questioning the rules: the experiences and beliefs of founders who start imitative versus innovative firms. Journal of Business Venturing 21, 633–663.

Coad, A., 2006. A closer look at serial growth rate correlation. LEM Working Paper Series 2006/29. Sant'Anna School of Advanced Studies, Pisa, Italy.

Cowling, M., 2004. The growth–profit nexus. Small Business Economics 22 (1), 1–9.
Cox, L.W., Camp, S.M., Ensley, M.D., 2002. Does it pay to grow? The impact of growth on profitability and wealth creation. Paper Presented at the Babson College/Kauffman Foundation Entrepreneurship Research Conference, Boulder, Colorado.
Davidsson, P., Delmar, F., 2000. Tillväxtföretag: var de finns, hur de växer, och vilka jobb de skapar. (Growth firms: where they are found, how they grow, and the jobs they create). Report No. 19, Nya Jobb & Företag (New Jobs & Companies). Rådet för Arbetslivsforskning, Stockholm.
Davidsson, P., Wiklund, J., 2000. Conceptual and empirical challenges in the study of firm growth. In: Sexton, D.L., Landström, H. (Eds.), The Blackwell Handbook of Entrepreneurship. Blackwell, Oxford, MA, pp. 26–44.
Davidsson, P., Delmar, F., Wiklund, J., 2002. Entrepreneurship as growth; growth as entrepreneurship. In: Hitt, M.A., Ireland, R.D., Camp, S.M., Sexton, D.L. (Eds.), Strategic Entrepreneurship: Creating a New Mindset. Blackwell, Oxford, MA, pp. 328–342.
Davidsson, P., Achtenhagen, L., Naldi, L., 2006. What do we know about small firm growth? In: Parker, S. (Ed.), Handbook of Entrepreneurship Research: The Live Cycle of Entrepreneurial Ventures, vol. 2. Springer, New York, NY, pp. 361–398.
Davidsson, P., Steffens, P., Fitzsimmons, J., 2007. Performance assessment in entrepreneurship research: is there a pro-growth bias? Manuscript Downloadable from http://eprints.qut.edu.au/archive/00012040.
Day, G.S., 1981. The product life cycle: analysis and applications issues. Journal of Marketing 45 (4), 60–67.
Delmar, F., 1997. Measuring growth: methodological considerations and empirical results. In: Donckels, R., Miettinen, A. (Eds.), Entrepreneurship and SME Research: On its Way to the Next Millennium. Ashgate, Aldershot, pp. 190–216.
Dierickx, I., Cool, K., 1989. Asset stock accumulation and sustainability of competitive advantage. Management Science 35 (12), 1504–1513.
Florin, J., Lubatkin, M., Schulze, W., 2003. A social capital model of high-growth ventures. Academy of Management Journal 46 (3), 374–384.
Geroski, P.A., 1995. What do we know about entry? International Journal of Industrial Organization 13, 421–440.
Gimeno, J., Folta, T.B., Cooper, A.C., Woo, C.Y., 1997. Survival of the fittest? Entrepreneurial human capital and the persistence of underperforming firms. Administrative Science Quarterly 42, 750–783.
Gupta, V., 1981. Minimum efficient scale as a determinant of concentration. The Manchester School of Economic and Social Studies 49, 153–164.
Hannan, M.T., Freeman, J.H., 1977. The population ecology of organizations. American Journal of Sociology 82 (5), 929–964.
Headd, B., 2003. Redefining business success: distinguishing between closure and failure. Small Business Economics 21 (1), 51–61.
Hill, C.W., 1988. Differentiation versus low cost or differentiation and low cost: a contingency framework. Academy of Management Review 13 (3), 401–412.
Hisrich, R.D., Peters, P.P., Shepherd, DA., 2005. Entrepreneurship, 6th ed. McGraw-Hill, New York, NJ.
Hoy, F., McDougall, P.P., Dsouza, D.E., 1992. Strategies and environments of

high growth firms. In: Sexton, D.L., Kasarda, J.D. (Eds.), The State of the Art of Entrepreneurship. PWS-Kent Publishing, Boston, MA, pp. 341–357.
Katz, M.L., Shapiro, C., 1985. Network externalities, competition, and compatibility. American Economic Review 75 (3), 424–440.
Kim, H., Hoskisson, R.E., Wan, W.P., 2004. Power dependence, diversification strategy, and performance in Keiretsu member firms. Strategic Management Journal 25, 613–636.
Kogut, B., Zander, U., 1992. Knowledge of the firm, combinative capabilities, and the replication of technology. Organization Science 3 (3), 383–397.
Kor, Y.Y., Mahoney, J.T., 2004. Edith Penrose's (1959) contributions to the resource-based view of strategic management. Journal of Management Studies 41 (1), 183–191.
Lieberman, M.B., Montgomery, D.B., 1988. First-mover advantages. Strategic Management Journal 9, 41–58.
Lieberman, M.B., Montgomery, C.A., 1998. First mover (dis)advantages: retrospective and link with the resource-based view. Strategic Management Journal 19, 1111–1125.
Lockett, A., Wiklund, J., Davidsson, P., 2007. Organic growth and acquisitive growth: re-examining and extending Penrose's theory. Paper Presented at the Academy of Management Meeting, Philadelphia, PA., August.
Markman, G.D., Gartner, W.B., 2002. Is extraordinary growth profitable? A study of Inc. 500 high-growth companies. Entrepreneurship Theory and Practice 27 (1), 65–75.
Marris, R., 1967. The Economic Theory of Managerial Capitalism. MacMillan, London, UK.
Mendelson, H., 2000. Organizational architecture and success in the information technology industry. Management Science 46 (4), 513–529.
Mishina, Y., Pollock, T.G., Porac, J.F., 2004. Are more resources always better for growth? Resource stickiness in market and product expansion. Strategic Management Journal 25 (12), 1179–1197.
Morrow, J.L.J., Sirmon, D.G., Hitt, M.A., 2007. Creating value in the face of declining performance: firm strategies and organizational recovery. Strategic Management Journal 28, 271–283.
Nicholls-Nixon, C., 2005. Rapid growth and high performance: the entrepreneur's "impossible dream?". Academy of Management Executive 19 (1), 77–89.
Peng, M.W., 2004. Outside directors and firm performance during institutional transition. Strategic Management Journal 25, 453–471.
Peng, M.W., Heath, P., 1996. The growth of the firm in planned economies in transition: institutions, organizations, and strategic choice. Academy of Management Review 21 (2), 492–528.
Penrose, E., 1959. The Theory of the Growth of the Firm. Oxford University Press, Oxford, UK.
Peteraf, M.A., Barney, J.B., 2003. Unraveling the resource-based tangle. Managerial and Decision Economics 24 (4), 309–323.
Porter, M.E., 1985. Competitive Advantage. The Free Press, New York, NY.
Porter, M.E., 1991. Towards a dynamic theory of strategy. Strategic Management Journal 12, 95–117.
Priem, R.M., Butler, J.E., 2001. Is the resource-based "view" a useful perspective for strategic management research? Academy of Management Review 26 (1), 22–40.

Ramezani, C.A., Soenen, L., Jung, A., 2002. Growth, corporate profitability, and value creation. Financial Analysts Journal 62 (6), 56–67.
Reid, G., 1995. Early life-cycle behavior of micro firms in Scotland. Small Business Economics 7, 89–95.
Roper, S., 1999. Modelling small business growth and profitability. Small Business Economics 13 (3), 235–252.
Sapienza, H.J., Korsgaard, M.A., Forbes, D.P., (2003). The self-determination motive and entrepreneurs' choice of financing. In: Katz, J., Shepherd, DA. (Eds.), Cognitive Approaches to Entrepreneurship Research. Advances in Entrepreneurship, Firm Emergence, and Growth (vol. 6, pp. 107–140). Elsevier/JAI Press, Oxford, UK.
Scott, J., Pascoe, G., 1986. Beyond firm and industry effects on profitability in imperfect markets. Review of Economics and Statistics 68, 284–292.
Sexton, D.L., Smilor, R.W., 1997. Growth strategies. In: Sexton, D.L., Smilor, R.W. (Eds.), Entrepreneurship 2000. Upstart, Chcago, IL, pp. 97–98.
Sexton, D.L., Pricer, R.W., Nenide, B., 2000. Measuring performance in high-growth firms. Paper Presented at the Babson College/Kauffman Foundation Entrepreneurship Research Conference, Babson College, MA.
Siegfried, J.J., Evans, L.B., 1994. Empirical studies of entry and exit: a survey of the evidence. Review of Industrial Organization 9 (2), 121–155.
Sirmon, D.G., Hitt, M.A., Ireland, R.D., 2007. Managing firm resources in dynamic environments to create value: looking inside the black box. Academy of Management Journal 32 (1), 273–292.
Stern, C.W., Stalk Jr., G. (Eds.), 1998. Perspectives on Strategy from the Boston Consulting Group. Wiley, New York, NY.
Stevenson, H.H., Jarillo, J.C., 1990. A paradigm of entrepreneurship: entrepreneurial management. Strategic Management Journal 11, 17–27.
Storey, D.J., 1994. Understanding the Small Business Sector. Routledge, London, UK.
Teece, D.J., Pisano, G., Shuen, A., 1997. Dynamic capabilities and strategic management. Strategic Management Journal 18 (7), 509–533.
Weinzimmer, L.G., Nystrom, P.C., Freeman, S.J., 1998. Measuring organizational growth: issues, consequences and guidelines. Journal of Management 24 (2), 235–262.
Wernerfelt, B., 1984. A resource based view of the firm. Strategic Management Journal 5 (2), 171–180.
Whetten, D.A., 1989. What constitutes a theoretical contribution? Academy of Management Review, 14 (4), 490–495.
Wickham, P.A., 2004. Strategic Entrepreneurship, 3rd ed. Pearson, Harlow, UK.
Wiklund, J., Davidsson, P., Delmar, F., 2003. What do they think and feel about growth? An expectancy-value approach to small business managers' attitudes towards growth. Entrepreneurship Theory and Practice 27 (3), 247–269.
Winn, J., 2004. Making it big. Entrepreneurship Theory and Practice 28 (1), 487–503.
Yudkin, P.L., Stratton, I.M., 1996. How to deal with regression to the mean in intervention studies. Lancet 347, 241–243.
Zahra, S., Sapienza, H., Davidsson, P., 2006. Entrepreneurship and dynamic capabilities: a review, model and research agenda. Journal of Management Studies 25 (4), 917–955.

# APPENDIX A

*Table 7.A.1a Combined 1-year and 3-year transition percentages for Australia.*

| | | Initial performance group | | | | | |
|---|---|---|---|---|---|---|---|
| | | Poor[a] | Middle[a] | Growth[a] | Profit[a] | Star[a] | Total |
| 1st row: aggregated 1-year transitions | | ($n$ = 2057) | ($n$ = 2964) | ($n$ = 1588) | ($n$ = 1499) | ($n$ = 2379) | ($n$ = 10469) |
| 2nd row: 1995–1998 transition | | ($n$ = 619) | ($n$ = 930) | ($n$ = 605) | ($n$ = 486) | ($n$ = 848) | ($n$ = 3488) |
| Final performance group | Exit | 9.1 | 4.2 | 6.4 | 7.8 | 4.6 | 6.1 |
| | | 31.5 | 17.2 | 26.3 | 28.4 | 20.5 | 23.7 |
| | Poor | 30.8 | 17.9 | **30.3** | **11.0** | 12.9 | 20.2 |
| | | 21.6 | 14.8 | **23.1** | **12.1** | 12.7 | 16.6 |
| | Middle | 21.4 | 45.9 | 22.8 | 19.7 | 19.8 | 27.9 |
| | | 20.4 | 37.4 | 18.8 | 15.6 | 19.0 | 23.7 |
| | Growth | 21.2 | 9.5 | 22.6 | 5.6 | 6.2 | 12.5 |
| | | 11.5 | 8.9 | 15.0 | 3.9 | 9.0 | 9.7 |
| | Profit | 6.0 | 8.8 | 6.2 | 26.3 | 25.4 | 14.1 |
| | | 5.8 | 10.6 | 6.4 | 23.5 | 15.7 | 12.1 |
| | Star | 11.5 | 13.6 | **11.6** | **29.6** | 31.1 | 19.2 |
| | | 9.2 | 11.0 | **10.2** | **16.5** | 23.1 | 14.2 |
| | Total | 100.0 | 100.0 | 100.0 | 100.0 | 100.0 | 100.0 |
| | | 100.0 | 100.0 | 100.0 | 100.0 | 100.0 | 100.0 |

*Note:* a. The table reports percentage of specified (initial state) performance group that transitions to specified (final state) performance group. The three 1-year transitions (1995–1996, 1996–1997 and 1997–1998) are aggregated. Percentage signs are removed for readability. Transitions related to the hypotheses are in bold font.

*Table 7.A.1b  Combined 1-year and 2-year transition percentages for Sweden.*

| | | Initial performance group | | | | | |
|---|---|---|---|---|---|---|---|
| | | Poor[a] | Middle[a] | Growth[a] | Profit[a] | Star[a] | Total |
| 1st row: aggregated 1-year transitions | | ($n$ = 590) | ($n$ = 846) | ($n$ = 434) | ($n$ = 407) | ($n$ = 675) | ($n$ = 2952) |
| 2nd row: 1998–2000 transition | | ($n$ = 295) | ($n$ = 429) | ($n$ = 226) | ($n$ = 195) | ($n$ = 337) | ($n$ = 1482) |
| Final performance group | Exit | 2.4 | 0.1 | 0.5 | 2.2 | 0.4 | 2.0 |
| | | 3.7 | 0.7 | 1.8 | 3.6 | 1.2 | 2.0 |
| | Poor | 21.6 | 14.8 | 23.1 | 12.1 | 12.7 | 16.6 |
| | | 33.6 | 20.0 | 26.1 | 19.0 | 11.0 | 21.5 |
| | Middle | 20.4 | 37.4 | 18.8 | 15.6 | 19.0 | 23.7 |
| | | 22.7 | 42.2 | 24.3 | 19.5 | 22.6 | 28.1 |
| | Growth | 11.5 | 8.9 | 15.0 | 3.9 | 9.0 | 9.7 |
| | | 21.0 | 7.5 | 24.8 | 7.2 | 9.5 | 13.2 |
| | Profit | 5.8 | 10.6 | 6.4 | 23.5 | 15.7 | 12.1 |
| | | 8.1 | 10.5 | 11.5 | 17.9 | 15.4 | 12.3 |
| | Star | 9.2 | 11.0 | **10.2** | **16.5** | 23.1 | 14.2 |
| | | 10.8 | 19.1 | **11.5** | **32.8** | 40.4 | 22.9 |
| | Total | 100.0 | 100.0 | 100.0 | 100.0 | 100.0 | 100.0 |
| | | 100.0 | 100.0 | 100.0 | 100.0 | 100.0 | 100.0 |

*Notes:* a. The table reports percentage of specified (initial state) performance group that transitions to specified (final state) performance group. The two 1-year transitions (1998–1999 and 1999–2000) are aggregated. Percentage signs are removed for readability. Transitions related to the hypotheses are in bold font.

# 8. Performance configurations over time: implications for growth- and profit-oriented strategies*

**Paul Steffens, Per Davidsson and Jason Fitzsimmons**[1]

## INTRODUCTION

Entrepreneurship research and practice places emphasis on company growth as a measure of entrepreneurial success. In many cases, there has been a tendency to give growth a very central role, with some researchers even seeing growth as the very essence of entrepreneurship (Cole, 1949; Sexton, 1997; Stevenson & Gumpert, 1991). A large number of empirical studies of the performance of young and/or small firms use growth as the dependent variable (see reviews by Ardishvili, Cardozo, Harmon, & Vadakath, 1998; Delmar, 1997; Wiklund, 1998). By contrast, the two most prominent views of strategic management – strategic positioning (Porter, 1980) and the resource-based view (Barney, 1991; Wernerfelt, 1984) – are both concerned with achieving competitive advantage and regard achieving economic rents and profitability relative to other competitors as the central measures of firm performance. Strategic entrepreneurship integrates these two perspectives and is simultaneously concerned with opportunity seeking and advantage seeking (Hitt, Ireland, Camp, & Sexton, 2002; Ireland, Hitt, & Sirmon, 2003). Consequently, both company growth and relative profitability are together relevant measures of firm performance in the domain of strategic entrepreneurship.

Yet firms' growth and profitability interact and evolve in complex, multidimensional ways that are not well understood. Growth, whether measured as sales or employee growth, is not always good news for a firm. As originally proposed by Penrose (1959), growth is not just a change in size, but also a process that may lead to challenges during managerial transitions (Arbaugh & Camp, 2000). Moreover, despite several theories (and perhaps popular notions) suggesting that growth leads to higher profitability, a review of the empirical evidence (see Davidsson, Steffens,

& Fitzsimmons, 2008, 2009) demonstrates there is no substantial, universal, and positive intraindustry relationship of that nature. While these two dimensions of performance sometimes move together, there are frequent other instances where the growth–profit relationship is either neutral or negative.

Indeed it is argued that younger, smaller firms are relatively more effective in identifying opportunities than their larger, established counterparts, yet they are less effective in developing competitive advantages to an appropriate value from those opportunities (Ireland et al., 2003). As such, the character of the relationship between a firm's profitability and growth can be expected to change over time as the firm develops.

This chapter extends earlier work by contextualizing the study of growth and profitability in two important ways. First, we use a configuration approach that simultaneously but separately considers both a firm's growth and profitability, rather than considering only one of them or lumping them together in a performance index. Second, we explore differences in growth-profitability dynamics across companies of different ages. We integrate multiple theoretical perspectives to suggest different ways the profitability–growth configuration of firms might evolve over time. To explore difference by company age we make one fundamental assumption, namely that younger firms tend to be stronger in 'discovery ability' while older firms tend to have better 'exploitation ability.' This point will be elaborated further later. Despite our emphasis on configuration and development over time, we do not position ourselves in the 'stages-of-development' tradition (e.g., Churchill & Lewis, 1983; Greiner, 1972; Kazanjian & Drazin, 1989). That literature tends to assume complex and often deterministic configurations of founder and firm characteristics that evolve and change along an unspecified timeline. By contrast, we focus on configurations of performance outcomes for companies in different, specified age groups and suggest or explore probabilistic rather than deterministic relationships between age and performance configurations.

In order to make the type of contributions that we intend, we employ a non-standard approach in this chapter. We do not derive ideas from one theory about a few variables' effects on a single performance variable. Instead, we use input from multiple theories and perform empirical analyses in order to make sense of the dynamic interplay between two aspects of firm performance: growth and profitability. To help explain the lack of consistent findings in previous research, we first review the principal theoretical arguments concerning the growth–profit relationship and then integrate these insights into a model outlining alternative performance pathways by company age. This means that we provide a broader theoretical context for our analysis than what is strictly needed for a narrow interpretation of our results. Empirically, we examine the prevalence of companies proceeding along these possible pathways using a large, longitudinal data set of Australian firms. We classify firms into configurations based on their profitability and growth relative to other firms in their industry and examine changes over time. The analysis consists of hypothesis testing, where we find sufficient theoretical justification. Where competing theoretical arguments occur, we employ a strong inference approach (Balkundi & Harrison, 2006; Platt, 1964) to examine whether either of the two alternative hypotheses can be rejected. For the purposes of this chapter, we refer to sales growth as our measure of growth; in the empirical work, profitability refers to return on assets (ROA).

It is our hope that the reader will accept these deviations from standard approaches in order to reach the goal of achieving a fresh, new perspective – and possibly the opening up of a new type of research stream – towards research on the role of growth and profitability in business performance.

## A MODEL OF GROWTH-PROFITABILITY DYNAMICS BY FIRM AGE

A number of theoretical perspectives provide insights into the development of growth and profitability by firm age. Figure 8.1 integrates many of these perspectives into a model of growth-profitability development. The model has five elements. First, there are the central performance variables – growth (VII) and profitability (VI). By the former we mean sales growth. Our preferred conceptualization of profitability would perhaps be surplus from operations above what is needed for maintaining operations on the same level; in the empirical analysis we will use the most suitable measure available, which is ROA. Second, we introduce our focal 'moderator,' firm age (I). While focusing on age, we note that company age is frequently correlated with size and ownership, and that empirical and theoretical works do not always distinguish between the three (cf. notions of 'the entrepreneurial firm,' often loosely referring to a young, small, and owner-managed entity). Third, we introduce four boxes denoting key company characteristics that are assumed to vary with age; characteristics that are also important elements of our theoretical analysis. Older firms tend to have larger resource stocks (II) leading to a superior 'exploitation ability' (IV), whereas younger firms tend to have advantages in terms of flexibility (III) and superior 'discovery ability' (V). We have adopted the terms 'discovery' and 'exploitation' from Shane and Venkataraman (2000). By 'discovery ability' we mean the ability of principal decision makers to conceive and/or recognize new, innovative

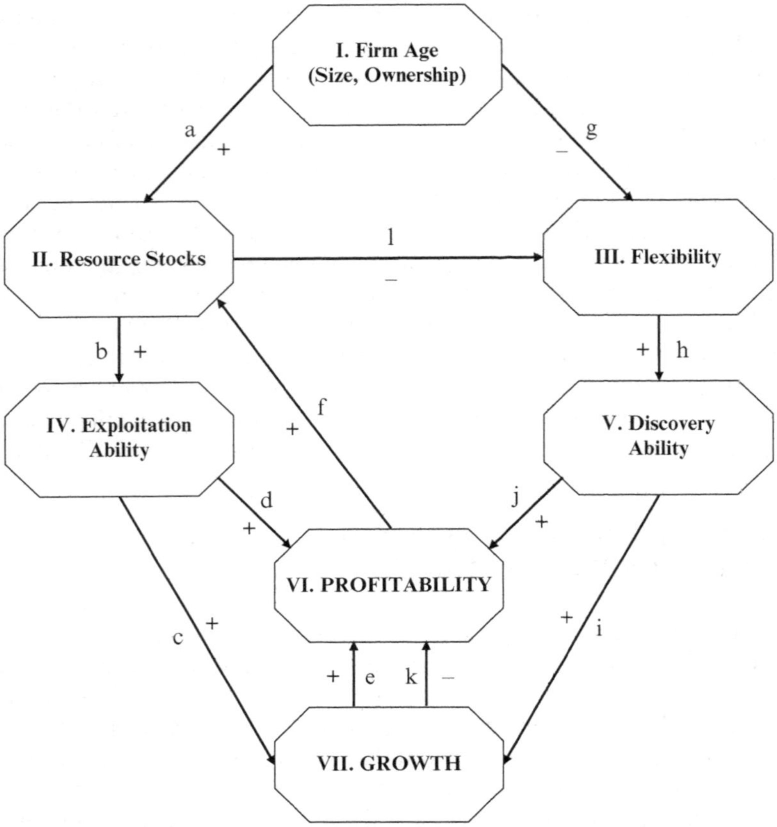


*Figure 8.1 An integrated model of growth–profitability dynamics*

ideas and bring them to the market quickly and at low development cost. Exploitation ability refers to the ability to realize the full potential of given ideas. This entails scaling them up and maximizing margins by employing efficient processes. Sometimes exploitation refers to the ability to bring an idea to market even when development costs and/or process complexity present insurmountable barriers for inexperienced and resource-starved organizations (cf. Arrow, 1983).

Strategic entrepreneurship, which makes sustained high growth and profitability possible, requires both discovery and exploitation ability. Firms with discovery ability alone are likely to be able to generate (short-lived) growth (i) and possibly profitability (j), but they are unlikely to be able to sustain either in the face of competition without effective exploitation. Conversely, exploitation ability alone most directly leads to profitability (d) as firms efficiently exploit current opportunities in the market. It may also result in short-term growth (c) when firms imitate opportunities identified by other companies that are unable to fully exploit those opportunities. However, when the potential of current opportunities is already exhausted, excellent exploitation ability alone cannot sustain continued high growth.

An underlying, empirically informed and fundamental assumption of the model is that the age of firms (alongside size and ownership characteristics) influences their growth–profitability dynamics. In short, the model holds that young firms suffer from resource disadvantages (a) and may therefore need infusion of external resources (e.g., through debt funding or venture capital) in order to expand and realize the full potential of their business ideas (b → c). Alternatively, when their discovery ability yields low cost/high value innovation, they may – seemingly against the odds – be able to build such resources themselves based on retained earnings (g → h → j → f). By contrast, old, large corporations are comparatively resource-rich, well-oiled machineries that are well suited for realizing the full commercial potential (a → b → d) of given, competence-enhancing business opportunities. But, they may have a problem when it comes to fast and/or radical changes and therefore need infusion (e.g., through acquisition) of ideas developed elsewhere in order to make continued growth possible (g; l). Using this model as the basis, we can elaborate on its implications for a greater understanding of the dynamics of firm growth and profitability. In further discussion, we explicate the model's underpinnings in theories and previous empirical work.

## Liabilities of Newness (and Smallness) – Limited Resource Stocks and Exploitation Ability

Young firms are associated with liabilities of newness (Aldrich & Auster, 1986; Stinchcombe, 1965). This is a fundamental reason why the virtuous sequence of growth leading to increased profitability, which in turn leads to further growth as indicated by the sequence e → f → b → c in Figure 8.1, is not always realized. Many young companies lack the most fundamental resource of all: a product with some inherent potential for profitable growth. The vast majority of new entrants are imitators in mature industries (Aldrich, 1999; Reynolds & Miller, 1992; Storey, 1994). In that context, older and larger firms may enjoy prohibitive cost advantages based on more efficient routines (Nelson & Winter, 1982), as represented by the sequence a → b → d in Figure 8.1. Reviews of the relevant empirical literature suggest that young firms/entrants/'entrepreneurial firms,' while often having a positive impact on industry efficiency through innovation, tend to have lower productivity with regard to the production of given products or services (Geroski, 1995; van Praag and Versloot, 2007). As a result, the majority of new firms never embark on a growth trajectory, nor do they reach any spectacular level of profitability.

The growth-limiting potential of resource deficiencies (along path [a] in Figure 8.1) ensures that, in many cases, a process of resource-driven growth – sequence b → c – does not take place. Perhaps the most frequently discussed resource deficiency is lack of financial capital. Indeed, empirical research supports the notion that initial capitalization is important for early growth (Cooper, Gimeno-Gascon, & Woo, 1994; Dahlqvist, Davidsson, & Wiklund, 2000). While young and small entrants may have the capacity for the fast action needed to secure first-mover advantages, the growth deemed necessary may still not be achieved unless there is also an infusion of external venture capital (Manigart & Sapienza, 2000). Penrose (1959) pointed out the importance of managerial capacity. Thornhill and Amit (2003) identified that new companies were most likely to fail due to deficiencies in managerial knowledge and financial management. Transition and stages-of-development models typically discuss the importance of both managerial and financial resources (Arbaugh & Camp, 2000; Churchill & Lewis, 1983; Greiner, 1972; Hambrick & Crozier, 1985; Kazanjian & Drazin, 1989). Furthermore, liabilities of newness (and smallness) also imply a lack of other types of 'resources' that are necessary for successful exploitation of the inherent potential in the firm's products. For example, ecological and institutional perspectives point out the lack of legitimacy, which makes it difficult for young firms to gain market acceptance (DiMaggio & Powell, 1983; Suchman, 1995). All in all, young firms suffer from an 'exploitation ability' disadvantage, i.e., limitations to their ability to scale up effectively and efficiently, so as to generate as much of the inherent potential in a *given* idea as possible.

Company founders may also refrain from pursuing perceived growth opportunities (Davidsson, 1989; Wiklund, Davidsson, & Delmar, 2003). This may be because of a focus on affordable loss rather than profit maximization (Sarasvathy, 2001). Such a lack of willingness to grow is, to a certain extent, related to the expected profitability of growth. For example, Davidsson found that 40 per cent of the owner-managers in his sample did not expect a doubling in company size to lead to a greater personal income stream, thus effectively removing one of the most important reasons for pursuing expansion. The willingness-to-grow issue may also be related to resources. It is a well-established fact that business owner-managers prefer financing through retained earnings to debt, and debt to external equity. This, which is referred to as (external) 'control aversion' and 'the pecking order hypothesis' in previous research (Cressy & Olofsson, 1996; Sapienza, Korsgaard, & Forbes, 2003), explains why the owners of young firms may forego growth opportunities.

### Advantages of Newness (and Smallness) – Flexibility and Discovery Ability

When growth and profitability are positively associated it may sometimes be because profitability drives growth rather than the other way round. This is what Sexton, Pricer, and Nenide (2000; cited in Markman and Gartner, 2002) concluded based on their analysis of a very large sample of U.S. firms. In terms of Figure 8.1, the virtuous sequence in this case starts with profitability (retained earnings), which provides the firm with the necessary resources for successful further growth, i.e., the f → b → c → e sequence. But what leads to high profitability in the first place? From Schumpeter (1934) and onwards, a recurring theme in the literature has been that young, entrepreneurial firms – while burdened by liabilities of smallness and newness – also have specific advantages that make them flexible and allow them to bring innovations to the market faster and at lower cost than large, incumbent firms are able to. This has been discussed under various labels such as 'incumbent inertia' (Lieberman & Montgomery, 1988), 'core rigidities' (Leonard-Barton, 1992), 'liabilities of obsolescence' (Henderson, 1999), and a range of other terms (Mosakowski, 2002; Tushman & Anderson, 1986). Thornhill and Amit (2003) found that while new firms were more likely to fail because of deficiencies in managerial knowledge and financial management, older firms were more likely to fail as a result of an inability to strategically adapt to changes in their external environment. Moreover, resources often bring with them resource dependencies that lock firms into particular directions (Pfeffer & Salancik, 1978).

Hence there may be a 'pure' age effect that makes it harder to come up with new ideas the more organizations are familiar with their current routines (path [g] in Figure 8.1), as well as an indirect effect suggesting that the management of large resource stocks itself directs attention away from new opportunities (path [l]). Arrow (1983) shows through theoretical analysis why small organizations – with their simple structures, closeness between market and decision-making power, and speed of implementation – often outperform large organizations in innovative activity as long as development costs are not prohibitive. Empirical results reported by Acs and Audretsch (1990) largely confirm Arrow's observations. The importance of structural smallness is also emphasized by authors like Hambrick and Crozier (1985), Stevenson and Jarillo (1986) and Stevenson and Gumpert (1991) who all take the tendency towards inertia by older and larger firms as their starting point (path [l] in Figure 8.1). While these authors focus more on size than on age, the two dimensions tend to be highly correlated and at least parts of the effect are likely attributable to age rather than size. For example, young, small firms are likely to have more flexible routines than old firms of the same size. Hansen (1992) made an explicit attempt to separate age and size effects and found that both tended to be negatively associated with innovative output. Another empirical result that supports the notion that young firms excel in 'discovery' whereas old firms specialize in 'exploitation' is the demonstration by Davidsson and Delmar (2006) that among 'high-growth firms,' the expansion of the young firms is almost entirely organic – i.e., presumably based on products developed in-house – whereas old firms grow predominantly through the acquisition of other firms.

While not all young firms are innovative or ever embark on a growth trajectory, some of them do come up with innovations that create much more value for the customers than what is needed to cover the costs of development, production, and distribution. This creates a potential for high profitability (g → h → j). The fact that a firm shows high profitability indicates that it has created a product that has a considerable value above cost for its customers, and that the firm has developed a business model that allows it to appropriate a substantial share of that value (cf. Alvarez & Barney, 2004; Amit & Zott, 2001). Subsequent growth can therefore be based on retained earnings, which coincides with widespread founder-owner preferences as discussed above. All in all, the economic effects would lead to a positive association between profitability and growth where – at least in the first instance – profitability drives growth rather than the other way around.

**Reasons for Growth Leading to Profitability**

This brings us to the lower part of the model in Figure 8.1. As indicated by arrow (e) several theories assume a positive effect of growth on profitability. Basic economic theory, assuming inverted U-shape cost curves, implies that firms grow until they have reached the size where average variable cost is at a minimum (Besanko, Dranove, & Shanley, 2004; Mansfield, 1979). Up to that point, increased size would, *ceteris paribus*, be associated with improved profitability; assuming rational behavior, the firm would refrain from expanding beyond that point. Applying the more realistic assumption of L-shaped cost curves (Mansfield, pp. 203–206), the same rationally behaving firm would grow to at least the size where the cost curve flattens out, which corresponds to the idea of *minimum efficient scale* in industrial economics (Gupta, 1981). In short, basic economic theory suggests that, at least up to a certain size, *economies of scale* ensure that growth is rewarded with increased profitability.

The strategy school emanating from the Boston Consulting Group (BCG) in the 1970s holds that *experience curve effects* (Amit, 1986; Stern & Stalk, 1998) pertaining to all aspects of the firm's operations can be the basis of cost advantages. According to this theory, the firm with the highest cumulative volume in any industry will have the lowest unit costs. This implies a positive relationship between market share and profitability (Buzzell, Gale, & Sultan, 1975). Based on evidence of a positive relationship also existing between industry market growth and profitability (Capon, Farley, & Hoenig, 1990), the recipe for profitable growth becomes to launch and secure large market shares for new products in high-growth markets. In a similar vein, and more closely related to the reality of young firms, literature on first-mover advantages (Lieberman & Montgomery, 1988) suggests that new entrants can create a lasting advantage by rapidly building a dominant position for themselves in the market. That is, size – and hence growth – is important for gaining high profitability.

Finally, in markets with substantial network externalities (Katz & Shapiro, 1985) the value of the offering is contingent on the number of users, so above-average growth should therefore lead to (a potential for) higher profitability. All in all, these theoretical perspectives demonstrate that a range of situations exists in which rational firms can gain profitability advantages from growth and hence enter a virtuous cycle where growth leads to resource accumulation that facilitates further, profitable growth (e → f → b → c, etc.).

## Reasons Why Growth May Not Lead to Profitability

While there are strong, theoretical reasons to believe that firm growth can lead to profitability, a review of the empirical literature does not support a substantial, universal, and positive intra-industry relationship of that nature (Davidsson et al., 2008, 2009). In part, this may be due to non-rational behavior. Economic theory suggests that growth beyond the minimum efficient scale is associated with unknown or reversed effects on profitability. Likewise, according to the BCG strategy school, pursuing a growth strategy in low-growth markets or attempting to increase sales for products with low initial market share is no guaranteed recipe for financial success. Thus, a low empirical correlation between growth and profitability is not that difficult to explain when actors do not have perfect foresight or are not perfectly rational for other reasons. Furthermore, assuming that the firm is not a powerless price-taker, one would, from a rationalistic theory-based view analogous to the monopolist model in microeconomics

(Mansfield, 1979), expect the firm to first service the most profitable customers or market segments. It would then continue to expand into gradually less and less profitable segments. Thus, unless the expansion into less attractive segments is accompanied by scale and/or experience effects, the firm's level of profitability would eventually fall as a result of expansion, even if total profits continue to increase.

Moreover, contemporary strategy theory tends to be based on much less of a pro-growth ideology than the theories reviewed earlier. Theoretical arguments from the resource- and knowledge-based views of the firm (Barney, 1991; Kogut & Zander, 1992) clearly suggest that growth would only enhance profitability if the expansion is aligned with the firm's unique resources and competences. Empirical research on expansion through more and less related diversification (Christensen & Montgomery, 1981; Montgomery, 1982; Rumelt, 1974) and mergers and acquisitions (Jensen & Ruback, 1983; Ravenscraft & Scherer, 1987) also underlines that many forms of expansion have questionable influence on financial performance. Furthermore, as pointed out by Penrose (1959), growth is not just a change in size, but also a process. In this process, the company may encounter an array of managerial challenges that reduce or reverse any profitability-enhancing effects of increased size. This is recognized in the literature on stages-of-development and managerial transitions (e.g., Churchill & Lewis, 1983; Greiner, 1972; Hambrick & Crozier, 1985; Kazanjian & Drazin, 1989). Although the resulting, larger firm may eventually reach higher profitability than the original, smaller firm, this line of reasoning suggests that in the process of reaching this state, there may be a trade-off between growth and profitability (Cowling, 2004; Marris, 1967; Zahra, 1991). In short, the positive effect of growth on profitability depicted by arrow (e) in Figure 8.1 demonstrates the potential that is reachable for rational actors in particular situations. Actual outcomes may be neutral or even negative, as indicated by arrow (k).

Some theorists and empirical works have highlighted the possibility of a negative influence of growth on profitability. For example, it has been noted that firms that do not possess any particular advantages and operate in stable markets are unlikely to achieve growth without employing profitability-reducing tactics such as price cutting and/or costly promotion (Peteraf & Barney, 2003). Even when based on value-creating innovation, growth does not always lead to a positive profit-growth trajectory. This may be the case when firms grow rapidly and therefore are subjected to time compression diseconomies, as discussed by Dierickx and Cool (1989). This is in line with the negative correlation between growth and profit that Markman and Gartner (2002) found in their study of rapidly growing firms. Apart from increased costs of resources, it is a well-known fact that rapid growth sometimes goes haywire and ends in financial disaster (Hambrick & Crozier, 1985). This is indicated by arrows (i; k) in Figure 8.1. This is the case when a firm innovates and as a result faces drastically increased demand, but fails to turn this into high profitability. This suggests that, at least in some cases, rapid growth should be taken as a sign not of astonishing success, but as indication that while the firm is evidently creating value for its customers (hence the very high demand), it is failing to appropriate enough of that value in order to secure its own survival.

## PERFORMANCE CONFIGURATIONS AND AGE-RELATED HYPOTHESES REGARDING THEIR PREVALENCE AND DEVELOPMENT

The previous section drew on multiple theoretical perspectives to develop a framework for exploring important differences in the growth–profitability trajectories between younger and older firms (Figure 8.1). In this section, we use the model to develop some hypotheses regarding differences expected between young and old firms.

Individual companies will navigate their course around this model in different ways. The different pathways traveled by the individual firms will depend on a range of factors, including their initial endowment of resources and discovery ability, their strategic behavior in terms of growth and profit orientation at any point in time, and industry conditions and trends. Since we are interested in strategic behavior of young firms as they develop, we investigate the impact on mid-term performance (3–5 years). Shorter-term performance (say 1 year) is likely to reflect outcomes of tactical decisions and fails to account for strategic investments for future performance gains, yet longer-term performance (>5 years) is likely to exceed the strategic horizon for young firms.

To assist in our understanding of these alternative pathways and develop some formal hypotheses based on the model, we introduce a profitability–growth configuration schema (Figure 8.2) adapted from Davidsson et al. (2009). The earlier model paints a picture of the relationship between growth and profitability that is theoretically complex and multifaceted. Clearly, if we are interested in the strategic development of young firms, both growth and profitability are important components of company performance. This also implies that a composite index that adds growth and profitability is in some way unsatisfactory for understanding the different profit–growth paths firms might undertake, along with their consequences. For example, high profitability at low growth

| | | Growth Tri-tile | | |
|---|---|---|---|---|
| | | 1st | 2nd | 3rd |
| Profitability Tri-tile | 1st | Poor | Low Profit | Growth Focus |
| | 2nd | Low Growth | Middle | High Growth |
| | 3rd | Profit Focus | High Profit | Star |

*Figure 8.2 Profitability–growth configurations*

is qualitatively very different from low profitability at high growth, or having medium performance in both dimensions.

Hence, firms were classified into a 3 × 3 configuration based on the two performance dimensions – sales growth and profitability. Specifically, firms were classified into three equal percentile groups (tri-tiles) for both sales growth and ROA. Since our focus is the behavior of individual firms, both dimensions are considered relative to other firms in their industry so as to eliminate the impact of external industry conditions. They were then divided into the nine growth–profitability configurations as shown in Figure 8.2. In preliminary work, we also used several other methods of categorizing firms to ensure our results were not an artifact of the categorization schema.

These nine profitability–growth configurations can also be considered to vary according to three levels of profitability–growth performance groups and three profit–growth orientations. We define the three upper-left configurations in Figure 8.2 (poor, low profit, and low growth) as Weak Performance; the three diagonal configurations (middle, profit focus, and growth focus) as Medium Performance, and the three lower-right configurations (star, high growth, and high profit) as Strong Performance.

Similarly, the configurations indicate whether the firm is orientated towards profitability or growth. We define high growth, growth focus, and low profit as growth-orientated firms; the diagonal configurations, poor, middle, and star as neutral orientations; and high profit, profit focus, and low growth as profit-orientated firms. Although this collapsing of performance categories is not optimal from the perspective of keeping growth and profitability separated, it simplifies the reporting of findings and is also necessitated by the need for statistical power.

A firm's initial endowment of resources and discovery ability will determine their initial performance with respect to growth and profitability. Subsequently, their performance will be determined by how they navigate pathways around Figure 8.1. We examine possible differences in development pathways for younger and older firms. In essence, our model suggests a tendency towards discovery advantages for young firms, and exploitation advantages for older firms.

We do not have data that allows us to test all implications of the theoretical model. However, in the following we will develop directional hypotheses concerning some aspects of the model where theory and data allow. For other features of the model, the theoretical input allows alternative predictions; we will then develop pairs of competing hypotheses that are tested using a strong inference approach.

First we consider young firms: as discussed in the previous section, there are sound theoretical reasons to suggest that, based on their strong discovery ability, young firms may be able to exploit the virtuous sequence of growth, represented by g → h → j → f → b → c → e in Figure 8.1, with potential for further f → b → c → e iterations if they operate in markets where there are significant scale or first-mover advantages, experience effects, or network externalities. In the latter situation the sequence g → h → i → e → f → b → c (and so on) is another possible – albeit riskier – route to simultaneous high performance in terms of profitability and growth. Older firms, while having become well-oiled machineries with respect to their original products should, according to our reasoning, have exploited their most profitable growth opportunities already. Further growth may not be unprofitable, but below the average profitability of the industry. In addition, at mature age they face a difficulty coming up with new, high margin opportunities (arrow i). Consequently, we argue that:

*Hypothesis 1:* *A greater proportion of younger firms than older firms will belong to the Star profitability–growth configuration.*

Using similar arguments, even if young firms do not have a sufficiently high discovery ability that enables them to simultaneously achieve above-average growth and profitability, we expect most would have at least sufficient discovery ability to avoid the lowest performance category (Poor). Moreover, due to their shorter existence, they have, on average, been subject to fewer external shocks that may lead to poor performance. This leads to the mirroring hypothesis:

*Hypothesis 2a:* *A smaller proportion of younger firms than older firms will belong to the Poor profitability–growth configuration.*

However, despite young firms as a category being overrepresented as innovators, research suggests that a majority of all start-ups are imitative ventures in mature industries (Aldrich, 1999). Such firms would likely struggle with scale and legitimacy disadvantages, suggesting they perform comparatively poorly. In addition, it may be argued that while the resources and experience of older firms may not help them excel simultaneously on both performance dimensions, these resources should give them some protection against performing poorly on both at the same time. This alternative reasoning suggests the opposite to hypothesis 2a:

*Hypothesis 2b:* *Asmaller proportion of older firms than younger firms will belong to the poor profitability–growth configuration.*

We have noted that in spite of strong theoretical arguments for growth leading to profitability (among rational actors), the empirical evidence is mixed at best. This suggests that many firms may be pursuing misguided growth, i.e., expanding in the absence of any real advantage by price cutting and/or incurring above-average marketing costs (c → k); that includes expansion based on expensive external capital, or associated by managerial and organizational cost increases in excess of what the market opportunities can pay for (other variants of c → k), or growth based on value-creating innovations while failing to appropriate a large enough share of the value created (i → k). It seems logical that because of their relative inexperience, young firms with limited exploitation ability would be more likely to pursue such dubious growth strategies, e.g., indiscriminately pursue growth opportunities whether they are very profitable or not. This would also concur with psychological research on expertise, which suggests that increased experience is accompanied by an improved ability to adapt the decision making to the characteristics of the task at hand (see Gustafsson [2004] for an application to a somewhat analogous entrepreneurship problem). Hence, we expect young firms to be overrepresented not only as Stars (hypothesis 1), but to be overrepresented among growth-orientated firms regardless of the level of profitability. Based on this we suggest the following hypothesis:

*Hypothesis 3:* *Relative to older firms, a higher proportion of younger firms will belong to the high growth and growth focus configurations.*

We now turn our attention to how firms maintain or improve their performance over time. The model proposes that older firms are better placed to utilize their exploitation advantages in order to initiate the virtuous sequence of growth and profitability represented by e → f → b → c in Figure 8.1. If we first consider the top-performing Stars, the model suggests these firms are successfully enacting this virtuous sequence. This is in contrast to young Star firms who are more likely to have yielded short-term profitability and growth through discovery advantages. We propose that older Star firms already enacting this virtuous sequence of growth and profitability are more likely to stay above average on both performance dimensions simultaneously than are younger Star firms who would first need to enter this virtuous sequence of growth and profitability. This line of thought is also supported by (unexpected) results reported by Durand and Coeurderoy (2001). They found that the pioneers that were able to sustain high performance (in their analysis of an index combining growth and profitability) were those aiming for cost leadership rather than innovative differentiation. Arguably, the former is indicative of superior exploitation ability while the latter indicates superior discovery ability. The overall implication is that 'Stardom' may be difficult to sustain based on discovery ability alone. Hence:

*Hypothesis 4: Older firms with a Star configuration are more likely than their younger counterparts to maintain their Star profitability–growth configuration over time.*

A further important distinction is the sequence in which firms develop profitability and growth. As argued above, companies might either (1) first develop growth as a mechanism to generate future profitability (e.g., economies of scale, first-mover advantages), or (2) first develop profitability as a mechanism to generate future growth (resource building). Furthermore, we know that too-rapid growth may lead to performance problems. Indeed, Davidsson et al. (2009) suggest that first developing profitability as a mechanism to generate future growth is more likely to result in more preferable future growth–profitability configurations. This said, our model suggests variations by firm age are likely to exist for each of the above mechanisms of growth–profitability dynamics. As we have already discussed, as companies get older there is a tendency for their discovery ability to decrease (g; 1 → h) and their exploitation ability to improve (a → b). Hence, we might expect younger firms to create initial first-mover advantages, yet older firms to be better placed to exploit these fully. Younger firms are likely to have a greater potential to improve profitability through economies of scale not yet utilized, yet older firms are more likely to be able to effectively exploit scale economies where they exist. Older firms are also more likely to be able to achieve growth through the exploitation of resources they already possess; i.e., at low marginal cost. Finally, the influence of age on the possible negative outcomes of rapid growth is unclear. In summary, while we expect age to have an impact on the likely profitability–growth dynamics of firms, the overall nature of this impact is unclear. Consequently, we present the following competing hypotheses:

*Hypothesis 5a: Younger firms adopting a profit orientation are more likely to have stronger future profitability–growth performance than older firms with the same orientation.*

*Hypothesis 5b: Older firms adopting a profit orientation are more likely to have stronger future profitability–growth performance than younger firms with the same orientation.*

*Hypothesis 6a: Younger firms adopting a growth orientation are more likely to have stronger future profitability–growth performance than older firms with the same orientation.*

*Hypothesis 6b: Older firms adopting a growth orientation are more likely to have stronger future profitability–growth performance than younger firms with the same orientation.*

In addition to testing the directional and competitive hypotheses we will also explore other patterns for which we found the theoretical input a priori too weak to suggest hypotheses in either direction.

## METHOD

### Data Source

We use a large, longitudinal secondary data source to test our hypotheses. The data is sourced from the Business Longitudinal Survey (BLS) conducted by the Australian Bureau of Statistics (ABS) from 1995 to 1998. This refers to financial years ending in July of the nominated year. The sampling frame was all employing businesses on the ABS business register employing fewer than 200 employees, excluding primary industries other than mining, government enterprises, utilities, and public services (education, health, libraries, museums, parks, etc.). The survey was designed to provide information on the growth and financial performance of Australian employing businesses and to identify selected economic and structural characteristics of these firms. A large cross-sectional survey of businesses was conducted in 1995. These businesses were randomly sampled from industry stratifications. Surveys were sent to approximately 13,000 businesses resulting in 8,375 responses (a response rate of 63.7

per cent). Of these, 1,949 firms reported no sales in either 1994 or 1995, resulting in a sample of 6,426 companies for our cross-sectional analyses. A subset of approximately half of these firms (4,508) was selected to be included in an ongoing panel. Completed responses were collected from between 84 per cent and 90 per cent of the panel for the surveys in 1996 to 1998. Of the 3,488 businesses that completed all years of the survey, 826 businesses exited. This resulted in a final sample size of 2,662 for our longitudinal analyses. Exiting businesses are an ambiguous category including not only financial failures but also voluntary closures and lucrative outright sales of firms to new owners (Gimeno, Folta, Cooper, & Woo, 1997; Headd, 2003). Consequently, we could not interpret these firms as a pure failure category. We note that failure to be able to classify this category correctly introduces a potential for survivor bias in our results; preliminary analysis revealed that the percentage of exits from the nine profit–growth configurations did not vary in a systematic way that indicates either higher or lower performing firms are more likely to exit. As such, it is highly unlikely that survivor bias has a substantial impact on our results.

**Measures**

The performance measures used in this chapter are sales growth and pretax ROA. Sales growth was preferred over employment growth, based on the emerging consensus that for most purposes, sales is the more relevant growth indicator (Davidsson & Wiklund, 2000; Delmar, 1997; Delmar, Davidsson, & Gartner, 2003; Hoy, McDougall, & Dsouza, 1992; Weinzimmer, Nystrom, & Freeman, 1998). The specific formula used was the change in sales from the previous year as a percentage of the sales in the previous year. Sales data for 2 years prior to the first survey year were reported. Hence, sales growth could be calculated in the first year (1995).

ROA was calculated as the net profit (operating profit or loss before tax and extraordinary items) as a percentage of total assets in each year. ROA was the preferred measure because it measures economic rents before accounting for taxes and extraordinary items. As such, it is the purest singular measure of the operational performance of the firm. Also, it is normalized relative to the capital employed.

We are concerned with how companies shape their performance with respect to growth and profitability and not external or industry effects on performance. It is well established that firm performance along these dimensions varies according to both firm-specific and industry effects (McGahan & Porter, 1997, 2002; Rumelt, 1991). To reduce the confounding influence of both industry effects and annual fluctuations, we use performance measures relative to other firms within the same industry for that year. Both growth and profitability measures were adjusted for industry variations by subtracting the industry median. Although some previous research suggests to subtract industry means (Waring, 1996), we chose to use industry medians in order not to give undue weight to a few extreme cases that are not typical of firms in that industry. The ANZSIC industry divisions were used as the basis for industry groupings. In preliminary work, we also used the subdivisions (two-digit code). The substantive results of the chapter were not affected.

### Analyses

Hypotheses 1–3 are tested using cross-sectional analyses, allowing the use of the larger first-year data set ($N = 6{,}426$). We compare the frequencies of young (≤8 years) and old (≥9 years) firms in the nine profitability–growth configurations.

Hypotheses 4–6 are tested using a longitudinal analysis of firm profitability-growth configurations over time. We examine the likelihood of transitions from one profitability–growth configuration to others over the four years of our longitudinal data set ($N = 2{,}662$). For hypothesis 4 we use a probit analysis to test whether young or old Star firms in year 1 are more likely to remain Star firms in year 4. To test hypotheses 5 and 6 we use an ordered probit analysis (Borooah, 2002) to examine the likelihood that a company will have weak, medium, or strong profitability–growth performance (as defined above based on Figure 8.2). Specifically, we examine the differences between young and old firms with a growth orientation or profit orientation (again defined above; based on Figure 8.2). We control for firm size and industry.

For those hypotheses where we have competing theoretical arguments (hypothesis 2, hypothesis 5, and hypothesis 6), we adopt a strong inference approach (Balkundi & Harrison, 2006; Platt, 1964) to examine whether either of the two alternative hypotheses can be statistically rejected.

## RESULTS

### Static Analysis of Profitability–Growth Configurations

Table 8.1 indicates the proportion of firms in each of our nine profitability-growth configurations for young (≤8 years) and old (≥9 years) firms. Tests of the differences in proportions of young and old firms belonging to each configuration are reported. Although our formal hypotheses 1–3 only refer to some of the differences, we report all significance tests as a heuris-

*Table 8.1 Proportion of Firms in Each Growth–Profitability Configuration: Variation by Firm Age*

| Performance configuration | Firm age† | |
|---|---|---|
| | ≤8 years (%) ($N = 2883$) | ≥9 years (%) ($N = 3543$) |
| Poor | 12.5 | 14.1* |
| Low profit | 9.1 | 9.3 |
| Low growth | 8.0 | 12.5*** |
| Growth focus | 11.5*** | 7.2 |
| Profit focus | 9.9 | 8.7 |
| Middle | 9.7 | 15.2*** |
| High growth | 11.4 | 10.5 |
| High profit | 11.3 | 11.3 |
| Star | 16.6%*** | 11.2% |
| Total | 100.0% | 100.0% |

*Notes:*
† For each age category, percentage of firms in each performance group is reported.
* $p < .05$; ** $p < .01$; *** $p < .001$ based on 1-tailed z test of column (age categories) proportions.

tic device in order to avoid over-interpretation of explorative results that have a high probability of being the result of random sampling error.

We find support for hypothesis 1, that a greater proportion of younger firms will belong to the Star configuration. The proportion of young firms that are in the Star configuration (16.6 per cent) is substantially higher than the proportion of old firms (11.2 per cent). The results support hypothesis 2a, that a smaller proportion of younger firms are found in the poor configuration, and thus do not support hypothesis 2b. The 12.5 per cent of young firms that are in the poor configuration is significantly lower than the proportion of poor old firms (14.1 per cent) in that configuration, although the difference is not impressively large in magnitude.

Some caution is advisable in interpreting this result because of potential survivor bias. Previous research suggests that young firms are less likely to survive than are older firms (Geroski, 1995), and are therefore more likely to exit the population and escape analysis. Therefore, the under-representation in the Poor configuration does not necessarily reflect a positive characteristic of young firms. Although preliminary analysis reveals no clear tendency in our data for young firms (and especially the low performers among them) to exit the population more frequently than older firms, the ambiguity of the exit category leaves room for alternative interpretations.

*Table 8.2 Probit Model of* Year-4 *Star Configuration for Firms Having Star Configuration in Year 1*

| Variable | Coefficient (Std. Error) | |
|---|---|---|
| Asymmetric age effect | | |
| Young firm | −.241 | (.118) |
| Old firm | 0† | |
| Intercepts | | |
| Year 4 not Star | .939*** | (.174) |
| Year 4 Star | 0† | |
| Control variables | | |
| Sales year 1 | −1.03E–5* | (.6E–5) |
| Manufacturing | .256 | (.183) |
| Other | .031 | (.211) |
| Property & business services | .335 | (.215) |
| Retail | −.291 | (.282) |
| Wholesale | 0† | |
| Model statistics | | |
| Chi-squared (d.f. =6) | 19.1** | |
| Nagelkerke R-squared | .047 | |

*Notes:*
† Redundant dummy variable.
* $p < .05$; ** $p < .01$;*** $p < .001$; 1-tailed tests.

The results provide mixed support for hypothesis 3 that as a result of their combination of high-discovery ability and low exploitation ability young firms should be overrepresented in high-growth configurations regardless of the level of profitability. We have already commented on the overrepresentation among Stars (16.6 per cent vs. 11.2 per cent). The difference in representation is more marked in the Growth Focus configuration (highest tri-tile in growth; lowest tri-tile in profitability). With 11.5 per cent in that configuration, the young firms have a representation that approaches twice that of old firms (7.2 per cent). However, while the proportion of young high-growth firms is slightly higher than old high-growth firms (11.4 per cent vs. 10.5 per cent) the difference is not statistically significant.

## Longitudinal Analyses of Profitability–Growth Configuration Transitions

Table 8.2 displays the results of a probit analysis predicting the likelihood that firms with Star profitability–growth configuration in year 1 remain in that configuration in year 4. We find support for hypothesis 4 that older firms are more likely to remain in the Star category than younger firms.

*Table 8.3 Ordered Probit Model of Year 4 Profitability–Growth Performance*

| Variable | Coefficient | (Std. Error) |
|---|---|---|
| Asymmetric age effect or profit-growth orientation | | |
| Growth orientation – young firm | −.306*** | (.079) |
| Neutral orientation – young firm | −.234** | (.078) |
| Profit orientation – young firm | −.004 | (.091) |
| Growth orientation – old firm | −.473** * | (.074) |
| Neutral orientation – old firm | −.201** | (.068) |
| Profit orientation – old firm | 0† | |
| Year 1 profitability–growth performance | | |
| Weak performance | −.469*** | (.055) |
| Medium performance | −.259*** | (.053) |
| Strong performance | 0† | |
| Intercepts | | |
| Year 4 weak performance | −.788*** | (.080) |
| Year 4 medium performance | −.019 | (.079) |
| Year 4 strong performance | 0† | |
| Control variables | | |
| Sales year 1 | −1.6E–7 | (1.0E–6) |
| Manufacturing | .020 | (.065) |
| Other | −.034 | (.076) |
| Property & business services | −.032 | (.082) |
| Retail | −.012 | (.088) |
| Wholesale | 0† | |
| Test of asymmetric age effects | | |
| Growth orientation: young vs. old firm | .166* | (.079) |
| Neutral orientation: young vs. old firm | −.033 | (.073) |
| Profit orientation: young vs. old firm | −.004 | (.091) |
| Model statistics | | |
| Chi-squared (d.f. = 18) | 120.4*** | |
| Nagelkerke R-squared | .050 | |

*Notes:*
† Redundant dummy variable.
* $p < .05$; ** $p < .01$; *** $p < .001$; 1-tailed tests.

The results of an ordered probit analysis to predict the likelihood of profitability–growth performance (weak, medium or strong) in year 4 are shown in Table 8.3. We see that for both young and old firms, the performance of firms that have a profit orientation in year 1 is higher than for both neutral and growth-orientated firms. In terms of our two sets of competing hypotheses, we find support for hypothesis 6a in favor of hypothesis

6b that younger firms with a growth orientation are more likely than older firms with the same orientation to have stronger future performance. However, we found no evidence in favor of either hypothesis 5a or hypothesis 5b – both young and old firms with a profit orientation appear to have equally strong future performance.

**The Early Years**

Having examined our hypotheses, we now turn to a holistic examination of all results by age class, including explorative examination of nonhypothesized relationships. In regards to the prevalence of profit–growth configurations (Table 8.1), a conventional analysis and interpretation indicates that young firms perform well. They are overrepresented as Stars and among firms showing above-average growth in general, and underrepresented among those showing low performance on both dimensions. However, other aspects of our results for performance configurations over time give reason to question whether the high performance of most of these young 'Stars' really reflect successful, strategic entrepreneurship. The results for hypothesis 4 demonstrate that young Star firms are less likely than their older counterparts to maintain that status. Furthermore, the results for hypothesis 3 indicate that young firms' overrepresentation among Stars reflects an overrepresentation among growth-orientated firms in general. In our dynamic analysis for young firms, those with a Profit or Neutral orientation perform better over time than those with a growth orientation. This all suggests that 'Star' status among young firms is often indicative not of competent management, but of luck (that will be short lived) on the part of some firms who show the same – perhaps indiscriminate – heightened tendency among inexperienced firms to go for growth opportunities regardless of whether they will be highly profitable or not. That is, young firms' overrepresentation among high-growth firms suggests that many of them may be pursuing misguided growth. Regarding young firms' underrepresentation among the Poor, it cannot be ruled out that their underrepresentation is due, in part, to a higher instance of (negative) exits from the population.

So, we see that young firms have a heightened tendency to be high-growth firms. However, unless these high-growth firms have above-average profitability, three years later they tend to perform poorly compared to other firms. With the possible exception of those already in the Star configuration, the best future performers among younger firms are those with high profit, but only low or medium growth. Overall, the results suggest high growth early on is associated with considerable risk.

**Older Firms**

With respect to the pattern of profitability–growth configurations amongst older firms, Table 8.1 illustrates they are more likely to have the medium or weak performance configurations of low growth and poor. This is not necessarily a sign of underperformance; it may also be a result of the ability to survive longer at low levels of performance than younger firms are capable of.

Like for young firms, the dynamic analysis (Table 8.3) indicates that the strong performance configurations in year 1 unsurprisingly perform better than those in the medium performance configurations, who in turn perform better than those in weak performance configurations. If we compare the three orientations for old firms, profit orientation performs stronger than neutral orientation, which in turn performs stronger than a growth orientation.

In all, old firms are overrepresented in low-performance configurations; however, to some extent this may be because of a superior ability to survive in such a state. Older firms with a Star configuration are more likely to sustain simultaneous high performance on both growth and profitability than younger firms in the Star category are. Other than Stars, the best future performing older firms are those with a profit orientation.

## DISCUSSION AND CONCLUSIONS

Strategic entrepreneurship has been conceived as simultaneous opportunity and advantage seeking. Successful firms will achieve high performance both in sales growth and profitability. In this chapter we investigated the growth and profitability dynamics of younger vs. older firms. First, we integrated numerous theoretical perspectives into a model of growth–profitability evolution, and used this to develop several hypotheses. We then tested these hypotheses and provided a further exploratory empirical examination of the dynamics of young firms using profitability–growth configurations to simultaneously examine their profitability and growth performance over time. Where we had competing hypotheses, we adopted a strong inference approach.

We now offer an interpretation of these results in light of the theoretical model developed in Figure 8.1. While many of them never really take off in the medium term, a substantial number of young firms are able to convert discovery ability advantages into short-lived high growth. There is, however, considerable diversity of young firms with respect to converting this discovery ability into profitability. Those firms that are more successful at initially generating growth than profitability on average tend to perform relatively poorly in the medium term. Thus, there appears to be a high prevalence of *misguided growth* among young firms. As a consequence, negative performance outcomes are common. This may indicate that liabilities of newness are particularly strong for firms that pursue a growth orientation.

For older firms, we again saw that a profit orientation, rather than growth orientation, was more likely to lead to future success. This we interpret as two phenomena jointly impacting a large proportion of firms. The virtuous sequence of growth leading to profits that build resources that in turn facilitate the pursuit of further growth remains an important factor. But for older firms, the inflexibility associated with age and resources (g; l) becomes more prevalent. If such firms try to 'force' further growth without newness, it is likely to occur in less profitable geographical markets or market segments than those originally served, or the growth is achieved via price cuts or increased marketing expenditure. In either case, growth would not be associated with high profitability. Other research suggests older firms are likely to turn to acquisitions if they want to continue to grow at all (Davidsson & Delmar, 2006). This would allow them to introduce innovations they now find difficult to develop in-house. Because we cannot distinguish between organic and acquisitive growth in our empirical analysis, we cannot be certain that this is the case in our sample. However, we can speculate that a substantial proportion of older firms that strive for growth suffer the negative consequences of growth because of the type of unforeseen integration costs that are highlighted in research on mergers and acquisitions among large corporations (e.g., Ravenscraft & Scherer, 1987).

For researchers of strategic entrepreneurship, the chapter highlights that growth–profitability of young firms remains a fertile area for research if one moves away from the simplistic analysis of factors assumed to universally lead to growth, and the assumption that growth unambiguously reflects good company performance. Because of the complexity of the phenomenon, a more contextualized and critical approach is advisable. For example, a conventional analysis on our data would likely lead to the conclusion that young firms generally perform well. Our analysis led to a more nuanced interpretation. Although young firms seem to find growth opportunities – something we ascribe to superior discovery ability – they do not seem very good at selecting among them and/or realizing/appropriating their full inherent value. Our theoretical model illustrates that many theoretical perspectives inform our understanding. While our empirical work provides some evidence of development pathways that can be interpreted with this model, the empirical work presented here remains just a first step. We hope this chapter will inspire other researchers to both investigate the scope of generalizability of our empirical findings, and to test other elements of the theoretical model that we did not directly examine. Specifically, research that simultaneously measures resource stocks and exploitation ability together with flexibility and discovery ability, how these change as firms develop, and how they affect performance outcomes over time would contribute substantially to the domain of strategic entrepreneurship.

For practitioners and educators, we hope that our findings will be useful in helping chart pathways that will maximize chances of longer-term success for young firms. Overall, we suggest that some caution is warranted before embarking on a high-growth strategy if starting from a state of low profitability. For young firms in particular, we suggest that inexperience may lead to over-optimistic growth expectations in the face of liabilities of newness. This has a clear implication for policy makers. Many policy initiatives are geared towards helping or incentivizing firms to grow, presumably in the hope that they will generate more employment and tax revenue. Especially when geared towards young firms, our results indicate that such policies can backfire, and that policies aimed at increasing the profitability of young firms are more advisable.

We also suggest older firms may find it hard to grow profitably because the most profitable growth opportunities for their original offering have already been utilized, and new opportunities may have to be gained through acquisitions that may be associated with costly integration processes. Regardless of age, however, we would recommend firms considering embarking on substantial growth pathways to carefully consider the negative impact such growth may bring, and carefully articulate the mechanisms by which they expect growth to lead to future success.

## NOTES

* Previously published as: Paul Steffens, Per Davidsson and Jason Fitzsimmons (2009), 'Performance configurations over time: implications for growth- and profit-oriented strategies', *Entrepreneurship Theory and Practice*, **33** (1), January, 125–48
1. We would like to thank the two anonymous reviewers and editor for their insightful comments that contributed substantially to the development of this chapter. We would also like to thank attendees of the Max Planck Ringberg Conference on Strategic Entrepreneurship, and Academy of Management meeting, Atlanta, August 2006, for their helpful suggestions. We are grateful for the data that was made available for the study by the Australian Bureau of Statistics.

# REFERENCES


Acs, Z.J. & Audretsch, D.B. (1990). *Innovation and small firms*. Cambridge, MA: MIT Press.

Aldrich, H.E. (1999). *Organizations evolving*. Newbury Park, CA: Sage Publications.

Aldrich, H.E. & Auster, E.R. (1986). Even dwarfs started small: Liabilities of age and size and their strategic implications. In B.M. Staw & L.L. Cummings (Eds.), *Research in organizational behavior* (Vol. 8, pp. 165–198). Greenwich, CT: JAI Press.

Alvarez, S.A. & Barney, J.B. (2004). Organizing rent generation and appropriation: Toward a theory of the entrepreneurial firm. *Journal of Business Venturing, 19*(5), 621–635.

Amit, R. (1986). Cost leadership and experience curves. *Strategic Management Journal, 7*, 281–292.

Amit, R. & Zott, C. (2001). Value drivers in e-business. *Strategic Management Journal, 22*, 493–520.

Arbaugh, J.B. & Camp, S.M. (2000). Managing growth transitions: Theoretical perspectives and research directions. In D.L. Sexton & H. Landström (Eds.), *The Blackwell handbook of entrepreneurship* (pp. 308– 328). Oxford, UK: Blackwell.

Ardishvili, A., Cardozo, S., Harmon, S., & Vadakath, S. (1998, May 21–23). *Towards a theory of new venture growth*. Paper presented at the 1998 Babson Entrepreneurship Research Conference, Ghent, Belgium.

Arrow, K. (1983). Innovation in small and large firms. In J. Ronen (Ed.), *Entrepreneurship* (pp. 15–28). Lexington, MA: Lexington Books.

Balkundi, P. & Harrison, D.A. (2006). Ties, leaders, and time in teams: Strong inference about network structure's effects on team viability and performance. *Academy of Management Journal, 49*(1), 49–68.

Barney, J. (1991). Firm resources and sustained competitive advantage. *Journal of Management, 17*(1), 99–120.

Besanko, D., Dranove, D., & Shanley, M. (2004). *Economics of strategy* (3rd ed.). New York: Wiley.

Borooah, V.K. (2002). *Logit and probit: Ordered and multinominal models*. Thousand Oaks, CA: Sage.

Buzzell, R.D., Gale, B.T., & Sultan, R.G.M. (1975). Market share: A key to profitability. *Harvard Business Review, 53*, 97–106.

Capon, N., Farley, J.U., & Hoenig, S. (1990). Determinants of financial performance: A meta-analysis. *Management Science, 36*(10), 1143–1159.

Christensen, H.K. & Montgomery, C.A. (1981). Corporate economic performance: Diversification strategy versus market structure. *Strategic Management Journal, 2*, 327–343.

Churchill, C. & Lewis, V.L. (1983). The five stages of small business growth. *Harvard Business Review, 61*(3), 30–50.

Cole, A.H. (1949). Entrepreneurship and entrepreneurial history. In *Change and the Entrepreneur*, prepared by the Research Center in Entrepreneurial History (pp. 85–107). Cambridge, MA: Harvard University Press.

Cooper, A.C., Gimeno-Gascon, F.J., & Woo, C.Y. (1994). Initial human and financial capital as predictors of new venture performance. *Journal of Business Venturing, 9*(5), 371–395.

Cowling, M. (2004). The growth-profit nexus. *Small Business Economics, 22*(1), 1–9.
Cressy, R. & Olofsson, C. (1996). The financial conditions for Swedish SMEs: Survey and research agenda. *Small Business Economics, 9*, 179–194.
Dahlqvist, J., Davidsson, P., & Wiklund, J. (2000). Initial conditions as predictors of new venture performance: A replication and extension of the Cooper et al. study. *Enterprise and Innovation Management Studies, 1*(1), 1–17.
Davidsson, P. (1989). Entrepreneurship – and after? A study of growth willingness in small firms. *Journal of Business Venturing, 4*(3), 211–226.
Davidsson, P. & Delmar, F. (2006). High-growth firms and their contribution to employment: The case of Sweden 1987–96. In P. Davidsson, F. Delmar, & J. Wiklund (Eds.), *Entrepreneurship and the growth of firms*. Cheltenham, UK and Northampton, MA, USA: Edward Elgar.
Davidsson, P. & Wiklund, J. (2000). Conceptual and empirical challenges in the study of firm growth. In D. Sexton & H. Landström (Eds.), *The Blackwell handbook of entrepreneurship* (pp. 26–44). Oxford, MA: Blackwell Business.
Davidsson, P., Steffens, P.R., & Fitzsimmons, J.R. (2008). Performance assessment in entrepreneurship and management research: Is there a pro-growth bias? Queensland University of Technology ePrints, http:// eprints.qut.edu.au/archive/00012040/
Davidsson, P., Steffens, P., & Fitzsimmons, J. (2009). Growing profitable or growing from profits: putting the horse in front of the cart? *Journal of Business Venturing, 24*(4), 388–406.
Delmar, F. (1997). Measuring growth: Methodological considerations and empirical results. In R. Donckels & A. Miettinen (Eds.), *Entrepreneurship and SME research: On its way to the next millennium* (pp. 190–216). Aldershot, UK and Brookfield, VA: Ashgate.
Delmar, F., Davidsson, P., & Gartner, W. (2003). Arriving at the high-growth firm. *Journal of Business Venturing, 18*(2), 189–216.
Dierickx, I. & Cool, K. (1989). Asset stock accumulation and sustainability of competitive advantage. *Management Science, 35*(12), 1504–1513.
DiMaggio, P. & Powell, W. (1983). The iron cage revisited: Institutional isomorphism and collective rationality in organizational fields. *American Sociological Review, 48*, 147–160.
Durand, R. & Coeurderoy, R. (2001). Age, order of entry, strategic orientation, and organizational performance. *Journal of Business Venturing, 16*, 471–494.
Geroski, P.A. (1995). What do we know about entry? *International Journal of Industrial Organization, 13*, 421–440.
Gimeno, J., Folta, T.B., Cooper, A.C., & Woo, C.Y. (1997). Survival of the fittest? Entrepreneurial human capital and the persistence of underperforming firms. *Administrative Science Quarterly, 42*, 750– 783.
Greiner, L.E. (1972). Evolutions and revolutions as organizations grow. *Harvard Business Review, 50*(4), 37–46.
Gupta, V. (1981). Minimum efficient scale as a determinant of concentration. *The Manchester School of Economic and Social Studies, 49*, 153–164.
Gustafsson, V. (2004). *Entrepreneurial decision-making*. Doctoral dissertation. Jönköping: Jönköping International Business School.
Hambrick, D.C. & Crozier, L.M. (1985). Stumblers and stars in the management of rapid growth. *Journal of Business Venturing, 1*(1), 31–45.

Hansen, J.A. (1992). Innovation, firm size, and firm age. *Small Business Economics*, *4*(1), 37–44.
Headd, B. (2003). Redefining business success: Distinguishing between closure and failure. *Small Business Economics*, *21*(1), 51–61.
Henderson, A.D. (1999). Firm strategy and age dependence: A contingent view of the liabilities of newness, adolescence and obsolescence. *Administrative Science Quarterly*, *44*, 281–314.
Hitt, M.A., Ireland, R.D., Camp, S.M., & Sexton, D.L. (2002). Strategic entrepreneurship: Integrating entrepreneurial and strategic management perspectives. In M.A. Hitt, R.D. Ireland, S.M. Camp, & D.L. Sexton (Eds.), *Strategic entrepreneurship: Creating a new integrated mindset* (pp. 1–16). Malden, MA: Blackwell Publishing.
Hoy, F., McDougall, P.P., & Dsouza, D.E. (1992). Strategies and environments of high growth firms. In D.L. Sexton & J.D. Kasarda (Eds.), *The state of the art of entrepreneurship* (pp. 341–357). Boston: PWS-Kent Publishing.
Ireland, R.D., Hitt, M.A., & Sirmon, D.G. (2003). A model of strategic entrepreneurship: The construct and its dimensions. *Journal of Management*, *29*(6), 963–989.
Jensen, M.C. & Ruback, R.S. (1983). The market for corporate control: The scientific evidence. *Journal of Financial Economics*, *11*, 5–50.
Katz, M.L. & Shapiro, C. (1985). Network externalities, competition, and compatibility. *American Economic Review*, *75*(3), 424–440.
Kazanjian, R.K. & Drazin, R. (1989). An empirical test of stage of growth progression model. *Management Science*, *35*(12), 1489–1503.
Kogut, B. & Zander, U. (1992). Knowledge of the firm, combinative capabilities, and the replication of technology. *Organization Science*, *3*(3), 383–397.
Leonard-Barton, D. (1992). Core capabilities and core rigidities. *Strategic Management Journal*, *13*(Summer), 111–125.
Lieberman, M.B. & Montgomery, D.B. (1988). First-mover advantages. *Strategic Management Journal*, *9*, 41–58.
Manigart, S. & Sapienza, H. (2000). Venture capital and growth. In D. Sexton & H. Landström (Eds.), *The Blackwell handbook of entrepreneurship* (pp. 240–258). Oxford, MA: Blackwell Business.
Mansfield, E. (1979). *Microeconomics: Theory and applications* (3rd ed.). New York: Norton.
Markman, G.D. & Gartner, W.B. (2002). Is extraordinary growth profitable? A study of Inc. 500 high-growth companies. *Entrepreneurship Theory and Practice*, *27*(1), 65–75.
Marris, R. (1967). *The economic theory of managerial capitalism*. London: MacMillan.
McGahan, A.M. & Porter, M.E. (1997). How much does industry matter, really? *Strategic Management Journal*, *18*(special summer issue), 15–30.
McGahan, A.M. & Porter, M.E. (2002). What do we know about variance in accounting profitability? *Management Science*, *48*(7), 834–851.
Montgomery, C.A. (1982). The measurement of firm diversification: Some empirical new evidence. *Academy of Management Journal*, *25*, 299–307.
Mosakowski, E. (2002). Overcoming resource disadvantages in entrepreneurial firms: When less is more. In M.A. Hitt, R.D. Ireland, S.M. Camp, & D.L. Sexton (Eds.), *Strategic entrepreneurship: Creating a new mindset* (pp. 106–126). Oxford, UK: Blackwell.

Nelson, R.R. & Winter, S.G. (1982). *An evolutionary theory of economic change*. Cambridge, MA: Belknap Press.
Penrose, E. (1959). *The theory of the growth of the firm*. Oxford: Oxford University Press.
Peteraf, M.A. & Barney, J.B. (2003). Unraveling the resource-based tangle. *Managerial and Decision Economics*, *24*(4), 309–323.
Pfeffer, J. and Salancik, G.R. (1978). *The external control of organizations*. New York: Harper & Row.
Platt, J.R. (1964). Strong inference. *Science*, *146*(3642), 347–353.
Porter, M.E. (1980). *Competitive strategy*. New York: Free Press.
Ravenscraft, D.J. & Scherer, F.M. (1987). *Mergers, sell-offs, and economic efficiency*. Washington, DC: Brookings Institution.
Reynolds, P.D. & Miller, B. (1992). New firm gestation: Conception, birth and implications for research. *Journal of Business Venturing*, *7*, 405–417.
Rumelt, R. (1974). *Strategy, structure, and economic performance*. Boston: Division of Research, Harvard Business School.
Rumelt, R.P. (1991). How much does industry matter? *Strategic Management Journal*, *12*(3), 167– 185.
Sapienza, H.J., Korsgaard, M.A., & Forbes, D.P. (2003). The self-determination motive and entrepreneurs' choice of financing. In J. Katz & D. Shepherd (Eds.), *Cognitive approaches to entrepreneurship research* (Vol. 6, pp. 107–140). Oxford, UK: Elsevier/JAI Press.
Sarasvathy, S. (2001). Causation and effectuation: Towards a theoretical shift from economic inevitability to entrepreneurial contingency. *Academy of Management Review*, *26*(2), 243–288.
Schumpeter, J.A. (1934). *The theory of economic development*. Cambridge: MA: Harvard University Press.
Sexton, D.L. (1997). Entrepreneurship research needs and issues. In D.L. Sexton & R.W. Smilor (Eds.), *Entrepreneurship 2000* (pp. 401–408). Chicago, IL: Upstart Publishing Company.
Sexton, D.L., Pricer, R.W., & Nenide, B. (2000). *Measuring performance in high-growth firms*. Paper presented at the Babson College/Kauffman Foundation Entrepreneurship Research Conference, Babson College, Wellesley, MA.
Shane, S. & Venkataraman, S. (2000). The promise of entrepreneurship as a field of research. *Academy of Management Review*, *25*(1), 217–226.
Stern, C.W. & Stalk, G., Jr. (Eds.) (1998). *Perspectives on strategy from the Boston Consulting Group*. New York: Wiley.
Stevenson, H.H. & Gumpert, D.E. (1991). The heart of entrepreneurship. In W.A. Sahlman & H.H. Stevenson (Eds.), *The entrepreneurial venture* (pp. 71–80). Boston: Harvard Business School.
Stevenson, H.H. & Jarillo, J.C. (1986). Preserving entrepreneurship as companies grow. *Journal of Business Strategy*, *6*, 10–23.
Stinchcombe, A.L. (1965). Social structure and organizations. In J.D. March (Ed.), *Handbook of organizations* (pp. 142–193). Chicago: Rand McNally.
Storey, D.J. (1994). *Understanding the small business sector*. London: Routledge.
Suchman, M.C. (1995). Managing legitimacy: Strategic and institutional approaches. *Academy of Management Review*, *20*, 571–610.
Thornhill, S. & Amit, R. (2003). Learning about failure: Bankruptcy, firm age and the resource-based view. *Organization Science*, *14*(5), 497–503.

Tushman, M.L. & Anderson, P.C. (1986). Technological discontinuities and organizational environments. *Administrative Science Quarterly*, *31*, 439–465.

van Praag, C.M. & Versloot, P.H. (2007). *What is the value of entrepreneurship? A review of recent research*. Amsterdam: Tinbergen Institute.

Waring, G.F. (1996). Industry differences in the persistence of firm-specific returns. *American Economic Review*, *86*(5), 1253–1265.

Weinzimmer, L.G., Nystrom, P.C., & Freeman, S.J. (1998). Measuring organizational growth: Issues, consequences and guidelines. *Journal of Management*, *24*(2), 235–262.

Wernerfelt, B. (1984). A resource based view of the firm. *Strategic Management Journal*, *5*(2), 171–180.

Wiklund, J. (1998). *Small firm growth and performance: Entrepreneurship and beyond*. Doctoral dissertation. Jönköping: Jönköping International Business School.

Wiklund, J., Davidsson, P., & Delmar, F. (2003). Expected consequences of growth and their effect on growth willingness in different samples of small firms. *Entrepreneurship Theory & Practice*, *27*(Spring), 247–269.

Zahra, S. (1991). Predictors and financial outcomes of corporate entrepreneurship: An explorative study. *Journal of Business Venturing*, *6*(4), 259–285.

# PART IV

# Theory-driven research on specific forms of growth

# 9. Asset specificity and behavioral uncertainty as moderators of the sales growth–employment growth relationship in emerging ventures*

**Gaylen N. Chandler, Alexander McKelvie and Per Davidsson**

## 1. EXECUTIVE SUMMARY

New venture growth is a central topic in entrepreneurship research. Although sales growth is emerging as the most commonly used measure of growth for emerging ventures, employment growth has also been used frequently. However, empirical research demonstrates that there are only very low to moderately sized correlations between the two (Delmar et al., 2003; Weinzimmer, et al., 1998). In addition, sales growth and employment growth respond differently to a wide variety of criteria (Baum et al., 2001; Delmar et al., 2003). In this study we use transaction cost economics (Williamson, 1996) as a theoretical base to examine transaction cost influences on the addition of new employees as emerging ventures experience sales growth.

We theorize that transaction cost economics variables will moderate the relationship between sales growth and employment growth. We develop and test hypotheses related to asset specificity, behavioral uncertainty, and the influence of resource munificence on the strength of the sales growth/employment growth relationship. Asset specificity is theorized to be a positive moderator of the relationship between sales growth and employment growth. When the behavioral uncertainty associated with adding new employees is greater than that of outsourcing or subcontracting, it is hypothesized to be a negative moderator of the sales growth/employment growth relationship. We also hypothesize that resource scarcity will strengthen those relationships.

We test our hypotheses in a sample of 1357 emerging firms that registered first sales in Sweden in 1994. The data were collected in four waves, with the final data collection occurring in 2004. We used confirmatory factor analysis and Cronbach's alpha scale analysis to provide evidence to support the reliability and validity of our measures. We used moderated hierarchical regression analysis to test our hypotheses.

Transaction cost theory predicts that if emerging ventures increase their sales, they will be either more or less likely to support that growth by adding employees depending on the transaction costs inherent in the employer/employee relationship (Williamson, 1985, 1996). That position is supported by our results. In the entire sample and the resource scarce sub-sample, each of our hypotheses is supported by the analysis. The increases in $R^2$ are all significant at the .05 level. When resources are abundant the interactions become insignificant, except for the case of difficulty of measuring performance which is significant but in a direction opposite that which we hypothesized. In addition we conducted a $Z$-test substantiating the difference between effect sizes for the resource scarce and resource munificent groups. In all six cases there are strongly significant differences ($p<.001$). Consistent with Coles and Hesterly (1998), the results consistently show that young and small firms tend to choose solutions consistent with the predictions of transaction cost economics when financial resources are scarce, but are less likely to do so when financial resources are more abundant.

In addition to the theoretical implications, our findings have practical implications. From a practical perspective our results indicate that emerging firms add new employees in accordance with the predictions of transaction cost economics under resource constrained situations but are less likely to do so in resource abundant situations. Awareness of this tendency can help practitioners more clearly evaluate the decision to add permanent employees. For policy-makers our results refine our understanding of why the firm level pursuit of growth as measured by sales often does not translate into increased employment. If employment growth is a desired societal outcome, policy-makers may focus on reducing the political and administrative hassles associated with creating and expanding employment.

## 2. INTRODUCTION

Firm growth is an important research topic in economics, strategy, and entrepreneurship. It is of interest to scholars for many reasons; however, the most often cited is that it has a fundamental impact on the performance of economies through the introduction of new products and the creation of new markets (Shane and Venkataraman, 2000), the generation of new jobs (Birch, 1979), and regional or national economic growth (Thurik and Wennekers 2004).

In this chapter, we focus specifically on the growth of emerging ventures. Most of the new venture growth research is contained in two streams. The first, and more prevalent of the two, is *why* some ventures grow while others do not (Gilbert et al., 2006). Researchers have examined this question at the individual level (Baum et al., 2001; Chandler and Jansen 1992; Wiklund and Shepherd, 2003), the firm level (Edelman et al., 2005; Chandler and Hanks, 1994; Dess and Davis, 1984), and the environmental level (Dess and Beard, 1984; Ensley et al., 2006; McDougall et al., 1992). Overall, the results suggest that factors from each of these levels of analysis are associated with new venture growth.

The second stream of venture growth research examines *how* firms grow and the internal consequences of growth (e.g. Hanks et al., 1993; Kazanjian and Drazin, 1990; McMahon, 2001). In this stream of research firm growth is assumed to be present, but there is no strong theoretical reason explaining why firms grow. Rather, it seeks to describe the processes associated with growth. Our research fits best within the latter stream. We do not attempt to predict firm growth, but rather whether employees will be added to support sales growth or whether sales growth will be supported by external contracting or other activities. For example, instead of adding permanent employees, an emerging company might subcontract for workers or with an existing manufacturer to produce its product. Alternatively, it might acquire technology and equipment to replace workers. Our integration of transaction cost economics provides a theoretical rationale for choosing to add permanent employees rather than choosing other solutions and thus makes a novel and noteworthy contribution to the literature.

Research focusing on *why* firms grow is frequently limited because only survivors are studied. However, that criticism does not apply equally to the study of *how* firms grow. In the introduction to her classic theory of the growth of the firm, Penrose (1959) acknowledges the tautological problem (survivor bias) associated with studying only growing firms when studying *why* firms grow. However, she points out that the study of defunct firms cannot inform us with regards to *how* firms grow. We believe Penrose's rationale also applies to our study. We are not studying *why* firms grow, but rather analyzing the relationship between sales growth and employment growth. Consistent with Penrose's reasoning, the study of failed firms does not inform that process.

Despite significant research interest concerning both the *why* and the *how* of firm growth, empirical results regarding those factors associated with growth are mixed (Davidsson and Wiklund, 2000; Weinzimmer et al., 1998; Delmar, 1997). This may occur because growth measures including changes in sales and employment have been used somewhat interchangeably (Delmar 1997; Ardichvili et al., 1998; Weinzimmer et al., 1998; Wiklund 1998). Although many studies have used sales and employment change as indicators of growth, in the few that reported correlations between sales growth and employment growth indicators, the correlations were relatively small, ranging from .09 in a sample of small firms in Sweden (Delmar et al. 2003) to .57 in a sample of publicly traded firms in the U.S. (Weinzimmer et al., 1998). For example in Delmar et al. (2003) some categories of 'high sales-growth firms' did not expand at all in terms of employment. Thus, sales growth and employment growth are not interchangeable measures of new venture growth. Rather, they are related, but largely independent constructs that respond differently to a variety of criteria (Weinzimmer et al., 1998).

In addition, different stakeholders do not view the benefits of different types of growth in the same way. For example, policy-makers generally view employment growth as an indicator of a healthy economy (Birch, 1979; Birch and Medoff, 1994; U.S. Small Business Administration, 2004; Zacharakis et al., 2001), yet managers of emerging firms often have more ambivalent attitudes towards expanding the work force (Delmar and Davidsson, 1999; Sapienza et al., 2003). Employment growth appears to be a particular dilemma for independent business owner-managers as it is associated with both desirable and undesirable expected consequences (Wiklund et al., 2003). For the managers of emerging ventures, hiring permanent employees may respond to opportunities to expand, gain market share, and provide employment. However, it may also be associated with considerable responsibility, front-loaded cost, and administrative hassle. As a result founders of new ventures may choose not to pursue growth or alternatively pursue growth in revenues only when it can be done without assuming the responsibility for additional permanent employees.

Therefore, the relatively small reported correlation between sales and employment growth in emerging ventures is not merely a technical issue that is solved by choosing the supposedly more appropriate indicator. If a new venture's sales growth is not accompanied by employment growth in the same organization, it has important implications for management and policy-makers alike. A focus only on sales growth neglects the possible societal benefit of increased employment (which may not result if owner-managers refrain from growth that can only be achieved if employment is also increased, or which may appear in subcontracted organizations in other regions or nations).

There is a dearth of theory-based research that analyzes the relationship or lack of relationship between sales growth and employment growth. Our research makes a unique contribution by applying a well-known theory, transaction cost economics (Williamson, 1996), to identify conditions that link employment growth and sales growth. Our research shows that venture founders make choices to increase employment consistent with the predictions of transaction cost economics when constrained by scarce financial resources. The research also makes a contribution to the transactions cost literature by applying the theory to the domain of new venture growth and by testing the theory's applicability to settings with scarce or abundant financial resources. Finally, we make a contribution to practitioners at both policy-making and management levels. The question of under what conditions it is possible to successfully grow in sales without or with only limited employment growth is a pertinent issue given business founders' documented reluctance to expand the workforce.

The chapter proceeds as follows. Using transaction cost economics (Williamson, 1996) as a theoretical background we derive testable hypotheses about the relationship between sales growth and employment growth. These hypotheses are tested in a large sample of Swedish firms that registered first sales in 1994 and have been tracked during their first decade of existence. We then summarize our results and discuss their implications.

## 3. THEORETICAL PERSPECTIVE

There are a variety of reasons why managers of firms with sales growth potential choose to add or not to add new employees. Evidence suggests that in industry specific sectors there is a significant amount of job creation, destruction, and reallocation (Davis and Haltiwanger, 1992). Indeed, in many cases, sales growth may be supported by advanced technology and equipment rather than the addition of employees or subcontracting for services (Dunne et al., 1996). However, the purpose of the current study is not to explain all discrepancies between sales growth and employment growth, but rather to show that transaction cost economics (Williamson, 1996) provides a theoretical rationale explaining part of the shared variance in the relationship between sales growth and employment growth.

According to the transaction cost perspective (Williamson, 1996), the benefits of having a larger organization and hierarchy come at a cost. In the framework of our study, employment growth is unlikely to occur unless sales and cash flows grow sufficiently to support employment expansion. However, even when sales are growing, it may or may not be desirable or feasible to add new permanent employees. Whenever a transaction is transferred from an external market to an internal organization function there are increased bureaucratic costs that may outweigh the efficiencies gained through such a transfer. In addition, the incentives to the individual decision maker are degraded as organizations become larger and necessarily more bureaucratic. Transaction cost economics predicts that under some conditions, it is more efficient for managers in growing firms to add long-term employees internally, while in others it is more efficient to contract externally. In the current research, we focus on two aspects of transaction cost economics: (1) asset specificity, and (2) behavioral uncertainty. These constructs have been shown in previous research to be related to the decision to grow sales concurrently with adding employees to the company structure (David and Han, 2004). Based on a review of the transaction costs literature (e.g. Rindfleisch and Heide, 1997; Anderson, 1985), we focus on four specific aspects of human asset specificity and two aspects of costs associated with behavioral uncertainty. In the following section we hypothesize their moderating affect on the relationship between sales growth and employment growth.

## 3.1 Asset Specificity

Williamson (1985) argues that a major force that drives the decision to add employees to the firm is the specificity of skills and abilities required. From a transaction cost perspective the more specific the inputs required in the firm's production process, the less likely these products or services will be satisfactorily available from the market. As the specificity of required human assets increases it influences firms to integrate by adding employees to support growth rather than engage in external contracting (David and Han, 2004). In addition, when assets are either not specific or cease to be specific, tasks that were formerly performed by employees are likely to be outsourced or disintegrated (Hesterly et al., 1990). Thus, as firms experience growth in sales, they may support that growth by adding employees, subcontracting externally, or using technologies that require fewer employees. Transaction cost economics provides a reasonable explanation of the moderating influence of human asset specificity on the relationship between sales growth and employment growth. Human asset specificity has been measured and applied with more consistent results than other transaction cost variables across a variety of research settings (Rindfleisch and Heide, 1997). The following constructs represent four different ways to view human asset specificity.

### 3.1.1 Product specific knowledge

Product specific knowledge involves the degree to which investments in human capital must be made to gain knowledge and expertise regarding the products and services provided by an organization (Anderson, 1985).

Specific human capital cannot be redeployed without losing productive value (Robertson and Gatignon, 1998). The time and effort required to get an employee up to speed with respect to unique products and services represents a significant investment in human capital that will not be recaptured unless the employment relationship is relatively permanent (Bac, 2000; Benson et al., 2004). Thus, the greater the degree of product specific knowledge required, the more likely that permanent employees will be added to support sales growth.

*Hypothesis 1. The degree of product specific knowledge required for new employees is a positive moderator of the relationship between sales growth and employment growth.*

### 3.1.2 Firm specific knowledge

Anderson (1985) identifies the amount of firm specific knowledge as a second dimension of human asset specificity. Firm specific knowledge refers to knowledge about the firm's specific process, practices, and procedures that are required for an employee to operate effectively. If extensive training and socialization is required before an employee can work effectively in a company, it requires a front-loaded expenditure of time, energy and often money on the part of the entrepreneur and management team that is not likely to pay off for some time in the future (Pfeffer, 1998). The investment in training and socializing new employees may be lost if the employee does not stay with the firm for an extended period of time (Bac, 2000; Benson et al., 2004). Hence, there is likely to be an emphasis on recruiting and hiring employees under a long time window, which suggests somewhat permanent rather than temporary employment arrangements.

*Hypothesis 2. The degree of firm specific knowledge required for new employees is a positive moderator of the relationship between sales growth and employment growth.*

### 3.1.3 Importance of excellent personalized service

The degree to which firm success depends on excellent customized service introduces another type of human asset specificity. This construct is relevant when personal relationships count, the identity of the person that provides the customer's contact point with the company matters to the customer, and the nature and quality of the interaction between employees and customers is relevant (Anderson, 1985). In such organizations, the customer relationship has been likened to a marriage in which the quality of the relationship depends on how well it is managed by the seller (Dwyer et al., 1987). Thus, when personalized service matters, there is an expectation that employees will be hired permanently and brought within the firm. This provides a greater opportunity to develop and maintain ongoing customer relationships.

*Hypothesis 3.* *The degree to which personalized customer service matters is a positive moderator of the relationship between sales growth and employment growth.*

### 3.1.4 Necessity of maintaining proprietary information

An emerging firm can build a competitive advantage because of proprietary information not possessed by other companies. In fact, specialized intellectual or technical resources may provide a sustainable source of competitive advantage (Barney, 2001). For a small firm, opportunistic hazards exist because individuals learning the proprietary information may be tempted to pursue self-interests (Zeng and Chen, 2003). Yet opportunistic hazards are expected to be less for permanent employees than for temporary employees or subcontractors. Thus, the more the success of the firm relies on maintaining proprietary information, the greater the likelihood that permanent employees will be added.

*Hypothesis 4.* *The importance of maintaining proprietary information is a positive moderator of the relationship between sales growth and employment growth.*

## 3.2 Behavioral Uncertainty

In addition to asset specificity, behavioral uncertainty is thought to influence the decision to add permanent employees or to contract externally. Behavioral uncertainty arises from the difficulties associated with assuring the performance of employees or external exchange partners (Williamson, 1985). Most studies conceptualize behavioral uncertainty as an issue of making sure the expected performance occurs (Heide and John, 1988; Rindfleisch and Heide, 1997), whether it is completed by regular employees, temporary or contract workers, or an external firm. The behavioral uncertainty associated with performance can take on two forms. The first form of behavioral uncertainty involves screening, hiring, and supervising employees. Although research indicates that more rigorous screening, hiring, and supervising policies are likely to lead to better performance (Koch and McGrath, 1996), it requires an upfront expenditure by the employer, with no guarantee that the hired permanent employees will perform as hoped. The second form of behavioral uncertainty is associated with accurate measurement of performance (e g., John and Weitz,

1989; Stump and Heide, 1996; Weiss and Anderson, 1992). When individual performance is difficult to measure, it makes it difficult to determine whether or not the hoped for performance has occurred.

### 3.2.1 Difficulty of screening and supervision

Costs accrue when it is difficult to screen potential employees and when the control of work processes requires substantial supervision. These internal transaction costs represent immediate cost outlays for firms. Small and young firms often operate in a resource strapped mode and payoffs from such hiring may require some time to develop. Therefore, consistent with the predictions of transaction cost analysis (Williamson, 1996) as the amount of screening and supervision for long-term employees increases, it discourages employment and leads to a greater likelihood of supporting sales growth through methods such as subcontracting or outsourcing (Anderson, 1985). If temporary employees are used, the screening function shifts to the agency. If a function such as manufacturing is outsourced, the emphasis would shift from supervising employees to inspecting the quality of incoming goods. Hence, screening costs, as we have formulated them, apply more specifically to permanent employees. If the cost of screening and supervising permanent employees is greater than the cost of hiring temporary employees through an agency, or monitoring a production contract, companies would be less likely to add employees. Thus, the relatively higher costs associated with screening and supervising permanent employees would have a negative influence on hiring.

*Hypothesis 5. The difficulty of screening and supervising employees is a negative moderator of the relationship between sales growth and employment growth.*

### 3.2.2 Difficulty of measuring employee performance

Behavioral uncertainty and potential hazard costs exist when it is difficult for a manager to determine how well an individual is performing. This occurs when much of the work occurs at a team level, outcomes are difficult to measure, or measurable outcomes do not reflect adequate performance (Anderson, 1985). In such a setting, workers can take advantage of the organization by not performing adequately and poor performance is likely to go undetected. Permanent employees are more likely to be influenced by culture and organizational norms, even when performance is hard to measure (Mintzberg, 1978). Thus, these opportunistic hazards exist for permanent employees, yet they are expected to be greater for temporary employees. In such a setting, permanent employees would be preferred over temporary employees or subcontracting. Thus, if individual performance is difficult to measure, companies are more likely to add permanent employees to support sales growth.

*Hypothesis 6. The degree to which it is difficult to measure employee performance is a positive moderator of the relationship between sales growth and employment growth.*

### 3.3 Contextual Factors

Coles and Hesterly (1998) explain that transaction cost explanations are subject to contextual factors. In their research the predictions of transaction cost economics were valid in a sample of for-profit hospitals, but not so in a sample of not-for-profit hospitals. They conjectured that the difference in results stemmed from less pressure to perform in market efficient ways in the not-for-profit hospitals. In general, the transaction cost approach is presented as resource neutral with an underlying assumption that firms will make efficient decisions. However, firms with abundant resources have no immediate pressures to perform in market efficient ways. The perceived risks involved in making a 'wrong decision', including failure, are less when resources are abundant (Yasai-Ardekani, 1989; Baum and Wally, 2003). Risk-averse actions, including actions that allow firms to maintain more control over potential losses, are therefore more likely in situations of resource scarcity (Singh, 1986). Thus, resource munificence (Castrogiovanni, 1991) is likely to moderate the relationship between human asset specificity and behavioral uncertainty on the one hand, and employment growth on the other. When financial resources are readily available, there is decreased pressure to operate in accordance with the predictions of transaction cost economics.

*Hypothesis 7. When resources are scarce the moderating effect of transaction cost variables is significantly stronger than will be encountered when resources are abundant.*

## 4. METHODS

### 4.1 Sample

This study employs a unique and well-developed data set. The sample frame for this study was a panel with an original size of 7256 new firms. The panel was created using a stratified random sample of all new business registrations in Sweden during 1994, representing 30 per cent of the entire target population. The sample covers the full spectrum of industries, with the exception of agriculture, and thus provides a representative indicator for sales and job creation in new businesses in Sweden. Since inception, we systematically surveyed the panel using telephone and mail surveys in 1995, 1998, and 2000. As the first two waves were in part mandatory surveys by a Government agency response rates were exceptionally high; well above 90 per cent of eligible firms. By the end of 2000, 42.8 per cent (N=3048) of the firms were no longer active and 2.9 per cent (N=210) of the firms were missing data. A number of firms had also requested to not be contacted again. Early in 2004 we sent an additional survey to the remaining 3451 firms that had continued to report sales through to the end of 2000. We received 2021 responses following two reminders; a response rate of 59 per cent. This is a very positive response, especially considering that a substantial number of non-responding firms are likely to have gone out of business (potentially due to recession in the global economy) and/or moved without leaving a forwarding address during the more than three years since last contact. Of the 2021 responses, 1357 had sufficient information across all waves of data collection for our analyses. The mean size of the firms in 2004 is slightly over 5.1 full-time equivalent employees (with standard deviation 55.9). The mean sales in 2003 (the last full year of sales data) was 2,100,000 SEK (during the time period of the study the exchange rate ranged between 6.6–10.6 SEK per 1 $US). We compared the means from the final survey to those in 2000 in which mean size of the firms was 1.8 FTE (standard deviation 2.79) and 866,000 SEK in mean sales. This indicates that average sales and employment growth increased significantly between the 2000 and 2004 surveys.

Relative to the U.S., Sweden is characterized by comparatively strict employment security legislation as well as by wage setting institutions leading to a compressed salary span (Henrekson and Johansson, 1999; Henrekson and Rosenberg, 2001; Henrekson, 2005). On the one hand, it may mean that the tendency for employment and sales growth to move together is weaker than in the U.S. On the other hand, this may make it a suitable context for testing our theory-based hypotheses. It is not particularly difficult to set up a business in Sweden. The legal requirements to set up a firm in Sweden are somewhat similar to those in the U.S.

## 4.2 Measurement

### 4.2.1 Dependent variable

The dependent variable is the change in employment. This is particularly relevant for this study because of our predictions that employment growth is more likely to accompany sales growth when human assets are highly specific and less likely to accompany sales growth when the costs associated with behavioral uncertainty costs are high. In addition, many studies of new venture performance use employment growth as an important indicator (Baum et al., 2001; Chandler and Hanks, 1993). In the 1995, 1998, 2001 and 2004 questionnaires respondents were asked to tell us the number of employees working less than 10 h, from 10–35 h, and 35 or more hours. Employees working ten hours or less are computed as 1/4 FTE (full-time equivalent), employees working between 10–35 h are computed as 1/2 FTE and employees working 35 or more hours are computed as 1 FTE. Although the preferred exact formula to use is debated (Delmar, 1997; Davidsson and Wiklund, 2000; Weinzimmer et al., 1998), we believe our aggregation to represent a reasonable approximation of employment. We calculate the change in employment as the difference between 2004 and 1995 levels, which results in a skewed distribution with extreme outliers. To avoid having a small number of cases drive the results we trim the most extreme outliers and use a natural log transformation (Box and Cox, 1964). The natural log transformation affects large values more than small values, and is a frequently used and time honored method to improve the characteristics of the distribution with regards to the assumption of normality inherent in ordinary least squares regression. To control for the influence of initial start size, we used the number of FTE employees in 1995 as a control variable. The start date of each company in the sample is controlled by the study design because all companies started in 1994.

#### 4.2.2 Sales growth

We test the relationship between sales growth and employment growth. Sales growth has been widely accepted as an important indicator of emerging venture performance (Chandler and Hanks, 1993; Davidsson and Wiklund, 2000; Delmar, 1997; Robinson and McDougall, 2001; Weinzimmer et al., 1998). Sales data were available through government sources for each year of the study. Sales growth in this study is the slope of the sales regression line over time. Because the distribution is skewed we employ a natural log transformation.

#### 4.2.3 Moderating variables

To develop the items measuring asset specificity and behavioral uncertainty, we followed the guidelines set out by Robinson et al. (1991). We developed multiple item asset specificity scales following the theoretical components first set out by Williamson (1985) and amended these issues with later theoretical advances. This task was simplified by the fact that both Anderson (1985) and Rindfleisch and Heide (1997) discussed scales for measuring human asset specificity and behavioral uncertainty.

Using these scales as prototypes, we added items and modified items to be appropriate for use in a sample of start-up firms. We initially rendered the items in English. The items were translated into Swedish by a native speaker. Another native speaker with extensive research experience double-checked the items. A team of native English and Swedish speakers then re-translated the items into English and they were checked against the original items. Additionally, we pre-tested the survey with ten local businesses from different industries in order to verify item relevance and respondent understanding across a variety of contexts.

We measured asset specificity and behavioral uncertainty variables using five-point Likert type scales. We analyzed item measures using confirmatory factor analysis (CFA). We employed several goodness of fit measures in order to assess the fit of the six factor model. The results for the CFA are presented in Table 9.1. The six factor model suggested by theory is superior to the null single-factor model (as well as 2, 3, 4 and 5 factor models). In this case the value of the root mean square error of approximation (RMSEA) in the six factor case is .042; values of less then 05 for RMSEA indicate good model fit (Byrne, 2001), while values as high as .08 may represent reasonable errors of approximation in the population (Browne and Cudeck,1993). The adjusted goodness off it index (AGFI) is .95 and indicates good model fit (Byrne, 2001).We also employed two comparative indices, the comparative fit index(CFI) and the incremental index of fit (IFI). The values of both indices are .96, once again indicative of good fit (Hu and Bentler, 1999). We did not employ the chi-square likelihood ratio test because of its sensitivity to large sample sizes (MacCallum et al., 1996; Bagozzi et al., 1991).

We assessed the internal consistency of each of the newly formed constructs. Reliabilities range from .69 to .90. Nunnally (1978) recommends that for decisional purposes alphas should be greater than .70; however, for research purposes, .60 may be adequate. Thus, for the purposes of this chapter, measures of all of these constructs meet his recommendations.

Four scales measure asset specificity: product specific knowledge, firm specific knowledge, importance of customer relationships, and importance of maintaining proprietary information. The appropriateness of each construct was discussed and justified in the theory and hypothesis development section of the chapter. The full text for each item is included in Table 9.1.

*Product specific knowledge* is intended to measure the time and energy required for a new employee to gain sufficient knowledge about the products and services offered to be effective in his/her role. It is measured using a four item scale. Key items reference the time and effort required for a new employee to gain adequate product expertise, achieve the ability

*Table 9.1 Confirmatory factor analysis results**

| Items | Null single factor model | 6 factor model |
|---|---|---|
| *1. Product specific knowledge: coefficient alpha=.85* | X | 1 |
| How much time, training and energy would it take for new employees to gain basic knowledge about the firm's products or services? | X | 1 |
| How much time, training and energy would it take for new employees to become proficient in using/selling your products and/or services? | X | 1 |
| How much time, training and energy would it take for new employees to become expert with regards to your products and/or services? | X | 1 |
| How much time, training, and energy would it take for a new employee to become fully qualified to deal personally with your customers on product/service issues? | X | 1 |
| *2. Firm specific knowledge: coefficient alpha=.80* | | |
| How much time, training and energy would it take for new employees to become proficient in your company's specific way of doing things? | X | 2 |
| How much time, training and energy would it take for new employees to learn how the firm works at a basic level? | X | 2 |
| How much time, training and energy would it take for new employees to learn specific company policies and procedures? | X | 2 |
| *3. Importance of customer relationships: coefficient alpha=.82* | | |
| How important would it be for your employees to be fully aware of the specific needs of very atypical customers? | X | 3 |
| How important would it be for customers to develop loyalty to a specific employee? | X | 3 |
| How important would it be for your employees to develop close working relationships with your customers? | X | 3 |
| How important would it be for your employees to have an in-depth understanding of what your customers need? | X | 3 |
| *4. Importance of trade secrets: coefficient alpha=.90* | | |
| How necessary would it be for you to share trade secrets with new employees about the processes and technology that the firm uses? | X | 4 |

| Items | Null single factor model | 6 factor model |
|---|---|---|
| How necessary would it be for you to share closely held information with new employees about business opportunities, knowledge of suppliers etc. that could impact your ability to compete? | X | 4 |
| How necessary would it be for you to trust new employees with confidential information about customers? | X | 4 |
| *5. Difficulty in screening and supervising: coefficient alpha=.69* | | |
| It is very difficult to find employees with the appropriate skills. | X | 5 |
| There is no way to know if a potential employee is good or bad until you have hired the person in question. | X | 5 |
| There is a lot of risk associated with hiring new employees. | X | 5 |
| If we hire someone, there is a strong likelihood they will not have appropriate knowledge. | X | 5 |
| It is costly and time consuming to make sure employees continue to work hard. | X | 5 |
| *6. Difficulty measuring performance: coefficient alpha=.71* | | |
| In our company, it is not easy to monitor whether or not an employee is doing a good job. | X | 6 |
| In our company it is easy to see individual employee performance results (RS). | X | 6 |
| AGFI | .58 | .95 |
| CFI | .47 | .96 |
| IFI | .48 | .96 |
| RMSEA | .15 | .04 |

to operate independently, and understand the details of the company's products. Coefficient alpha for the scale is .85.

*Firm specific knowledge* is intended to measure the time and energy required for a new employee to gain sufficient knowledge about the processes, procedures and practices of the business to work effectively. The specific statements in this three item scale focus on the time and energy required for new employees to learn specific company practices, how the business works, and the rules and procedures they are expected to follow. Coefficient alpha for the scale is .80.

*The importance of customer relationships* is intended to measure how important employee/customer relationships are for the success of the business. Such relationships became asset specific because it takes substantial time and energy to develop such relationships. This variable is measured using a four item scale. Example items include the importance of employees understanding customer needs, developing loyalty between customers and specific employees, and forming cooperative working relationships. Coefficient alpha for the scale is .82.

*The importance of maintaining proprietary information* is the fourth measure of asset specificity included in our study. It is intended to measure how important it is for employees to know and maintain proprietary information. It is measured by a three item scale that includes items referencing the necessity of giving proprietary information to employees regarding products, procedures and practices. Coefficient alpha for the scale is .90.

The remaining items were intended to measure the costs associated with the behavioral uncertainty of hiring permanent employees. The *difficulty in screening and supervising* employees is measured by a five item scale. Key items for the scale focus on issues such as the uncertainty in knowing whether or not an employee will turn out to be good or bad, the costs associated with dismissing an employee that doesn't live up to expectations, and the cost in time and money of supervising employees. Coefficient alpha for the scale is .69.

Our final scale in this section assesses the *difficulty of measuring performance*. This construct is measured using a two item scale. As can be seen in Table 9.1, the items are straightforward statements directly addressing the difficulty of measuring performance. Coefficient alpha for the scale is .71.

While sales growth and employment growth variables were measured at multiple times throughout the study, asset specificity and behavioral uncertainty variables were measured in 2004. The validity of this approach requires an assumption that differences among firms on variables such as the importance of firm specific knowledge, building and maintaining customer relationships, and the difficulty of measuring employee performance are relatively stable over time. While this is a reasonable assumption as long as firms do not completely change industries or core businesses, it is also an admitted weakness of our design.

In addition to the asset specificity and behavioral uncertainty variables, we hypothesize that *resource munificence* will be a moderating contextual variable. Resource munificence is the scarcity or abundance of resources a firm has access to (Castrogiovanni, 1991). Prior research has shown resource munificence to influence transaction cost impacts (Coles and Hesterly, 1998). Because financial resources are often substitutable for other forms of resources (Chandler and Hanks, 1998), we focused specifically on the availability of financial resources. Resource munificence is measured using a two item scale referencing the availability of resources. The specific items are: (1) the capital we need is readily available, and (2) it is generally very easy for us to get the resources we need. Coefficient alpha for the scale is .86.

#### 4.2.4 Controls

Because of the large sample size we were able to control for industry differences. We use dummy variables for 26 industries with 15 or more companies represented per industry as determined by the Swedish industrial classification system (similar to SIC codes in the U.S). We aggregate twenty of these at the five digit industry code, while six remaining industries are aggregated at the two digit level. We chose this approach rather than aggregating all industries into two digit codes because we believe industry differences may be obscured by excessive aggregation. These industries accounted for 71 per cent of the companies. We categorize the remaining companies as 'other' (these were industry codes with fewer than 15 companies at the two digit level) and use them as the hold-out group in the regression analysis. We also control for the initial size (number of full time equivalent employees).

In Table 9.2 we report descriptive statistics and correlations for the key independent and dependent variables in the study. Of particular note, our measures of sales growth and employment growth are correlated only at the .22 level, which suggests that only about 5 per cent of the variance in employment growth is explained by sales growth. Although there is some relationship between the two, they do not appear to be jointly determined. A Durbin-Wu-Hausman test of endogeneity as described by Davidson and McKinnon (1993) was performed to assess the appropriateness of the OLS model. The test is conducted by developing a two stage least squares model. In the first stage, sales growth is estimated using instrumental variables. In the second stage, the regression coefficient associated with the standardized residual from the first equation is not significantly different from zero ($p = .26$). Thus, the results of this test (available from the authors) fail to provide evidence of endogeneity and support the use of OLS regression to estimate our models.

In the correlation matrix, the transaction cost variables are only modestly correlated with each other, with product specific knowledge and firm specific knowledge being the most strongly correlated at $r = .58$ ($p < .001$). As might be expected the interaction terms are significantly and strongly correlated with the variables from which they are composed. For example, the interaction of product specific knowledge*sales growth is correlated at the .99 level with product specific knowledge. Southwood (1978) suggests

*Table 9.2 Descriptive statistics and correlations for key variables*

| Variable | Mean | SD | 1 | 2 | 3 | 4 | 5 |
|---|---|---|---|---|---|---|---|
| 1. Ln employees 1994 | −.06 | .86 | | | | | |
| 2. Product specific knowledge | 3.91 | .79 | .11 | | | | |
| 3. Firm specific knowledge | 3.34 | .83 | .12 | .58 | | | |
| 4. Customer relationships | 3.90 | .81 | .00 | .31 | .25 | | |
| 5. Proprietary information | 2.68 | 1.12 | .01 | .31 | .31 | .31 | |
| 6. Difficulty screening/supervision | 3.47 | .72 | .10 | .25 | .32 | .16 | .18 |
| 7. Difficulty measuring performance | 1.74 | .78 | −.04 | −.11 | −.10 | −.19 | −.06 |
| 8. Prod specific know*ln sales growth | 33.1(0) | 6.80 | .12(.11) | .99(−.06) | .58(−.06) | .30(−.02) | .31(−.04) |
| 9. Firm specific know*ln sales growth | 28.33(0) | 7.08 | .13(.14) | .58(−.04) | .99(−.06) | .25(−.02) | .31(−.04) |
| 10. Customer relations* ln sales growth | 33.05(0) | 6.93 | .01(11) | .31(−.04) | .25(−.04) | .99(−.07) | .32(−.05) |
| 11. Proprietary info*ln sales growth | 22.72(0) | 9.55 | .02(.10) | .31(−.03) | .32(−.04) | .31(−.02) | .98(−.05) |
| 12. Screening * ln sales growth | 29.44(0) | 6.17 | .10(−.17) | .26(−.01) | .33(.02) | .16(−.01) | .19(.03) |
| 13. Measuring perf*ln sales growth | 14.76(0) | 5.78 | −.03(.15) | −.09(−.03) | −.09(−.04) | −.19(−.01) | −.06(−.04) |

| 6 | 7 | 8 | 9 | 10 | 11 | 12 | 13 | 14 |
|---|---|---|---|---|---|---|---|---|
| −.21 | | | | | | | | |
| .24(−.01) | −.10(.03) | | | | | | | |
| .30(.01) | −.09(.02) | .60(.92) | | | | | | |
| .15(−.02) | −.18(.00) | .33(.77) | .27(.76) | | | | | |
| .18(.02) | −.06(.02) | .32(−.91) | .32(.91) | .32(.77) | | | | |
| .98(−.04) | −.20(.03) | .27(−.61) | .34(−.67) | .18(−.54) | .19(−.69) | | | |
| −.21(.02) | .99(.02) | −.08(.87) | −.08(.95) | −.17(.73) | −.05(.92) | −.19(−.79) | | |

*Table 9.2* (continued)

| Variable | Mean | SD | 1 | 2 | 3 | 4 | 5 |
|---|---|---|---|---|---|---|---|
| 14. Ln sales growth | 8.46 | .26 | .06 | .06 | .07 | .02 | .05 |
| 15. Ln employees added | .92 | .54 | .00 | .09 | .13 | .02 | .00 |

*Notes:*
( ) centered interaction terms.
Correlations >.05 significant $p<.05$.
Correlations >.07 significant $p<.01$.
Correlations >.09 significant $p<.001$.

mean centering variables before computing the interaction term to reduce the degree of collinearity. In the correlation matrix we report the uncentered interaction term on the left and the centered interaction on the right. The signs on the uncentered terms are consistent with intuitive expectations. After centering, the correlations among variables are substantially lower, consistent with Southwood (1978) and the signs on the centered interaction terms are less intuitive because of the centering.

## 5. ANALYSIS AND RESULTS

We use hierarchical linear regression analysis to test the moderating influence of asset specificity and behavioral uncertainty. We enter industry membership as a block to control for industry differences. The industry variables explain approximately 5 per cent of the variance in the full sample; about 12 per cent in the sub-sample of firms reporting scarce financial resources, and approximately 6 per cent of the variance in the sub-sample of firms reporting abundant financial resources.

The second block included initial employment size as a control variable, sales growth and each of the asset specificity and behavioral uncertainty variables in turn. Our hypotheses focused on the moderating influence of asset specificity and behavioral uncertainty. Venkatraman (1989) suggests that this form of moderation can be successfully modeled as an interaction. Thus, in the third block we entered the interaction terms: (1) sales growth*product specific training, (2) sales growth*firm specific training, (3) sales growth*importance of customer relationships, (4) sales growth*importance of trade secrets, (5) sales growth*difficulty of screening and supervision, and (6) sales growth*difficulty of measuring

| 6 | 7 | 8 | 9 | 10 | 11 | 12 | 13 | 14 |
|---|---|---|---|---|---|---|---|---|
| −.02 | .04(.03) | .12(−.64) | .17(−.65) | .17(−.54) | .10(−.72) | .15(54) | .12(−.72) | |
| .01 | .07 | .13(−.01) | .16(−.03) | .06(−.01) | .02(−.03) | .05(.01) | .09(−.02) | .22 |

performance. We estimated the models in separate equations because each interaction term shared the sales growth component which resulted in high levels of multicollinearity.

Because of the size of the sample we were able to model the moderating influence of financial munificence by splitting the sample, which is an appropriate way to show that predictive ability of a variable differs across different conditions (Venkatraman, 1989). The median and mode of the financial munificence variable was 3.0, with 383 companies represented at that value. We used a decision rule 'larger or equal to the median' as the cutoff, resulting in 481 firms in the resource scarce subgroup and 876 firms in the resource munificent subgroup. Some of the regressions were done with slightly smaller sample sizes because of missing data for independent variables. Results are displayed in Table 9.3.

All of our hypotheses are supported by the analyses for the full sample and for the resource scarce sub-sample. Each investigated aspect of asset specificity and behavioral uncertainty influences the relationship between sales growth and employment as hypothesized. Although these relationships are significant, the effect sizes are relatively small. $f^2$ is the appropriate effect size measure to use in the context of an F-test for multiple correlation or multiple regression (Cohen, 1988). The effect size measure for multiple regression is defined as:

$$f^2 = R^2/1 - R^2$$

By convention, $f^2$ effect sizes of 0.02, 0.15, and 0.35 are considered small, medium, and large, respectively (Cohen, 1988). Each of the effect sizes in our study is considered to be small. Effect sizes for statistically significant results are also displayed in Table 9.3.

When resources are abundant the interactions become insignificant, except for the case of difficulty measuring performance which becomes significant in the opposite direction. Note that we conservatively made the resource munificent group the larger one, so the lack of significant results for that group is due to no or smaller estimated effect and not an artifact

*Table 9.3 Moderated hierarchical regression analysis*

| Variables | Importance of proprietary information | | | Difficulty screening/ supervision | | | Difficulty measuring performance | | |
|---|---|---|---|---|---|---|---|---|---|
| | Full sample | Scarce | Abundant | Full sample | Scarce | Abundant | Full sample | Scarce | Abundant |
| *Block 1* | | | | | | | | | |
| Manufacture food products 15xxx | −.01 | −.04*** | .02 | −.01 | −.04 | .02 | −.00 | −.05 | .02 |
| Publishing and printing 22xxx | −.02 | −.05 | .00 | −.01 | −.05 | .03 | −.01 | −.05 | .03 |
| General mechanical engineering 28520 | −.01 | −.03 | −.00 | −.01 | −.03 | .00 | −.01 | −.03 | .00 |
| Demolition and earth moving 45110 | −.00 | .06 | −.04 | −.00 | .06 | −.04 | −.00 | .08 | −.05 |
| General construction of buildings 45211 | .08* | .17*** | .02 | .08* | .17*** | .02 | .08* | .17 | .02 |
| Installation of electrical wiring 45310 | .04 | .04 | .04 | .04 | .04 | .04 | .05 | .05 | .04 |
| Painting 45441 | −.00 | −.03 | .01 | −.00 | −.03 | .01 | −.00 | −.03 | .01 |
| Sales/maintenance of motor vehicles 50000 | −.05 | −.06 | −.04 | −.05 | −.06 | −.04 | −.05 | −.06 | −.04 |
| Wholesale trade 51000 | .06 | .01 | .08* | .06* | .01 | .08* | .07* | .01 | .10** |
| Retail trade 52000 | −.02 | .03 | −.05 | −.02 | .03 | −.05 | −.03 | .03 | −.06 |
| Restaurants 55300 | .02 | −.02 | .04 | .02 | −.02 | −.04 | .01 | −.02 | .04 |
| Taxi operation 60220 | .02 | .00 | .05 | .03 | .00 | .05 | .03 | .00 | .06 |
| Freight transport by road 60240 | .01 | .15*** | −.06 | .01 | .16** | −.06 | .01 | .02 | −.07 |
| Financial intermediation 65000 | −.06* | −.04 | −.07 | −.06* | −.05 | −.07* | −.06* | −.04 | −.06 |

| | | | | | | | | | |
|---|---|---|---|---|---|---|---|---|---|
| Software consultancy and supply 72201 | −.07* | −.07 | −.07* | −.07* | −.07 | −.07* | −.07* | −.05 | −.07* |
| Other business activities 74000 | .01 | .05 | −.01 | .01 | .05 | −.01 | .01 | .06 | −.01 |
| Accounting, bookkeeping, auditing 74120 | −.06* | −.01 | −.09* | −.06* | −.01 | −.08* | −.06* | .01 | −.09 |
| Business consulting 74140 | −.07* | −.08 | −.07 | −.07* | −.08 | −.07 | −.07* | −.07 | −.07 |
| Construction engineering 74202 | −.06* | −.08 | −.05 | −.06* | −.07 | −.05 | −.06* | −.06 | −.06 |
| Advertising agencies 74401 | −.03 | −.04 | −.02 | −.03 | −.04 | −.02 | −.03 | −.04 | −.02 |
| Education 80000 | −.04 | −.04 | −.05 | −.04 | −.04 | −.04 | −.04 | −.03 | −.05 |
| Medical practice activities 85120 | .01 | .05 | −.00 | .01 | .06 | −.00 | .01 | .06 | −.00 |
| Other human health activities 85140 | −.06* | −.04 | −.08* | −.06* | −.04 | −.08* | −.06* | −.03 | −.08* |
| Artistic and literary creation 92310 | −.06* | −.08 | −.04 | −.06* | −.09 | −.03 | −.05 | −.06 | −.04 |
| Hairdressing 93021 | −.08* | −.06 | −.09* | −.07** | −.06 | −.08* | −.08* | −.06 | −.09* |
| Physical well-being activities 93040 | −.07* | −.11 * | −.04 | −.07* | .10* | −.04 | −.06* | −.011 | −.03 |
| Block 1 change *R*-square | .05*** | .12*** | .06** | .05*** | .12*** | .06** | .05*** | .12*** | .07*** |
| *Block 2* | | | | | | | | | |
| #Employees in 1995 | −.07** | −.07* | − .13*** | −.07* | −.07 | − .13*** | −.06* | −.07* | −.11 * |
| Natural log of the slope of the sales line | .20*** | .16*** | .30*** | .20*** | .16*** | .30*** | .20*** | .16*** | .30*** |
| Product specific knowledge | .09*** | .01 | .12*** | | | | | | |
| Firm specific knowledge | | | | .12*** | .04 | .15*** | | | |
| Importance of customer relations | | | | | | | .04 | .02 | .04 |
| Importance of trade secrets | | | | | | | | | |
| Difficulty supervision/screening | | | | | | | | | |

*Table 9.3* (continued)

| Variables | Importance of proprietary information | | | Difficulty screening/ supervision | | | Difficulty measuring performance | | |
|---|---|---|---|---|---|---|---|---|---|
| | Full sample | Scarce | Abundant | Full sample | Scarce | Abundant | Full sample | Scarce | Abundant |
| *Block 2* | | | | | | | | | |
| Difficulty measuring performance | | | | | | | | | |
| Block 2 change R-square | .05*** | .03*** | .10*** | .06*** | .03*** | .11*** | .05*** | .03*** | .08*** |
| *Block 3* | | | | | | | | | |
| Ln sales*product specific knowledge | .24*** | .57*** | .007 | | | | | | |
| Ln sales*firm specific knowledge | | | | .23*** | .47*** | −.07 | | | |
| Ln sales*customer relations | | | | | | | .15*** | 1.28*** | −.04 |
| Ln sales*importance of trade secrets | | | | | | | | | |
| Ln sales*supervision/screening | | | | | | | | | |
| Ln sales*difficulty measuring perf. | | | | | | | | | |
| Block 3 change *R*-square | .03*** | .04*** | .00 | .03*** | .03*** | .00 | .02*** | .04*** | .00 |
| Adjusted *R*-square for total model | .16*** | .14*** | .13*** | .12*** | .13*** | .14*** | .09*** | .13*** | .12*** |
| $f^2$ effect size | .032 | .043 | | .028 | .034 | | .015 | .036 | |
| Total model *F* | 6.85*** | 3.56*** | 5.16*** | 6.95*** | 3.44*** | 5.58*** | 5.23*** | 3.21*** | 4.67*** |
| *Z*-test for scarce vs. abundant | | | 3.26*** | | | 4.02*** | | | 4.09*** |
| *N* | 1346 | 477 | 868 | 1358 | 481 | 876 | 1284 | 449 | 834 |

| Variables | Importance of proprietary information | | | Difficulty screening/ supervision | | | Difficulty measuring performance | | |
|---|---|---|---|---|---|---|---|---|---|
| | Full sample | Scarce | Abundant | Full sample | Scarce | Abundant | Full sample | Scarce | Abundant |
| *Block 1* | | | | | | | | | |
| Manufacture food products 15xxx | −.00 | −.04*** | .02 | −.00 | −.05 | .02 | −.01 | −.05 | .01 |
| Publishing and printing 22xxx | −.01 | −.05 | .03 | −.01 | −.05 | .03 | −.01 | −.05 | .03 |
| General mechanical engineering 28520 | −.01 | −.03 | −.00 | −.02 | −.03 | .00 | −.01 | −.03 | .00 |
| Demolition and earth moving 45110 | −.01 | .06 | −.05 | −.00 | .08 | −.05 | .01 | .06 | −.05 |
| General construction of buildings 45211 | .08* | .17*** | .02 | .08* | .17*** | .02 | .08 | .17*** | .02 |
| Installation of electrical wiring 45310 | .04 | .04 | .05 | .04 | .04 | .04 | .04 | .04 | .04 |
| Painting 45441 | −.00 | −.03 | .01 | −.01 | −.03 | .01 | −.00 | −.03 | .01 |
| Sales/maintenance of motor vehicles 50000 | −.04 | −.07 | −.02 | −.05 | −.06 | −.04 | −.05 | −.06 | −.04 |
| Wholesale trade 51000 | .06 | .00 | .09** | .07* | .01 | .10** | .07* | .01 | .10** |
| Retail trade 52000 | −.02 | .03 | −.05 | −.03 | .02 | −.05 | −.02 | .03 | −.05 |
| Restaurants 55300 | .02 | −.02 | .04 | .01 | −.02 | .04 | .02 | −.02 | .05 |
| Taxi operation 60220 | .03 | .00 | .06 | .02 | .00 | .05 | .02 | .00 | .05 |
| Freight transport by road 60240 | .01 | .16*** | −.06 | .01 | .16*** | −.07 | .01 | .16*** | −.06 |
| Financial intermediation 65000 | −.06 | −.05 | −.06 | −.06 | −.05 | −.06 | −.06* | −.04 | −.07 |
| Software consultancy and supply 72201 | −.07 | −.06 | −.07 | −.06* | −.06 | −.07 | −.07 | −.06 | −.07* |

*Table 9.3* (continued)

| Variables | Importance of proprietary information | | | Difficulty screening/ supervision | | | Difficulty measuring performance | | |
|---|---|---|---|---|---|---|---|---|---|
| | Full sample | Scarce | Abundant | Full sample | Scarce | Abundant | Full sample | Scarce | Abundant |
| *Block 1* | | | | | | | | | |
| Other business activities 74000 | .02 | .05 | −.01 | .01 | .06 | −.02 | .01 | .06 | −.02 |
| Accounting, bookkeeping, auditing 74120 | −.07 | −.03 | −.08* | −.07* | −.02 | −.09** | −.07* | −.02 | −.09* |
| Business consulting 74140 | −.07 | −.08 | −.07 | −.07* | −.08 | −.07 | −.07* | −.07 | −.07 |
| Construction engineering 74202 | −.07 | −.08 | −.06 | −.07* | −.08 | −.06 | −.06* | −.08 | −.06 |
| Advertising agencies 74401 | −.03 | −.04 | −.02 | −.03 | −.04 | −.02 | −.03 | −.04 | −.02 |
| Education 80000 | −.04 | −.05 | −.04 | −.04 | −.05 | −.04 | −.04 | −.03 | −.04 |
| Medical practice activities 85120 | .01 | .06 | −.00 | .01 | .06 | −.00 | .01 | .06 | −.00 |
| Other human health activities 85140 | −.06 | −.03 | −.08* | −.06* | −.02 | −.08* | −.06* | −.04 | −.08* |
| Artistic and literary creation 92310 | −.05 | −.09 | −.03 | −.05 | −.06 | −.04 | −.06* | −.09 | −.04 |
| Hairdressing 93021 | −.08 | −.06 | −.09* | −.08* | −.06 | −.08* | −.07* | −.05 | −.09* |
| Physical well-being activities 93040 | −.06 | −.11 * | −.03 | −.06* | −.11 * | −.03 | −.06* | −.11 * | −.03 |
| Block 1 change *R*-square | .05*** | .12*** | .06*** | .05*** | .12*** | .06** | .05*** | .12*** | .07*** |
| *Block 2* | | | | | | | | | |
| #Employees in 1995 | −.06 | −.07 | −.10** | −.06* | −.07 | −.107** | −.06* | −.06 | −.11** |
| Natural log of the slope of the sales line | .21 | .16*** | .30*** | .21*** | .16*** | .30*** | .20*** | .17*** | .29*** |

| | | | | | | | | | |
|---|---|---|---|---|---|---|---|---|---|
| Product specific knowledge | | | | | | | | | |
| Firm specific knowledge | | | | | | | | | |
| Importance of customer relations | | | | | | | | | |
| Importance of proprietary information | .02 | −.03 | .03 | | | | | | |
| Difficulty screening/supervision | | | | .00 | −.01 | −.01 | | | |
| Difficulty measuring performance | | | | | | | .06 | .04 | .07* |
| Block 2 change R-square | .04*** | .03*** | .08*** | .04*** | .03*** | .08*** | .05*** | .03*** | .08*** |
| *Block 3* | | | | | | | | | |
| Ln sales*product specific knowledge | | | | | | | | | |
| Ln sales*firm specific knowledge | | | | | | | | | |
| Ln sales*customer relations | | | | | | | | | |
| Ln sales*importance of trade secrets | .26*** | .75*** | −.06 | | | | | | |
| Ln sales*difficulty screening/ supervision | | | | .16*** | −.34*** | .03 | | | |
| Ln sales*difficulty measuring perf. | | | | | | | .30*** | .56*** | −.32*** |
| Block 3 change *R*-square | .03*** | .06*** | .00 | .02*** | .04*** | .00 | .038*** | .05*** | .03*** |
| $f^2$effect size | .032 | .066 | | .017 | .039 | | .040 | .056 | .027 |
| Adjusted *R*-square for total model | .11 | .16 | .12 | .09 | .14 | .11 | .12 | .15 | .15 |
| Total model *F* | 6.11*** | 3.93*** | 4.65*** | 5.29*** | 3.34*** | 4.46*** | 6.92*** | 3.71*** | 5.86*** |
| *Z*-test for scarce vs. abundant | | | 5.18*** | | | 3.88*** | | | 5.89*** |
| *N* | 1293 | 452 | 840 | 1283 | 450 | 832 | 1319 | 462 | 856 |

*Notes:* *$p$<.05; **$p$<.01; ***$p$<.001.

of smaller sample size. In addition we conducted a $Z$-test as proposed by Cohen (1983) substantiating the difference between effect sizes for the resource scarce and resource munificent groups. In all six cases there are strongly significant differences ($p < .001$). These results consistently show that young and small firms are less likely to choose solutions consistent with TCE prescriptions when resources are abundant.

## 6. DISCUSSION

This is the first study that measures asset specificity and behavioral uncertainty constructs and applies them to the relationship between sales growth and employment growth in emerging businesses. Our results suggest that transaction cost based explanatory variables have a significant moderating influence on employment growth.

Our results provide answers to our initial research question. When does employment growth accompany sales growth? According to our results and the logic of transaction cost economics (Williamson, 1996), employment growth accompanies sales growth in emerging companies when human asset specificity is relatively high and the costs and uncertainty associated with screening for potential employees and monitoring performance are lower than the cost of external contracting. The results of this study provide support for the hypotheses we derived from the predictions of transaction costs economics as framed by Williamson (1985, 1996). Our four measures of human asset specificity; (1) product specific knowledge, (2) firm specific knowledge, (3) the importance of protecting trade secrets, and (4) the importance of maintaining personalized customer relationships, are positive moderators of the relationship between sales growth and employment change in the full sample and when financial resources are relatively scarce. Although not hypothesized, product specific knowledge and firm specific knowledge have a positive direct effect on employment growth. On this basis it may be speculated that firms requiring specialized company and product related skills appear to find it preferable to hire and train new employees to guarantee a certain service level, as opposed to sub-contracting this work to external parties. These results are consistent with the findings of Anderson (1985) when she examined the propensity to employ or contract salespeople (see Table 9.4).

In contrast, the cost of screening for and supervising employees is a negative moderator of the sales growth/employment relationship, suggesting that under resource constrained conditions firms are more likely to seek ways, other than adding employees, to provide their product or service when screening and supervising costs are high. This finding is in a reverse

*Table 9.4 Summary of results*

| Hypothesis | Results | | |
|---|---|---|---|
| | Full sample | Resource scarce | Resource abundant |
| 1. The degree of product specific knowledge required for new employees will be a positive moderator of the relationship between sales growth and employment growth. | Supported | Supported | Not supported |
| 2. The degree of firm specific knowledge required for new employees will be a positive moderator of the relationship between sales growth and employment growth. | Supported | Supported | Not supported |
| 3. The degree to which personalized customer service matters will be a positive moderator of the relationship between sales growth and employment growth. | Supported | Supported | Not supported |
| 4. The degree to which proprietary information needs to be shared with employees is a positive moderator of the relationship between sales growth and employment growth. | Supported | Supported | Not supported |
| 5. The difficulty of screening and supervising employees is a negative moderator of the relationship between sales growth and employment growth. | Supported | Supported | Not supported |
| 6. The degree to which it is difficult to monitor employee performance is a positive moderator of the relationship between sales growth and employment growth. | Supported | Supported | Reversed |
| 7. When resources are scarce the moderating effect of transaction cost variables is significantly stronger than will be encountered when resources are abundant. | Supported | | |

direction from the others. The costs and hassles of screening permanent employees are not the same with temporary employees or with outsourced agreements. For example, when temporary employees are employed, the temp agency assumes the role of screening employees. Likewise, if an emerging firm contracts with an external company to manufacture its product, it is only required to screen the manufacturer once, in contrast to the screening required for each permanent employee. Thus, the results of this hypothesis are consistent with practice.

Finally, when it is difficult to measure performance, firms are more likely to hire employees than to engage in external contracting. When outcomes are hard to measure, clan based controls (Mintzberg, 1978) are likely to take their place. Permanent employees will respond to controls based on culture more readily than temporary or subcontracted workers.

Also consistent with Coles and Hesterly (1998), TCE does not appear to be a resource neutral theory. Our findings suggest that managers of emerging firms often make choices inconsistent with the prescriptions of TCE with respect to employment. If they have access to sufficient financial resources they tend to avoid the sometimes undesirable expected consequences of hiring and managing employees (Wiklund et al., 2003). These results are consistent with those reported by Coles and Hesterly (1998). This has implications for the theory's applicability in the studied context, but in conjunction with findings from Coles and Hesterly (1998) who found support for transaction cost predictions in for-profit hospitals, but not in not-for-profit hospitals, it seems reasonable to assume that the applicability of transaction cost economics is also more generally contingent on scarcity or abundance of resources. In the subgroup of firms with less than median financial munificence – those claiming financial resources were scarce – the relationships are significantly and consistently in harmony with the predictions of transaction cost economics. In contrast, transaction cost predictions become weaker when resources are perceived to be abundant.

One might well ask: if firms are not making market efficient choices, how do they have munificent resources? In our case these are young and small firms and resource availability may be a function of things other than the efficient operation of the business. For example, they may have had some sort of windfall or high profits due to competitive effectiveness rather than efficiency. In addition, if a founder has another source of income such as significant savings, a pension, a working spouse, an inheritance, or proceeds from the sale of a property or a previous business, the psychic costs associated with increasing employment may be deemed not worthwhile even if it would make sense from a business perspective. Only when resources are scarce are individuals more likely to make resource efficient choices.

## 6.1 Significance and Effect Size

In the full sample and the resource scarce sub-sample our results are all statistically significant. However, based on Cohen's (1988) guidelines, the effect sizes (ranging from .015 to .066) are all considered small. The effect sizes, however, must be viewed in light of the theory. TCE is not intended to explain *why* firms grow. In fact, it only states that firms will tend to choose whether to hire permanent employees or to outsource or seek other options based on the relative costs of the transaction. Given this restricted scope of the theory our results are quite strong. In fact, the degree of support for hypotheses in this study is substantially greater than much of the transaction cost research that has been carried out previously (David and Han, 2004). A reason for this may be that young and small firms tend to be more resource constrained, and thus are less likely to be insulated from TCE effects.

## 6.2 Limitations

From the initiation of this data set in 1994, approximately 75 per cent of all the firms were confirmed to have gone out of business. An additional 5 per cent are suspected to have gone out of business for one reason or another. Clearly, we are studying survivors. However, as discussed in the introduction, because we are interested in addressing *how* emerging firms grow, we do not believe survivor bias to be a damaging limitation. We did not attempt to predict *why* firms grow.

While the sample covers the full spectrum of new firms started in 1994 in Sweden, the average size of the firms involved are quite small. Indeed the average size of the firms involved in the study in 2004 was slightly over 5 FTE. The mean sales in 2003 (the last full year of sales data in the study) were approximately 2,988,241 SEK (during the time period of the study the exchange rate ranged between 6.6–10.6 SEK per 1 $US). When data were collected in 2000, average size of the firms was 1.8 FTE (standard deviation 2.79) and 866,000 SEK in mean sales. Thus, there may be growth bias, yet there is a strong argument for focusing on growing firms in entrepreneurship research, not only based on the economic value created by employing more people, but also that growing firms survive over longer periods of time (Phillips and Kirchhoff, 1989). Further, as we emphasized in the Introduction with reference to Penrose (1959): in order to study *how* firms expand, growing (rather than dissolved) firms need to be studied.

Another limitation is that the sample is limited to Sweden. As noted in the Method section the particularities of Swedish employment security and wage setting institutions may lead to amplified TCE effects because business founders are more reluctant to let employment growth follow sales development. Our results concerning munificence show that the TCE effects do not apply equally in all contexts. Hence, to improve the generalizability of our results the study should be replicated in other settings.

In addition, all of our measures except sales come from a single source. CEOs were asked to report employment growth, perceived asset specificity and behavioral uncertainty variables, and perceived resource munificence. The threat of same source variance is mitigated somewhat because our measures refer to verifiable firm characteristics rather than unobservable individual feelings (Podasakoff et al., 2003). For example, sales growth and employment growth are factual and verifiable measures. However, our asset specificity, behavioral uncertainty, and resource munificence variables are perceptions of the situation rather than hard measures. Note, however, that tests of our hypotheses do not rely on correlations among perceptual variables. Moreover, common method bias would not explain the interactive relationships between predictor and outcome variables, nor would it explain why results are not significant in the resource munificent subset. To further help mitigate the threat of same-source bias, we used Harman's One-Factor Test as described by Podasakoff et al. (2003). We entered the 21 items measuring sales growth, employment growth, and TCE factors into an exploratory factor analysis. The first factor accounted for only 13.5 per cent of the total 65.1 per cent variance and no single factor accounted for the majority of the covariance, suggesting that common method variance is not solely responsible for our findings.

Another measurement-related limitation of our study is 'when' the TCE constructs were assessed. Such 'prediction of the past' designs have been rather common in research on firm growth (Davidsson and Wiklund, 2000). It can be argued that a fair amount of temporal stability appears a reasonable assumption for these variables. Nonetheless, a true longitudinal assessment of these variables as possibly time-varying constructs to be re-assessed repeatedly during the studied period is a more recommendable approach for future studies.

Finally, our theoretical model specifies a direction of causality – employees are added to support sales growth. The direction of causality could be reversed and the addition of employees would then drive sales growth. However, in that scenario TCE factors would have a direct, but not a moderating role on employment growth. As can be seen in Table 9.3, direct effects are significant with product specific knowledge and firm specific knowledge in the full sample and in the resource constrained sub-sample. However, results are not significant with respect to any of the other variables. Although we acknowledge that causality could be reversed, the conception of our model is consistent with the rationale inherent in transaction cost economics, and the results are consistent with the direction of causality we have theorized.

### 6.3 Implications for Future Research

The limitations associated with this study also provide opportunities for future research. It is possible to speculate that in some cases, the levels of high asset specificity in the firm worked as a source of competitive advantage for the firm (Barney, 2001) and therefore provided the basis for survival. At the same time, misuse, opportunism, overtraining or other problems with employing new individuals could be the reason for the firm to go out of business. It would therefore be valuable for future studies measuring growth and industry characteristics to address whether the same asset specificity measures associated with a positive relationship between sales growth and employment growth are also associated with survival in some way.

Also raised is an intriguing question of direction of causality. Our research is consistent with the literature (e g. Delmar, 1997; Davidsson and Wiklund, 2000) in providing evidence that the relationship between sales growth and employment growth in emerging firms is smaller than might be anticipated. However, it will require more fine-grained longitudinal research to determine for the part of the population where these two measures move together, whether employment growth occurs to meet the demands of sales growth, or alternatively whether employment growth provides opportunities for future sales growth.

Finally, the interaction between sales growth and transaction cost variables explains a relatively small proportion of the variance in employment growth. Additional research will be required to identify other variables that influence that relationship.

## 7. CONCLUSIONS

This is the first study to apply transaction cost economics to explain the relationship between sales growth and employment growth in emerging ventures. It provides evidence that the predictions of transaction cost economics are consistently significant with this sample of emerging firms. In addition, it sheds further light on the influence of resource scarcity and the application of transaction cost economics.

This chapter makes a significant contribution by adapting measures of asset specificity and behavioral uncertainty for application in emerging firms. It provides substantial evidence supporting the reliability and validity of the measures.

For policy-makers our results give input to a refined understanding of why the firm level pursuit of growth as measured by sales does not always translate into increased employment. The psychic and monetary costs of adding employees may deter many startup businesses from adding employees. Thus, if employment growth is a desired societal outcome, policy-makers may focus on reducing the political and administrative obligations associated with creating and expanding employment

These primary conclusions are useful for understanding how transaction cost economics predictions apply to sales growth and employment in emerging firms. We note that the total amount of variance accounted for is small; however, it must be understood that the transaction costs model does not purport to be the major theoretical explanation of *why* firms add employees, but rather explains a portion of *how* sales growth and employment growth are associated. The implication of transaction cost theory for emerging firms is that *if* they have sales growth opportunities, and *if* the psychic and other intangible costs of adding employees are not too high, then it is more efficient to add permanent employees when human asset specificity is high and the behavioral uncertainty associated with hiring permanent employees is less than the behavioral uncertainty of subcontracting, outsourcing, or hiring temporary employees (Williamson, 1985, 1996).

# NOTE

* Previously published as: Gaylen N. Chandler, Alexander McKelvie and Per Davidsson (2009), 'Asset specificity and behavioral uncertainty as moderators of the sales growth–employment growth relationship in emerging ventures', *Journal of Business Venturing*, **24** (4), July, 373–87.

# REFERENCES

Anderson, E., 1985. The salesperson as outside agent or employee: A transaction cost analysis. Marketing Science 4, 234–254.

Ardichvili, A., Cardozo, S., Harmon, S., Vadaktah, S., 1998. Towards a theory of new venture growth. Paper presented at the 1998 (May 21–23) Babson Entrepreneurship Research Conference. Ghent, Belgium.

Bac, M., 2000. On-the-job specific training and efficient screening. Journal of Labor Economics 18, 681–701.

Bagozzi, R.P., Yi, Y., Phillips, L.W., 1991. Assessing construct validity in organizational research. Administrative Science Quarterly 36, 421–458.
Barney, J.B., 2001. Resource-based 'theories' of competitive advantage: a ten-year retrospective on the resource-based view. Journal of Management 27, 643–650.
Baum, J.R., Locke, E.A., Smith, K.G., 2001. A multidimensional model of venture growth. Academy of Management Journal 44, 292–303.
Baum, J.R., Wally, S., 2003. Strategic decision making speed and firm performance. Strategic Management Journal 24, 1107–1129.
Benson, G.S., Finegold, D., Mohrman, S.A., 2004. You paid for the skills, now keep them: tuition reimbursement and voluntary turnover. Academy of Management Journal 47, 315–331.
Birch, D.L., 1979. The job generating process. MIT Program on Neighborhood and Regional Change, Cambridge, MA.
Birch, D.L., Medoff, J., 1994. Gazelles. In: Solmon, L.C., Levenson, A.R. (Eds.), Labor markets, employment policy and job creation. Westview Press, London, pp. 159–168.
Box, G.E.P., Cox, D.R., 1964. An analysis of transformations. Journal of the Royal Statistical Society, Series B 26 (2), 211–252.
Browne, M.W., Cudeck, R., 1993. Alternative ways of assessing model fit. In: Bollen, K.A., Long, J.S. (Eds.), Testing structural equation models. Sage, Newbury Park, CA, pp. 445–455.
Byrne, B.M., 2001. Structural equation modeling with AMOS: basic concepts, applications, and programming. Lawrence Erlbaum Associates, Mahwah, NJ.
Castrogiovanni, G.J., 1991. Environmental munificence: a theoretical assessment Academy of Management Review 16, 542–565.
Chandler, G.N., Hanks, S.H., 1993. Measuring the performance of emerging businesses: a validation study. Journal of Business Venturing 8, 391–408.
Chandler, G.N., Hanks, S.H., 1994. Market attractiveness, resource-based capabilities, venture strategies, and venture performance. Journal of Business Venturing 9, 331–349.
Chandler, G.N., Hanks, S.H., 1998. An examination of the substitutability of founders' human and financial capital in emerging business ventures. Journal of Business Venturing 13, 353–370.
Chandler, G.N., Jansen, E., 1992. The founder's self-assessed competence and venture performance. Journal of Business Venturing 7 (3), 223–236.
Cohen, A., 1983. Comparing regression coefficients across subsamples: a study of the statistical test. Sociological Methods & Research 12 (1), 77–94.
Cohen, J., 1988. Statistical power analysis for the behavioral sciences, 2nd Edition. Lawrence Erlbaum Associates, Hillsdale, NJ.
Coles, J.W., Hesterly, W.S., 1998. The impact of firm-specific assets and the interaction of uncertainty: an examination of make or buy decisions in public and private hospitals. Journal of Economic Behavior and Organization 36, 383–409.
David, R.J., Han, R.J.A., 2004. Systematic assessment of the empirical support for transaction cost economics. Strategic Management Journal 25, 39–48.
Davidson, R., MacKinnon, J.G., 1993. Estimation and inference in econometrics. Oxford University Press, New York.
Davidsson, P., Wiklund, J., 2000. Conceptual and empirical challenges in the study of firm growth. In: Sexton, D., Landström, H. (Eds.), The Blackwell handbook of entrepreneurship. Blackwell, Oxford, MA, pp. 26–44.

Davis, S.J., Haltiwanger, J., 1992. Gross job creation, gross job destruction, and employment reallocation. The Quarterly Journal of Economics 107 (3), 819–863.
Delmar, F., 1997. Measuring growth: methodological considerations and empirical results. In: Donckels, R., Miettinen, A. (Eds.), Entrepreneurship and SME research: On its way to the next millennium. Ashgate, Aldershot, pp. 190–216.
Delmar, F., Davidsson, P., 1999. Firm size expectations of nascent entrepreneurs. In: Reynolds, P.D., Bygrave, W.D., Manigart, S., Mason, C, Meyer, G.D., Sapienza, H.J., Shaver, K.G. (Eds.), Frontiers of entrepreneurship research 1999, vol. 19. Babson College, Wellesley, MA, pp. 90–104.
Delmar, F., Davidsson, P., Gartner, W., 2003. Arriving at the high-growth firm. Journal of Business Venturing 18,189–216.
Dess, G.G., Beard, D.W., 1984. Dimensions of organizational task environments. Administrative Science Quarterly 29 (1) 52–73.
Dess, G.G., Davis, P.S., 1984. Porter's generic strategies as determinants of strategic group membership and organizational performance. The Academy of Management Journal. 27 (3), 467–488.
Dunne, T., Haltwanger, J., Troske, K.R., 1996. Technology and jobs: secular changes and cyclical dynamics. Economic Studies 96-7 US Census.
Dwyer, F.R., Schurr, P.H., Oh, S., 1987. Developing buyer-seller relationships. Journal of Marketing 2 (51), 11–27.
Edelman, L.F., Brush, C.G., Manolova, T., 2005. Co-alignment in the resource-performance relationship: strategy as mediator. Journal of Business Venturing 20, 359–383.
Ensley, M.D., Pearce, C.L., Hmieleski, K.M., 2006. The moderating effect of environmental dynamics on the relationship between entrepreneur leadership behavior and new venture performance. Journal of Business Venturing 21, 243–263.
Gilbert, B.A., McDougal, P.P., Audretsch, D.B., 2006. New venture growth: a review and extension. Journal of Management 32 (6), 926–950.
Hanks, S.H., Watson, C.J., Jansen, E., Chandler, G.N., 1993. Tightening the life-cycle construct: a taxonomic study of growth stage configurations in high-technology organizations. Entrepreneurship Theory and Practice 18 (2), 5–30.
Heide, J.B., John, G., 1988. The role of dependence balancing in safeguarding transaction-specific assets in conventional channels. Journal of Marketing 52, 20–35.
Henrekson, M., Johansson, D., 1999. Institutional effects on the evolution of the size distribution of firms. Small Business Economics 12 (1), 11–23.
Henrekson, M., Rosenberg, N., 2001. Designing efficient institutions for science-based entrepreneurship: lessons from U.S. and Sweden. Journal of Technology Transfer 26 (3), 207–231.
Henrekson, M., 2005. Entrepreneurship: a weak link in a welfare state. Industrial and Corporate Change 14 (3), 437–467.
Hesterly, W.S., Liebeskind, J., Zenger, T.R., 1990. Organization economics: an impending revolution in organizational theory? Academy of Management Review 15, 402–420.
Hu L -, T., Bentler, P.M., 1999. Cutoff criteria for fit indexes in covariance structure analysis: conventional criteria versus new alternatives. Structural Equation Modeling: A Multidisciplinary Journal 6, 1–55.
John, G., Weitz, B., 1989. Sales force compensation: an empirical investigation

of the factors related to use of salary versus incentive compensation. Journal of Marketing Research 26 (1), 1–14.
Kazanjian, R.K., Drazin, R., 1990. A stage-contingent model of design and growth for technology based new ventures. Journal of Business Venturing 5 (3), 137–150.
Koch, M.J., McGrath, R.G., 1996. Improving labor productivity: human resource management policies do matter. Strategic Management Journal 17 (5), 335–354.
MacCallum, R.C., Browne, M.W., Sugawara, H.M., 1996. Power analysis and determination of sample size for covariance structure modeling. Psychological Methods 1,130–149.
McDougall, P.P., Robinson Jr., R.B., DeNisi, A.S., 1992. Modeling new venture performance: an analysis of new venture strategy, industry structure, and venture origin. Journal of Business Venturing 4 (7), 267–289.
McMahon, R.G.P., 2001. Growth and performance of manufacturing SMEs: the influence of financial management characteristics. International Small Business Journal 19 (3), 10.
Mintzberg, H., 1978. Patterns in strategy formation. Management Science 25, 934–948.
Nunnally, J.C, 1978. Psychometric theory. McGraw-Hill, New York.
Penrose, E., 1959. The theory of the growth of the firm. Oxford University Press, Oxford.
Pfeffer, J., 1998. Seven practices of successful organizations. California Management Review 40 (2), 96–124.
Phillips, B., Kirchhoff, B., 1989. Formation, growth and survival: small firm dynamics in the U.S. economy. Small Business Economics 1, 65–74.
Podasakoff, P.M., MacKenzie, S.B., Lee, J.Y., Podsakoff, N.P., 2003. Common method biases in behavioral research: a critical review of the literature and recommended remedies. Journal of Applied Psychology 88 (5), 879–903.
Rindfleisch, A., Heide, J.B., 1997. Transaction cost analysis: past, present, and future applications. Journal of Marketing 61, 30–54.
Robertson, T.S., Gatignon, H., 1998. Technology development mode: a transaction cost conceptualization. Strategic Management Journal 19, 515-531.
Robinson, K.C., McDougall, P.P., 2001. Entry barriers and new venture performance: a comparison of universal and contingency approaches. Strategic Management Journal 22, 659–685.
Robinson, J.P., Shaver, PR., Wrightsman, L.S., 1991. Criteria for scale selection and evaluation. In: Robinson, J.P., Shaver, P.R., Wrightsman, LS. (Eds.), Measures of personality and social psychological attitudes. Academic Press, San Diego, CA, pp. 1–6.
Sapienza, H.J., Korsgaard, M.A., Forbes, D.P., 2003. The self-determination motive and entrepreneurs' choice of financing. In Advances in entrepreneurship, firm emergence and growth: Cognitive approaches to entrepreneurship research, vol 6. J. Katz, J, Shepherd D, (eds). Oxford, UK: Elsevier/JAI Press; 107–140.
Shane, S., Venkataraman, S., 2000. The promise of entrepreneurship as a field of research. Academy of Management Review 25 (1), 217–226
Singh, J., 1986. Performance, slack, and risk taking in organizational decision making. Academy of Management Journal 29, 562–585
Southwood, K.E., 1978. Substantive theory and statistical interaction: five models. American Journal of Sociology 83, 1154–1203.

Stump, R.L., Heide, J.B., 1996. Controlling supplier opportunism in industrial relationships. Journal of Marketing Research 33 (4), 431–441.

Thurik, A.R., Wennekers, S., 2004. Entrepreneurship, small business and economic growth. Journal of Small Business and Enterprise Development 11 (1), 140–149.

U.S. Small Business Administration, 2004. The small business economy: a report to the President. United States Government Printing Office, Washington.

Venkatraman, N., 1989. The concept of fit in strategy research: toward verbal and statistical correspondence. Academy of Management Review 14, 423–444.

Weinzimmer, L.G., Nystrom, P.C, Freeman, S.J., 1998. Measuring organizational growth: issues, consequences and guidelines. Journal of Management 24, 235–262.

Weiss, A.M., Anderson, E., 1992. Converting from independent to employee sales forces. Journal of Marketing Research 29 (1), 101–115.

Wiklund, J., 1998. Small Firm Growth and Performance: Entrepreneurship and Beyond. Doctoral dissertation. Jönköping: Jönköping International Business School.

Wiklund, J., Davidsson, P., Delmar, F., 2003. Expected consequences of growth and their effect on growth willingness in different samples of small firms. Entrepreneurship Theory & Practice 27, 247–269.

Wiklund, J., Shepherd, D., 2003. Knowledge-based resources, entrepreneurial orientation and the performance of small and medium-sized businesses. Strategic Management Journal 24, 1307–1314.

Williamson, O.E., 1985. The economic institutions of capitalism. The Free Press, New York.

Williamson, O.E., 1996. Economics and organization: a primer. California Management Review 38, 131–146.

Yasai-Ardekani, M., 1989. Effects of environmental scarcity and munificence on the relationship of context to organizational structure. Academy of Management Journal 32, 131–156.

Zacharakis, A.L., Neck, H.M., Bygrave, W.D., Cox, L.W., 2001. Global Entrepreneurship Monitor 2001 Executive Report Babson College, Wellesley, MA

Zeng, M., Chen, X., 2003. Achieving cooperation in multiparty alliances: a social dilemma approach to partnership management. Academy of Management Review 28, 587–605.

# 10. Organic and acquisitive growth: re-examining, testing and extending Penrose's growth theory*

**Andy Lockett, Johan Wiklund, Per Davidsson and Sourafel Girma**

## INTRODUCTION

*The Theory of the Growth of the Firm* by Edith Penrose, first published in 1959, is a seminal contribution to the field of management. Penrose's intention was to create a theory of firm growth which was logically consistent and empirically tractable (Buckley and Casson, 2007). Much attention, however, has been focused on her unintended contribution to the resource-based view (henceforth RBV) (e.g. Kor and Mahoney, 2004; Lockett and Thompson, 2004) rather than her firm growth theory. We feel that this is unfortunate because despite a rapidly growing body of empirical work, conceptual advancement in growth studies has been limited (Davidsson and Wiklund, 2000; Davidsson et al., 2006; Delmar, 1997; Storey, 1994). The growth literature frequently references Penrose's work, but little explicit testing of her ideas has been undertaken. This is surprising given that Penrose's work remains the most comprehensive theory of growth to date. One explanation is that she did not formally present her arguments, favouring verbal exposition over formalized models (Lockett, 2005; Lockett and Thompson, 2004). However, the central propositions and conclusions of her theory can be operationalized and empirically tested.

Central to Penrose's growth theory are the adjustment costs (henceforth AC) of growth and the productive opportunity set (henceforth POS) facing the firm. The ACs of growth consist of the time and effort required to integrate new managers and operations in expanding the activities of the firm. The development of managerial resources takes time, which sets an ultimate limit to how fast firms can grow. ACs, however, only relate to firms that have been able to identify and exploit a growth opportunity. The identification and exploitation of growth opportunities is inextricably linked to managers' subjective assessment of their productive opportunity set, which is influenced by the resources of the firm (Penrose, 1959, p. 85), including its knowledge base. Even operating with the same set of resources, different managers may generate entirely different services from these resources (Kor et al., 2007; Penrose, 1959). To date, empirical tests of Penrose's theory have been limited to the ACs of growth. We argue that a focus on ACs of growth, to the exclusion of any consideration of POSs, will provide only partial and potentially inaccurate insights into the growth of firms (see Geroski, 2005, for a critique of the focus on ACs).

To address this limitation we investigate the relative impact of ACs and POSs arising from a strategy of organic (internal) growth vs. acquired (external) growth. Penrose made it clear that organic growth (henceforth OG) and acquisitive growth (henceforth AG) are two different strategic options facing the managers of a firm. She outlined clearly the effects of OG on ACs and POSs, and their subsequent effects on future organic growth. However, she was largely silent about the effects of AG. Central to Penrose's theory is that opportunities for, and limits to, future growth are generated by the resource accumulation of past growth. The past use of one mode of growth has consequences for future organic growth. Penrose was clear that previous OG may act as a constraint on current OG. Furthermore, she wrote that: 'The significance of merger [and acquisition] can best be appraised in the light of its effect on and limits to internal growth' (Penrose, 1959, p. 5). Penrose did not, however, explain *how* AG influences ACs and POSs, and subsequently the future OG of the firm.

In revisiting Penrose's writings it is important to acknowledge that they are a product of her time (Lockett and Thompson, 2004), which necessitates a re-examination of her ideas when applying them to a contemporary context. Her ideas were informed by inductive reasoning based on her own observations of businesses and their environment. The 1950s was a period of sustained economic growth. Consequently, she explicitly states that her theory assumes that there are no external limits to the growth opportunities of firms. The assumption of unlimited growth opportunities does not hold today given slower economic growth and increased international competition. In comparison to the 1950s, economic growth for European nations was much slower at the end of the 20th century.[1] In addition, financial liberalization and innovation during the last 20 years of the 20th century led to an increase in the availability of inexpensive debt. Low costs for debt encourages debt-financed takeovers just as a booming stock market cuts the cost of capital. Hence it became easier for firms to pursue a strategy of growth through acquisition.

We develop our arguments in relation to the OG and AG of firms by revisiting and extending Penrose's work in light of recent developments in the areas of the RBV (see Barney, 1986, 1991; Dierickx and Cool, 1989, Wernerfelt, 1984); the RBV interpretation of acquisitions (see Harrison et al., 1991, 2001); and the organizational literature on path dependency and inertia (see Cyert and March, 1963; Miller, 1994; Vermuelen and Bakerma, 2001). Consistent with Penrose, our theoretical and empirical focus is on the growth of firm resources. Specifically, we focus on employment growth because we are primarily interested in extending Penrose's theory of growth, which concerns 'the expansion of human and other resources' of the firm (Penrose, 1995, p. xi).

Our contribution is threefold. First, we conceptually and empirically separate OG from AG. To our knowledge this is the first, broadly based empirical study to do so. Second, we theoretically explain *how* previous OG and AG affect future organic growth in terms of their relative effects on ACs and POSs. We feel that a major contribution of our work is the focus we bring to bear on the issue of POSs and their potential effects on the growth of the firm. Third, we empirically validate our model employing a ten-year panel of commercially active enterprises in the private (non-government) sector in Sweden, which had 20 employees or more in the final year of our panel. Consequently, privately owned SMEs constitute the vast majority of our sample studied. Our dataset is unique in that we are able to decompose employment growth into its constituent elements, organic and acquisitive, and hence examine their interrelationships.

The remainder of the chapter unfolds as follows. In Section 2 we outline our theoretical background and derive hypotheses in relation to both OG and AG. In Section 3 we present our data and methods. The results of our analysis are presented in Section 4. Finally, in Section 5 we discuss our results and highlight the implications and limitations of our work.

## THEORETICAL BACKGROUND

The origins of Penrose's work on growth can be traced back to her 1952 paper published in the *American Economic Review* (Penrose, 1952). In the paper she criticized the use of biological analogies of growth, reasserting the importance of economic principles and human motivation for explaining firm growth. These principles were introduced in a subsequent paper in the same journal (Penrose, 1955). The culmination of her growth research was the publication of her seminal book *The Theory of the Growth of the Firm* and the associated case study on the Hercules Powder Corporation (Penrose, 1960).

Penrose's interest lay in the growth of firms as institutions. Influenced by the writings of Barnard (1938), Cyert and March (1955), and Simon (1947), she considered firms to be administrative entities, with the control over potentially valuable resources. It is the managers of the firm who make decisions about how firm activities and resources are deployed (Penrose, 1960, pp. 2–3). The current and historical activities of the firm shape the firm's future resources and knowledge – i.e. the firm's resource base is unique and path dependent. In addition to highlighting the importance of firm-specific managerial knowledge, Penrose identifies two types of firm-specific capabilities: entrepreneurial and managerial (Penrose, 1959, p. 35). Entrepreneurial capabilities are a function of imagination. Managerial (or administrative) capabilities are largely practical in orientation, and are associated with the execution of ideas. Entrepreneurial capabilities are a necessary but not sufficient condition for firm growth as they must be accompanied by managerial capabilities for growth to occur.

Penrose's emphasis on the importance of managerial capabilities was based on her view that the firm is not just a collection of individuals but 'a collection of individuals who have experience working together' (Penrose, 1959, p. 46). The need for shared experience in order for managers to be effective has important implications for the rate at which a firm can expand its activities. The expansion of the management team, and hence the development of managerial capabilities, is inherently limited in the short run. Any expansion of managerial resources will require effort on the part of existing managers to train new managers and creates the ACs of growth. We define the ACs of growth, consistent with Penrose (1959) and Geroski (2005), as the costs of managing the growth process, i.e. the time and effort required to integrate new people into the firm, not the direct costs of acquisition. Both organic and acquisitive employment growth creates ACs, which are negatively related to the future OG rate of the firm.

Penrose proposed that the size of a firm's POS is positively related to the ability of the firm to grow. The POS is determined by the ways in which managers are able to combine resources at their disposal to produce productive services. At any given point the known productive services arising from a given bundle of resources are unlikely to exhaust its full potential. This is particularly the case with large firms relative to small firms because of the sheer diversity of resources they comprise. There is always the potential for firm expansion.

The POS of the firm may be influenced by two different resource-usage activities. First is the search for novel uses of existing resources. A firm's resources are never utilized fully and hence there is always some resource slack, which creates an opportunity for firm growth. In order for any excess capacity of existing resources to be exploited, the resources may need to be combined with other available resources in order to generate productive services. Penrose highlights that firms attempt to discover more about the potential uses of their existing resources via research and other types of proactive search. She represents this by arguing that managers frequently reflect: '. . . there ought to be some way in which I can use that' (Penrose, 1959, p. 77).

Second, existing resources may be used as a basis for growth through the application of the entrepreneurial judgement, or entrepreneurial capabilities, of managers. Managers make subjective evaluations of market conditions which are influenced by their perceptions. Based on the discovery of changes in customer preferences and innovation, managers choose to engage in the recombination of existing resources to satisfy this perceived demand. Hence, opportunities for expansion are limited by the extent to which the managers of a firm perceive opportunities, are willing to act on them, and able to capitalize on them by using their own resources (Penrose, 1959, p. 84). Thus, the growth of the firm involves discovering new market opportunities and changing and using existing resources to match these opportunities.

The growth rate of a firm therefore is influenced by two factors. First, firms incur ACs when they grow because of the need to train and integrate new managers and employees into the business. ACs relate to the utilization and development of managerial capabilities. Penrose argued that the rate at which the firm can develop its managerial capabilities sets an ultimate limit to its growth, even if the productive opportunity set is immense (which has become known as the Penrose effect; Marris, 1964). Second, and arguably of greater importance, the ability of a firm to grow is influenced by its POS. Penrose defines the POS of the firm as 'all of the productive possibilities that its "entrepreneurs" see and can take advantage of' (Penrose, 1959, p. 31). Penrose viewed people as being the most important resource in any business, because it is their knowledge and insights that determine the future POS of the firm. She continues to argue that a theory of the growth of firms is essentially an examination of the changing POSs of firms (Penrose, 1959, pp. 31–2). The larger the POS of the firm, the greater its potential for growth.

Managers face two strategic growth options: OG and AG. OG involves the internal generation of resources, e.g. by employing and training new staff. However, as many resources are non-standard, complex, involve tacit knowledge, and are firm specific, they are difficult to trade individually. Consequently, AG (one firm buys controlling interest in another firm and the acquired business is integrated within current operations or becomes a subsidiary of the acquirer's portfolio) may provide an attractive alternative to organic growth because it enables managers to acquire 'bundles' of resources (Barney, 1986; Rumelt, 1987). Furthermore, a strategy of acquisition may enable a firm to take advantage of growth opportunities by accessing resources that are complementary in nature to the resources that the firm already controls (Harrison et al., 1991, 2001).

We anticipate therefore that the diversity of resources developed through strategies of OG and AG, respectively, are likely to be different. Furthermore, the ACs and POS associated with OG and AG are likely to be different, which has consequences for the future growth of the firm. We now explore how the firm's past OG and AG affects its future OG by re-examining and extending Penrose's arguments. Specifically, we examine the relative change in the ACs and POSs, and the subsequent effect on future organic growth, arising from the different strategies of OG and AG.

Before presenting our model of firm growth we feel it is important to position our work relative to two dominant growth literatures in management and economics: merger and acquisition (henceforth M&A) and diversification (interestingly both literatures explicitly, or implicitly, draw on ideas that are central to the RBV – see Lockett and Thompson, 2001). The M&A literature, overwhelmingly focusing on samples of large publicly listed companies, indicates that the financial returns to M&A activity are, on average, negligible at best (see King et al., 2004, for a review and meta-analysis of the evidence). Similarly, the diversification literature, overwhelmingly drawing on studies of publicly listed companies, suggests that there is a curvilinear relationship between diversification and financial performance. The performance of the firm improves for increasing levels of diversification, up to a relatively modest level, and then tails off (see Palich et al., 2000, for a review and a meta-analysis). Whilst these two bodies of literature are impressive, we view them as being tangentially related, but not core, to our research on growth for two main reasons.

First, our empirical context is the population of Swedish firms, which is dominated by private small and medium sized enterprises (henceforth SMEs). Interestingly, recent evidence suggests that the financial returns to M&A activity of private firms may be much better than public firms (Fuller et al., 2002). Performance differences of M&A activity across public and private firms may be due to the nature of the acquisition bidding process and the existence of private information in the valuation of companies. Large public firms face the problem that the bidding process is likely to be more visible, attracting increased competition, and the potential synergies from an acquisition are less likely to be private, hence the target price of the firm will be bid up (Barney, 1988). This argument is consistent with Denrell et al.'s (2003) RBV argument that firms can only acquire other firms at less than their full market value if they have idiosyncratic resources which will add value to the acquired firm's resources (in the absence of serendipity). For this reason we anticipate that the M&A performance problems faced by larger public firms may be less prevalent with smaller private firms where the bidding process will be conducted in a less public manner and with a greater degree of private information. Similarly, private SMEs are more likely to be non-diversified in comparison to larger public firms, and so the negative performance implications of diversifying above a relatively modest level are less likely to affect SMEs. Second, both literatures focus on the financial performance implications of growth, whereas we focus on the implications of previous growth on current growth. Hence, the M&A and diversification literatures employ a different dependent variable (financial performance) to our study (employment growth).

**Previous Organic Growth and Its Effect on Future Organic Growth**

Organic growth creates ACs for a firm because of the need to bring in and train new managers, which will be correlated to the rate of organic growth. The quicker a firm tries to grow, the more costly growth may be due to time compression diseconomies (Dierickx and Cool, 1989). Although positive (i.e. $AC_{organic} > 0$), the magnitude of AC is subject to debate. Penrose viewed AC as potentially significant, arguing that even if the productive opportunity set facing a firm is immense, the rate at which the firm can develop its managerial capabilities sets an ultimate limit to its growth. More recently, however, Geroski (2005), through his review of the empirical evidence on firm growth, has argued that the ACs of expanding a business do not appear to be very high and may have been overstated by Penrose. Arguably of more importance is the issue of the growth opportunities facing the firm, which we view as the dominant constraint on growth.

As a firm grows it accumulates resources, which in principle increases its potential resource combinations. There are many more ways of combining *2n* resources than *n* resources. However, because the POS is limited to those possibilities for combining resources that managers are able to see and willing to act upon, past growth does not necessarily provide the firm with an increasing number of new opportunities over time (Moran and Ghoshal, 1999). Firm growth requires the successful matching of perceived opportunities with combinations of resources. It is the matching of resources to perceived opportunities, rather than the size of the resource stock *per se*, which determines the scope of the firm's POS. The POS can be expanded by increasing the knowledge base of a firm, which may lead to new insights into how to better utilize existing resources, and/or expanding the resource base of a firm, which may lead to more potential resource combinations, in turn creating new growth opportunities.

It is unlikely, however, that the exact same set of resources can be used to expand the firm's POS *ad infinitum*. Over time firms develop routines of limited scope, which constrain their ability to recombine existing resources (Nelson and Winter, 1982), and previous activities and resource uses limit the possibility for learning outside of areas where the firm already holds prior knowledge (Cohen and Levinthal, 1990; Teece, 1987). Winter and Szulanski (2001) note that managers develop their business practices by honing increasingly detailed routines, adjusting and fine-tuning the same actions over and over again. Such path dependence leads firms to becoming increasingly myopic in their search for new ways of recombining existing resources (Levinthal and March, 1993). When searching for new opportunities, managers tend to search close-in before moving into uncharted terrains (Cyert and March, 1963). Over time, organic growth will lead to the repeated exploitation of existing resources, which may result in firms becoming 'simple and inert' (Vermeulen and Bakerma, 2001). Rigidities created by the repeated use of resources (Miller, 1994) will potentially hinder the future organic growth rate of the firm, especially in the face of a dynamic environment.

Furthermore, the development of new resources through organic growth will be limited, in terms of both quantity and variety, in the short run. Penrose argues that the new resources will be close in to their existing operations because of path dependency (Penrose, 1960, pp. 2–3). This point is echoed by Wernerfelt (1984) when he argues that tomorrow's strengths tend to be built on today's strengths. The development of similar, not complementary, resources will arguably hinder the expansion of the firm's productive opportunity set. This argument is consistent with the literature on acquisitions that argues that it is complementarities and not similarities that create new opportunities for firms' improved performance (see Harrison et al., 1991, 2001).

Consequently, we believe that the POS of the firm may be smaller and more difficult to expand than Penrose predicted. The problem facing firm managers is that previous organic growth will only permit an incremental expansion of the firm's POS (i.e. $\Delta POS_{organic} \geq 0$), while simultaneously they exploit the POS through current organic growth. Consequently, firm managers will find it increasingly difficult to maintain a high rate of organic growth from one period to the next because firms that have exhibited high organic growth rates in the past will have already harvested the closer and easier growth opportunities. In order to sustain a strategy of organic growth, firms need to search further from their existing operations. However, due to path dependence and associated organizational rigidities, the pursuit of growth opportunities in new fields of activity is inherently costly and difficult.

In summary, previous organic growth will have the dual constraining effects of imposing ACs of managing the growth process and permitting only an incremental expansion of the firm's increasingly exhausted POS. Consequently, the managers of the firm will find it increasingly difficult to maintain the firm's current rate of organic growth. Hence:

*Hypothesis 1: The greater the rate of organic growth in previous periods, the lower the rate of organic growth in the current period.*

**Previous Acquisitive Growth and Its Effect on Future Organic Growth**

Although Penrose did not argue that firms limiting themselves to OG may exhaust all their growth opportunities, she did note that AG could allow firms to break new paths of development and access new growth opportunities: 'Acquisitions can be a means of obtaining the productive services and knowledge that are necessary for a firm to establish itself in a new field' (Penrose, 1959, p. 126). Furthermore, she argued that AG may be best suited for those companies that lacked the ability to expand organically. However, she never explicated *how* AG would affect the firm's ability to continue to expand organically. Interestingly, later resource-based conceptualizations of firm growth have also failed to address this issue. In this section we re-examine and extend Penrose's arguments regarding the relationship between AG and OG. We focus our arguments, as in the previous section, on the effect of AG on the ACs and the POS of the firm.

On the downside, Penrose (1959) argued that AG creates ACs arising from the integration of two firms. ACs arise because managers' time (and hence managerial capabilities) will have to be devoted to integrating the resources of the acquired firm. Consequently, the diversion of managerial resources to managing the integration of the acquired firm, rather than to OG, may potentially retard post-acquisition OG (Penrose, 1959, p. 195). As with OG, we feel that Penrose may have overstated the problems associated with ACs of AG, i.e. the costs of managing the process of AG not the costs of the acquisition, for two main reasons.

First, firms may have spare managerial resources, which is probable if the firm has not utilized its OG potential fully in the past. The spare managerial resources may be employed in managing the integration of the new operations, and hence the ACs of AG will have less impact on the future OG of the firm. Second, AG will result in an influx of managerial resources, from the acquired firm, which should help reduce the AC incurred by the acquirer. Interestingly, Penrose articulates this argument herself stating that: 'Not only does a firm inherit the potentialities of growth of the firms it acquires, but a merger tends also to leave pools of unused productive services available to the combined firm which would not have been available in the independent firms' (Penrose, 1959, p. 195). Empirical support for this argument has been provided by Graebner (2004), who in a case study of eight acquisitions, found that the continued engagement by the acquired firm's leadership was crucial to post-acquisition performance. Consistent with the above, Geroski's (2005) review of the empirical evidence on growth suggests that not only have the ACs of growth been overstated (i.e. are lower than Penrose predicted), but their magnitude is not directly related to the level of previous growth.

We argue that the dominant effect of AG will be felt in terms of the expansion of the firm's POS. In highly competitive environments, which mirror more closely the present time than when Penrose was writing, there is an increasing acceptance that it is difficult for a single firm to try and possess all the resources required to compete effectively (Child and Faulkner, 1998; Dyer and Singh, 1998; Pfeffer and Salancik, 1978). As a consequence, acquisitions have become an increasingly popular means for firms looking to reshape their resource and knowledge bases (Ireland et al., 2001). AG will lead to an influx of new resources *and* new knowledge, which increases the diversity of the resource base of the firm *and* enables managers to gain new insights into how they can utilize their existing and new resources. As such, AG may be viewed as a strategy to reshape a firm's resource base and the resulting resource combinations.

AG involves the acquiring firm buying a bundle of productive resources (i.e. the acquired firm), which when combined with the acquiring firm's resources, creates new resource-combination possibilities. In contrast to OG, with its development of path dependent resources, AG presents an opportunity for the firm to bring in new non-path dependent resources. The effect of an influx of new resources on the firm, creating resource diversity and the potential for new resource synergies, will lead to an expansion of the firm's POS (Harrison et al., 2001; Wang and Zajac, 2007). We believe that the effect will be particularly pronounced for SME's because, due to their limited resource bases, any influx of new resources will lead to a non-incremental increase in the diversity of an SME's resource base and hence its POS.

As highlighted above, a firm's POS is a function of its resource base *and* knowledge about how to use it. Managers do not have perfect information and believe that there is more to know about the resources they have at their disposal at any given time (Penrose, 1959). An increase in knowledge will enable managers to utilize their existing resources more effectively. New knowledge generated via OG, e.g. through the introduction of new products (Kor and Mahoney, 2000), will be path dependent in nature and close to the firm's existing knowledge base. In contrast, AG may lead to the introduction of new non-path dependent knowledge to the firm. The new knowledge will better enable managers to engage in 'resource learning' (Mahoney, 1995) and to conceive new resource combinations. Consequently, new knowledge from AG may play an important role in the development of new productive services, and shaping the POS of the firm (Penrose, 1959, p. 77).

It is important to note, however, that the effects of acquisition will not be permanent. The increase in knowledge and resources will lead to a one-off expansion in the POS of the firm. Over time the new POS will be capitalized on and so the effect of the acquisition on current OG will diminish. AG therefore will have a short run effect on the OG rate of the firm, but in the long run its effects will be diminished.

The arguments above suggest that the ACs of AG, while positive (i.e. $AC_{acquisition} < 0$), may have been overstated by Penrose. We believe that the dominant effect of previous AG on the future OG of the firm will be in terms of the change in the firm's POS. A strategy of acquisition, particularly for SMEs, may also enable the firm to discover new paths of resource combinations and thus open up new growth opportunities for the firm that are different from those previously pursued. Furthermore, previous AG will not lead to the exhaustion of the increased POS because it is the result of bringing together established operations. Thus, we expect that the negative effect of the AC of previous AG will be more than offset by the potential positive effect from the increase in the firm's productive opportunity set, which will not be exploited by previous AG (i.e. $AC_{acquisition} < \Delta POS_{acquisition}$). Consequently, we argue that current acquisitive growth will have a positive effect on future organic growth. Hence:

*Hypothesis 2: The greater the rate of acquisitive growth in previous periods, the greater the rate of organic growth in the current period.*

Our model is summarized in Figure 10.1

## DATA AND METHODS

### The Sample

The dataset comprises a 10-year panel (1987–96) of all commercially active enterprises in the private (non-government) sector in Sweden that had 20 or more employees in the last period of our study and which had appeared

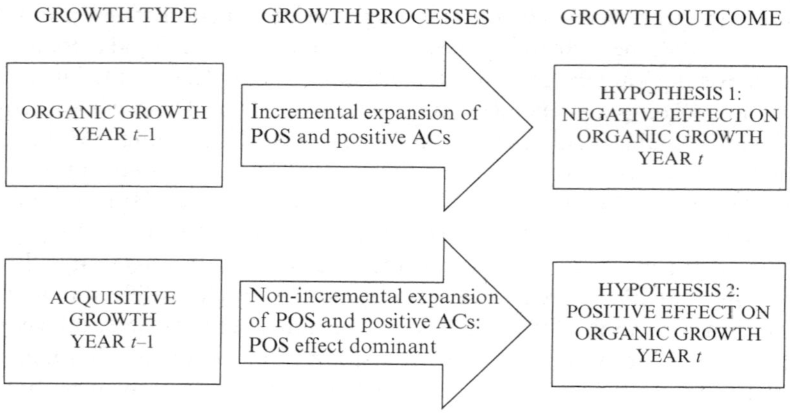


*Figure 10.1 Model of firm growth*

in the underlying database for at least one year prior to the last period. There are 11,525 such enterprises. Annual data for all enterprises have been compiled for every year of the period. Start-ups during this period are included if they fulfil the size criterion for the final year, as are a small number of previous government sector firms that by the final year have transferred to the private sector. Firms that dissolve during the period are excluded regardless of their previous size and growth, as are surviving firms that previously may have had more than 20 employees but do not reach that number in the final period. No upper size limit has been employed but because of the typical, skewed, distribution of firm sizes, SMEs dominate the data and will drive the results.

**The Data**

The data were taken from *Statistics Sweden* (i.e. the official 'Bureau of Census'). Their registers are complete in the sense that all legal commercial activity is represented, whether run as sole proprietorship, partnership, limited liability company, or some other legal form. Data originate from different sources such as tax authorities and mandatory surveys. Updating is frequent, and generally speaking, the registers are of a very high standard by international comparison. Data from three different registers, and 10 annual versions of each, have been utilized in developing the dataset. For a more elaborate description of the dataset see Davidsson (1997).

The unit of analysis in our study is the enterprise (or firm). Codes for enterprises, however, may be changed because of an ownership change, industry reclassification, or spatial relocation. This may make what in reality is an ongoing business to appear in the registers as a close-down and a start-up. Identification codes for establishments are relatively more insensitive to changes of the mentioned kind. We have therefore not accepted company code as the criterion for tracking enterprises over time. Rather, constellations of establishments (and their employment) associated with a certain company code are regarded as 'the same' company if they appear together in the next annual version of the register under a different company code. Specifically, for us to accept at t1 that firm $A_{t0}$ is the same unit as firm $B_{t1}$ the following has to apply: (1) at least 50 per cent of the former employment in A is now found in B; and (2) this same employment constitutes at least 50 per cent of B's total employment. This criterion is programmable and can establish unique links in the great majority of cases. Because of mergers and splits the above criteria do not always lead to a unique and satisfactory solution. In these cases the two foremost business data experts at Statistics Sweden used a manual procedure for deciding, according to their best collective judgement, which of several links should be used, or neither. For any individual year 0.7 per cent was the maximum fraction of cases for which a link was accepted on the basis of manual inspection rather than fulfilling both of the '50 per cent' criteria.

In order to investigate the growth of firms we focus on employment as a measure of the growth in firm resources. In the literature, the most common indicators of growth are sales and employment (Delmar, 1997). In the choice between these indicators we favour employment growth for four reasons. First, employment growth reflects, more closely than sales growth, the expansion of the resources and managerial capacity of the firm as emphasized in Penrose's theory. Penrose explicitly states that her theory concerns the expansion of 'human and other resources' (Penrose, 1995, p. xi). Total asset value is a conceivable but, as we see it, weaker alternative, as it is more sensitive to industry differences in capital intensity and therefore arguably scores worse on measurement invariance (Byrne and Watkins, 2003). Second, adjustment costs as defined by Penrose are largely attributable to the time and effort needed to integrate new people into the organization. Thus, employment growth has the advantage of being directly related to adjustment costs. Third, in their recent assessment of different growth indicators, Shepherd and Wiklund (2009) found that among five different growth indicators (employment, sales, equity, assets, and profits), employment growth was the measure showing most instances of concurrent validity, having higher generality and robustness than the other measures. They also advised against the use of multi-item growth indicators because the correlation among growth indicators is typically low. Fourth, while sales growth data is available for a subset of our data (approx. 50 per cent), it is a non-random subset by firm size, industry, and time period, so relying on sales growth data would introduce biases.

## The Model

In this section, we describe the empirical strategy we used to identify the conditional (direct) and unconditional (indirect) effects of acquisition growth on organic growth. The model we estimate is as follows:

$$OG_{it} = \beta_1 OG_{t-1} + \beta_2 AG_{t-1} + \gamma'\mathbf{X} + \delta D + \varepsilon_{it}. \quad (3.1)$$

In the above equation *i* and *t* represent firms and time periods, respectively, OG denotes organic growth, AG is acquisition growth, D is the full set of time and industry dummies, and ε is a random error term. **X** is a vector of control variables hypothesized to impact on firm growth, including terms for firm age and initial size, and dummy variables indicating if the firm is foreign-owned and if it is part of a corporate group. The quadratic relationships between age and growth and size and growth are well documented in the literature (e.g. Evans, 1987), hence we include linear and quadratic terms for both age and size.

The lagged dependent variable $OG_{it-1}$ captures the effects of past organic growth on current organic growth. Negative and significant coefficients on these variables would be consistent with Hypothesis 1, which postulates that past organic growth constrains current organic growth.

The coefficients on $AG_{it-1}$ give the unconditional effects of past acquisition growth on current organic growth. Positive and significant coefficients on these variables would lend empirical support for Hypothesis 2, which posits that past acquisition growth has beneficial effects on future organic growth.

## The Measures

The different measures that we employed in our analysis are detailed below and summarized in Table 10.1. All variables are italicized.

Our study has the unique feature of being able to separate organic growth from acquisitive growth. The partition of the different types of growth was achieved by keeping track over time of the status and size changes of all establishments that are associated with a firm and classifying them into five categories: original, previously acquired, previously created, acquired the current year, and created the current year. *Organic growth* is measured as total employment$_{(t)}$ – total employment$_{(t-1)}$: the change in employment in associated establishments acquired in the

*Table 10.1 Descriptive statistics for continuous variables*

| Variable | Definition | Mean | SD | Minimum | Maximum |
|---|---|---|---|---|---|
| Organic growth | Change in the log of organic employment | 0.054 | 0.352 | –4.060 | 7.091 |
| Acquisitive growth | Log of employment due to acquisition | 0.103 | 0.637 | 0.000 | 9.455 |
| Size | Log of total employment (organic and acquisition) in the past year | 3.740 | 1.146 | 0.000 | 10.331 |
| Age | Years since establishment | 12.077 | 6.984 | 0.000 | 24.000 |
| Number of total observations | | 103 136 | | | |

current year, i.e. acquisition growth$_{(t)}$. *Acquisitive growth* is measured as the addition to employment through acquisition (or merger) in year *t*. Employment changes in these units in subsequent years will then form part of the firm's organic rather than acquisition-based growth.

*Size* was chosen based on its supposed importance to growth and employment creation (Dunne and Hughes, 1996; Storey, 1995; Wagner, 1992). We measure firm size in terms of the total number of employees, which we log transformed, in the initial year of our study.

*Age* is a recurrent variable in most studies of growth. Normally, younger firms are more prone to grow than older more established firms. Further, one study found that young firms that grow have twice the probability of survival to that of young non-growing firms (Phillips and Kirchhoff, 1989). We measure the age of the firm in years since the firm started operations. This variable is truncated at 24 years because the underlying database was first set up in 1972, i.e. 24 years prior to our end year, 1996.

*Foreign owned firm* was a dummy variable which we coded 1 if the company was a subsidiary of a foreign firm and 0 if it was not. Related to the business structure is the question of how the organizational form of the firm affects its growth performance, i.e. is the firm acting as an independent actor or is it part of a business group, and how does this affect its possibilities to grow? It can be assumed that independent firms are more flexible, whereas firms affiliated with a group have better access to resources. Therefore the implications for growth are mixed (cf. Barney, 1991; Morris and Trotter, 1990).

*Corporate ownership* is a dummy variable we coded 1 if the company was part of a corporate group and 0 otherwise. The inclusion of this variable could be important because corporate management considerations are likely to affect the growth strategy of the firm.

*Industry dummies* were included for two reasons. First, the absolute majority of research on growth firms has been performed on firms in the manufacturing industry (Delmar, 1997), and little has been done on the service industry. Second, the importance of the service industry as employment creator has increased drastically during the last decades. In order to control fully for industry differences we constructed a range of industry dummies using a classification that included the following industries (the proportion of observations in each category is given in parentheses): high-tech manufacturing (2.7 per cent); wood, pulp, and paper (5.6 per cent); engineering industry (14.7 per cent); mining and steelworks (1.8 per cent); other manufacturing (11.7 per cent); technical consultants (4.6 per cent); other knowledge-intensive services (3.2 per cent); banking, insurance, and finance (3.4 per cent); construction (8.8 per cent); retail and wholesale (24.6 per cent); hospitality (4.2 per cent); transportation and communication (6.7 per cent); education and healthcare (3.5 per cent); other services (2.8 per cent); farming, fishery, and forestry (1.1 per cent); and other/unclassified (0.6 per cent). The variables were coded 1 for being in the industry sector and 0 for not being in the industrial sector. Retail and wholesale, containing the largest number of cases, was the base category as recommended in the literature. Due to the large number of industry dummies we do not report individual industry dummies in our analysis.

*Year dummies*: as with industry we created dummy variables for each year covered by the dataset to control for time related effects. We chose to make the first period of the study the base group (1987). Due to the large number of year dummies we do not report individual year dummies in our analysis.

## RESULTS

The descriptive statistics for the continuous variables are presented in Table 10.1. The mean rate of organic growth was 0.054 (SD 0.352), and the mean rate of acquisitive growth was 0.103 (SD 0.637). The mean (log of) initial size is 3.74, with 64.4 per cent of the sample having 20–49 employees, 29.4 per cent 50–249 employees, and 6.2 per cent of the sample ≥250 employees. The average age of firms in the sample was 12 years (SD 6.984). In terms of ownership, 38 per cent were independent firms and 62 per cent were part of a larger corporate group. Finally, 87.6 per cent of the firms were Swedish owned, with only 12.4 per cent being foreign owned.

Table 10.2 presents evidence relating to the frequency of acquisition for

*Table 10.2 Frequency of acquisition of growers and non-growers*

| | No acquisitive growth year *t* | Acquisitive growth year *t* |
|---|---|---|
| No organic growth year *t* | 32177 | 830 |
| Organic growth year *t* | 23193 | 611 |
| No organic growth year *t* – 1 | 32717 | 901 |
| Organic growth year *t* – 1 | 22653 | 540 |

*Note:* As growth rates can only be calculated for surviving firms and firms with two or more consecutive observations, the number of observations in this table is smaller than the total number of observations.

firms that are organic growers and organic non-growers. We performed this analysis to identify whether or not there are systematic differences in the propensity of organic growing vs. non-organic growing firms to undertake a strategy of acquisitive growth. Specifically, we tabulated organic growth in years $t$ and $t - 1$ against acquisitive growth in the current period. The descriptive statistics do not suggest any systematic differences.

Our empirical strategy involves simultaneously controlling for two potential sources of bias: selection and individual firm differences. First, to address the problem of selection bias, as firm growth is observed only in firms that have survived, it is necessary to assess and correct the selection bias due to survivorship. A popular method for correcting selection bias is the Heckman approach (1976, 1979). However, this method is only appropriate in cross-sectional models and cannot be used with panel data where different firms drop out of the sample at different points during the sample period. Fortunately, Wooldridge (1995) modifies Heckman's approach to panel data models with unobserved firm-specific effects. The procedure involves two steps: in the first step, the selection equation is estimated by standard probit for each time period $t = 1, 2, \ldots T$ and the inverse Mills ratio for surviving firms, say, $\hat{\lambda}_{it}$, is generated. In this chapter we include firm size and age as well as ownership and industry dummies in the probit regressions. Thus for each time period we estimate the equation $Pr[S_{it} = 1] = F(x_{it}\delta_{\tau})$ using standard probit, where $S$ is a binary variable indicating whether the firm survives at time $t$ or not, and $F$ denotes the standard normal cumulative distribution function. Based on the estimates from the probit regression, the inverse Mills ratio can be constructed (again for each time period) as $\hat{\lambda}_{it} = \frac{f}{1 - F}$, where $F$ is as defined above and $f$ is the standard normal probability distribution function. In the second step of the estimation, the matrix of inverse Mills ratio defined for each time period as $\Lambda_{it} = (0\ 0\ \hat{\lambda}_{it}\ 0\ 0)$ is included in the original model: first, to correct for the selection bias – the extended equation is estimated using firm-specific fixed effects (the within estimator); and second, to control the problem of unobserved firm differences (our analysis employs firm-specific effects).

Finally, we also test the robustness of our results by investigating whether the relationships between organic and acquisitive growth vary by firm size and age. To this end, we divide our dataset into young and old, and small and big firms, and estimate our model on each sub-group separately. Small (big) firms are defined as those below (above) the median employment level in the data. Similarly, young (old) firms are defined as those below (above) the median age in the data. The results of our regression models, which include selection-bias corrected estimates with firm-specific effects, are presented in Table 10.3.[2] All specifications include the full set of time and industry dummies. We discuss these results below.

First, the results indicate that organic growth in the previous period exerts detrimental effects on current growth. The full sample Model 1 shows that the coefficient is negative and statistically significant at the 1 per cent level. Furthermore, the negative and statistically significant result holds across Models 2–5, i.e. across small, large, young, and old firms. In terms of the substantive significance of the result, Model 1 suggests that a 10 percentage point increase in the organic growth ($t - 1$) will lead, on average, to a 0.958 percentage point reduction in organic growth in the current period. The results are consistent with Hypothesis 1.

Second, the results indicate that acquisitive growth in the previous period exerts a positive effect on organic growth in the current period. The coefficient for acquisitive growth ($t - 1$) is positive and significant at the 1 per cent level. Furthermore, the positive and significant relationship is robust as it holds across Models 1–5, i.e. across small, large, young, and old firms. The substantive significance of the result, based on Model 1, suggests that a 10 percentage point increase in the acquisitive growth ($t - 1$) will lead, on average, to a 0.917 percentage point increase in organic growth in the current period. Interestingly, the effect size is more than 2.5 times higher for small firms (Model 2) than for large firms (Model 3). This result attests to the importance of resource diversity in promoting organic growth. The results are consistent with Hypothesis 2.[3]

## Curvilinear Effects

Although Hypotheses 1 and 2 hypothesize linear relationships, between $OG_t$ and $OG_{t-1}$ and $AG_{t-1}$, respectively, as an additional robustness check for our model we also tested for presence of curvilinearity by including a quadratic term for both $OG_{t-1}$ and $AG_{t-1}$ and re-ran the

*Table 10.3 Acquisition growth and organic growth: selection bias corrected estimates with firm-specific fixed effects*

| Coefficient | Model 1: All | Model 2: Small firms | Model 3: Big firms | Model 4: Young firms | Model 5: Old firms |
|---|---|---|---|---|---|
| Organic growth | –0.0958*** | –0.0671*** | –0.0756*** | –0.0975*** | –0.0953*** |
| ($t-1$) | (–25.2) | (–12.1) | (–14.4) | (–17.8) | (–17.8) |
| Acquisition | 0.0917*** | 0.223*** | 0.0865*** | 0.0942*** | 0.0904*** |
| growth ($t-1$) | (46.3) | (25.4) | (48.0) | (25.6) | (43.9) |
| SIZE ($t-1$) | –0.390*** | –0.633*** | –0.230*** | –0.463*** | –0.205*** |
| | (–54.5) | (–49.8) | (–22.6) | (–80.4) | (–35.6) |
| SIZE ($t-1$) | 0.0345*** | 0.0593*** | 0.0173*** | 0.0416*** | 0.0167*** |
| squared | (42.3) | (24.0) | (17.9) | (60.3) | (27.3) |
| Age | –0.0521*** | –0.0232*** | –0.0310*** | –0.102*** | –0.0318 |
| | (–6.60) | (–7.01) | (–5.12) | (–6.60) | (–0.46) |
| Age squared | 0.000902*** | 0.000394*** | 0.000540*** | 0.00337*** | 0.000598 |
| | (7.38) | (5.87) | (5.88) | (6.32) | (0.39) |
| Foreign-owned | 0.0134 | 0.0144* | 0.00366 | 0.0170** | 0.0184*** |
| | (1.54) | (1.68) | (0.50) | (2.00) | (5.06) |
| Corporate | 0.00633 | –0.00207 | 0.0407*** | 0.0179** | 0.0382*** |
| | (0.69) | (–0.15) | (5.31) | (2.52) | (8.18) |
| Selection bias | –0.655*** | –0.265*** | –0.380*** | –0.393*** | 0.0480 |
| correction term | (–5.42) | (–5.87) | (–4.17) | (–5.87) – | (–0.61) |
| Observations | 103 136 | 49 980 | 53 156 | 57 846 | 45 290 |
| R-squared | 0.16 | 0.25 | 0.11 | 0.19 | 0.14 |

*Notes:*
Robust t statistics in parentheses.
*** $p < 0.01$, ** $p < 0.05$, * $p < 0.1$, two-tailed tests.
All specifications include the full set of time and industry dummies.
Small (big) firms are defined as those below (above) the median employment level in the data.
Young (old) firms are defined as those below (above) the median age in the data.

*Table 10.4 Acquisition growth and organic growth: selection bias corrected estimates with firm-specific fixed effects*

| Coefficient | Model 6: All |
|---|---|
| Organic growth ($t-1$) | –0.117*** |
| | (–31.0) |
| Organic growth ($t-1$) squared | 0.0880*** |
| | (39.4) |
| Acquisition growth ($t-1$) | 0.0967*** |
| | (16.9) |
| Acquisition growth ($t-1$) squared | –0.00162 |
| | (–1.33) |
| SIZE ($t-1$) | –0.545*** |
| | (–67.1) |
| SIZE ($t-1$) squared | 0.0433*** |
| | (46.0) |
| Age | –0.0670*** |
| | (–3.56) |
| Age squared | 0.000984*** |
| | (3.14) |
| Foreign-owned | 0.0304*** |
| | (4.45) |
| Corporate | 0.00545 |
| | (0.60) |
| Selection bias correction term | –0.783*** |
| | (–4.25) |
| Observations | 103 136 |
| R-squared | 0.19 |

*Notes:*
Robust t statistics in parentheses.
*** $p < 0.01$, ** $p < 0.05$, * $p < 0.1$, two-tailed tests.
All specifications include the full set of time and industry dummies.

analysis on the complete sample, the results of which are presented in Table 10.4.

Interestingly the results indicate the presence of a curvilinear relationship between $OG_t$ and $OG_{t-1}$ (significant at the 1 per cent level), but no curvilinear relationship between $OG_t$ and $AG_{t-1}$. Although the linear relationship between $OG_t$ and $OG_{t-1}$ (Hypothesis 1) indicates, on average, that there is a trade-off between previous and current organic growth, the positive and significant coefficient of the quadratic term suggests that for firms with very high growth rates, on average, the trade-off does not exist. A plot estimate of the linear and quadratic marginal effects relationships

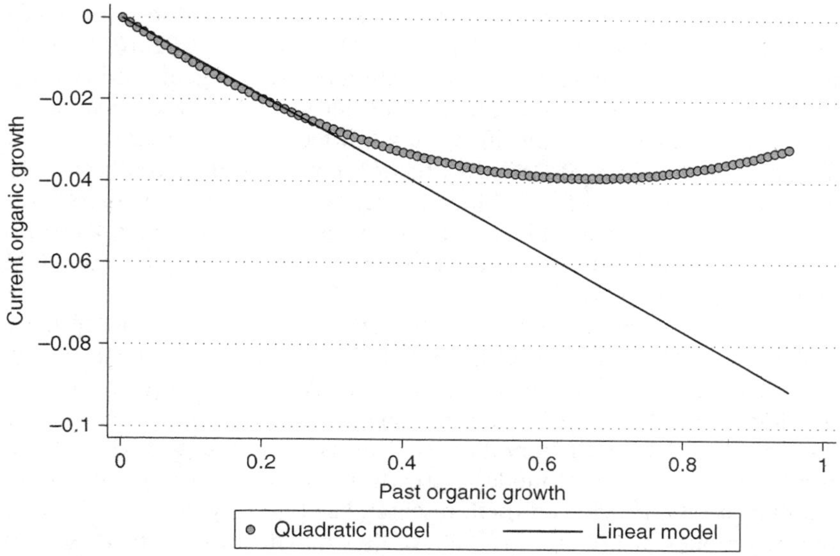


*Figure 10.2 Linear and quadratic models of the relationship between previous and current organic growth*

between $OG_t$ and $OG_{t-1}$ are presented in Figure 10.2. The U-shaped quadratic relationship indicates that for $OG_{t-1}$ growth rates of 0–30 per cent, the linear and quadratic relationships are the same. Therefore, the linear relationship holds for the vast majority of firms in our study. However, for the more exuberant growers the growth constraint is less pronounced through the $OG_{t-1}$ range 30 per cent through to the turning point of 66 per cent, with the marginal effect becoming positive thereafter for the very rapid growers. The presence of a U-shaped relationship $OG_t$ and $OG_{t-1}$ indicates that the very fast growing firms may not be subject to the Penrose effect. We discuss the theoretical implications of curvilinearity in the discussion section.

## DISCUSSION

In this chapter we have revisited Penrose's ideas to examine how the resource/capability accumulation process influences firm growth. Specifically, we have examined how the adjustment costs and productive opportunity set of the firm in terms of past organic and acquisitive growth influence current organic growth, both directly and indirectly. In doing so, we have followed in the footsteps of Penrose and her intentions for developing a theory of the growth of the firm. Our reading of Penrose's work tells us that she clearly makes the distinction between organic and acquisitive growth and that the main interest of her work lies in understanding how past organic and acquisitive growth affects future organic growth. To date, applications of Penrose's theory have typically been limited to a focus on the effects of AC, which has led to a number of scholars criticizing the lack of applicability of Penrose's growth theory (e.g. Geroski, 2005; Marris, 2002). Consistent with Penrose's theory, we utilized a dual focus on ACs and POSs.

In order to appropriately deal with both these issues, we conceptually and empirically separated OG from AG. We hypothesize and empirically find that the effects of organic growth and AG on subsequent OG are qualitatively different. We interpret this as reflecting differences in the AC and POS that result from these two forms of growth. Consequently, a firm's strategic choice of mode of growth has consequences for its future amount of OG. Previous growth research has typically failed to separate the two modes of growth. We believe that our delineation of these two modes of growth is an important contribution to the literature interested in applying and testing Penrose's growth theory, but also to growth research in general. Therefore, we encourage future studies to pay much greater attention to the differences between OG and acquisitive growth in order to further our understanding of firm growth. These two modes are fundamentally different. Others have noted that there are several conceptual and empirical challenges to the study of firm growth (Davidsson and Wiklund, 2000). Our conceptual and empirical separation and clarification of organic and acquisitive growth address some of these challenges.

In revisiting Penrose's theory, we also believe her theory of growth does need modification. We believe that the nature of the modification relates to bringing to the fore aspects of her theory that are currently less emphasized.

First, our results are robust and consistent with Hypothesis 1, indicating a direct and negative relationship between previous OG and current OG. Firms that have expanded organically in the past will find it more difficult to expand organically in the current period. This finding supports that argument that ACs do matter for the growth of firms (e.g. Garnsey et al., 2006; Tan and Mahoney, 2007). However, irrespective of the magnitude of ACs we feel that Penrose overestimated the ease at which the management of a firm can extend its POS set by recombining the existing resources and those generated by the internal growth process. Expressed differently, industrial firms in the post-World War II era, on which Penrose bases her theory, operated in an environment where growth opportunities were immense and competition limited. They did not face the external growth restrictions that firms face today. In comparison, contemporary firms need to extend their operations into new areas in order to continue their OG, which is difficult and costly due to myopia and path dependence. Therefore, there is a need to relax Penrose's assumption that growth opportunities always exist and can be pursued – as long as firms are able to match these opportunities with combinations of resources. We argue that it is more realistic to assume that growth opportunities are restricted. Therefore, in order to continue to grow, firms need to devote attention and effort to developing and extending their POS. AG is one strategic option for firms wishing to increase the POS of their firm.

Second, we argued and found that the problems associated with the ACs of AG will be outweighed by the increase in the POS of the firm. Our results are robust and consistent with Hypothesis 2, indicating a positive relationship between previous AG and current OG. To some extent this finding counters Penrose's original formulation of the theory, suggesting that she overestimated the ACs associated with acquisitions. If the AC associated with acquisitions were substantial, the firm would not be able to develop its managerial capacity to simultaneously acquire another firm and foster OG. Initially, management would be occupied with conducting the acquisition, and later they would need to devote substantial time and effort to integration. We have argued and found empirical support for the counter-argument that acquisitions can lead to diversification of the firm's resource and knowledge bases, which expands the POS set of the firm. The firm can then benefit from this extended opportunity set by growing organically. In Penrose's treatment of acquisitive growth, she did not explicitly examine the relationship between AG and OG. Our results demonstrate clearly that previous AG, on average, has positive effects on future OG. AG can stimulate OG. For this to be the case the ACs of AG must be outweighed by the corresponding increase in the firm's POS.

Third, as Penrose notes, entrepreneurial capabilities are needed in order to find ways of recombining resources to take advantage of growth opportunities. Similar to Shepherd and Wiklund (2009), we believe that entrepreneurial capabilities and resource recombination can explain our finding of positive implications of acquisitions. Given that the acquisition literature finds that, on average, acquisitions have neutral or negative effects on the financial performance of the acquiring firm (see the meta-analysis by King et al., 2004), our positive results of acquisitions may be surprising. To some extent, our results can be explained by methodological differences between this study and studies aimed at explaining acquisition performance, including the sample studied (mainly small, non-listed firms instead of large, listed firms) and the outcome variable (organic growth instead of stock market performance). Our results comparing small and large firms are consistent with the argument that acquisitions may have a greater liberating growth effect on small firms with narrow resource bases than larger firms with more diversified resource bases (see Models 2–3 in Table 10.3). It is the ability of the acquiring firm to discover and conduct productive resource combinations which determines the extent to which the growth potential of an acquisition becomes realized (Shepherd and Wiklund, 2009).

Fourth, we argue that Penrose's theory in relation to how new resources and knowledge are developed or acquired needs updating. The problems of path dependence and myopia are likely to be pervasive in a way that Penrose did not foresee when the assumption of unlimited growth opportunities is relaxed. The importance of previous growth (organic or acquired), and the characteristics of the resources thus brought into the firm, are related to the future POS facing the firm. For example, March (1991) demonstrates that there are strong pressures within organizations to exploit already existing competencies, technologies, and resources rather than exploring new ones, leading to limitations in the variety of the resource and knowledge bases of the firm. One way of overcoming this homogenization of resources is to bring outsiders into the firm. Similar to Penrose, March (1991) notes that these newcomers are likely to be less knowledgeable than existing staff about the firm's operations, but the variety of their knowledge that they bring outweighs their lack of knowledge. This speaks to the qualitative differences between OG generating limited variety in the resource base and AG generating greater variety and thus greater chances of extending the POS of the firm. We argue that these insights from organizational learning will hold important insights into the differences between OG and AG and their effect on the future growth of the firm.

## Future Extensions to Penrose's Work

In this section we outline potential future extensions of Penrose's work. We begin by returning to the U-shaped relationship between previous OG and current OG and then comment on relaxing the assumption that the firm is the appropriate unit of analysis for examining growth.

As part of our robustness checks we found the existence of a U-shaped relationship between previous OG and current OG, whereby for very exuberant growers (over 66 per cent growth) the growth constraint was relaxed (but still present). This finding extends Penrose's work, which assumed a linear relationship, and opens up interesting theoretical implications for future research. We suggest that the U-shaped relationship may be due to two factors.

First, in addition to AC being lower than Penrose (1959) predicted, the magnitude of AC is not directly related to the level of previous growth (Geroski, 2005). Therefore, the AC associated with high levels of previous growth may be proportionally lower, on an employee-by-employee basis, than low levels of previous growth. The magnitude of ACs is determined by the managerial capabilities of the firm. Firms which have engaged in high levels of AG may be better able to develop the skills to manage such transactions and so face relatively lower ACs.

Second, and arguably of more importance, is the nature of the firms' POS. Firms which are able to grow rapidly will have large POSs. Where the POS is sufficiently large, the firm will be able to capitalize only on a small proportion of available growth opportunities in the short run. Consequently, the firm will be insulated from the problem of their POS becoming increasingly exhausted, with its associated constraint on future organic growth in the short run.[4] This raises the question: What determines the POS of firms? There are two possible explanations. First, certain competitive environments will present greater growth opportunities than others and hence, *ceteris paribus*, act to increase a firm's POS. Second, and arguably of more importance, is the firm's ability to expand its POS irrespective of its current competitive environment. This relates back to Penrose's key distinction between the managerial and entrepreneurial capabilities of the firm, and her emphasis on entrepreneurial capabilities being central to firm growth. As managerial capabilities are practical in orientation they are more easily developed than entrepreneurial capabilities, which are a function of the imagination (Penrose, 1959). Consequently, entrepreneurial capabilities are the key resource (being valuable, rare, imitable, and non-substitutable in RBV parlance) that differentiates a firm's abilities to overcome a growth constraint.

The importance of managers' subjective assessments of the resources at their disposal, allied to their imagination, raises interesting issues for both future developments of Penrose's growth theory and the RBV (Kor et al., 2007). We feel that researchers need to attend more closely to the processes by which managers make decisions about resources and growth. To date insights from cognitive theory have been applied to modelling managers' mental models of the competitive landscape (see Hodgkinson, 1997; Porac and Thomas, 1994; Porac et al., 1989, 1995). We contend that a cognitive perspective on firm growth and the RBV can help to overcome these limitations and can open avenues for further research. Future work needs to embrace the importance of managers' subjective decisions about the functionality of resources at their disposal rather than reify resources as objective entities waiting to be discovered through some formal analysis. In reality resources may only exist in the eye of the beholder, which is consistent with Wernerfelt's (1984) argument that a resource is *anything* that is a strength or weakness of the firm. Resource functionality remains an under-researched aspect of the RBV (Lockett et al., 2008).

In this chapter, building on the work of Penrose, we have taken the firm as the unit of analysis; however, recent developments in economics and management have highlighted that organizational boundaries are becoming increasingly blurred (Powell, 1990). An interesting direction for future developments of Penrose's growth theory will be to relax the assumption that the firm is the unit of analysis to examine the role of alliances and networks between firms. Below we outline the implications of two specific forms of network arrangement (which incorporate alliances): relational networks and modular production networks (see Sturgeon, 2002, for a review).

Relational networks are based on organizations with complementary strengths, recognizing their interdependence on one another, and linking together for mutual benefit in an open-ended manner (see Powell, 1990, for a review). In many knowledge-rich environments, such as high-tech industries, relational networks have developed (which are commonly geographically clustered) to promote knowledge flow between firms and hence foster innovation (e.g. in the case of Silicon Valley, see Saxenian, 1991, 1994). The access to more diverse sources of information may have a positive impact on expanding the POS of the firm as managers become more aware of new market opportunities and/or are able to access complementary knowledge. As such, relational networks may enable firms to avoid making acquisitions in order to gain access to new sources of information in order to expand the POS of the firm. Arguably future studies on firm growth should examine the potential role of relational networks (which encompass alliances) in relaxing the growth constraint on firms.

In modular production networks, the lead firm (e.g. Apple) engages in the innovation, design, and marketing of new products but outsources production, on the basis of market relationships, to turn-key suppliers who engage in contract manufacture (Sturgeon, 2002). As such, the lead's sole attention is focused on how to develop the POS of the firm whilst outsourcing many of the problems of managing the growth process of manufacturing operations to external firms. By outsourcing production the lead firm may be better able to reap the value from innovation while spreading the risks from volatile demand (Venkatesan, 1992). In modular production networks the full employment effects of the lead firm's activities will not be fully accounted for in their change in employment. Therefore, future research into firm growth may need to embrace the changing nature of production, and the role of modular production networks, by focusing on employment effects across the whole network.

## Managerial Implications

We feel that our work has implications for managers. First, our empirical evidence suggests that the important role the POS of a firm may play in constraining or enabling the future organic growth of the firm, and the importance of the ACs of growth may have been overstated by Penrose (1959). Therefore, managers need to focus their attention on how they can influence the expansion of the firm's POS over time. If diversity and synergy within a firm's resource base will lead to a larger POS, and hence enhanced opportunities for future growth, firm managers need to think how they can achieve diversity and synergies within their resource base. If firms exclusively rely on organic growth then managers need to be alert to the potential problems of the path dependence, and the potential for limited learning outside of areas where the firm already holds prior knowledge (Cohen and Levinthal, 1990; Teece, 1987).

Second, and related to the above point, our findings attest to the importance of acquisitive growth as a means of expanding the firm's POS and hence future organic growth. We feel that acquisitive growth may be a strategy for overcoming the problems of path dependence associated with an exclusive focus on organic growth. The acquisition, in effect, should be viewed as a strategic option for managers to break the path dependence of the firm, and its associated development of close-in resources, to permit broadening of the resource base and the potential to create new synergies. The issue facing firm managers is how to develop the necessary skills to a strategy of acquisitive growth, and hence stimulate future organic growth, in a profitable manner. Clearly, any strategy of acquisition should be predicated on the existence of resource synergies between the two companies, which if private will be more likely to lead to positive financial returns (Harrison et al., 1991, 2001). This will require managers to have a good understanding of the nature of both their own firm's resource base and the target firm's resource base, which is a fundamental element of any RBV-based strategy (Lockett et al., 2009).

Finally, the existence of a curvilinear relationship between previous and current organic growth suggests that some firms may have sufficiently large POS that they do not face a growth constraint. Furthermore, the ACs of organic growth do not appear to be problematic for hindering future growth. In the growth rate range 0–66 per cent (see Figure 10.1), there is a trade-off between previous organic growth and current organic growth (the quadratic and linear relationship being effectively the same up to a growth rate of 30 per cent per annum). However, for growth rates above 66 per cent, the growth constraint does not bite. This finding raises interesting managerial issues as to why some firms are able to develop much larger POSs than others, and to what extent they are able to sustain very high growth rates in the medium to long run. Anecdotal evidence of firms such as Microsoft and Google indicates that a small number of firms in fact achieve extraordinary growth rates over extended periods of time, exploiting opportunities that appear more or less inexhaustible. These firms also face managerial challenges, but these are different in nature – more closely associated with the problems of integrating new people into the business (cf. e.g. Hambrick and Crozier, 1985). Stated differently, the managerial problems of these firms are more similar to those noted by Penrose.

**Limitations**

As with all empirical research there are limitations associated with our work. First, on the basis of theory, we make assumptions concerning the nature of the resources that are added to the firm through organic and acquisitive growth, respectively, but these resources remain unobserved. We share this limitation with the vast majority of growth studies. More detailed information about the nature of resources involved in growth (e.g. resource complementarities) would have provided a deeper understanding of how previous growth mode can help fuel future OG. The nature of resources falls into the category of unobserved heterogeneity together with other unobserved variables (see the comment below about control variables). The effect of this is attenuation of results, i.e. results are weaker than they would have been had these variables been included. The risk that it would lead to spurious results, however, is small. For example, the issue of resource complementarities is likely to influence the decision of whether to acquire a firm or not. This effect is absorbed in our acquisitive growth variable. Further, firms are likely to differ in their ability to select and integrate acquired firms. Variance in this ability would lead to spurious results only if it systematically affected the ability to generate OG in future periods and not in present and past periods (we control for the latter). This is an unlikely scenario. The limited evidence on firm growth based on samples dominated by small and medium sized firms suggests that penetration and related diversification strongly dominate (Levie, 1997). Therefore, we feel confident that our results are not driven by the omission of the variables measuring the nature of resources acquired in the growth process.

The second limitation relates to the generalizability of our data. The data includes all commercially active enterprises in the private (non-government) sector in Sweden from 1987 to 1996 and raises issues about the age of the data and its geographic focus. First, the age of the data is only problematic if the conditions in Sweden during that period deviate from other contexts where the theoretically suggested relationships are supposed to hold. Second, the geographic focus of the data means that Swedish firms may pursue growth across national borders in ways that we fail to observe. This, however, is likely to have a limited influence on our results. Swedish exports can be largely attributed to a small number of very large multinationals, whereas our sample mainly consists of small firms, many of them in the service industries. We note that in a similarly composed sample of Swedish firms used by Naldi (2008), the average export share of sales was 12 per cent. Clearly, the reliance on data from a single economy also limits statistical generalization to other countries. Although we have derived our hypotheses from theory and found support for them, care must be taken in generalizing findings beyond Sweden or countries with similar features.

Finally, due to the panel nature of our data we were only able to collect data for a limited number of control variables in our analysis (e.g. size, age, foreign, and corporate). Ideally we would have liked to include a greater range of control variables to account for the potential influence of other firm level factors. However, our panel data approach employing fixed effects means that we minimize any potential problems arising from the omission of relevant control variables if they are constant over time and correlated with the independent variable.

## CONCLUSIONS

Although Penrose's theory is the most comprehensive theory of firm growth to date, surprisingly little work has been focused on extending and testing her theory. Relying on Penrose's central concepts of ACs and the firm's POS, we argue and find that OG and AG are qualitatively different phenomena and have different effects on the future OG of the firm. This leads us to conclude that these elements of Penrose's theory have received insufficient attention in the literature on firm growth to date. At the same time, on the basis of our findings and recent theoretical development, we suggest specific extensions to Penrose's theory.

## ACKNOWLEDGEMENTS

The authors would like to thank Deniz Ucbasaran, Mike Wright, and Erik Stam for their helpful comments and suggestions.

## NOTES

* Previously published as: Andy Lockett, Johan Wiklund, Per Davidsson and Sourafel Girma (2009), 'Organic and acquisitive growth: re-examining, testing and extending Penrose's growth theory', *Journal of Management Studies*, **48** (1), January, 48–74.

1. Annual growth in GDP per capita across the 16 most industrialized nations (13 of which were European) was 3.8 per cent from 1950 to 1973, but only 2.1 per cent from 1989 to 1999 (Kranz, 2004). However, the recent turmoil on financial markets has led to a restriction in credit, and a corresponding increase in the price of credit, which is having a detrimental impact on the ability of firms to raise credit in order to engage in acquisitive activity (see: http://www.businessweek.com/investor/content/jul2009/ pi2009077-750192.htm; accessed 15 August 2009).
2. By employing a fixed effects model we control for time-invariant unobserved firm heterogeneity which is correlated with the independent variables. Note that the within-transformation removes the time-invariant components of the model.
3. We have experimented with using further lags of growth in our model ($t - 2$ and $t - 3$), and found that the conclusions of this chapter are robust to such changes of specifications. However, we chose to confine our analysis to the case of one lag ($t - 1$) because the use of further lags entails the loss of a substantial number of observations.
4. We state in the short run because we only look at the effect of period $t - 1$ on period $t$. It is important to note that our analysis does not employ a time series approach.

## REFERENCES


Barnard, C.I. (1938). *The Functions of the Executive*. Cambridge, MA: Harvard Business School Press.

Barney, J. (1986). 'Strategic factor markets: expectations, luck and business strategy'. *Management Science*, **42**, 1231–41.

Barney, J. (1988). 'Returns to bidding firms in mergers and acquisitions: reconsidering the relatedness hypothesis'. *Strategic Management Journal*, **9**, Special Issue, 71–8.

Barney, J. (1991). 'Firm resources and sustained competitive advantage'. *Journal of Management*, **17**, 99–119.

Buckley, P.J. and Casson, M. (2007). 'Edith Penrose's theory of the growth of the firm and the strategic management of multinational enterprises'. *Management International Review*, **47**, 151–73.

Byrne, B. and Watkins, D. (2003). 'The issue of measurement invariance revisited'. *Journal of Cross-Cultural Psychology*, **34**, 155.

Child, J. and Faulkner, D. (1998). *Strategies of Cooperation: Managing Alliances, Networks and Joint Ventures*. Oxford: Oxford University Press.

Cohen, W. M. and Levinthal, D. A. (1990). 'Absorptive capacity: a new perspective on learning and innovation'. *Administrative Science Quarterly*, **35**, 128–52.

Cyert, R.M. and March, J.G. (1955). 'Organization structure and pricing behavior in an oligopolistic market'. *American Economic Review*, **45**, 129–39.

Cyert, R.M. and March, J.G. (1963). *A Behavioral Theory of the Firm*. Englewood Cliffs, NJ: Prentice-Hall.

Davidsson, P. (1997). 'High-Growth SMEs: Feasibility Analysis for the Swedish Study'. Mimeo prepared for the OECD Working Party on SMEs. Paris: OECD.

Davidsson, P. and Wiklund, J. (2000). 'Conceptual and empirical challenges in the study of firm growth'. In Sexton, D. and Landström, H. (Eds), *The Blackwell Handbook of Entrepreneurship*. Oxford, MA: Blackwell Business, 26–44.

Davidsson, P., Achtenhagen, L. and Naldi, L. (2006). 'What do we know about small firm growth?'. In Parker, S. (Ed.), *Handbook of Entrepreneurship Research: The Life Cycle of Entrepreneurial Ventures*, Vol. 2. New York: Springer, 361–98.

Delmar, F. (1997). 'Measuring growth: methodological considerations and empirical results'. In Donckels, R. and Miettinen, A. (Eds), *Entrepreneurship and SME Research: On Its Way to the Next Millennium*. Aldershot, VA: Avebury, 190–216.

Denrell, J., Fang, C. and Winter, S.G. (2003). 'The economics of strategic opportunity'. *Strategic Management Journal*, **24**, 977–90.

Dierickx, I. and Cool, K. (1989). 'Asset stock accumulation and sustainability of competitive advantage'. *Management Science*, **35**, 1504–11.

Dunne, P. and Hughes, A. (1996). 'Age, size, growth and survival: UK companies in the 1980s'. *Journal of Industrial Economics*, **XLII**, 115–40.

Dyer, J.H. and Singh, H. (1998). 'The relational view: cooperative strategy and sources of interorganizational competitive advantage'. *Academy of Management Review*, **23**, 660–79.

Evans, D.S. (1987). 'The relationship between firm growth, size and age: estimates for 100 manufacturing industries'. *Journal of Industrial Economics*, **35**, 567–81.

Fuller, K., Netter, J. and Stegemoller, M. (2002). 'What do returns to acquiring firms tell us? Evidence from firms that make many acquisitions'. *Journal of Finance*, **57**, 1763–93.

Garnsey, E., Stam, E. and Heffernan, P. (2006). 'New firm growth: exploring processes and paths'. *Industry and Innovation*, **13**, 1–20.

Geroski, P. (2005). 'Understanding the implications of empirical work on corporate growth rates'. *Managerial and Decision Economics*, **26**, 129–38.

Graebner, M.E. (2004). 'Momentum and serendipity: how acquired leaders create value in the integration of technology firms'. *Strategic Management Journal*, **25**, 751–77.

Hambrick, D. and Crozier, L. (1985). 'Stumblers and stars in the management of rapid growth'. *Journal of Business Venturing*, **1**, 31–45.

Harrison, J.S., Hitt, M.A., Hoskisson, R.E. and Ireland, R.D. (1991). 'Synergies and post-acquisition performance: differences versus similarities in resource allocation'. *Journal of Management*, **17**, 173–90.

Harrison, J.S., Hitt, M.A., Hoskisson, R.E. and Ireland, R.D. (2001). 'Resource complementarity in business combinations: extending the logic to organizational alliances'. *Journal of Management*, **27**, 679–90.

Heckman, J. (1976). 'The common structure of statistical models of truncation, sample election, and limited dependent variables and a simple estimator for such models'. *Annals of Economic and Social Measurement*, **5**, 475–92.

Heckman, J. (1979). 'Sample selection bias as a specification error'. *Econometrica*, **47**, 53–161.

Hodgkinson, G. (1997). 'The cognitive analysis of competitive structures: a review and critique'. *Human Relations*, **50**, 625–54.

Ireland, R.D., Hitt, M.A., Camp, S.M. and Sexton, D.L. (2001). 'Integrating entrepreneurship and strategic management thinking to create firm wealth'. *Academy of Management Executive*, **15**, 43–57.

King, D.R., Dalton, D.R., Daily, C.M. and Covin, J.M. (2004). 'Meta-analysis of post-acquisition performance: indications of unidentified moderators'. *Strategic Management Journal*, **25**, 187–200.
Kor, Y.Y. and Mahoney, J.T. (2000). 'Penrose's resource-based approach: the process and product of research creativity'. *Journal of Management Studies*, **37**, 99–139.
Kor, Y. and Mahoney, J. (2004). 'Edith Penrose's (1959) contributions to the resource-based view of the strategic management'. *Journal of Management Studies*, **41**, 183–92.
Kor, Y.Y., Mahoney, J.T. and Michael, S. (2007). 'Resources, capabilities and entrepreneurial perceptions'. *Journal of Management Studies*, **44**, 1187–212.
Kranz, O. (2004). *Economic Growth and Economic Policy in Sweden in the 20th Century: A Comparative Perspective*. Available at: http://www.ratio.se/pdf/wp/ok_growth.pdf) (accessed 16 October 2008).
Levie, J. (1997). 'Patterns of growth and performance: an empirical study of young, growing ventures in France, Ireland and Scotland'. In Reynolds, P.D., Bygrave, W.D., Davidsson, P., Gartner, W.B., Carter, N.M., Mason, C. and McDougall, P.P. (Eds), *Frontiers of Entrepreneurship 1997*. Wellesley: Babson College, 419–43.
Levinthal, D.A. and March, J.G. (1993). 'The myopia of learning'. *Strategic Management Journal*, **14**, 95–112.
Lockett, A. (2005). 'Edith Penrose's legacy to the resource-based view'. *Managerial and Decision Economics*, **26**, 83–98.
Lockett, A. and Thompson, S. (2001). 'The resource-based view and economics'. *Journal of Management*, **27**, 723–54.
Lockett, A. and Thompson, S. (2004). 'Edith Penrose's contributions to the resource-based view: an alternative perspective'. *Journal of Management Studies*, **41**, 193–204.
Lockett, A., O'Shea, R. and Wright, M. (2008). 'The development of the resource-based view of the firm: reflections from Birger Wernerfelt'. *Organization Studies*, **29**, 1125–411.
Lockett, A., Thompson, S. and Morgenstern, U. (2009). 'The development of the resource-based view of the firm: a critical appraisal'. *International Journal of Management Reviews*, **11**, 9–28.
Mahoney, J. T. (1995). 'The management of resources and the resource of management'. *Journal of Business Research*, **33**, 91–101.
March, J. G. (1991). 'Exploration and exploitation in organization learning'. *Organization Science*, **2**, 71–87.
Marris, R. (1964). *The Economic Theory of Managerial Capitalism*. London: Macmillan.
Marris, R. (2002). 'Edith Penrose and economics'. In Pitelis, C. (Ed.), *The Growth of the Firm: The Legacy of Edith Penrose*. Oxford: Oxford University Press, 61–80.
Miller, D.M. (1994). 'What happens after success: the perils of excellence'. *Journal of Management Studies*, **31**, 325–58.
Moran, P. and Ghoshal, S. (1999). 'Markets, firms, and the process of economic development'. *Academy of Management Review*, **24**, 390–412.
Morris, M.H. and Trotter, J.D. (1990). 'Institutionalizing entrepreneurship in a large firm: a case study at AT&T'. *Industrial Marketing Management*, **19**, 131–9.

Naldi, L. (2008). *Growth through Internationalization: A Knowledge Perspective on SMEs*. JIBS Dissertation Series No. 47. Jönköping: Jönköping International Business School.
Nelson, R.R. and Winter, S.G. (1982). *An Evolutionary Theory of Economic Change*. Cambridge: The Belknap Press.
Palich, L., Cardinal, L. and Miller, C. (2000). 'Curvilinearity in the diversification-performance linkage: an examination of over three decades of research'. *Strategic Management Journal*, **21**, 155–74.
Penrose, E.T. (1952). 'Biological analogies in the theory of the firm'. *American Economic Review*, **42**, 804–19.
Penrose, E.T. (1955). 'Limits to the growth and size of firms'. *American Economic Review*, **45**, 531–43.
Penrose, E.T. (1959). *The Theory of Growth of the Firm*. Oxford: Blackwell.
Penrose, E.T. (1960). 'The growth of the firm: a case study: the Hercules Powder Company'. *The Business History Review*, **34**, 1–20.
Penrose, E. (1995). 'Foreword to the third edition'. In Penrose, E. (Ed.), *The Theory of the Growth of the Firm*, 3rd edition. Oxford: Oxford University Press.
Pfeffer, J. and Salancik, G.R. (1978). *The External Control of Organizations*. New York: Harper and Row.
Phillips, B.D. and Kirchhoff, B.A. (1989). 'Formation, growth and survival; small firm dynamics in the US economy'. *Small Business Economics*, **1**, 65–74.
Porac, J.F. and Thomas, H. (1994). 'Cognitive categorization and subjective rivalry among retailers in a small city'. *Journal of Applied Psychology*, **79**, 54–66.
Porac, J.F., Thomas, H. and Baden-Fuller, C. (1989). 'Competitive groups as cognitive communities: the case of Scottish knitwear manufacturers'. *Journal of Management Studies*, **26**, 397–416.
Porac, J.F., Thomas, H., Wilson, F., Paton, D. and Kanfer, A. (1995). 'Rivalry and the industry model of Scottish knitwear producers'. *Administrative Science Quarterly*, **40**, 203–27.
Powell, W.W. (1990). 'Neither market nor hierarchy: network forms of organization'. *Research in Organizational Behavior*, **12**, 295–336.
Rumelt, R. (1987). 'Theory, strategy and entrepreneurship'. In Teece, D. (Ed.), *The Competitive Challenge*. Cambridge, MA: Ballinger, 137–58.
Saxenian, A. (1991). 'The origins and dynamics of production networks in Silicon Valley'. *Research Policy*, **20**, 423–37.
Saxenian, A. (1994). *Regional Advantage: Culture and Competition in Silicon Valley and Route 128*. Cambridge, MA: Harvard University Press.
Shepherd, D. and Wiklund, J. (2009). 'Are we comparing apples with apples or apples with oranges? Appropriateness of knowledge accumulation across growth studies'. *Entrepreneurship Theory and Practice*, **33**, 105–23.
Simon, H.A. (1947). *Administrative Behavior*. New York: Macmillan.
Storey, D.J. (1994). *Understanding the Small Business Sector*. London: Routledge.
Storey, D.J. (1995). 'Symposium on Harrison's "lean and mean": a job generation perspective'. *Small Business Economics*, **7**, 5–8.
Sturgeon, T.J. (2002). 'Modular production networks: a new American model of industrial organization'. *Industrial and Corporate Change*, **11**, 451–96.
Tan, D. and Mahoney, J.T. (2007). 'The dynamics of Japanese firm growth in U.S. industries: the Penrose effect'. *Management International Review*, **47**, 259–79.
Teece, D.J. (1987). 'Technological change and the nature of the firm'. In Teece, D. (Ed.), *The Competitive Challenge*. New York: Harper and Row, 256–81.

Venkatesan, R. (1992). 'Strategic sourcing: to make or not to make'. *Harvard Business Review*, **70**, 98–108.

Vermeulen, F. and Bakerma, H. (2001). 'Learning through acquisitions'. *Academy of Management Journal*, **44**, 457–76.

Wagner, J. (1992). 'Firm size, firm growth and persistence of chance. Testing GIBRAT's law with establishment data form lower Saxony, 1978–1989'. *Small Business Economics*, **4**, 125–31.

Wang, L. and Zajac, E.J. (2007). 'Alliance or acquisition? A dyadic perspective on interfirm resource combinations'. *Strategic Management Journal*, **28**, 1291–317.

Wernerfelt, B. (1984). 'A resource based view of the firm'. *Strategic Management Journal*, **5**, 171–80.

Winter, S.G. and Szulanski, G. (2001). 'Replication as strategy'. *Organization Science*, **12**, 730–43.

Wooldridge, J.M. (1995). 'Selection corrections for panel data models under conditional mean independence assumptions'. *Journal of Econometrics*, **68**, 115–32.

# Index

*Introductory Note: References such as '178–9' indicate (not necessarily continuous) discussion of a topic across a range of pages. Wherever possible in the case of topics with many references, these have either been divided into sub-topics or only the most significant discussions of the topic are listed. Because the entire work is about 'firm growth', the use of this term (and certain others which occur constantly throughout the book) as an entry point has been minimized. Information will be found under the corresponding detailed topics.*


abilities 55–8, 61–2, 76–7, 84–6, 104, 154–5, 223–6
  discovery 8, 222–5, 227–8, 231–3, 235, 240, 243–5
  exploitation *see* exploitation ability
above-average growth 203, 209, 229, 233, 242
above-average profitability 193, 195–6, 203, 242
ABS *see* Australian Bureau of Statistics
absolute growth 119, 121–2, 126–7, 129–31, 133
  assets 116, 126, 129, 132–3, 136
  employees/employment 93, 115, 123, 126–7, 129–33, 136
  equity 126, 129, 131–3
  profits 126–7, 129, 133
  sales 93, 116, 123, 126–7, 129, 131–4, 136
absolute measures 122, 124, 126–7, 130, 133
  of growth 119, 121, 124, 126–7
    concurrence with relative measures 123, 130
acquired growth 162
acquisition-based growth 178, 305
acquisitions 146–8, 154–6, 163–5, 292–4, 298–301, 305–7, 313–14
  strategy of 296, 301, 317
acquisitive growth 9, 147, 152, 154, 156, 159, 169
  and organic growth 291–319
    data and methods 301–6
    discussion 311–18
    hypotheses 293, 299, 301–2, 304, 308, 310, 312–13
    limitations 318–19
    managerial implications 317–18
    measures 304–6
    model 304
    results 306–11
    sample 301–2
    theoretical implications 311, 314
  previous 299–301
  rate 301, 306
  strategy of 307, 317
ACs *see* adjustment costs
actual control 59
actual growth 1, 3–4, 60, 68, 71, 75–7, 84
adjustment costs 9, 156, 291–7, 299–303, 311–13, 315, 317
  of growth 291–2, 294, 299–301, 313, 317
age 91, 123–8, 222–4, 228, 235, 304–5, 307–10
  asymmetric effect 240–41
  business/company 66–8, 123–5, 131–3, 135, 203, 222–3, 225
  CEOs 93–4, 96, 98, 100
age-related hypotheses, and performance configurations 231–6
agency 157, 159–60, 261, 263, 282
  theory 162

Ajzen, I. 3, 57–9, 61, 75, 83–7, 90, 104
alliances 22–3, 159, 165, 316
strategic 22, 157–9
Alvarez, S.A. 21–2, 39, 190, 193
Amit, R. 193, 226–7, 229
analyses
appropriateness of knowledge accumulation 121–3
aspirations and growth achievement 68–70
cross-lagged regression 83, 92
cross-sectional 237–8
dynamic 242–3
empirical 2, 141, 208, 222–3, 244
growth and profitability
primary 199–201
samples 201–3
sub-samples 203
meta-analysis 85, 164, 191, 208, 296, 313
performance configurations over time 222–3, 237–8, 240–43
sales growth-employment growth relationship 272–80
Anderson, E. 258–9, 261, 264, 280
annual reports 63, 121
appropriateness of knowledge accumulation *see* knowledge accumulation
appropriation *see* value appropriation
Arend, R.J. 190, 199, 212
artistic and literary creation 275, 278
aspiration–growth relationship 61, 75
aspirations 1, 3, 40, 83, 90, 103, 181
and growth achieved 3, 56–77, 145, 162, 179
discussion 70–77
future research and implications 74, 77
hypotheses 58, 60, 62–3, 68–9, 73
independent effects only model 68–9
limitations 73–4
research design 57, 63–4
research methods 63–8
results and analysis 68–70
sample 63–4
variables and measures 64–8
and small business managers 62–3, 75, 77
asset growth 116, 123–7, 130, 132–3
absolute 116, 126, 129, 132–3, 136
relative 127–9, 132–3, 136
asset specificity 8–9, 253–86
controls 269–72
human 258–9, 262–3, 280, 286
hypotheses 253–4, 257, 259–63, 272–3, 280, 282–4
implications for future research 285
limitations 283–5
measurement 263–72
moderating variables 264–9
research design 264, 268, 284
research methods 262–72
results 272–80
sample 262–3
significance and effect size 283
theoretical implications 254
assets 5, 28, 115, 118, 121, 130–33, 156–7
complementary 158–9
human 258, 263
relative 132–3
total 121, 199, 237
attitude 18, 23–5, 30
growth *see* growth attitude
objects 30
and small business growth 39–40
Audretsch, D.B. 20, 22, 141, 227
Australia 187–214, 219
Australian Bureau of Statistics (ABS) 198, 236, 245
sample 198–9, 204–5

Bagozzi, R. 57, 61, 82, 86–7, 103, 265
Bamford, C.E. 22, 145, 148
Bandura, A. 86–7
Barnard, C.I. 294
Barney, J.B. 190, 192–5, 199, 221, 228, 230, 296
base models 31–2, 68–9, 93, 100
Baum, J.A. 23, 82, 84–5, 143, 150, 178, 191
behavioral control 58–61, 75
perceived 3, 103
behavioral uncertainty 8, 253–86
controls 269–72
hypotheses 253–4, 257, 259–63, 272–3, 280, 282–4
implications for future research 285

limitations 283–5
measurement 263–72
moderating variables 264–9
research design 264, 268, 284
research methods 262–72
results 272–80
sample 262–3
significance and effect size 283
theoretical implications 254
variables 265, 268, 272, 284
behaviors 23, 28, 56–61, 72–3, 82–7, 101–7, 228–9
goal-directed 82, 86, 103
predictors of 83–4, 102
strategic 193, 231
beliefs 30, 208, 210
bias
selection 91, 307–10
survivor 4, 74, 91, 136, 237, 239, 255
bidding process 296–7
big picture model 15–16, 31
biological metaphors 150–51, 169
bookkeeping 275, 278
Boston Consulting Group (BCG) 229
boundary conditions 5, 8–9, 26, 116, 131, 134, 213
Bowman-Upton, N. 23, 57, 59, 61–3, 71, 76
Bullvåg, E. 18, 24, 39, 57, 59–60, 82, 84–5
Burke, K.L. 121–2
business age 66–8, 123–5, 131–3, 135, 203, 222–3, 225
business environment 19, 37, 63
business founders *see* founders
business growth, *Introductory Note*
Business Longitudinal Survey (BLS) 198, 236
business models 18, 192, 228
business owners *see* owners
business size 26, 66–8

capabilities 21–2, 57, 159, 162, 294
dynamic 21–2, 192
firm-specific 153, 294
managerial 153–4, 156, 294–5, 297, 299, 315
capital 52, 66–7, 69, 77, 157, 211, 237
external 195–7, 234
financial 3, 22–3, 38, 62–3, 66–9, 73, 195–6
human *see* human capital (HC)
social 23, 29, 39
venture 144–5, 213, 225–6
Capon, N. 191, 208, 229
categorization schema 194, 214, 232
causal mechanisms 160, 166–7
causality
direction of 284–5
dual 92
Granger 89
reverse 4, 41
centered interaction terms 272
CEOs, age 93–4, 96, 98, 100
CFA (confirmatory factor analysis) 254, 265–6
CFI (comparative fit index) 265, 267
Chandler, G.N. 6, 22, 63, 74, 152–3, 255, 264
choices 3, 5–6, 83–4, 117–21, 148, 156–7, 161–2
efficient 282–3
measurement 117–20, 128
strategic 25, 35, 61, 103, 118, 208, 312
Coad, A. 140–41, 151, 160, 162, 197
coefficients 34, 68, 78, 100, 240–41, 266–7, 308
correlation 122–3, 126–8
path 27, 31–3
regression *see* regression coefficients
significant 100, 304, 310
Cohen, J. & P. 65, 68–9, 107, 121–2, 273, 280, 283
Coles, J.W. 254, 262, 268, 282
common method variance 89, 106, 284
company age *see* business age
comparability 27–8, 117
comparative fit index (CFI) 265, 267
competition 20, 51, 63, 103, 193, 224, 313
international 168, 292
price 51
competitive advantage 21, 187–8, 192–3, 195, 197, 207–9, 260
resource-based 187, 196
competitive environment 42, 300, 315
competitors 3, 19, 28–9, 49–52, 63–4, 191, 199

complementary assets 158–9
concurrent validity 116–17, 120–23, 126–36, 303
across indicators of growth 131–3
across time spans 133
high 120, 122–3, 126–8, 130, 132–3
and knowledge accumulation 128–30
low 116, 120, 122, 127, 130, 132–6, 148
confirmatory factor analysis (CFA) 254, 265–6
consistency 117, 121
construction 274–5, 277–8, 306
contingent relationships 72–3, 211
continuous variables 73, 305–6
contracts 158–9, 162, 258, 260, 282
control variables 4, 27, 66–8, 91, 100, 240–41, 318–19
corporate groups *see* groups
correction models, Heckman-type 91
correlation coefficients 122–3, 126–8
correlation matrix 269, 272
cost-of-capital effects 195–6, 211
costs 23–4, 228–9, 257–8, 261, 268, 280, 282–3
adjustment *see* adjustment costs
development 158, 224, 227
potential hazard 147, 261
transaction *see* transaction costs
creativity 40, 54
crisis survival 54–5
Cronbach's Alpha values 28, 64–6, 90
cross-lagged analysis of growth and growth motivation 88
cross-lagged regressions 4, 83, 89, 92–3
cross-sectional analyses 237–8
Crozier, L. 146, 226–7, 230–31, 318
culture 73, 105–6, 261, 282
curvilinear effects/relationships 296, 308–11, 317
customer relations/relationships 259–60, 265–6, 268, 270, 272, 275–6, 279–80
customers 51, 53–5, 193–5, 228, 230–31, 259, 266–8
Cyert, R.M. 22, 155, 293–4, 298
Czech, D.R. 121
data sources 198–9, 236–8
debts 226, 292
demolition 274, 277
dependent variables 27, 31, 74, 90–91, 117–18, 142–3, 263–4
design *see* research designs
Dess, G.G. 2, 19, 21, 28, 255
development costs 158, 224, 227
development models 151, 164, 226
direct effects 2, 32, 34–9, 41, 73, 284
discovery 22, 223–4, 228, 295
ability 8, 222–5, 227–8, 231–3, 235, 240, 243–5
advantages 233, 235
discriminant validity 65, 92
diversification 6–7, 10, 152, 176, 179, 230, 296
literature 146, 296–7
diversity 51, 155, 243, 294, 300, 317
resource 296, 300, 308
dual causality 92
dummy variables 91, 93, 206, 240–41, 269, 304–6
industry 304, 306–10
year 306
dynamic analysis 242–3
dynamic capabilities 21–2, 192
dynamic environments 20, 35, 63, 69, 72, 298
dynamics 8, 20, 63, 200, 213, 225, 243
dynamism 2, 33–6, 38, 41, 51, 67, 71
environmental 3, 29, 63, 66, 69

earth moving 274, 277
economic growth 19, 75, 104, 255, 292
economics 141, 180, 254, 296, 316
industrial 191, 228
education 3–4, 16, 29, 52, 61–2, 67–72, 75
higher 69, 72, 77
highest level of completed 52, 65, 71–2, 91
effect sizes 78, 254, 273, 280, 283, 308
and significance 283
effects of growth 93, 100, 178, 182, 228, 230
efficient choices 282–3
Eisenhardt, K.M. 19, 21, 23, 41, 157, 178
elementary school 91, 94, 96, 98

emerging firms 253–4, 283, 285–6
managers of 256, 282
empirical analysis 2, 141, 208, 222–3, 244
empirical literature 116, 164, 190, 229
empirical research 6–7, 141, 149–50, 188–9, 225–6, 230, 245
previous 60, 85, 101, 177
empirical studies 92, 177–8
empirical tests 36, 292
employee growth 28, 116, 118, 123–5, 130–31, 221
absolute 115, 123, 126–7, 129–33, 136
relative 123, 127–9, 136
employee performance, difficulty of measuring 261–2, 268
employees 52–5, 64–5, 89–91, 198, 257–61, 263–4, 266–70
full-time equivalent (FTEs) 49, 263–4, 283
new 103, 162, 253–4, 257, 259, 265–7, 280–81
permanent 254–62, 268, 282–3, 286
potential 261, 267, 280
supervising 260–61, 268, 280–81
temporary 260–61, 282, 286
employment 4–5, 92–3, 101, 118, 256–7, 263–4, 303–5
increasing 189, 254, 256, 282, 286
total 303–4
employment creation *see* job creation
employment growth 100–103, 253–64, 268–9, 280–81, 284–6, 293–4, 303
absolute 93, 115, 123, 126–7, 129–33, 136
motivation 96, 100, 103, 107
and sales 90–91
relationship to sales growth *see* sales growth, and employment growth relationship
endogeneity 269
energy 40, 259, 265–8
entrepreneurial activities 18
entrepreneurial capabilities 60, 153–5, 294–5, 313, 315
entrepreneurial firms 190, 225, 227
entrepreneurial orientation 2, 16, 18–22, 25–9, 31–42, 49–50
direct effect of 26, 31
entrepreneur resources 32–3
growth 32–3
predicting 31–2
and small business growth 18–19, 34–5
entrepreneurial strategic orientation 39, 41
entrepreneurs 22, 32–3, 40, 60, 106, 145, 168–9
entrepreneurship 19, 21, 73, 77, 82, 182, 189–90
domain of strategic 221, 245
journals 139, 141
research 7, 21, 39, 73–4, 76, 82–3, 189–90
scholars 60, 165
theory 82–3
entrepreneurship literature 23, 59, 190
environmental conditions 25, 37
environmental dynamism 3, 29, 63, 66, 68–9, 72, 77
environments 18–21, 24–7, 29, 31, 35–8, 41, 50–51
business 19, 37, 63
competitive 42, 300, 315
dynamic 20, 35, 63, 69, 72, 298
external 21, 227
hostile 20–21, 25
and small business growth 19–20, 35–8
and strategic fit 35–8
task 16, 20, 29, 32, 34–8, 41, 51
equity growth 123–5, 127, 130–33
absolute 126, 129, 131–3
measures 123, 130, 132
relative 123, 127–33
exit 88, 151, 200, 214, 219–20, 237, 239
expansion 58, 85, 105–6, 154–5, 162–3, 230, 293–5
incremental 298–9
experience 3–4, 22–3, 29, 61–3, 65–73, 75, 77
effects 191, 213, 230, 233
explained variance 26, 31–3, 69, 161, 211
exploitation 207, 223–5, 228, 233–5, 292
ability and limited resource stocks 225–7
opportunity 22, 39

external capital 195–7, 234
external contracting 255, 258, 280, 282
external environments 21, 227
external investors 188, 197, 210

factor loadings 33, 49
failure 74, 83, 86, 104, 169, 237
families 53–4
feedback 30, 42, 75, 82–3, 86, 92, 105–6
  loops 75, 102–3
financial capital 3, 22–3, 38, 62–3, 66–9, 73, 195–6
financial intermediation 274, 277
financial management 226–7
financial performance 164, 191, 230, 236, 296–7, 313
financial resources 18, 38, 254, 257, 268–9, 272, 282
firm heritage 94, 96, 98
firm-specific effects 307–8
firm-specific knowledge 259
first-mover-advantages (FMAs) 191, 193, 197, 210, 213
Fitzsimmons, J.R. 149, 222
FMAs *see* first-mover-advantages
focus 5–6, 15–16, 21–2, 159, 176–7, 254–6, 292–3
  geographic 319
  growth 232, 234, 239–40
  profit 232, 239
formulae 5, 93, 115, 118–21, 128, 134, 136
  relative 119–20, 122, 129
founders 4, 24, 56, 222, 226, 256–7, 282
France 144
franchising 157–9, 163, 167–8
freight transport 274, 277
FTEs *see* full-time equivalent employees
full-time equivalent employees (FTEs) 49, 263–4, 283
Fuller, T. 17–18, 104, 296

Garnsey, E. 146–7, 153, 312
Gartner, W.B. 83, 89, 139, 165, 180, 189, 191
geographic focus 319
Gilbert, B.A. 141, 143, 146, 148, 150, 162, 255
goal-directed behaviors 82, 86, 103
goals 24, 30–31, 40–41, 56, 84–5, 143–5, 157–9
  personal 24, 40, 56
  terminal 5, 211
government enterprises 198, 236
governments 75, 104, 198
Graebner, M.E. 164, 300
Granger causality 89
groups 17, 77, 93, 136, 214, 219–20, 304–6
  age 203, 222
  performance 200, 202, 204–6, 219–20, 232, 239
  resource munificent 254, 273, 280
  resource scarce 254, 273, 280, 283
growth *see Introductory Note and detailed entries*
growth aspirations *see* aspirations
growth attitude 2, 25, 39, 41
  and small business growth 23–4
growth constraint 311, 314–17
Growth firms 195–7, 201–3, 206
growth focus 232, 234, 239–40
growth from profits and profitability *see* profitability, and growth from profits
growth measures 4–5, 74, 116–17, 120–21, 126–36, 148–9, 167–8
  absolute 119, 121–2, 126–7
    and relative 123–6, 130–31
  with different time spans 127–8
  relative 122–3, 126–7
growth mode focus 139–69
  research agenda 160–66
  theoretical implications 166–7
growth models *see* models
growth modes, choice 160, 162
growth motivation 4, 71, 75–6, 82–107
  antecedents 75, 103
  comparison of size effects 101
  discussion 101–4
  effect on actual growth 84–5, 87, 93, 100–102
  feedback of past growth on 86
  future research 106–7
  hypotheses 83–4, 86–8, 92–3, 100–101, 107

independent impact 86–7
limitations 105–6, 319
measures 89
practical implications 104–7
prediction 93–100
predictions 93–100
research design 87–9
research methods 87–92
results 92–101
samples 87–9
and small business managers 4, 82–107
stability of 83–4, 107
theoretical implications 102–4
theory and hypotheses 83–7
growth opportunities 18–20, 22–3, 25, 194, 292, 296–9, 312–15
most profitable 233, 245
new 38, 61–3, 155–6, 298–9, 301
growth-orientated firms/businesses 63, 105, 232, 234, 241–2
growth-oriented and profit-oriented strategies 221–45
growth processes 17, 24, 84, 105, 152–3, 165–6, 180–81
theory 165
growth–profit relationship 7, 187–245
growth–profitability configurations *see* profitability-growth configurations
growth-profitability dynamics 8, 191–2, 199, 207–8, 213, 235, 243–4
by firm age 223–31
growth rates 5, 10, 90, 139–69, 295, 307, 317
industry 20, 66
variation over time 147–8
very high 19, 310, 318
growth research 5, 10, 255, 293, 312 *see also* growth mode focus
advancing 139–69
streams of 139–43, 156, 161
growth strategies 163, 167, 229, 234, 245, 292, 306
resource-intensive 38, 62
growth theories 10, 116–17, 134, 153, 160
Penrose's *see* Penrose, Edith, growth theory
hairdressing 275, 278
Hambrick, D.C. 146, 226–7, 230–31, 318
hard-to-copy strategies 192–3, 195, 197
HC *see* human capital
Heckman selection 91, 96, 98
Heide, J.B. 258, 260–61, 264
heritage, firm 94, 96, 98
heterogeneity 2, 20, 27, 29, 33–8, 51, 74
resources 192–3, 208
unobserved 136, 318
heterogeneous nature of growth 152, 167
hi-tech firms 37, 150
hierarchical approach 69, 78
high growth 7–8, 187–90, 194–7, 207, 210–11, 224–5, 232
and high profitability 203, 214
and low profitability 193–4
high-growth firms/businesses 40, 146, 148, 190, 207, 240, 242 *see also* Growth firms
high profitability 7–8, 187–8, 190, 194–7, 207–10, 227–9, 231
and low growth 193–4
high school 91, 94, 96, 98
hiring 153, 157, 162, 256, 260–61, 267–8, 286
Holt, R. 140–42, 153, 160
homogeneous samples 3, 178, 181, 189
hospitals
for-profit 262, 282
not-for-profit 262, 282
hostility 20, 27, 29, 33–8, 51
human asset specificity 258–9, 262–3, 280, 286
firm specific knowledge 259
human capital (HC) 3–4, 16, 22, 38–9, 61–3, 72, 258–9
general 61–2, 65
specific 65–6
human health activities other than medical practice 275, 278
hybrid growth 156, 158, 161–2, 167–8
hybrid models 139–40, 162–3, 165, 167
hybrid modes, of growth 140, 156–61, 165

hypotheses 8–10
age-related 231–6
aspirations and growth achieved 58, 60, 62–3, 68–9, 73, 78
asset specificity and behavioral uncertainty 253–4, 257, 259–63, 272–3, 280, 282–4
competing 233, 241, 243
formal 231, 238
growth motivation 83–4, 86–8, 92–3, 100–101, 107
and integrative model building 15, 24
knowledge accumulation 120, 131
organic and acquisitive growth 293, 299, 301–2, 304, 308, 310, 312–13
performance configurations over time 223, 231, 233–6, 238–43
profitability vs. growth from profits 188–90, 196–7, 201–2, 206–7, 211–13

ideology 8, 209, 214, 230
IFI *see* incremental index of fit
incorporated companies 87, 120–21
incremental index of fit 265, 267
independence 24, 55–6, 149
independent effects only model 68–9
independent firms 198, 300, 305–6
independent variables 74, 115, 130, 142, 145, 161–2, 319–20
indicators 8–9, 28–9, 66, 118–21, 129–30, 132–3, 135–6
employment growth 256
important 86, 264
manifest 26, 33
indices 28–30, 33, 64–6, 90, 135, 235, 265
indirect effect 16, 31, 34–8, 227
indirect positive effect 35–6, 38–9
industrial economics 191, 228
industry differences 269, 272, 303, 306
industry dummies 304, 306–10
industry variables 38, 272
inference approach, strong 223, 233, 238, 243
initial endowment of resources 231–2
initial state 200, 219–20
innovation 18, 20, 25, 50–51, 154–5, 225–8, 316
value-creating 230, 234
innovativeness 28, 50, 92
installation of electrical wiring 274, 277
integrative framework 6–7, 176–7, 179, 181–3
integrative framework for future research 176–82
methodological implications 167–8
integrative model building 2, 15–42, 49
conflicting views and integration of perspectives 24–5
discussion and limitations 40–42
entrepreneurial orientation (EO) and small business growth 18–19, 34–5
entrepreneurial orientation perspective 18–19
environment and small business growth 19–20, 35–8
environment perspective 19–20, 35–8
growth attitude and small business growth 23–4
growth attitude perspective 23–4
and hypotheses 15, 24
measures and variables 27–30
resource perspective 21–3
resources and small business growth 21–3, 38–9
sample and design 26–7
strategic fit and small business growth 20–21, 35–8
strategic fit perspective 20–21
intellectual property 157–8, 168 *see also* proprietary information
intentions 30, 59, 90, 103, 144, 312
growth 30, 41, 55, 59, 90, 103–4
interaction effects 68, 69–70, 72, 178, 199
interaction terms 69, 78, 269, 272–3
centered 272
internal growth 152, 154, 292
internal modes of growth 157–8
international competition 168, 292
internationalization 176, 179
interviews 26–7, 66, 88–91, 181
inverse Mills ratio 307

investments 29, 211, 231, 258–9
in growth 201, 203
investors, external 188, 197, 210
Ireland 144

Jarillo, J.C. 19, 25, 190, 227
job creation 257, 263, 305
joint ventures 158–9, 163, 165

Kimmel, S.K. 82, 86–7, 103
knowledge 130–36, 157–9, 258–9, 265–70, 279–81, 293–5, 299–301
accumulation 5, 115–37, 149
across growth studies 5, 115, 117, 119, 121, 123, 137
analysis 121–3
and concurrent validity 128, 128–30
discussion 128–36
hypotheses 120, 131
implications for future research 133–5
limitations 134–6
measurement choices 117–20
research methods 120–23
results 123–8
sample 120–21
bases 155, 292, 297, 300–301, 313–14
managerial 226–7
new 122, 134–5, 155, 163, 300–301
prior 155, 298, 317
product specific 258–9, 265–6, 269–70, 275, 279–81, 284
knowledge-intensive manufacturing 26
Kogut, B. 163, 192, 194
Kolvereid, L. 18, 20, 23–4, 39–40, 56–7, 59–60, 84–5
Kor, Y.Y. 23, 192, 291–2, 301, 315

labor-intensive manufacturing 26
large firms 36, 146–7, 152, 162, 167, 225, 314
large samples 2, 180, 227, 257
lenders 54–5
Levie, J. 6, 144, 146, 179, 318
licensing 156, 158–9, 168
strategy 158, 167
life cycle 37, 179, 182, 191
models 19, 150–51, 160
linear growth 147
linear model 311
linear regression analysis 32–3, 272
linear relationships 147, 308, 310–11, 314
literature 6–7, 15–18, 21–4, 139–43, 158–60, 162–4, 296–8
diversification 146, 296–7
entrepreneurship 23, 59, 190
merger and acquisition 162, 164, 296–7
reviews 27, 42, 120–21
streams of 2, 140, 142–3, 150, 152, 160, 164
Locke, E.A. 30, 40, 58, 82, 143, 178, 212
longitudinal analyses 237–8
of profitability-growth configuration transitions 240–42
longitudinal research designs 2, 24, 58, 74, 76, 92, 180
low growth 8, 118, 188, 190, 196–7, 203, 231–2
low profitability 8, 187–8, 190, 195–7, 203, 207, 211
and high growth 193–4
low-profitability firms 187, 195, 207
Lumpkin, G.T. 2, 19, 21, 28

Macpherson, A. 141–2
Mahoney, J.T. 192, 291, 301, 312
main effects model 69
management 7, 29, 35, 102–3, 141–2, 151, 312–13
challenges 9, 178, 182
experience 16, 62, 65
financial 226–7
practice 181–2
team 23, 52, 259, 294
managerial capabilities 153–4, 156, 294–5, 297, 299, 315
managerial capacity 156–7, 160, 226, 303, 313
managerial challenges 7, 163, 230, 318
managerial knowledge 226–7
managerial resources 147, 154, 156, 291, 294, 299
managers 3–4, 38–40, 75, 153–7, 256–8, 294–301, 315–17
new 144, 154, 157, 291, 294–5, 297

managing directors 27, 52, 87–8
manufacturing 22, 26, 64, 66, 68, 204–5, 240–41
  high-technology 306
  knowledge-intensive 26
  labor-intensive 26
March, J. 19, 22, 25, 155, 293–4, 298, 314
market conditions 57, 157, 295
market demand 35, 168
market potential 163, 195
market share 148–9, 192, 195, 197, 229, 256
marketing 40, 50, 54, 153, 158, 195, 234
markets 18–20, 51, 63–4, 156–9, 195, 224–5, 229
  new 24, 103, 210, 254, 295, 316
Martin, J.A. 21, 41
maturity model 163
measurement 3, 26, 73, 106, 145, 160, 260
  asset specificity and behavioral uncertainty 263–72
  decisions 116–18
measures
  absolute *see* absolute measures
  aspirations and growth achieved 64–8
  direct 189–90, 209
  growth *see* growth measures 4–5, 28, 116–17, 120–21, 126–36, 148–9, 167–8
  growth motivation 89
  integrative model building 27–30
  performance configurations over time 237–8
  profitability and growth from profits 199
  relative *see* relative measures
  sales growth 131, 269
measuring growth 88, 115, 159, 285
medical practice activities 275, 278
merger and acquisition literature 162, 164, 296–7
mergers 7, 121, 154, 176, 214, 230, 244
meta-analysis 85, 164, 191, 208, 296, 313
methodological choices 115–17, 119–20, 134, 136
Miller, D. 18–19, 25, 28–9, 32, 36, 63, 293
mining 198, 236, 306
misguided growth 234, 242, 244
Mishina, Y. 153, 195–6, 211
model fit 32–3, 93, 100, 265
model(s) 15–18, 31–3, 38–42, 68–71, 91–3, 96–102, 307–10
  business 18, 192, 228
  development 151, 164, 226
  of growth-profitability dynamics by firm age 223–31
  hybrid 139–40, 162–3, 165, 167
  independent effects only 68–9
  integrated 2, 8, 26, 31, 224
    of small business growth 26–34
  integrative 15–17, 31–2, 40
  linear 311
  main effects 69
  maturity 163
  quadratic 311
  selection 91, 93
  six factor 265–7
  theoretical 3, 16, 211, 233, 243–5, 284
  total 276, 279
moderating effects 57, 258, 264–9, 273, 280
  resources 3, 56, 76–7
    and opportunities 61–3
  transaction cost variables 262, 281
moderators 8, 61, 178, 223, 253, 286
  negative 253, 261, 280–81
  positive 9, 253, 259–60, 262, 280–81
  of sales growth 253–86
modes of growth 2, 5–10, 139–69, 176–7, 179, 181–2, 312
  differences in 146–7
  hybrid 140, 156–61, 165
  internal 157–8
modular production networks 316
Moran, P. 17–18, 297
Morrow, J.L.J. 193, 195–7
motivation 1, 3–4, 56–60, 73, 77, 82–7, 101–7 *see also* growth motivation
  task 93
  theories 39, 83, 85–7, 90, 101, 103, 168
myopia 313–14

Naldi, L. 319
negative correlations 5, 230
negative effects 9, 35–7, 93, 100, 301–2, 313
negative moderators 253, 261, 280–81
net profit 199, 237
network externalities 191, 197, 211, 213, 229, 233
network resources 18, 22, 27, 32–4, 42, 53
networks 17–18, 22–3, 38–9, 42, 316
  modular production 316
  relational 316
new firms 63, 105, 116, 121, 132, 144, 226–7
new markets 24, 103, 210, 254, 295, 316
new products 19, 30, 40, 103, 147, 153, 155
new ventures 40, 132, 256
newness
  advantages of 227–8
  liabilities of 225–7, 244–5
normative theory 188, 209

OG *see* organic growth
old firms 8, 222–3, 227–8, 231, 233–6, 238–45, 308–9
ontology of small businesses 17–18
operationalization of growth 29, 34, 120, 212
opportunistic hazards 260–61
opportunities *see also* growth opportunities
  market 234, 295, 316
  moderating effect 61–3
  moderating role 3, 56, 61–3, 76–7
  new growth 38, 61–3, 155–6, 298–9, 301
opportunity exploitation 22, 39
opportunity set *see* productive opportunity set
organic growth 154–6, 164, 292–3, 295–302, 304–5, 307–15, 317–19
  and acquisitive growth *see* acquisitive growth, and organic growth
  future 297–301
  hypotheses 293, 299, 301–2, 304, 308, 310, 312–13
  rate 297–9, 301, 306
organizational boundaries 17, 316
orientation 35–7, 40, 236, 241–3, 294, 315
  entrepreneurial *see* entrepreneurial orientation
  profit 231, 236, 238, 241–4
  profit–growth 232, 241
outcomes 5–7, 40–41, 82–6, 102–6, 142–3, 161, 166–7
  of growth 2, 6, 56–7, 86, 142, 150–52, 163–4
  growth as outcome 143–50, 152, 156, 161–3
  societal 254, 286
owner-managers 1, 3, 106, 209–10, 226, 256
owners 18, 25, 87, 144, 157, 209–10, 227
ownership 156, 158, 223–4, 305–7

partial least square analysis 26, 32–3
past growth 4, 86–7, 101–2, 292, 297
path coefficients 27, 31–3
path dependence 35, 202, 298, 313–14, 317
Pearson correlations 92
Penrose, Edith 5–6, 9, 38, 62, 149, 153–6, 165
  future extensions to work of 314–16
  growth theory 9–10, 134, 153–4, 160–61, 165, 291–320
    theoretical background 293–301
performance 6, 19, 21, 161, 164, 223, 297
  configurations 208, 221–3, 231, 235–7, 239, 241–3, 245
    and age-related hypotheses 231–6
    over time 221–45
      analyses 222–3, 237–8, 240–43
      hypotheses 223, 231, 233–6, 238–43
      implications for growth-oriented and profit-oriented strategies 221–45
      measures 237–8
      research method 236–8
      results 238–43
  dimensions of 192, 200, 211, 222, 232, 234–5
  employee *see* employee performance

financial 164, 191, 230, 236, 296–7, 313
group 200, 202, 204–6, 219–20, 232, 239
growth 200, 241, 243, 305
high 21, 25, 91, 196, 200, 233, 242–3
low 197, 200, 242
measurement 254, 261–2, 267–8, 270, 273–4, 276–8
medium 232, 241
profitability–growth 236, 238, 241
strong 232, 241
weak 232–3, 241, 261
permanent employees 254–62, 268, 282–3, 286
personal goals 24, 40, 56
personalized service, importance 259–60
Phelps, R. 140–41, 150–51, 163–4, 169
planned behavior theory 57, 58–63, 70–73, 75–7, 85–6, 90, 103
PLS (partial least square) analysis *see* partial least square analysis
Podasakoff, P.M. 284
policy-makers 168–9, 188–9, 210, 245, 254, 256, 286
Poor firms 193–4, 196–7, 200–203, 205–6, 219–20, 233, 239
Porter, M.E 208, 221
POS *see* productive opportunity set
positive effects 24–5, 34, 84–6, 105, 168, 301–2, 308
indirect 35–6, 38–9
positive relationships 35, 57, 59–60, 82, 85, 187, 229
positive theory 188, 209
potential hazard costs 147, 261
predictions, growth 31–4, 102
previous growth 35, 64, 83, 297–300, 314–15, 317
price 7, 51, 195, 230, 234, 244, 296
competition 51
proactiveness 28, 50
probit analysis 238, 240–43, 307
process, growth as 152–6
product specific knowledge 258–9, 265–6, 269–70, 275, 279–81, 284
production networks, modular 316
productive opportunity set (POS) 9, 154–5, 291–302, 311–19
productive services 155, 294–5, 299–301
productivity 103, 226
professional services 26, 51, 64, 87, 91, 198
Profit firms 194–7, 202, 206
profit focus 232, 239
profit growth 123–6, 130, 133
absolute 126–7, 129, 133
relative 127–8
profit–growth orientations 232, 241
profit-oriented strategies 8
profit-oriented strategies/profit orientation 8, 221–45
profitability 7, 148, 153, 157, 221–35, 240–41, 243–5
above-average 193, 195–6, 203, 242
advantages 195, 229
data 198–9
and growth from profits 187–214, 228–9, 231
analysis of samples 201–3
analysis of sub-samples 203
discussion 207–13
hypotheses 188–90, 196–7, 201–2, 206–7, 211–13
implications for practitioners 209–10
measures 199
primary analysis 199–201
research agenda 210–13
research methods 198–201
results 201–7
supplementary analysis 201, 206–7
high *see* high profitability
low *see* low profitability
profitability-growth configurations 191, 193, 207, 222, 231–5, 237, 238–43
profitability-growth performance 236, 238, 241
profitability-reducing tactics 195, 230
profitable growth 160, 168, 210, 225, 229
and resource-based view 192–8
profits 5, 118, 121, 133, 149, 187–215, 219–20
above-average 189, 206
growth from 187–214

high 54, 232, 239, 242, 282
low 200, 232, 239
net 199, 237
property & business services 240–41
proprietary information 158, 260, 265–6, 268, 270, 274, 276–9 *see also* intellectual property
public services 198, 236

quadratic model 311
quadratic relationships 304, 311
quadratic terms 304, 308, 310

Ramezani, C.A. 189–90, 209
rapid growth 52, 188, 231, 235
RBV *see* Resource-Based View
realized growth 74–7
reasoned action, theory of 58, 85
regression analysis 92, 96, 98, 102, 119, 147, 199
regression coefficients 69, 92–3, 100–101, 119, 269
standardized 32–3, 68
regression weights 33, 52, 54
relational networks 316
relative formulae 119–20, 122, 129
relative growth 129, 131
assets 127–9, 132–3, 136
employees 123, 127–9, 136
equity 123, 127–33
profits 127–8
sales 5, 93, 127, 129, 132–3
relative measures 29, 119, 121–3, 126–7, 130–31, 133
of growth 122–3, 125–7, 130, 133
concurrence with absolute measures 123, 130
of sales 130, 132
replications 130, 134, 178
research agenda 2, 6, 8
changing 113, 115–82
growth mode focus 160–66
profitability and growth from profits 210–13
research designs 7
aspirations and growth achieved 57, 63–4
asset specificity and behavioral uncertainty 264, 268, 284
growth motivation 87–9
integrative model building 26–7
longitudinal 2, 24, 58, 74, 76, 92, 180
research methods
acquisitive growth and organic growth 301–6
aspirations and growth achieved 63–8
asset specificity and behavioral uncertainty 262–72
growth motivation 87–92
knowledge accumulation 120–23
profitability and growth from profits 198–201
research streams 140, 160–61, 165–6, 169, 176, 223
resource-based advantages 187, 194–7
resource-based mechanism 189, 208, 212
resource-based rationale 212–13
resource-based theory 21, 165, 190
Resource-Based View (RBV) 18, 187–8, 190, 207–8, 211–12, 296, 315–17
and profitable growth 192–8
resource bases 145, 158–9, 294, 298, 300, 314, 317
resource combinations 154–6, 297–8, 300–301, 313–14
resource complementarities 318
resource deficiencies 158, 226
resource diversity 296, 300, 308
resource functionality 315–16
resource heterogeneity 192–3, 208
resource-intensive growth strategies 38, 62
resource munificence 253–4, 262, 268–9, 273, 280
resource scarce groups 254, 273, 280, 283
resources 21–7, 37–42, 57–62, 153–6, 280–84, 292–301, 312–16
effect 25–6
financial 18, 38, 254, 257, 268–9, 272, 282
and growth aspirations 76
initial endowment 231–2
managerial 147, 154, 156, 291, 294, 299
moderating role 3, 56–77

network 18, 22, 27, 32–4, 42, 53
new 155, 298, 300, 314
opportunities and moderating effect 61–3
and small business growth 21–3, 38–9
results
acquisitive growth and organic growth 306–11
aspirations and growth achieved 68–70
asset specificity and behavioral uncertainty 272–80
growth motivation 92–101
knowledge accumulation 123–8
performance configurations over time 238–43
profitability and growth from profits 201–7
robustness 8, 105–6, 128, 188–9, 201, 203, 308
retail sector 26, 66, 203–5, 240–41, 274, 277, 306
retained earnings 195, 211, 225–8
reverse causality 4, 41
Rindfleisch, A. 258, 260, 264
risk 19, 50, 155, 157, 197, 200–201, 242
Robinson, J.P. 65, 264
robustness of results 8, 105–6, 128, 188–9, 201, 203, 308
Rosenthal, R. 93

sales 28, 64–5, 101–2, 130–33, 256–8, 276, 279
and employment growth motivation 90–91
sales growth 100–103, 123–8, 130–31, 148–9, 153, 199–200, 253–86
absolute 93, 116, 123, 126–7, 129, 131–4, 136
annual 52, 66
data 303–4
and employment 89–90, 280
measures 131, 269
moderators 253–86
motivation 96, 100, 107
relationship with employment growth 8, 89–90, 253–86
analysis and results 272–80
discussion 280–85
measurement 263–72
research methods 262–72
sample 262–3
relative 5, 93, 127, 129, 132–3
support 255, 259, 262, 284
samples
aspirations and growth achieved 63–4
asset specificity and behavioral uncertainty 262–3
full 9, 203, 272–4, 276–8, 280, 283–4
growth motivation 87–9
homogeneous 3, 178, 181, 189
integrative model building 26–7
knowledge accumulation 120–21
large 2, 180, 227, 257
organic growth and acquisitive growth 301–2
sizes 203, 214, 265, 269, 273, 280
scale economies 20, 191, 193, 213, 229, 235
Scotland 144
screening 260–61, 267–8, 270, 280, 282
difficulty 261, 270, 272, 274, 276–8, 281
selection
bias 91, 307–10
Heckman 91, 96, 98
model 91, 93
self-selection 91
services 19, 50–51, 54–5, 66, 68, 257–9, 265–6
productive 155, 294–5, 299–301
professional 26, 51, 64, 87, 91, 198
public 198, 236
Sexton, D. 23, 57, 59, 61–3, 71, 74, 221
Shane, S. 38, 73, 82, 118, 156–7, 223, 254
Simon, H. 61, 73, 141, 294
single factor model 266–7
six factor model 265
small- and medium-sized enterprises *see* SMEs
small business growth *see Introductory Note and detailed entries*
small business managers 23–4, 39–41, 60–64, 70–72, 75–7, 83–7, 101–5
goals 24, 56

growth aspirations *see* aspirations, and growth achieved
growth motivation *see* growth motivation
small business owners 18, 20, 23
smallness
advantages 227–8
liabilities 225–7
SMEs (small- and medium-sized enterprises) 35, 187–8, 193, 197–8, 207–10, 296–7, 300–302
social capital 23, 29, 39
software consultancy and supply 275, 277
sound growth 187, 190
Southwood, K.E. 269, 272
Spearman correlations 67
stability of growth motivation 83–4, 107
stable growth 147, 155
stages of development models 151
standardized regression coefficients 32–3, 68
Star firms 194–6, 200–204, 206, 219–20, 232–5, 238–40, 242–3
start-up experience 62, 65–6
start-ups 62, 73, 146–7, 158, 233, 265, 302–3
statistics, descriptive 66, 94, 269–70, 305–7
Statistics Sweden 198–9, 302–3
Steffens, P.R. 149, 221
Stevenson, H.H. 19, 25, 190, 227
strategic alliances 22, 157–9
strategic behaviors 193, 231
strategic choices 25, 35, 61, 103, 118, 208, 312
strategic decisions 60, 64
strategic entrepreneurship 221, 224, 242–5
strategic fit 20–21, 25, 35–8, 41
strategic orientation *see* orientation
strategies 2, 40–41, 54, 106, 151, 195–6, 206–8 *see also* orientation
finance 187, 207
growth *see* growth strategies 163, 167, 229, 234, 245, 292, 306
growth first 188, 206, 211, 213
growth-oriented and profit-oriented 8, 221–45
licensing 158, 167
subcontracting 253, 257–8, 261, 286
subsequent growth 60, 72, 103, 145, 149, 228
subsidiaries 27, 32–3, 93, 97, 99, 144, 295
success 82, 104, 145, 149–50, 187–9, 244–5, 259–60
supervision 260–61, 268, 270, 272, 274, 276–81
difficulty 261, 270, 272, 274, 276–8, 281
suppliers 53–5, 267
survivor bias 4, 74, 91, 136, 237, 239, 255
Sweden 52, 63, 73–4, 87, 187–214, 253–86, 318–19
data 198–9, 202–3, 206
sample 199, 201, 204–5, 214
Statistics Sweden 198–9, 302–3
Szulanski, G. 298

task environment 16, 20, 29, 32, 34–8, 41, 51
task motivation 93
TCE *see* transaction cost economics
temporary employees 260–61, 282, 286
theoretical arguments 187, 190, 192–3, 208, 211, 222–3, 230
theoretical constructs 15–16, 21, 24, 26–7, 29–31, 65
theoretical perspectives 2, 5, 15–26, 30, 40, 161, 243–4
multiple 143, 222, 231
theory development 83, 116–17, 134
theory-driven research on specific forms of growth 251, 253–319
Thornhill, S. 226–7
time-compression diseconomies 196, 212, 230, 297
time periods/spans 5, 28, 118–21, 126–7, 200–201, 304, 307
1-year 116, 122–7, 133, 136
3-year 89, 116, 122–3, 127, 133, 136
trade school 91, 94, 96, 98
trade secrets *see* proprietary information

training 29, 162, 182, 259, 266, 272, 295
transaction cost economics (TCE) 9, 153, 168, 253, 257–8, 282–3, 285
  predictions 149, 254, 257, 262, 282, 285–6
transaction costs 168, 254, 257–8, 261, 280, 286
transition matrices 200–201, 206, 212, 214
transitions 151, 161, 163, 194–7, 200–207, 214, 219–20
  1-year 188, 201–6, 219–20
  managerial 221, 230
  tests of 204–5

UC-Select 26, 63
United Kingdom 73
United States 73, 263
university degree 29, 91, 93, 100
utilities 198, 236

validity 11, 65, 177, 254, 268, 286
  concurrent *see* concurrent validity
  discriminant 65, 92
value appropriation 189–90, 193–4, 197
value creation 189–90, 193–5, 197, 208–9, 211
variables 30–31, 57–9, 64–6, 91–2, 142–3, 284–5, 304–6
  aspirations and growth achieved 64–8
  continuous 73, 305–6
  control 4, 27, 66–8, 77, 100, 240–41, 318–19
  dependent 27, 31, 74, 90–91, 117–18, 142–3, 263–4
  dummy 91, 93, 206, 240–41, 269, 304–6
  integrative model building 27–30
  moderating 264–9
variance 2–4, 10, 31–4, 121–2, 142–3, 150, 272
  common method 89, 106, 284
  explained 26, 31–3, 69, 161, 211
variance inflation factor (VIF) 68
Venkataraman, S. 38, 73, 82, 223, 254, 272–3
venture capital 144–5, 213, 225–6
virtuous sequence of growth 225, 233–5, 244
volitional control 56–8, 72, 84–5
  limited 57, 72, 85, 104

Weinzimmer, L.G. 28, 89, 115–17, 120, 130, 255–6, 264
Wernerfelt, B. 165, 192–3, 221, 293, 298, 316
Whetten, D.A. 83, 210–13
Williamson, O.E. 156, 253–4, 257–8, 260–61, 264, 280, 286
willingness to grow, differences in 149–50
Wilson, M.J. 121
Winter, S.G. 298
work experience 61–2

year dummies 306
young(er) firms 222–3, 225–9, 231, 233–6, 239–40, 242–5, 305

Z-tests 254, 280
Zahra, S. 18–19, 21–2, 28, 35, 37, 63, 159